4-09

The
Centennial Senator

The Centennial Senator

TRUE STORIES OF STROM THURMOND
FROM THE PEOPLE WHO KNEW HIM BEST

By

R.J. Duke Short

This document was prepared under grant number 2001-DD-BX-0077 from the Office of
Juvenile Justice and Delinquency Prevention (OJJDP), U.S. Department of Justice.

Points of view or opinions expressed in this document are those of the author/s and do
not necessarily represent the official position or policies of OJJDP or the U.S. Department
of Justice.

Graphic Design by Anne Matthews

ISBN 0-9778870-0-6

Manufactured in the United States of America
First Edition

For

the good people
of the state of South Carolina,
who gave the nation a great gift
when they sent Strom Thurmond to Washington

and for

my beautiful wife Dee,
who blesses me with her love
and has made my life complete

Contents

CONTENTS

THE CENTENNIAL SENATOR

Acknowledgements

This book would not have been possible without the support of my dear friends Robbie Callaway and Steve Salem. Their encouragement and unshakable faith in this project have made it a reality.

I am also tremendously grateful to all the individuals who contributed to this book by so unselfishly sharing their time and their memories of Senator Thurmond. For your consideration and generosity, I am most appreciative.

I owe a debt of gratitude as well to my good friend Senator Bob Dole who agreed to write the foreword to this book. He is a great leader, a true patriot, and a good man, and it has been my great fortune to have known him these many years.

I would also like to thank the members of Senator Thurmond's staff, many of whom I count among my closest friends. I was very proud to work with you.

Thanks to Coy Barefoot, my assistant and researcher, who devoted countless hours to this project and provided invaluable support at every stage. My thanks to Alison Bell, who edited numerous drafts of the manuscript and helped to bring the project to completion. And thanks to the talented team at Clemson University: Neil Cameron, Gregory Hawkins, Alan Burns, Shannon Hays, and Michael Kohl.

I am sincerely grateful as well to Dr. David McLeod, one of Walter Reed Medical Center's finest physicians, and to Dr. David Bernake and Dr. Alan Ansher of Alexandria, two of Virginia's ablest physicians. They saw me through some tough times so that I could continue to help the Senator and the people of South Carolina.

I am also grateful to the American Leadership Foundation for providing critical logistical support throughout my work on this project.

I want to pay a special tribute as well to my mother, Eloise Strom, who passed away at age 90 on June 3, 2005, nearly two years to the day after we lost Senator Thurmond. I cannot find the words to adequately express the devastating loss I felt at her death. My mother, or "Red" as I called her, was one of my very best friends. Her love, encouragement, and strength guided me my entire life. I miss you, Red.

My greatest thanks goes to my beautiful wife, Dee. Senator Thurmond used to call Dee the "Queen of the Senate." She was one of his dearest friends during the last fifteen years of his life. Not many people know how Dee looked after him, cooked his dinners, and even did his laundry. He cherished her, as I know she cherished him.

It was Dee's idea to write this book, and her determination that saw it through to the end. She has been there at every step in the process — tracking down old friends, digging up rare photos, and helping to edit the many drafts. She even took time to share her own memories of the Senator, each one told through heartfelt tears. Dee, you have brought the sunshine into my life and for that I am forever grateful.

  – R.J. Duke Short
    Alexandria, Virginia
    June, 2006

Foreword

BY SENATOR BOB DOLE

The Centennial Senator is a rare behind-the-scenes portrait of one of the most enduring political leaders of the twentieth century, Senator J. Strom Thurmond of South Carolina. This book is not a biography or a political history. It is a uniquely private account of Senator Thurmond — Thurmond the man, the politician, the war hero, the boss, the generous friend, the doting and committed father — as told by the men and women who knew this legendary person first-hand. Whether offered by presidents, senators, Supreme Court judges, ambassadors, former staff, or constituents, these unforgettable anecdotes and reflections are at once touching, hilarious, and fascinating.

Only one man could have written this book. No one but R.J. Duke Short could have brought all of these people together for the first time to so unselfishly share their memories of Senator Thurmond. Duke spent three decades at Thurmond's side, as his closest advisor, confidant, and friend. He served as the Chief Investigator and Staff Director on the Senate Judiciary Committee as well as Thurmond's Chief of Staff, overseeing countless professional and personal details until the Senator's very last day in office.

Affectionately known on Capitol Hill as the "101st Senator," Duke was an unfailing supporter of Senator Thurmond and a stalwart servant to the people of South Carolina. He is a former Army officer and an Honorary Major General in the InterAllied Military Forces. Duke is a graduate of North Georgia Military College and a graduate of Palmer College of Chiropractic. He worked at one time as a chiropractor and has been one of the profession's most steadfast advocates. Duke also served as a Special Agent with the Treasury Department and has the distinction of being one of the nation's first Sky Marshals, having been appointed under then President Nixon.

It is my honor and pleasure to introduce readers to Duke Short, who for many years has been one of democracy's greatest friends in Washington. Duke has given us a wonderful book of which I'm confident my dear pal ol' Strom would have been mighty proud. *The Centennial Senator* is not only a joy to read from start to finish, but will prove to be a valuable historic document as well. In my opinion, it will be remembered as the most important and definitive book written on the life and legacy of Senator J. Strom Thurmond.

An old lady came in to the office one day and said that her older sister had taught

Senator Thurmond in the first grade. She told me her sister used to thump Senator

Thurmond on the head when he was a first grader and say, "Strom! If you don't

straighten up, you'll never amount to anything!"

– Judge Dennis W. Shedd, a former Administrative Assistant to Senator Thurmond –

Introduction

Shortly before I retired from almost thirty years of working with Senator Strom Thurmond, the last fifteen years of which I served as his Chief of Staff, I was asked to write a book about my experiences in Washington. I preferred to write a book about the Senator instead. At one time, the Senator and I had even discussed the prospect of writing a book together. He was a remarkable man who led an amazing life. He was one of my closest friends, and in many ways he was a father figure to me. So I wanted to create something of which he would have been proud. We all have our shortcomings, and Senator Thurmond certainly had his. But I refused to write a critical or insider-tells-all book.

At the same time I wanted people to know what he was really like. I wanted the people who didn't have an opportunity to meet him and know him personally like I did to get a sense of the man behind the legend. But I knew my memories would only go so far. So in my efforts to paint as complete a portrait as possible of this extraordinary man, I opened the door to a host of his friends, colleagues, and staff to share their own memories — their most unforgettable Strom Thurmond moments.

Nearly all of these stories were shared in person or over the phone. A handful were submitted in writing. This book, then, can be understood as an oral history of James Strom Thurmond as told by the people who knew him best.

In the stories that follow you will meet Strom Thurmond the politician, Strom Thurmond the boss, Strom Thurmond the ladies' man, the fitness advocate, the backseat driver, the soldier, the dancer, the friend, and much more. My only regret is that Holly Richardson did not live long enough to share her own stories. Holly worked for the Senator for nearly a quarter of a century, many of her last years as his most trusted personal secretary. She passed away in September of 2002, shortly before the Senator's retirement. The absence of her voice in this book is a loss to us all.

You will not find much at all in this book about Senator Thurmond's first daughter. I believe that story is better told by others. Many years ago the Senator chose to confide in me the true nature of his relationship with the young African-American woman who was his daughter. I know he cared for her and her family very much and that he made every effort to assist them whenever he could. The decision to go public with the relationship must not have been an easy one. I personally do not have much to say about the subject because frankly, it was none of my business. But I did admire the manner in which the revelation was handled by everyone involved, including the Senator's wife Nancy and their children.

The
Centennial Senator

U.S. Treasury Dept. Intelligence Division, National Training Center, Special Agent Basic School #41, March 6-April 21, 1967. Duke Short is second row, fourth from the right.

DENISE SHORT

Because so many young people applying for jobs did have "connections," I tried to convey the message that there's nothing wrong with someone helping you to get a job. But, in the end, you had better work hard, because you and only you can keep it.

– R.J. Duke Short –

Welcome Aboard!

GOING TO WORK FOR SENATOR THURMOND

I graduated from North Georgia College (the Military College of Georgia) in 1956 and received my commission as a brand-new second lieutenant in the United States Army. That was one of the proudest days of my life. While in college I spent three years in the Army Reserve and, after receiving my commission, I was on active duty for five years. I later learned that one of my assignments was with the same unit that Senator Thurmond had served with during World War II, the 325 Airborne Infantry of the 82nd Airborne Division. Needless to say, Senator Thurmond was there with the greatest generation and during the time that really counted.

After leaving the Army, I went to work as a Special Agent with the Intelligence Division of the U.S. Treasury Department in Atlanta, Georgia. This was a very interesting, fulfilling job, and I really enjoyed the work. At one point as an agent I was assigned to the Organized Crime Strike Force in Miami, but I continued to work out of Atlanta. At times we did undercover work in the process of gathering intelligence on organized crime leaders. My particular focus was on investigating illegal gambling activities.

During this time, I considered myself fortunate to have been selected as one of the first nineteen Special Agents in the Intelligence Division to be called up by President Nixon to help protect U.S. airlines against hijacking. As one of the first "Sky Marshals," I traveled all over the world in an undercover capacity. Our job was to prevent terrorists from taking over aircraft. Those duties were later incorporated into the Federal Air Marshal Service which is now under the Department of Homeland Security.

I came to Washington in the early 1970s as the National Chief of Investigations for the

Federal Protective Service. After years of exciting work, my first job in Washington with the FPS was a bit of a disappointment. I found myself sitting behind a desk most of the time pushing papers. So I asked my stepfather if he could help me find something a little better, preferably on Capitol Hill.

The next thing I know, Senator Strom Thurmond had hired me as the Senior Investigator for the Senate Subcommittee on Internal Security. That was 1974. I worked closely with Senator Thurmond and began to understand what he wanted from a staffer. Later I became the Chief Investigator and Staff Director for the Senate Judiciary Committee. In 1988 I joined his office as his Chief of Staff. I was there when we turned out the lights and closed the door nearly thirty years later. That was in January of 2003 when we both retired from the United States Senate.

People frequently ask me how I started to work for Senator Thurmond. I jokingly tell them I was hired for my ingenuity, ability, skill, knowledge, and intelligence. In addition to that was the fact that my stepfather, Lou Strom, and Senator Thurmond were first cousins! I would go on to say, I know that relationship had nothing to do with the reason I was hired! This was my way of stressing the fact that of course the family connection was the very reason I was hired. Because so many young people applying for jobs did have "connections," I tried to convey the message that there's nothing wrong with someone helping you to get a job. But in the end, you had better work hard, because you and only you can keep it.

FRANKI ROBERTS
is a former Legislative Aide to Senator Thurmond.
She is now married to Senator Pat Roberts of Kansas.

Let me tell you how I was hired by Senator Thurmond. It was 1965, and I was doing my graduate teaching in Hartsville, South Carolina. It was two weeks before graduation. I was not sure what I was going to be doing after graduation. Everybody was giving me a hard time about not having a job. One night I got a call from somebody saying he was Senator Strom Thurmond and would I like to come to work for him in his office. Well, I thought it was somebody teasing me. I told him sure, I'd think about it and let him know in a couple of days. Then I hung up and tried to figure out which one of my friends was playing the joke on me. But I checked the phone number he left me, and oh my gosh, it was for real! It really was Strom Thurmond!

It turned out the Senator had an opening at the time and had called the college for a recommendation. That's how he came to call me. I graduated on a Saturday morning and my parents drove me up to Washington that afternoon. I stayed with Rose Smith, who was the Senator's personal secretary at that time. I stayed with her until I got an apartment on Capitol Hill, one block from the Senate Office Building. Like I said, it was 1965, right after the Senator had switched parties. It was a wonderful opportunity and a very

Senator Thurmond and Duke Short at a hearing of the
Subcommittee on Internal Security. This was one of
Duke's first hearings with the Senator.

interesting time to be in Washington, that's for sure. I thought I'd come up to D.C. for a few years and then go home. But I ended up meeting my husband in Washington, and I've been here ever since!

WILLIAM W. WILKINS

*is the Chief Judge of the United States Court of Appeals for the
Fourth Circuit. He has the distinction of being the first Federal
Judge appointed by President Reagan (1981). Judge Wilkins
served as a Legal Assistant to Senator Thurmond from 1970-71.*

When I left active duty with the Army I went to work for Judge Clement F. Haynsworth, Jr., who was then the Chief Judge of the Fourth Circuit Court of Appeals. While I was working for him, he was nominated by President Nixon to the United States Supreme Court. I traveled to Washington a good deal as Judge Haynsworth's representative, to meet with the Justice Department lawyers who were overseeing his nomination. When people needed to talk with him about issues, I would relay the messages and get the answers back and forth. I met Senator Thurmond on several occasions when I was in Washington.

After the nomination was defeated, I was in my office in Greenville one day finishing my term with Judge Haynsworth. I will never forget that day. Everybody had gone to lunch. I was the only one in the office. I looked up from my desk and there stood Strom Thurmond. He had come to Greenville on business and had dropped by the courthouse unannounced to pay his respects to Judge Haynsworth. Back then we didn't have any security and the offices weren't locked. Senator Thurmond just came on in and walked around until he found somebody. We talked for probably 30 or 40 minutes. I didn't know it at the time, but he was looking for a lawyer to hire on his staff in Washington.

As we finished the conversation, he said, "Billy, how much does Judge Haynsworth pay you?" I said "$12,000 a year, Senator." He said, "I'll give you a $500 raise if you come to work for me." It wasn't because of the $500 raise, but I did go to work for him. I moved to Washington shortly after that conversation. And that's how I went to work for Senator Thurmond.

MELINDA KOUTSOUMPAS

worked for Senator Thurmond for almost 20 years, from 1984 until his retirement in 2003. She served as the Chief Clerk of the Senate Judiciary Committee and then later as Chief Clerk for the Senate Armed Services Committee.

When the Senator took over the Armed Services Committee, one of the first hires that I knew we had to make was a computer person. I had gotten word that there was one available from the Commerce Committee. I told Duke about it. So she came over one afternoon for an interview with the Senator. Well, she was in blue jeans; so we scrounged around and got her a skirt, a blouse, and a jacket.

We brought her in, and she sat down. She told the Senator she had relatives in South Carolina. He was in one of those bad moods that day. He said, "Why do you want to work?" She gave her background. He looked at her résumé. She had been working on the Hill for about twelve years at that point, and had started out with Senator Laxalt. Senator Thurmond kept at it. "Why do you want to work? You have children." She said, "Yes sir, I do, but I enjoy working. My children are little, and my mother and father take care of them." He said, "I just don't understand. Little kids need their parents."

Finally she said, "Senator, I need the money." He didn't say anything for a few minutes. Duke and I were looking at each other like, please God, just let her out of here. He asked, "What did you do for Senator Laxalt?" She told him, "I did input for letters." That was kind of an entry-level job.

Duke evidently knew what was coming, because he stepped out and called Senator Laxalt to give him a head's up. Senator Thurmond just wouldn't stop. He kept firing questions at this poor woman, and all of this simply to run the computer system. You'd have thought he was hiring a new Chief Counsel. At one point he said, "I think I'll call Senator Laxalt."

He got Laxalt on the phone and said, "I've got this young girl in here and she says she worked for you." Now this was twelve years ago. There's no way Senator Laxalt would have remembered an entry-level staffer from that long ago. But Duke had called him, so he said, "Oh yes, she's a fine worker. You should hire her!" The Senator hung up the phone and said, "He said you're a fine worker. You're hired!"

That woman turned out to be just that, a fine worker. Senator Thurmond usually wasn't at all like that when it came to hiring people, but if you caught him on one of those days when he was in a mood, you just never knew.

MICHAEL MISHOE
was a Legislative Assistant for Senator Thurmond, 1976-77.

My actual job interview with the Senator was down at Myrtle Beach in the summer of 1976. The Senator and his family were staying at a hotel there, and I was to meet him in the lobby. Not having ever met him before, I was certainly intimidated. When he came down to the lobby, he started by saying, "Mr. Mishoe, you come highly recommended. We'd like for you to come to work with us." Then he talked a little bit about salary. It wasn't much.

Then he added, "I know Washington is an expensive place to live. But we have a lot of receptions in Washington, so you'll be able to eat a lot of your food for free." I would later learn that there was some truth to that. He was essentially saying, "I can't pay you much, but you'll eat for free." And he was right! I'll never forget that.

JOHN DECROSTA
is a former Senior Policy Advisor and Press Secretary for Senator Thurmond. He worked for the Senator from 1991 to 2001.

When you started with Senator Thurmond, the very first thing you'd do is go in and meet Mr. Short. Then Mr. Short takes you in to meet the Senator, and the Senator welcomes you aboard. The first thing Senator Thurmond told me after I came to Washington in 1991 is, "Mr. DeCrosta, you're here to help the people. That's what we do here.

If somebody calls this office, they're calling to get help, and we're going to do whatever we can." That was it. Those were my marching orders. And that was typical for the Senator. Everybody I know that went to work for him got the same speech: "The whole reason we're here is to serve the people of South Carolina."

Funny thing is, I was a media guy. I was a Deputy Press Secretary. I wasn't going to work in Projects or Constituent Service. But to Senator Thurmond, it was all the same. To him, everyone on his staff did the same thing in a different way: they helped people. That's what it was all about.

DAVID BLACK

is the former Assistant Office Manager for Senator Thurmond. He
worked from 1999 until the Senator retired.

I remember my first day when Mr. Short took me in to meet the Senator. Mr. Short said, "Senator, here's a new staffer. I'd just like to introduce you to him. He's going to be your Assistant Office manager." The Senator said, "We got work for him to do?" Mr. Short said, "Sure do." The Senator looked at me and said, "Well, get back to work then!"

KEVIN SMITH

served initially as Senator Thurmond's personal driver, then later
as a Deputy Projects Director. He worked for the Senator from
2000 until 2002.

On the day I was hired, I was talking with Mr. Short in his office, which can be pretty intimidating. Once he had officially asked me if I was interested in the job and I said yes, he said, "Let's go in and I'll introduce you to the Senator." I was really nervous. On the way in, Mr. Short gave me all this advice, "Don't put your hands in your pockets; speak loudly so he can hear you; always look right at him." It was scary.

We walked in. The Senator stood up and looked at me. Mr. Short said, "Senator, this is Kevin Smith. He's from Florence, South Carolina. He's going to be your driver for awhile. We think he's going to do a good job; he comes highly recommended." The Senator kind of looked me over and asked, "Are you a good driver?"

It was like I was in a state of shock. I'm thinking, oh my God! I don't want to say the wrong thing here! I said, "Yes sir. I'm going to do my best." He said, "All right, you're hired! Glad to have you on board!" And he sat back down. I was thinking, get me out of here! My heart was racing so fast.

The first month or so when I drove for him was probably the biggest thrill of my life. I pretty much went wherever he did, other than the Senate Floor. It was an unbelievable experience. He was an amazing person.

BILL TUTEN

is a former Projects Director for Senator Thurmond. He worked from 1997 until January of 2003.

The first few times I went in to see the Senator in his office people asked me, "Did you see such and such a picture on the wall?" Heck no! From the time you walked around that corner and saw him there behind that massive desk, all your focus was on him! He was all I could see.

The very first time I went in to interview with him, he wanted to know where I was from. I was so nervous, I said, "South Carolina." He said, "I know that! Where in South Carolina?" "Oh! Yes sir, Columbia, sir." I guess I was in there about ten minutes or so. I had thought I might get a handshake or a nod or a welcome aboard, but he wanted to sit down and chat. It was great. I told him I'd done some coaching. He liked that. He told me how he used to coach, and how he really enjoyed it. When I walked out of there, I could not have told you one damn thing that was on the walls. I was looking right at him the entire time. He blew me away.

CRAIG METZ

served as Senator Thurmond's Counsel on the Labor and Human Resources Committee from 1988 to 1990. He was also Deputy Assistant Secretary for Congressional Liaison at the Department of Education, and later served as Chief of Staff to Congressman Floyd Spence of South Carolina.

Whenever anyone new would start with Senator Thurmond, he used to have all the staff come together to meet them. He'd get everybody gathered around and say, "Tell them a little bit about yourself." If the person was a man, he'd always say, "All you women look him over; he'd be a good target." The Senator was always interested in matching people up. He really wanted people to get married and have children. He was very focused on that.

Another thing he would tell new people is, "You're here to help people. If you can't help people, we're going to help you go somewhere else real quick." Senator Thurmond didn't like to fire people, especially if the person's dad was a state senator or someone well-connected back home. If there was a big reason, he didn't hesitate to fire someone for cause, but usually he tried to avoid having to send them home. If we had someone who wasn't pulling their weight he'd call the Administration, if the Republicans were in power, and arrange for them to be taken on as a Schedule C away from his office.

He'd send for the person to come to his office and tell them, "I've got wonderful news for you! The President needs you to come into his Administration, so you'll be starting at the Department of Agriculture on Monday! Congratulations! Good luck to you, and thank you so much for all you've done!"

SCOTT FRICK

served as a Legislative Assistant and then as Senator Thurmond's
Chief Counsel on the Senate Judiciary Subcommittee on the
Constitution from 2000 until 2003.

Of course I talked with Mr. Short first. And then he took me in to meet the Senator and have him approve of hiring me. I sat down to talk with him, but he only asked me one question. He said, "Have you ever failed a course?" I was thinking, wow, the bar's set pretty low here! I said, "No sir." He seemed to be pleased with that. And that was pretty much of the extent of my interview with the Senator.

PATRICIA RONES SYKES

managed Senator Thurmond's Charleston office from 1995 until
he retired in 2003.

In 1987 I came home to Charleston from Washington to work for Congressman Arthur Ravenel, a great man. He ran for governor on the Republican party ticket but did not get the nomination. So I went to work in his successor's office and was there for eight months. About a month later I got a call from a friend in Senator Thurmond's Charleston office who said there was a position opening up on Thurmond's staff. I called Congressman Ravenel and told him about it, and I asked if he could please make a courtesy call for me.

At that time I was at my mother's house recuperating from a broken foot. The phone rang one day; I picked it up, and there was the voice of Senator Thurmond. He said, "This is Senator Strom Thurmond calling. Is Patricia there?" I said, "Yes sir, this is Patricia." He said, "I hear you need a job." "Yes sir, I do."

He said, "Now tell me, are you a single gal?" I said yes sir. "Well, you got yourself a job, bye-bye!" And he hung up. And that was it! That's all there was to the interview. Truly I thought somebody must be playing a joke on me because that was too strange. I had heard of the Senator's constituent service before, but that went way beyond.

So I got back on the phone and called the Washington office and introduced myself. I told them, "I think I just spoke with Senator Thurmond. I am trying to find out for sure if that was him or not." The receptionist put me through to Mr. Short. Mr. Short came on the phone and said, "Hi Patricia. Welcome aboard." I said, "Sir, would you mind if I just asked you, is this job to be in the Charleston office or the Washington office?" Mr. Short said, "Well, where would you like the job to be?" I told him I would love to stay home in Charleston. He said, "That'll be just fine. When do you want to start?"

So I went on to work for the Senator for the next eight years. It was an amazing job. But that's how it happened, just a quick phone call from the Senator: "You got yourself a job, bye-bye!"

SHELL SUBER
is a former Staff Assistant for Senator Thurmond, 1990 to 1993.

When my dad graduated from the University of South Carolina Law School, he served as a JAG Officer in the Air Force. About the time he got out, Senator Thurmond had just gotten named to the Judiciary Committee and was looking to hire some lawyers. So Senator Thurmond heard about my dad, got in touch with him, and offered him a job to help him out on the Judiciary Committee.

My dad called his grandfather, Judge Martin from Greenville, to get his opinion. He said, "Granddaddy, the Senator just called me and asked about this job. What do you think?" The Judge told him not to go and get hooked up with Thurmond. "He is too old," the Judge said, in classic Judge Martin form. "And he doesn't have what it takes to last in politics. He'll be gone in no time flat. If you get hooked up with him, you'll go down with him. Son, I recommend you go ahead and get your law practice set up there in Columbia."

Thirty years later the Senator offered the same job to me that he'd once offered to my father. I called my dad at his office, at the law firm he'd set up when he didn't go to Washington. I said, "Dad, I just got off the phone with Senator Thurmond. He's offered me a job." My dad said, "Son, pack your bags now, you're going to Washington! You can't get on the train fast enough! Senator Thurmond could last another thirty years!"

The Last Staff Standing: Senator Thurmond's final staff.
This photograph was taken on his 100th birthday,
December 5, 2002.

U.S. SENATE PHOTO

He cut me off and said real quick, "The computer didn't make the mistake!" I walked out of
there feeling about two-feet tall. But he was exactly right.

– Bill Tuten –

"I Am the Senator"

WORKING FOR SENATOR THURMOND

My good friend the late Brigadier General Emory Sneeden, a former Administrative Assistant to Senator Thurmond and a great human being, once asked me, "Hey Duke, has Thurmond given you the 'I Am the Senator!' speech yet?" I said, "No Emory. I don't even know what it is." He said, "Well, you'll know it when you hear it." He was right.

Senator Thurmond attended a meeting of the American Bar Association one year; I believe it was in Louisiana. Apparently he heard someone at the conference make the comment, "If you need anything on the Senate Judiciary, you go see Duke Short. He's the guy who handles all the nominations." The Senator came back and shared that with me. He said, "Now Duke, I am the Senator! I'm the one that has to run for office!" I said, "Yes sir." That's basically all I could say. I hadn't done anything to encourage that comment he'd heard at the meeting. He went on, "They didn't even mention me one time! And I am the Senator!" I said, "I sure am sorry about that, Senator." That's all I could say. Senator Thurmond was absolutely right. It didn't matter to him that I did the best job I could and gave him all the credit. He frowned on the idea of any of his staff receiving credit or praise from anyone other than him.

Years later, after I became Chief of Staff, I put out a notice that went to every member of the Senator's staff. It basically said, "If you do something wrong or something goes wrong, then you must accept responsibility. If something goes right or happens like it's supposed to, then Senator Thurmond gets the credit. We take the blame and he gets the credit. That's how it works. That's the nature of working for a public official."

That said, I wasn't just there to agree with Senator Thurmond. He and I disagreed on many issues. In all honesty, we argued like cats and dogs numerous times over the years. That's one of the reasons I believe I was able to do my job so well, because I didn't just say "yes sir" every time. I told him what I thought. I gave him my opinion. He didn't have to take my advice, and many times he didn't. But I'd make sure he knew what I thought. A good leader wants to know what you think. He wants to know that you believe in what you say, and that you will defend it. Strom Thurmond was a good leader.

Strom Thurmond was an exceptional person to work for, as the anecdotes from this chapter demonstrate. He cared deeply about every member of his staff, past and present. He unselfishly opened many doors of opportunity for people who were close to him, whether it was simply to meet the President of the United States or get appointed to the Federal bench. The people who worked for him were family. We were all very close. To a person the Senator treated us with respect, appreciation, and devotion.

At the same time, Strom Thurmond could be incredibly demanding. He would accept no less than quality work. He wanted a sense of urgency attached to every task. He used to say, "Got something to do? Then let's get it done now so we can move on to the next thing!"

I know that all of us who worked for Senator Thurmond felt the same way: it was like no other job. It was unique even for the U.S. Senate. We all felt like we were a part of something special. We had a real sense of purpose. We were making a difference. It was a remarkable experience that I, like many others, am so fortunate to have had.

SHELL SUBER

I was originally assigned to what Senator Thurmond called "Projects." For all practical purposes, that office would be called "Constituent Service," but the Senator liked the word "Projects." Most everybody who worked for the Senator over the years at one time or another held that title: Staff Assistant, Projects. That's where you started out, unless you were a girl. Most of the girls would start out in the front office answering the phones. The Senator had two desks out front for receptionists. He always wanted pretty young girls sitting out there. So the girls almost always started out front, and the guys always started back in Projects. Now, if you had a law degree, you'd start over working in legislation. Every new guy while I was there started out in Projects unless they were a lawyer. That's how the Senator had it all set up.

BILL TUTEN

The first letter I took in to the Senator had a misspelled word in it. Nobody caught it but him. It was one of those words that you can spell two different ways, depending on the context. So even Spell Check won't catch it. The Senator got his pen out and started going through the letter. I remember it so clearly. He would go line by line, study every word. All of a sudden he stopped and the pen went back. He looked at me. "That's not how you spell that word." I looked at it and I said, "Yes it is." But then I read it in context. He was right. I said, "Senator, I'm sorry. I was working on the computer. I apologize, you know, the computer didn't —." He cut me off and said real quick, "The computer didn't make the mistake!" I walked out of there feeling about two-feet tall. But he was exactly right.

ELIZA EDGAR

was Assistant to the Chief of Staff in Senator Thurmond's office as well as the Page and Intern Coordinator from 1996 until 2003.

The Senator had an unbelievable schoolteacher's mind, right up until his last day. It never ceased to amaze me. I remember taking letters in there for him to look over. Right there on his desk was a little pencil cup that one of his kids had made when they were little. He'd reach in there and get a black felt tip pen, which he signed letters with, and a red felt tip pen, which he used for corrections.

He read the letters holding the black pen, having it ready to sign. But sometimes he would put that pen down and reach for the red. I'd say to myself, uh-oh, he found something. It didn't matter how many of us had reviewed the letter; he always managed to find something. It might be a comma or misspelled word. More likely, it was something that nowadays is acceptable to either omit or leave in, but according to the Old School rules, you should do something else. He would find those kind of things all the time.

I recall one letter that one of the girls took in for him to sign. We must have had four or five people read it before she took it in there, but wouldn't you know he found something. The Senator got that red pen out and made a big red circle and told her she needed to fix it. We actually had to go look it up because it wasn't a rule any of us had learned. It was very Old School. But that's how he wanted it done, and there was no way he was going to sign until it was fixed. He edited all his letters like that until the very last days in office. It was just unbelievable.

JOHN DECROSTA

Everything that was prepared for his approval went through a series of readers before it ever got to the Senator. I'd look at it. My immediate supervisors would look at it. Mr. Short would look at it. There would be edits and corrections at each step of the way. But something would happen to it as I walked through the door of his office. Some gremlin would reach out and scramble stuff, misspell a word. And God help you if you had an error; the Senator would nail you on it. He always had his red pen and his black pen ready to go.

I remember one day there was some document I kept having to change because he kept finding more errors. He was getting frustrated with me. I think I was getting frustrated with him. At some point he sensed my exasperation. I may have even said something like, "What's the difference?" He said, "Well, I can't help it! I was a school teacher my first job! Things have to be right!" Then he added, "I went to a military school too. I'm a military man. I've got to do things a certain way John! It's just my training!"

MATTHEW J. MARTIN

*was a Military Assistant to Senator Thurmond from 2000
until January of 2003.*

I'll never forget the first letter I took in for Senator Thurmond to sign. I had only been working for him for a few months at the time. It was a letter to President Clinton about the Junior ROTC program, which the Senator championed. This was the very first letter I'd prepared for him, so I was very nervous. I had everyone in the chain of command review the letter before I took it in to the Senator. I thought it was in good shape. But when I took the letter to him, he started marking it up. At that point, I thought I was going to be fired. He had this look on his face like, *Did you really just hand me this piece of paper?*

On one of the corrections, I told him I thought it should be the other way. He said, "Mr. Martin, it doesn't matter what you think. Whose name is at the bottom of this piece of paper?" He didn't say it in a stern or scolding voice. He said it in a very friendly voice. But his point was clear. The Senator knew his grammar. He always had that Old School teacher's mind and never hesitated to point that out to you.

GEORGE LAUFFER,

*Lieutenant Colonel, U.S. Army (ret.), worked for Senator
Thurmond from 1989 to 2002 as his Designee on the Senate
Armed Services Committee.*

Senator Thurmond wanted a statement for every hearing, whether he was going to be there or not. So I prepared these statements for him and took them over to his office for him to review. Nearly every time, he'd find some word I misused or misspelled. "That's not the right word," he'd say. "Senator, I think it's correct." "Get the dictionary!" So I would haul out one of those big Cambridge dictionaries, put it on his desk, and we'd look it up. And wouldn't you know it, he was right, every time.

To sort of soften the blow, he'd say, "Don't worry about it. You've got to remember, I was an English teacher and I know these things." I don't think, in all the time that I worked for him, he ever chastised me harshly for anything. He let me know where I screwed up, but it was in more of a fatherly tone. He was demanding; there was no doubt about that. And if you didn't have stuff in time for him, he'd let you know he was disappointed. But he was always a gentleman about it.

ED KENNEY

was an Administrative Assistant to Senator Thurmond. He
worked for the Senator from 1960 to 1970 and later served
for over a decade as a Professional Staff Member on the Senate
Armed Services Committee.

If I had a spelling error in a speech, the Senator would find it. He'd often say something like, "Ed, why are you bringing this to me? It's not ready. You've got a misspelled word here." He was always gentle about it, yet he got his point over. He was the kind of guy that would only rarely come down on somebody about something. And when he did, he was so gentle about it, you'd only realize later that hey, he's on my case.

CHRIS KELLEY CIMKO

served as Senator Thurmond's Press Secretary from 1993 to 1997,
and also worked as Communications Director for the Senate
Armed Services Committee.

I didn't know the Strom Thurmond from the 1940s. The Strom Thurmond I knew was warm, inspiring, smart, kind, a demanding boss, and the last gentleman I think I've known in my life. He could be a hard taskmaster. I can say, as a Communications Executive, that my writing style today is very different from what it was when I first started working for him.

One never forgot that the Senator started out life as an English teacher. He liked things clean and crisp. He had the same incisive, questioning mind as a reporter would, so press releases and other documents that we would give out to the media had to be very well thought out. And yet when you gave him quality work, he would always let you know that you'd done a good job, that he appreciated your work, and that he was proud of you.

BECKY FLEMING

*served as Senator Thurmond's Press Secretary. She worked
in his office from 1997 until January of 2003.*

I took something back for the Senator to sign off on. He read it over very closely and discovered that I'd left out two commas. Nothing got by him. He would catch any misspellings too, every time. When he corrected a word, he'd always say, "As a child, I was an excellent speller." He was very proud of that.

MELINDA KOUTSOUMPAS

Dennis Shedd and I used to carpool together when we worked for the Senator. We got to work one morning a little before nine o'clock. Dennis said to me, "Do you want me to run for coffee or do you want to?" I told him to go ahead because I was retyping a speech or something. A few minutes later the phone rang, and it was Senator Thurmond. "Is Mr. Shedd there?" I said, "No sir, he's not. He's just stepped out for some coffee."

Uh-oh. That was the wrong answer. At that point it was about ten minutes after nine. Senator said, "Coffee?! It's after nine o'clock! If you all want coffee or breakfast, then you get up early enough in the morning to do that before you come to work. At nine o'clock I want you to be at your desk working!" He was very adamant about that. He wanted everybody at their desks at the stroke of nine, no excuses.

TERRY L. WOOTEN

*worked with Senator Thurmond for over a decade,
beginning in 1986. Before he left the Senate, Mr. Wooten held
the title of Minority Chief Counsel and Staff Director for the
Senate Judiciary Committee. He is now a Federal District
Judge in Florence, South Carolina.*

Before I came to Washington, I had only seen Senator Thurmond a few times in South Carolina. I may have had an opportunity to shake his hand at some point, but I don't recall that I ever met him. So the first time that I ever had to talk to the Senator about an issue was as a member of his staff. I was told to meet him in the hallway, that he would come out of his office and I could talk to him then on his way to the Senate Floor.

Well, the Senator finally came out of the door. Here I was a young staffer, kind of uptight and nervous to talk to the Senator; I mean, here I am advising a powerful man. I didn't really know quite what to say or how to say it.

I remember the Senator was walking real fast. I was trying to think about what I was doing, and I guess I wasn't walking as fast as he was. I was talking a little bit too loud perhaps, because I was nervous. Anyway, at one point the Senator stopped, turned and looked at me, and said, "You walk too slow and you talk too loud! I got to go!" And he walked right off. That's just the way he did it. That's the way he was. He didn't have time for you to be nervous around him. He wanted you to say what you had to say and move on, because he had a lot to do.

CRAIG METZ

Senator Thurmond worked hard, and he expected everybody on his staff to work hard. I recall a time when a staffer from the Armed Services Committee came in to brief him on a Monday morning. He started out by saying, "Senator, how was your weekend?" If you're from the South, you usually start out with a few pleasantries before you ever get into your work. That was okay, but it went on a little bit longer than the Senator would have liked. The Senator finally said, "Get to the point!" So the staffer briefed him on the issue.

As soon as he left, the Senator called his AA [Administrative Assistant] and said, "Call over to the Committee and tell what's his name that we're here to work! We don't have time to chit chat." That's the way the Senator was. He didn't want any idle conversation. When you went in to brief him, he wanted to know what you had to say then thank you very much, and he moved on to the next thing. He was very disciplined about that.

JOHN L. NAPIER

is a former U.S. Congressman from South Carolina (1981-83), and was appointed to the U.S. Court of Federal Claims by President Reagan. Mr. Napier served as Counsel and Legislative Assistant to Senator Thurmond, 1972-79. He now practices law in Washington, D.C. and South Carolina.

In 1975 I had been promoted through the staff as Senator Thurmond's Counsel. He called me into his office one day to ask how he could fly on a certain plane to a certain location, and whether or not that conformed to the new campaign finance laws that had just been written. I said "No sir, the way you just described it, it does not conform to the new campaign finance laws. You can't do it." He said, "I didn't call you in here to tell me how not to do something. I called you in here to find me a legal way to get it done. Now, you go back and figure out the legal way to do it."

That was my first experience with him as his lawyer. And we found a legal way for him to do just what he wanted to do. If something was not going to work within the law, he wanted to know. But he didn't want a lawyer around him who was a "No" person. He wanted a lawyer who would say "Yes," but only if there was a legal way to do it.

FRANKI ROBERTS

He was busy! He was on the go all the time. We all worked very hard. It was like we had to beg for time off sometimes just to get our laundry done because we all worked such long hours. We'd be there till 11 or 12 o'clock at night. The Senator was there too, every night. Some nights he'd even walk back through the office with orange juice and oatmeal cookies for us.

WILLIAM W. WILKINS

In his office in Washington, Senator Thurmond used to have a buzzer system. It was a less-sophisticated communication system than the kind you see today. I remember he had a series of buttons next to each staff member's name. If he buzzed you, it would ring at your desk. That meant you were to drop everything and run to his office. He didn't want to waste any time. Of course, he's legendary about jogging down the halls on his way to the Senate. It was like working in an atmosphere of urgency. There was no time to waste. That was the way he worked.

MICHAEL MISHOE

Senator Thurmond didn't tolerate anybody wasting his time. He could be difficult if you went up to talk to him about something that was unimportant because he knew there were other things that needed his time. On the other hand, if you didn't tell him the things you needed to tell him, he wasn't happy about that either. So there was always that fine line you had to walk: do you tell him or don't you? Well, I'll never forget the time I made the wrong decision.

We had an issue come up where several counties in South Carolina had been declared disaster areas on account of dry weather. That made the farmers in those coun-

Coy Short, the author's brother, Senator Thurmond, and Duke Short in 1985.

ties eligible for certain programs. I was the one who got the call that the counties had just been so designated. The Senator was busy on the Floor at the time, so I decided I would tell him when he got back to the office.

But I never got around to telling him until later that afternoon. He said, "When did you find this out?" "This morning about 10 o'clock." He said, "Why Mr. Mishoe, you should have told me right away. What if I'd gotten a call about this? We don't do things this way. This is not acceptable."

The next day he called me into his office and lectured me about it again. Then all of a sudden, he told the AA to call all the staff into his office. I'll never forget this. Here I am sitting in the chair in front of the Senator's desk. I look up, and there's about 25 people standing around looking at me. The Senator says, "I wanted y'all to come in here. Y'all are not to do what Mr. Mishoe did. I don't want something like this to happen again. Make sure you don't do what Mr. Mishoe did." I'll never forget that moment. But at least I can say that I've been lectured by the best of them!

SUSAN PELTER

is a former Press Secretary for Senator Thurmond. She worked for him in the mid 1980s and again from 1990 to '93.

As a boss, Strom Thurmond could be very demanding. He wanted you to be prepared, have your facts straight, and know all the details. But he could also be quite caring. He was sort of like the patriarch of this extended family of staffers. Occasionally he'd have these big staff meetings, and he'd always go around and ask about everyone's spouses, children, and parents. He wanted to know how everyone's family was doing. And if a woman on the staff had a baby, Strom Thurmond would go visit her at the hospital.

JOHN R. STEER

is a former Legislative Director and Administrative Assistant to Senator Thurmond. He is now a Member and Vice Chair of the U.S. Sentencing Commission, having been appointed by President Clinton in 1999.

Here's the story of the only time the Senator ever chewed me out. This happened in Washington shortly after I came back to work in his office after law school. He was being sworn in as President Pro Tempore. He'd arranged to go down to the Old Executive Office Building where Vice President Mondale was going to swear him in. He asked me to drive him down to the building, which I did. When I dropped him off he said, "This is not the entrance where I need to be, but you wait right here anyway." I said, "Senator, I can drive around to the other entrance." He said, "No, I want you to wait right here." So he got out of the car and went in.

I decided to take it on my own initiative and try to get back to that closer entrance where the Senator would be coming out. But I got caught up in traffic, and I couldn't get back in time. So when the Senator finally came back, I was not there where I was supposed to be. Somehow or another, he got a ride back to the Capitol. To this day, I don't know how he got back there. But by the time I could get back he was already there. I had to go trooping into his office and explain.

He said, "I told you exactly what I wanted you to do. I wanted you to stay right where you were. I saw you pull away." I said, "Senator, I was trying to get closer to the entrance." He said, "Next time you do exactly what I tell you to do." I deserved to be chewed out. Although my intentions were good, and he knew that, nevertheless, I had blatantly done exactly what he told me not to do.

I don't think the Senator was afraid to chew staff out if it was warranted. And it did-n't matter who it was, whether your were a retired Major General in the Army or the receptionist. If you deserved it, he would dress you down and straighten you out. And if he did that, he didn't hold it against you. He just moved on to the next thing. He wasn't angry at you forever. He expected you to learn from it.

MARK GOODIN

*worked as Senator Thurmond's Press Secretary and Spokesman
for the U.S. Senate Judiciary Committee, 1981-87. He later served
as Deputy Assistant Secretary of Transportation under Ronald
Reagan and as George H.W. Bush's Campaign Spokesman.*

As Press Secretary you walk a fine line between being a servant of the press and being a servant of the Senator. The one thing that can't happen, if you're going to do your job, is for the Senator to show you up in front of the press. Well, Senator Thurmond dressed me down one time in front of a bunch of reporters. I waited until the elevator doors closed and I said, "Senator, that was embarrassing to me. And let me say this sir, if you do that to me again sir, I'm going to have to quit because I can't work under these circumstances." I didn't yell. I said it very calmly. He turned away, looked straight ahead, and didn't say another word. He cleared his throat a couple of times. We walked back to the office.

I guess an hour or so went by. The little buzzer went off at my desk. He said, "Come in here." I walked in. He said, "I want to apologize." I was taken aback. That's not at all like Senator Thurmond to apologize to his staff for anything. "Sir?" He said, "You were right to say something to me back there. You've got to be able to do your job, and basically, I put you in a bad situation." He actually used the words, "I apologize." I thought, damn!

DAVID BLACK

Senator Thurmond would often walk back to each section of the office, to make sure you were working and see what you were up to, that kind of thing. We had a system going where the person in one section would call back to the other and say, "Senator's coming back! Get off the Internet!" You always knew he was coming because there'd be a succession of phone calls throughout the office. Ring-ring-ring. Then all of a sudden you'd look up and the Senator would be standing there. "What you working on?" He was just genuinely curious. He would say, "If I need to help, you be sure and let me know."

Can you imagine that? There he is, almost 100-years old, walking through the office to see how he can help.

MANSEL LONG, JR.

served as a Legislative Director for Senator Howell Heflin
in the 1980s.

I came to know Senator Thurmond as an individual who placed a lot of confidence in his staff. He surrounded himself with highly competent staff members. They were very loyal to him, and he in turn was very loyal to them. I remember specifically when Duke Short was going to Walter Reed Hospital for surgery. I had heard that Senator Thurmond told the hospital officials to treat Duke just as if he was a Senator. That's an example of how loyal he was to his staff. Usually people speak about how loyal the staff members are to the elected official. But Senator Thurmond was very, very devoted to his staff and very concerned about them.

MICHAEL MISHOE

The Senator always tried to give you opportunities to do things that you wouldn't otherwise have. I remember coming in one morning, in the fall of '76. I'd only been on the job for about two months. His personal secretary said, "Michael did you drive in today?" I told her I did. "Would you like to take the Senator to the White House for a bill signing ceremony?" I said, "Sure I would!" The Senator and I drove down to the White House and up to the South Gate.

The officer waved us in, and I drove my car up the driveway just like I was going to someone's house. I couldn't believe it. In less than ten years I went from a kid on a tobacco farm on a dirt road in the country to pulling my car up to the White House with Senator Strom Thurmond. It's just an example of how the Senator would make an effort to include members of the staff in things so they could experience history. I'll never forget that.

BECKY FLEMING

I had worked for the Senator for about a year and a half when my dad got sick. I decided I needed to come back and be closer to home. I talked to Mr. Short and the Senator, and they both agreed. There was an opening in our Columbia office, so they said

I could work there. I remember it was Christmas time. I was coming home for Christmas and then going to work in the Columbia office after that.

When I went in to say goodbye to the Senator, I started crying. I was just sobbing. Holly was sitting right there at her desk, and she started crying because I was crying. So we were both crying. The Senator looked at me, looked at Holly, and said, "Pretty girl, if you just won't cry, I'll give you whatever you want." There are so many little moments like that which I'll never forget.

DENNIS W. SHEDD

started working for Senator Thurmond after law school in the summer of 1978. He held various posts for the next ten years, including Legislative Director, Chief Counsel and Staff Director of the Senate Judiciary Committee, and finally Administrative Assistant. Mr. Shedd is now a Judge on the United States Court of Appeals for the Fourth Circuit.

When I first worked for Senator Thurmond, a constitutional issue came up that was very important. I suggested that he call some other Senators together to try and devise a strategy on how to approach the issue. So I went ahead and set that meeting up. But being as busy as he always was, Senator Thurmond never had any time for me to meet with him and brief him on the issue before that meeting came around. So all the other Senators came right in his door one day for that meeting. They were certainly not going to wait outside for me to brief him. He had five or six Senators sitting around his desk, and he had no idea what the meeting was about. He got up and walked into his bathroom.

He must have been in there for two or three minutes. Then he stuck his head out the door and said, "Ah, Mr. Shedd, can you come in here please?" I said to myself, he is brilliant! He knows that he doesn't know what this meeting is all about; he knows he doesn't know anything about this issue, and he wants me to get in there and brief him because I'm so smart on the issue. He is brilliant!

So I went in the bathroom. There he was standing there messing with his fly. He said, "Mr. Shedd, this zipper's broken; can you help me please?" Right then and there I learned my importance as a young staffer.

ERNIE COGGINS

*is a former Legislative Assistant for Senator Thurmond, 1999
to 2003. He is now on Active Duty as a Lieutenant Colonel
with the U.S. Army Reserves.*

Working for Senator Thurmond was more like being part of a winning team than merely having a job. That may sound corny, but it was really true. The staff enjoyed an incredibly close bond. The Senator had been managing people for so long, he just knew how to bring out the best in people. You truly wanted to do well for him; not because it was your job, but because you knew you were really helping people and making a difference in the world. Senator Thurmond was one of the best there ever was.

JASON ROSSBACH

*served as a Special Assistant to Senator Thurmond
from 1995 until 2001.*

The Senator was truly loyal to Holly and Duke, and they were loyal to him in return. It was such an amazing relationship because they were three distinctly different types of people. For me, it was a real privilege because I learned so much from each one of them. When I took the job, I took it under the thought that, well, here's a good opportunity. I'll do it for six months or a year then bounce on to something else. Then six years later, wow.

Senator Thurmond was so easy to be around. He made you feel like an integral part of what was happening in that office. Whatever your job title was, it didn't matter. You were a part of his team. I knew of other Senators on the Hill who let it be known that their staff was replaceable; that there was only one important person in the office, the Senator. I knew other staffers who loathed their boss. But I don't think you'd ever find someone who worked for Senator Thurmond who felt that way.

JOHN A. GASTRIGHT, JR.

served as Projects Director for Senator Thurmond, 1995-2002.
He is now Deputy Assistant Secretary of State for South
Asian Affairs.

If you worked for Senator Thurmond, you got used to him calling you on the phone just to say, "You're doing a good job. Keep up the good work!" Or sometimes you'd look up and he'd come walking through, chatting with everyone. He'd want to know what you were working on and how he could help.

The best part about it was the fact that the work you did really mattered. We were totally focused on helping people. The Senator didn't let his office staff get involved in politics. There's that side to politics which is all about raising money and treating the right people well. He never let any of that enter your brain. That's not why we were there. He would say, "Treat everyone well," and he meant it.

I know a lot of people who worked for him felt like they were part of something special. It wasn't like a regular job where you go to work so you can pay your bills. We had a real sense of purpose. We were making a difference. It was a remarkable experience.

JASON ROSSBACH

The Senator meant a great deal to me. He was not like a regular boss. Consider the fact that Duke Short was with him for so many years, and Holly as well, and Mr. Abernathy down in South Carolina. This business doesn't elicit that kind of loyalty unless there's something else there. We had genuine affection for the Senator. He was like family.

I remember the first time I realized there was something very special about him. I had only been working there a couple of months. My parents were up visiting my grandmother in Baltimore. My grandfather had recently passed away, and they wanted to get her out of the house. I asked Holly if I could take a little bit of time off to go to lunch with them. She said, "Oh no, Senator Thurmond wants to take you and your family out to lunch." I told her, "That's okay; it's not necessary." She said, "No, it's a done deal." And if you knew Holly, well, that was that. We were all going to lunch.

My family came in. Of course, they were very impressed with the Senator and his office. It was a literal museum unto itself. You could have spent hours studying all the things on the walls. The Senator was great. He said, "Hey! I hear we're going to lunch!"

We started to walk over to the Capitol to the Senate Dining Room. My grandmother and parents were walking slowly, thinking that the Senator would need to. He was being polite, but secretly giving me this look like, boy, your family's kind of addled, aren't they? I was thinking, come on: pick it up; the old man can move pretty good.

We got to the Dining Room, and we're sitting there looking at the menus. The Senator looked at my grandmother and said, "I want to tell you something right now. Your grandson means a great deal to my office. I can't get along day to day without him. We're happy to have him. He speaks so highly of his family, and he speaks so highly of you. I know your husband must have been a wonderful man." Right then and there he won my loyalty and gratitude for years to come.

DENNIS W. SHEDD

Several years ago when we had a Strom Thurmond staff reunion, an African-American woman came over to me. She said, "Mr. Shedd, I'm so and so and I came over to thank you. I came a long way to come to this meeting. I know I was a lot of trouble in the office. But I know you had faith in me. I'm straightened out now. I finished college. I became a nurse. I'm married, and I have children. I wanted to thank you for not giving up on me."

I told her, "Thank you for saying that. But there's Strom Thurmond right over there, you need to go tell him that story. It was Strom Thurmond who saw the good in you. It was Strom Thurmond who gave you a second chance."

I remembered that girl. She had serious financial problems when she worked for us. As a matter of fact, Senate Disbursing called me and said they wouldn't even cash any more of her checks because she was bouncing them. I went in and told Senator Thurmond, "Senator, she's kind of a problem in the office, kind of hard to get along with. And her financial record is so bad, I think you have to think about dismissing her."

So I took her in to talk with the Senator. They chatted for awhile. Then he said, "Your trouble really isn't that there's anything wrong with you; you're just having financial trouble." He stood up right at that moment, opened his wallet, took money out, and gave it to that girl on the spot. Later, at some point in her life, because of how she was treated in that office, she turned her life around. She tried to give me credit for it, but truthfully, it was Strom Thurmond.

SONIA HOLMES PRICE

*is a former Staff Assistant and Law Clerk. She worked
for Senator Thurmond from 1991 to 1995 and again in 1997.
She is now a practicing attorney in D.C.*

I think the most difficult part of my time working on the Hill was when I had to tell Senator Thurmond goodbye. I gave my resignation in August of 1995. When I first started working for him, I committed to just one year. It was immediately after college. I told the Senator that I wanted to go to law school, so I was only going to commit to one year. He said that was fine, and he applauded my efforts not only for moving so far away from South Carolina at a young age but also for wanting to excel. I loved working in that office. It was by far the best experience in my professional life. I can't even begin to tell you how rewarding it was for me to be able to see him first hand. He was an icon, a legend. But he was also a person who cared about each of his staff members on a personal level.

I was accepted by Howard Law School. The first person I told at the office was Duke Short. The evening that I told the Senator, I rode with him over to the Capitol on the subway. He was going over for a vote. It was extremely difficult for me to tell him I was leaving. I thanked him for the opportunity. I thanked him for his trust and faith in me. Then I told him that I thought it was my time to move on.

One of the first things the Senator said to me was, "Did someone make you unhappy? Did something happen?" I said, "No, no Senator. It wasn't that." He was always very cognizant of how each staff member was feeling personally. He wanted everybody to be happy. He said, "You know, I'm going to hate losing you, but I understand." He knew that law school was my passion, and that's what I wanted to do. So he was happy for me. But part of me really hated to leave. I really adored that man.

ELIZA EDGAR

I started working for Senator Thurmond a month after I graduated from college. I planned to work there for a year, but ended up staying there until he retired. If you would have asked me when I first started if I would be there at the end, I never would have said I would. I was just fortunate to have had that experience. That's a difficult set of shoes to fill when that's your first job right out of college. Everywhere I go people still ask me, "What was it like to work for Strom Thurmond?" I always have the same answer: "It was incredible. He was such an unbelievable, amazing man."

Duke Short at his desk working
on issues important to the Senator.

*We were there to help people, period. I wish I could say that about everybody that goes to
Washington, but it's not true. Senator Thurmond was very unusual in that respect.*

– R.J. Duke Short –

Doing the People's Work

STROM THURMOND'S CONSTITUENT SERVICE

*S*enator Thurmond's constituent service was legendary. One of his biographers observed, "If every member of Congress was as good as Strom Thurmond on constituent service, the Congress of the United States would have a much higher rating." What a true statement.

We helped people with their Social Security checks. We helped people get passports in a hurry so they could go on vacation. We helped countless men and women in the Armed Forces with a variety of issues. Senator Thurmond called it "doing the people's work."

We got letters asking for help from all over the country -- from New York, Chicago, California, and from U.S. military bases around the world. We honestly didn't care where they were from; we tried to help. We didn't care if you were black, white, brown, or purple. We never asked whether you were a Republican or a Democrat. We never asked if you'd contributed money. We didn't care. We were there to help people, period. I wish I could say that about everybody that goes to Washington, but it's not true. Senator Thurmond was very unusual in that respect.

I remember one time sitting with the Senator in his office. We'd been discussing the particulars on a long list of constituent service projects the staff was diligently working on. At one point during the discussion Senator Thurmond said to me, "You know Duke, I know this really isn't our job. I know I wasn't sent to Washington to do this kind of thing. But if we don't help these people, who else will do it?"

The Senator would often come into my office, which was always to him "a mess." He would say, "Duke look at your desk; now go in and look at mine. It's clean." I would always reply, "Yes sir, but the reason your desk is clean is the reason mine is such a mess."

BOB DOLE

*was a United States Senator from Kansas, 1969-1996. He served
as either Majority or Minority Leader from 1985 to 1996, and was
the Republican Nominee for President in 1996.*

Senator Thurmond probably had the best constituent service of anyone who had ever served in the Senate. When he came to the Senate Floor to vote, he would vote then head immediately for the Cloak Room and make calls back to South Carolina: happy wedding, happy anniversary, happy birthday, you've just been nominated federal judge, whatever it was. He was always on the phone congratulating somebody for something, and Duke Short was always there with him.

One of the keys to Senator Thurmond's success was that he never wasted one minute. He was one person you would never see sitting around shooting the breeze. He showed us all that hard work can get you some place. Senator Carlson, who was my predecessor, told me, "Keep an eye on Senator Thurmond and Senator Stennis. Those guys are real workhorses. They don't have an agenda. They're not trying to make the news. They're just doing their work for the folks back home. You pay attention to them. They can really teach you something."

I don't care how you vote on some of these big issues. You can stay in the Senate forever if you have good constituent service; if you really let people know you're concerned about veterans, farmers, people on welfare. You answer their mail. You stay in touch with them. We're really going to miss Strom. He was my buddy, and in many ways, he was my mentor too. There was nobody like Senator Thurmond, and there probably never will be again.

DR. NED CATHCART

*is a prominent doctor, friend, and a life-long supporter
of Strom Thurmond. He practices obstetrics and gynecology
in Spartanburg, South Carolina.*

He was such an unusual and outstanding person. Above all, Strom was a servant of the people. I had many patients who never hesitated to call Strom for help. Each one of them was always so graciously greeted like a personal friend, whether they knew him or not. And action in their favor was immediate. We were incredibly fortunate to have him represent us.

JESSE HELMS
was a United States Senator from North Carolina, 1972-2003.

Strom's notable career was built on his remarkable service to his fellow citizens. He was a leader, and he used his gift for leadership to rally others to his side — and his side was always the side of doing good, of assisting those who needed it.

DOUG JENNINGS
represents District 54 in the South Carolina House of Representatives. He has continuously served in that capacity since he was first elected in 1991.

Senator Thurmond will go down in history as a unique, compassionate person who truly cared about everybody. He saw his role in Washington as one of making sure that little ol' South Carolina and his constituents got a fair shake and as big a piece of the pie as possible. The way he conducted himself personally on behalf of his constituents, and the way that he obviously carried that message through the years to his staff, speaks volumes about the kind of man he was.

There is no equal to Strom Thurmond on our delegation, never has been and never will be again. He set the standard for constituent service and for taking care of the people that he loved so much. I don't think it ever mattered a bit in the world to him what party anybody was from or what their station in life was. He just cared about taking care of them.

JIM DEMINT
is a United States Senator from South Carolina, elected in 2004. He previously represented South Carolina's 4th District in the U.S. House of Representatives.

If I had to suggest an alternate title to this book it would be, *Let Me Know How I Can Help You.* Every time I saw Senator Thurmond, and I mean every single time, he would shake my hand and say, "Let me know how I can help you." And he was serious; he wasn't just saying it. He meant it. He honestly wanted to help every single person he met.

GEDNEY HOWE III

and his family were long-time friends and supporters of Senator
Thurmond. He practices law in Charleston, South Carolina.

Senator Thurmond was a powerful but selfless individual. A lot of people take on that mode in life where they're out gathering nuts, and they want all the nuts for themselves. That's not what Thurmond was about at all. He literally saw it as: I represent the people of my state, so I've got to do as much as I can for them. He was a genuinely selfless guy. Whenever you talked with him he always asked, "Is there anything I can do for you?" It was almost like a next-door neighbor asking you if you wanted to borrow the lawn mower. He sincerely wanted to help. They weren't just words to him. It was very real and reflective of his tireless spirit of giving.

DON FOWLER

is a former Chairman of the Democratic National Committee.
He is now President of Fowler Communications.

To my knowledge, Senator Thurmond never turned anybody down, friend or foe. It was said by many that he'd rather do an enemy a favor than a friend, because he already had a friend and he was always looking to make a friend of an enemy. And when I say an enemy, I mean someone who didn't support him politically. There are thousands of stories of how attentive he and his staff were to constituents. I believe his legacy will be service to the people of South Carolina without regard to party or economic status or race or anything else.

CHRIS KELLEY CIMKO

Senator Thurmond's office was a well-oiled machine. It had been running practically 24-hours-a-day since the 1950s. They had it down to a science. The root of it all was the Senator's passionate commitment to servicing the people of the state of South Carolina in whatever ways he could. No matter what it was, he was going to give it his all. I don't even think the staff had to be instilled with that commitment. I think the fact that you worked for Strom Thurmond, you understood who he was and what he stood for and you wanted to be a part of it. It wasn't a job. It was a calling. You understood that you were his agent in serving the people of South Carolina.

I can't imagine you will ever see an office like that on the Hill again. One thing that made it work is that so many of us were from South Carolina. These were South Carolinians working for the "god" of South Carolina, helping the people from South Carolina. I just don't think you'll be able to replicate something like that in any other office.

Too often politicians lose sight of the fact that the people need to be served. It is the people, after all, who put them in office. Strom Thurmond never forgot that. He may not have been the author of landmark legislation that changed the world, but quietly every day he was changing the lives of people in South Carolina, either by helping them person-ally or through the various assets that he brought to the state. For Senator Thurmond, first, last, and always it was the people of South Carolina.

SUSAN PELTER

Every single time we got together as a staff the Senator would say, "I want you to remember you're here to serve the people of South Carolina. You need to work as hard as you can to do the best job that you can for them because that's why we're all here." He never missed an opportunity to underscore that.

ROBERT R. SMITH

was a Staff Assistant in the Columbia, South Carolina office and handled Constituent Affairs. He worked for Senator Thurmond from 1995 until 2001.

I often went out to meet the Senator when he flew into the Columbia airport. On one occasion we met up at the Lizard's Thicket, right near the airport, to get something to eat. After we ate, he walked around the entire restaurant introducing himself to everybody. Of course, everybody already knew who he was. They'd shake his hand, smile and say, "Yep, we know who you are Senator." He wouldn't leave until he had shaken everybody's hand in the restaurant. Folks gave him letters, asking for help on various things. They wrote on napkins even, anything that was handy. He stuck them all in his pockets as he walked around.

When we got back to the office he divvied them up to various staff members. He always took a particular interest in those folks that you could just tell had had some rough times. He would sit and listen to them for as long as they wanted to talk. I can remember some times when his schedule didn't permit him to sit and listen to folks, but he did it anyway. I person-ally saw Strom Thurmond keep some of the most powerful men in the nation waiting so he could sit and visit with some of the poorest, most impoverished folks in South Carolina.

SHELL SUBER

I'll always have this image in my mind of Senator Thurmond coming in to work on Monday mornings. He'd go right up to the first person he ran into, reach into his pockets, and start pulling out little pieces of paper. Sometimes he had matchbooks and gum wrappers; I'm not kidding! They were all little notes from constituents that had been handed to him over the previous weekend during a visit home to South Carolina.

Thurmond was one of the few Senators who went home every weekend. And everybody from South Carolina knew that if you asked Senator Thurmond for some kind of help on something, he'd follow up on it. Most times people didn't expect to see him, so they didn't have a formal letter prepared. They would jot down their name and number on whatever was handy and give it to him. Sometimes in the rush they'd even forget to write their names. All we'd get is a phone number with an 803 area code scribbled on a gum wrapper.

At the end of the day on Monday, he'd usually want a report about what progress had been made with each one of those cases. They were all special priority to him, because people had taken the time to talk to him directly. So I'd sit down with him and say something like, "Senator, you met with Joe Smith this weekend who was asking you about the bridge in Aiken County." He would nod and say, "Oh yes, Joe Smith, go ahead." All he would need is the name. He talked to hundreds of people in a weekend. But you give him a name of somebody who had asked for help, and he'd remember the conversation.

I recall one time Duke came around handing out those little notes the Senator had picked up one weekend. Duke said, "This guy talked to the Senator; see what we can do for him." And he handed me a pack of Salem Lights with a phone number on it.

LEE BANDY

is a reporter and columnist with The State *newspaper of Columbia, South Carolina. He covered Strom Thurmond for over forty years.*

Strom Thurmond had the best constituent service in Washington, bar none. That is a fact. I don't know of anybody on the Hill who offered that degree of service like Strom did. He would always say, "This seat doesn't belong to me; it belongs to the people." They hired him by electing him. And he knew he was to be held accountable to them for his actions.

Anytime you asked him what he enjoyed most, he would always say helping people, or as he put it, "hep'n people!" And he helped people regardless of their color, their political affiliation, or their religious faith. As a result of that he touched a lot of lives in South Carolina. It's hard to find someone in South Carolina who hasn't had their life touched by Strom. That was the true secret of his strength. South Carolinians knew that if they needed help in Washington, on both minor and major things, the go-to person was Strom Thurmond. He would always deliver.

DENNIS W. SHEDD

Most people would say that Senator Thurmond considered constituent service his job. Interestingly enough, that was not his view. So many people think that is the case. This is what he told me one time about constituent service. He said, "You have to understand this first of all: when these people contact us about something, they have pot holes or they can't get their trash picked up or their son can't get into school. That may not be very important to you, and quite frankly, it might not be the most important thing to me, but if anybody takes the time to write me or to call me about something it is in fact the most important thing in their life at that moment. And we need to do something to help."

He also said one time, "I know, Mr. Shedd, that I was sent up here to be a legislator. I know what my job is. My primary job is not really to help constituents with their problems. I know that. But the truth is, these people are fighting a bureaucracy and if I don't help them, nobody will; they will never get government to be responsible to them." He knew constituent service was not his primary job. But he felt an obligation to make government responsible to people. Imagine how well government would function if everybody in Washington felt that way.

TERRY L. WOOTEN

The most Senator Thurmond ever got upset with me was over a constituent service case. Somebody from South Carolina had written us a letter asking for help on a matter. As I recall, it was a very complicated issue. I was looking into it. After five days of getting nowhere on the case, I took the letter to him to talk about it. I said, "Senator, here's a letter you got from some constituents. I'm making some calls, but I haven't quite been able to get to the bottom of it. I wanted to see what you wanted me to do."

He looked at the letter and saw the date it arrived in the office. He said, "Have you contacted these people to let them know you're going to talk to me about this and look into this for them?" I said, "Well, no sir, not yet." He said, "Don't you know that I expect this office to contact anybody who sends me a letter or calls me within 48 hours?!

I want everyone to get a response! Now, why didn't you give them a response?" I said, "Well, I thought I'd need some more time to work on this." He said, "I don't want to hear it! You go call these people right now and tell them you have talked to me and I am going to look into it for them. But understand, I don't want anything that comes into this office to sit for more than 48 hours without a response to the constituent!"

That's probably one of the most direct conversations he ever had with me. He was upset and adamant that I had to respond to a constituent within 48 hours. That's just how it was done in that office, and there weren't going to be any exceptions.

CRAIG METZ

Here's a little lesson Senator Thurmond taught me about constituent service. Whenever he met with a constituent, he would quite often have a person from the department or agency involved come and join them in his office. That person would always say, "Well Senator, we're certainly going to try and do this for you." To which he would invariably respond, "When? When are you going to have this done?" He would get them to commit to a specific timeframe, and if they didn't, they knew he was going to continue to call every day until they did. It was common knowledge in Washington that Senator Thurmond could be very, very persistent when it came to matters of constituent service.

MARK GOODIN

The thing Strom Thurmond enjoyed the most was helping the little guy. He honestly saw the people as the boss of the government, and he didn't like the fact that government often ended up in the other capacity. He never liked that. He was a conservative, and yet he had a streak of populism the size of Utah running down his back.

He distrusted large institutions, including government. He distrusted large industry, and he instinctively knew the larger and more powerful something got, the more vulnerable individuals became. He had a classic sense that the primary mission of government was simply to help the common man, the common person. He believed as Calhoun did that the ultimate reservoir of sovereignty was the individual. The individual cedes some of their sovereignty to create the state, and the state gives up some of its sovereignty to create the federal government. But the parent of them all is the individual. And ultimately, the individual's rights were paramount.

Senator Thurmond was in many ways a ward politician, yet on a grander scale. His mission in life was to do favors for people. He grew up in that South Carolina populist tradition where politicians were the ones who built farm-to-market roads for all the farmers.

Politicians were the ones who made sure the mail got delivered on time. They kept the law and order. They kept you from having your chickens stolen. So he grew up around that, where a politician was someone who was always there to help, and I think that stayed with him forever.

JOHN DECROSTA

There is something to be said about Senator Thurmond's generation having a deeper appreciation, understanding, and devotion to public service. But even among those of his own generation, Senator Thurmond had an even higher devotion to public service. At some point in his life, he made a conscious decision: he didn't want to be a businessman; he didn't want to be a lawyer; he didn't want to be a judge; he wanted to be somebody who could do the greatest good for the people of South Carolina. And the best place he could do that was in the United States Senate. That was it. While he was responsible for making laws, advising and consenting on nominations, voting on budgets, and basically doing all the things that Senators do, his real priority was in fact using his office to help South Carolinians who needed help, and to help the government of South Carolina create a state that's a good place to live.

DEE SHORT,

the wife of Duke Short, was one of Senator Thurmond's dearest friends
in the last fifteen years of his life. The Senator used to call her the
"Queen of the Senate." She was, as he used to say, "family."

We went to lunch with the Senator nearly every Sunday for many years. His favorite place to go was Elsie's Magic Skillet down Route 1 in Alexandria. I'll never forget the last time we went there. It was Sunday, December 15, 2002. We were driving back and Duke and Senator Thurmond started reminiscing about their years together and all the things they had done to help people.

The Senator said, "Duke, we sure have helped a lot of them, haven't we?" And Duke said, "Yes sir, we sure have." The Senator thought about that for a moment and said, "How many? How many do you think we helped?" He really wanted to know a number. Duke said, "I don't know Senator, hundreds of thousands." Senator Thurmond was amazed. "Really?" he said. "That many?" Duke said, "Yes sir." I said, "Senator, I know you've helped all the folks in upstate." He said, "Oh Miss Dee, you're a flatterer." I said, "No sir, I'm a truth teller!" We'd go back and forth like that.

DAVID WILKINS

is Ambassador to Canada and Former Speaker of the House of
Representatives, State of South Carolina. He served on every one
of Senator Thurmond's campaigns for the U.S. Senate, beginning
in 1972, and was Chairman of his last campaign in 1996.

I believe Strom Thurmond's desire to help people came straight from his heart. He genuinely loved people, and he wanted to help them. All politicians like to talk about doing that, but I think Strom Thurmond really enjoyed it. Most other Senators are focused on passing a specific bill or defending a certain position. But Senator Thurmond's ultimate goal in the United States Senate was to help the people of South Carolina in any way he could, as best he could, every day of the week. He excelled at that better than anybody who's ever served in Washington or ever will.

SHELL SUBER

Senator Thurmond got paid to go to committee meetings and vote on legislation. That was his job. But he did constituent services for nothing. Constituent service is not in the Constitution. It's not among the official duties of a United States Senator. That was his hobby, and quite frankly, that was his passion. He certainly cared a great deal about matters of legislation, particularly as it applied to the Judiciary, to Armed Services, or to Veterans. But those issues were not his true passion. His passion was helping people.

Now, I defy any South Carolinian who claims to know everything about Senator Thurmond — and believe me, there are Thurmond buffs from the coast to the mountains in this state — I defy anyone to tell me what the Thurmond Bill is. They can't name one. They can't name a single piece of legislation for which he is remembered. Of course, Senator Hollings had his name on several bills; that was his claim to fame. But Senator Thurmond's passion, his hobby, his avocation, was constituent service. Simply put, he got a huge charge out of it.

I have to imagine that if you are a Congressman or a Senator, there's not a lot of personal satisfaction at the end of the day if all you care about is legislation because how many pieces of meaningful legislation get passed in a session? But if you focus on constituent service like Senator Thurmond's office did, you can help one hundred people a day. That's what put his head on the pillow at night and got it up first thing in the morning. It was his love for that. He loved helping people.

It meant a lot to the staff as well. We'd get to know some of these families during the process of helping them out. We'd talk to them several times on the telephone. They'd get on the phone and say, "Thank you, thank you Shell so much for following up on this!" And I would always say, "The Senator appreciates your thanks, and he's glad he could help you."

The truth is, Shell Suber helped no one. Strom Thurmond helped them. Think about it. What if I had called over to the Department of Defense and said, "Hey, this is Shell Suber; I need a little help with something!" They would have hung up on me. But I would say, "This is Shell Suber calling for Senator Thurmond's office." Every single time the response was the same: "Yes sir, what can I do for you?"

PHIL JONES

was a Correspondent for CBS News for 32 years,
which included his tenure as the Chief Congressional
Correspondent on Capitol Hill.

Strom Thurmond was a young, vibrant guy in his late 60s when I first met him. But unlike the other Senators on the Hill, he never really seemed to enjoy the floor speeches and debates all that much. He would do it, but it was not the most comfortable thing for him. What he did enjoy, and what he was the king of in Washington, was constituent service. That's what made him.

He was not the eloquent speaker on the Senate Floor. He was not the engaging debater. He didn't seem to have time for that. He was hustling around, always going to committee meetings or votes, but otherwise he was back in his office taking care of and meeting with constituents.

He wasn't the type of guy to seek television coverage or go after the headlines. All he wanted to do was take care of the people back home. I'm sure that's all he wanted on his tombstone: "I took care of my people." And that was the secret to his longevity in office. He would have certainly lost that last election had it not been for what he'd already accomplished for people. Even though he had the checkered Civil Rights record, he had come around. He may have fooled me, but from what I witnessed it didn't make a damn bit of difference what color someone was. If they lived in South Carolina, he was going to take care of them.

He was unique. I never saw anyone else on the Hill that enjoyed constituent service that much or who did it with such enthusiasm. He was almost ferocious with it. It wasn't an act. As far as he was concerned, that was the reason he went to Washington.

JOHN A. GASTRIGHT, JR.

Every elected official in Washington tries to do constituent service. Everybody has people in their office assigned to do just that. The difference is that Thurmond personally liked to do it, whereas in other offices, I think it's a little more challenging to get the Senator personally involved. If we ran into a roadblock on something, Strom Thurmond didn't hesitate to make a phone call and help us out. This might sound a bit cynical, but in some other offices in Washington, Congressmen and Senators save their "aces" for people who are their friends, or helper bees, people who are really big supporters. But Thurmond didn't believe in any of that. He'd make a call anytime to help anyone. He'd make those calls all day long if he had to. He honestly enjoyed it. And there was never a sense that the well was going to run out of water.

The bottom line in Senator Thurmond's office was this: there's an individual who's pinned down by the bureaucracy, needs help, and we're going to help them. The Senator would make a quick phone call and cut right through the bureaucracy. He'd tell the secretary of some department, "Fix this matter for John Doe down there in Aiken." And of course the secretary would get off the phone and quickly tell his staff, "Fix this thing so Strom Thurmond doesn't call me anymore!" All of a sudden the wheels would move into action and the red tape would fall away.

You know, a rich guy can call a lawyer and get his problem litigated, but the people who called us, the vast majority of them, were not rich people. They were people who had no place else to turn. The bureaucracy was beating them down. The Senator considered it his duty to be that last resort. If there was going to be a system, that system needed to work. And if it didn't work, he would make it work. He liked that. He would say all the time, "There's no better work than hep'n people!"

"Hep'n People! All the People!"

UNFORGETTABLE MOMENTS FROM STROM THURMOND'S CONSTITUENT SERVICE

Despite the fact that Senator Thurmond was extremely healthy even into his late 90s, the media quite often acted like he had one foot in the grave. The very young reporters, especially, used to ask him questions that were more appropriate for an obituary than a news story, which I suppose is understandable given the fact that he was old enough to be their great-grandfather. They frequently asked, "Senator Thurmond, how do you want to be remembered?" He'd wave his finger in the air for emphasis and give the same answer every time in that wonderful Edgefield County accent: "Hep'n people! All the people!"

Our office handled every constituent service scenario imaginable, as the stories from this chapter will illustrate. Though we had one part of the office specifically set up for constituent service — the Senator called it "Projects" — everyone in the office knew that was their primary duty. As Senator Thurmond would often say during our staff meetings, "It doesn't matter to me what your job is. We're here to help people. And if you can't help people, we're going to help you go somewhere else real quick."

Strom Thurmond always enjoyed meeting with his constituents. He is shown here with Bub, Ada, Lori, and Ronnie Vickers from Chesnee, S.C.

SHELL SUBER

Of course, Strom Thurmond was South Carolina's Senator. But when you're as famous as he was, nationally recognized, the whole world thinks you're their Senator. We got letters from people all over the country asking for help. When it came to Grandma's social security check in New York or a problem with a passport in California, Senator Thurmond was more likely to get a letter asking for help than any other Senator in Washington. He had that reputation and the word got around.

A great deal of the time we would get letters from veterans. They'd write, "Senator Thurmond, I've always known that we can trust you to help us." And they were right. The Senator would do anything he could to help a veteran. I mean anything. We'd help a veteran out in Oregon who had a problem with a pothole in front of his house. It didn't matter. The veteran community is very tight, particularly the World War II generation. They read a lot; they're very politically astute, and they pay a lot of attention to what's going on. I'm sure they heard Senator Thurmond's name come up over and over again as being someone they can count on. So many of them would write to us.

Everyone who wrote would try to come up with any possible South Carolina connection. We'd get letters like, "Dear Senator Thurmond, I lived in South Carolina from 1964 to 65 when I was stationed at Fort Jackson, and you were my Senator. Now I live in Wisconsin. Here's my problem." I'll say this about Senator Thurmond: the only liberal thing about Strom Thurmond was his definition of who was from South Carolina.

If you're from South Carolina, you're in. If you went to college in South Carolina, you're in. If you had kin in South Carolina, you're in. If you could come up with any connection to South Carolina, you'd be as in as the guy who was born and raised in Edgefield County. And once you were in, he was going to do anything in his power to help you. Once he had determined, through his very liberal definition of a South Carolinian, that you were a South Carolinian — and it's sort of like a credit union, they're going to find a way to make you eligible — then the full powers of his office were at your disposal.

LINDSEY GRAHAM

is a United States Senator from South Carolina, 2003- present.
He succeeded Senator Thurmond in office.

I was at the Peach Festival in Trenton, South Carolina one time with Senator Thurmond. We were walking through the crowd, and this man came up to the Senator to say hello. The man was probably in his mid 50s. He thanked Senator Thurmond for getting his disability started, getting his mother into a nursing home, and getting his grandson into the Air Force Academy. That was one family who had three generations touched by Senator Thurmond. There are countless stories like that all around South Carolina.

WILLIAM W. WILKINS

Senator Thurmond's constituent service is legendary on Capitol Hill and in South Carolina. All sorts of people went to him for help, and he felt it was his duty, responsibility, and privilege to serve anybody who asked. He expected his staff members to treat each problem very seriously and to see to it that it was favorably resolved.

I remember an Airman stationed overseas with the Air Force who wanted to go to graduate school. But in order to attend school in the United States, he would have to be back a few weeks before he was set to be discharged. Even the Air Force had agreed to discharge him early so he could start school, but the red tape was slowing the process down so much, it looked like he was not going to meet the deadline. He contacted

Senator Thurmond. Senator Thurmond immediately called the Secretary of the Air Force. That Airman was on a plane headed home the very next day.

BECKY FLEMING

A woman called into the office one day and said she'd seen the Senator several times and that he'd always said to her, "If I can ever do anything for you please don't hesitate to call." Well, she was calling.

A dog had been hit out in front of her house in Darlington. I guess she had tried to get Animal Control a couple of times already and nothing happened. So she called Senator Thurmond. She told us about how this dead dog needed to be moved from out in front of her house. I got her name and address and phone number. I called Darlington Animal Control and gave them the information. They went right out and picked up the dog.

The woman called back and profusely thanked the Senator for always being there for the people of South Carolina. From that point on, I was never amazed at what the people would call the office for help with. Senator Thurmond would do anything to make the people of South Carolina happy; he'd even get rid of dead dogs!

DENNIS W. SHEDD

Here's a true story that's fairly well known among Thurmond staffers. It took place back during the Vietnam War. A father had passed away in Columbia, South Carolina. The family desperately wanted the son home for the funeral, but he was serving in Vietnam. So they contacted their Congressional delegation for help, which included Senator Thurmond. On the day of the funeral, one of their elected officials called the family to tell them that he had tried as hard as he could, but there was just no way to get the son home from Vietnam. When he called the house to tell them the bad news, he said, "I'm Congressman so and so. I'm sorry but there's just no way we can get Johnny home for his daddy's funeral." And the voice on the other end of the phone said, "Congressman, this is Johnny. Senator Thurmond got me home."

I was told later that Johnny said he was in Vietnam when a helicopter came in and lifted him out, took him to an aircraft carrier where they strapped him into the back of a two-seater airplane and flew him off to the Philippines or somewhere, where he caught a military flight to get home in time for the funeral. Strom Thurmond had set that all up for him.

JOHN A. GASTRIGHT, JR.

When I left Senator Thurmond's office, I moved across the Hill to work as the Chief of Staff to Congressman Jack Kingston of Georgia. On one of my first orientation trips for the Congressman, I traveled to the Brunswick Naval Station in Georgia. They did the typical dog and pony show where they walk you around, pretending like you're someone very important. They took me to see a submarine that was in the refurbishment phase. The sub commander was there. He was just gushing with kindness; he spent a lot of time with me, and even had a nice lunch prepared. He went way beyond what you'd expect. At one point he pulled me aside and asked to speak with me alone. I was like, uh-oh, something must be wrong. So we walked into his stateroom. There on his wall was a framed letter from Strom Thurmond. He said to me, "You don't know me, but I know you." Then he starts telling me this story.

He said, "Several years ago, my daughter was hit by a car. We almost lost her. It was a real pain getting the system to take care of her properly, and to get her the treatment that she needed. I'm not from South Carolina. I'm from Illinois. And to be quite frank, I'm not even a Republican. I'm a Democrat. But I'd always heard that Strom Thurmond really cared. So I called Strom Thurmond's office. And as it turned out, I got you on the phone. You never asked me any questions other than the information you needed to help my daughter. I had run into all the walls. I thought we were going to lose. But somehow you made it all happen."

At this point, the Navy Captain started to break down into tears telling me this story about his little girl. He said, "Strom Thurmond stood up for me. He didn't know me from Adam. I wasn't even one of his constituents. But he saved my daughter's life."

I said, "Sir, we were just doing our job. Strom Thurmond always said that every person in the U.S. military was his constituent. I know that he'd be glad he could help."

GEORGE LAUFFER

In 1992 Hurricane Andrew hit the U.S. Customs folks at Homestead Air Force base really hard. They were essentially wiped out, all their facilities and everything. The Director of Customs wanted the Senator to go down and see for himself what had happened. So we flew down to Homestead in Florida. The Senator toured the whole complex. He spent some time with the troops. And he even visited some private homes that had been devastated. Now, keep in mind, none of these folks were from South Carolina. But that didn't matter to him. These were people who needed help; that's all he cared about.

I vividly remember our visit to a private little airport right outside Homestead. There were about a dozen airplanes in a hangar that had been completely smashed against the back wall. They were just a pile of rubble. We stood there in amazement. At one point two ladies with the Red Cross came over to us. It turned out one of them was from Oregon and the other was from Washington state. They asked if they could talk to Senator Thurmond. I said sure.

So they went over and spent a few moments talking with the Senator, thanking him for being there. And of course, he thanked them for everything they were doing to help. These women were not constituents. They were from way out west. But they knew Senator Thurmond, and they appreciated the fact that he came down there to lift the spirits of those folks. None of the people he saw that day could vote for him. But like I said, that's not what was important to him. What was important was the fact that there were people who needed help, and he was going to do whatever he could to make sure they got it.

DON FOWLER

The one thing that everybody recognized about Senator Thurmond was his keen sense of taking care of people's needs. I remember one case specifically from a few years ago. There was a good friend of mine who has since passed away. His name was Pete Stathakis. He was an active, noted Democrat in Anderson, South Carolina. Pete was a dogged economic development person. He worked hard, without really any compensation, to bring industry to Anderson and create jobs. Stathakis is a great name in South Carolina.

One of Pete's relatives back in Greece had a child. There was some question about the care of this child, and Pete had decided to adopt him. Pete had exhausted every avenue he could to get that child from Greece to the United States. He tried all of his contacts in the Administration, in Washington, but nobody could get it done. He finally decided to ask Senator Thurmond. And Senator Thurmond went to work on it. Within about two weeks that child was in the United States. Pete was obviously overjoyed and very impressed that Senator Thurmond would work on something that hard. That baby is now an adult and living in Anderson.

WILLIAM W. WILKINS

As each case came into Senator Thurmond's office it would get assigned to a particular staff member. That staff member would then go to work on the problem in an attempt to resolve it favorably. If we reached an impasse with an agency with whom we were dealing, the Senator would immediately get the director of that agency on the phone and take care of it. He never hesitated to pick up the phone and call a top Cabinet official on a minor problem — minor only in the big picture of things, but a major problem to a South Carolinian who'd come to the Senator for help.

I remember a young Marine who'd been wounded in Vietnam and had a permanent disability. He was going to law school at the time. He received a letter from the Department of the Navy stating that they were going to terminate his disability and pay him a lump sum instead of the monthly payment that he desperately needed. I was assigned the case, and I just couldn't get anywhere. I told the Senator that they were just not going to budge on the issue.

He turned to his secretary right then and said, "Get Commandant so-and-so on the phone!" The Senator got him on the phone and said, "General, I have a young man in my office, Billy Wilkins, and he's coming to see you right now and I want you to solve his problem." That's all he said. I got in the car, went over there, and they treated me like I was a four-star general. The young Marine's problem was solved that very day.

ROBBIE CALLAWAY

is President and Chief Executive Officer of Technology Investors, Inc. and is also Chairman of the National Center for Missing and Exploited Children. Robbie was for many years a close and devoted friend to Senator Thurmond.

Steve Salem and I were waiting outside Senator Thurmond's office one time; we always stopped by to visit with Duke and say hi to the Senator. So we're waiting there in the reception room, and there was no one out there at the time. Now, this was obviously before 9-11, because a woman walked in the office with two old and very dirty shopping bags. She came in very quietly and put her stuff down behind a door and then left. We didn't quite know what to do. Who was this lady? Steve and I were kind of looking at each other, wondering what the deal was. She just put her bags down and left. Was it a bomb? Some kind of a protest? We had no idea.

The receptionist came back to her desk, and I mentioned to her what had just happened. She said, "Oh that's what's her name." Senator Thurmond had seen her on the street one day. He walked up to her and told her she could leave her things in his office during the day if it made things easier for her. It got to be a regular thing that she dropped her stuff off there in his office.

Now, there are a lot of offices up there on Capitol Hill, with a whole lot of folks who talk about helping people. But how many of them would walk up to a street person and offer something like that? Senator Thurmond did. He was that kind of a man.

Whenever I hear people talk negatively about Strom Thurmond, about what he might have done or said in the distant past, I always remember that woman. She was not invisible to a powerful man like him. He went up to her on his own and asked her how he could help. She said she'd like to have a place to keep her bags during the day; so he said no problem. As far as I'm concerned, the people who might have something negative to say about Senator Thurmond are people who didn't know him. He was a great, kind man.

DONALD BALDWIN

has been a lobbyist in Washington since the 1960s. He and his family were friends of Senator Thurmond's for many years.

I recall a time when I was representing Mack Trucks. They had recently opened a plant in South Carolina. At that time it was the largest truck assembly plant in the world. We were having some trouble getting parts in there, so we wanted to extend the public airfield to make it possible to bring in planes that would carry some of the parts that we needed. But our request was getting nowhere. A delegation from the area came up to discuss this with Senator Thurmond. They had asked me to arrange the meeting.

We were sitting outside his office, waiting to get in and see the Senator. I happened to notice that the Chairman of the Federal Aviation Administration was also there in the waiting room. A staffer came up and said, "Mr. Baldwin, if you don't mind waiting, this gentleman asked to see the Senator first." I said no problem.

A few minutes later, when we went in to the Senator's office, the Chairman was there. The Senator introduced everybody. Then he said, "Before we start our meeting, I think the Administrator has something to say." The Chairman looked at us and said, "We have upgraded your application. You will get the financial assistance you were looking for." And it was done, just like that, before any of us said a word.

That's the way Senator Thurmond worked. He had a reputation in Washington as the man who could get things done. It didn't matter what it was; Strom Thurmond could make it happen. That said, I never saw him throw his support behind something he didn't believe in. If he believed in what you were trying to do, and he knew that it would ultimately help the people of South Carolina, he would go to great lengths to help.

DENNIS W. SHEDD

There's a woman named Frances Rast. Her husband was Ed Rast, and he was a part-time, volunteer baseball coach of mine when I was in high school. Ed was an agent for the Bureau of Alcohol, Tobacco, and Firearms. I saw Frances one time in Washington when she was on a school trip, and she told me she was trying to get Ed's ATF badge back. She said he had died of a heart attack just a week or two short of twenty years of service. They had a policy that if you hadn't served at least twenty years, your family was not allowed to keep your badge.

I asked her what she was doing to try and get the badge back. She said she'd asked everybody she could think of for help. I said, "Have you talked to Senator Thurmond?" She said no. I said, "You ought to deal with Senator Thurmond on this. He's really good at this kind of stuff." So she wrote a letter to Senator Thurmond. Senator Thurmond contacted the ATF. It required a change in the law, which Senator Thurmond made happen. And this woman got her husband's badge back for the family to keep in his memory.

JAMES B. EDWARDS

was Governor of South Carolina from 1975 to 1979.
He later served as the President of the Medical University
of South Carolina from 1982 to 2000.

Senator Thurmond had some outstanding staff people, and I have never heard a negative word about the Senator from any staff person that worked for him, not one. I'll tell you one little story that shows the incredible organization he had in place in that office.

I was sitting at home one Sunday afternoon. The phone rang, and this man was on the phone. He was almost hysterical, very distraught. He said, "Dr. Edwards! I'm at my wit's end! I don't know what to do. We have a daughter who's in Greece. She's been harassed by some Algerians. At this present time, they're knocking on her door trying to get in. They're trying to break in her house!" This was in Greece! I didn't know what to do, so I tried to get Strom on the phone. I couldn't get him, so I called Holly and told her what the situation was.

In less than an hour, and this is a true story, I got a call from this girl's father again saying, "Dr. Edwards, I can't thank you enough! I just can't believe what you've done for me." I said, "Well, I haven't done anything. I just notified some of Strom's staff what the problem was." The man said, "My daughter told me it wasn't 30 minutes after I talked to you that the Embassy sent a contingent of Marines out to her house. She's at the Ambassador's home now."

Only Strom Thurmond had the organization to make something like that happen. I never even spoke to him directly. All I had to do was mention the problem to a member of his staff. Everybody in that office knew what Strom Thurmond was committed to, and they were committed to the very same things — the patriotic virtues and values of constituent service.

JOHN A. GASTRIGHT, JR.

A man came to us once for help. His daughter had been in an accident on the Chattahoochee River, which runs through South Carolina right up on the northern border of Georgia. It's a pretty rough, rapid river. This man's daughter slipped on a rock and was sucked into the rapids. Evidently when all the water converges on a spot it creates this huge amount of suction. The water had pinned her to the bottom of the Chattahoochee, and she unfortunately drowned.

The parents wanted to recover her remains, but because the rapids were so intense, they simply couldn't reach her to pull her body out. Everybody had told the parents that the river would eventually drop, usually in the winter. They said the suction would let up such that they could finally pull her body out. But that could be months. You know, if you're a parent, that's not what you want to hear. You want to get your child. So this father, he was from Pennsylvania, picked up the phone and called us.

I remember he said this, "I can't get anyone to help me. But I heard Senator Thurmond will help." So I took the case into Duke and explained it to him. He said, "Let's go talk to the boss." I explained the case to Senator Thurmond. You can just imagine his reaction. Here's a man who's lost his own daughter. If anyone understood what this family might be going through, it was him. The Senator said, "Whatever we have to do to get that girl's remains out of that river, that's what we're going to do."

Now, there's a whole cottage industry built up around rapids, and there are a lot of environmentalists who don't want you to disturb the water. There were a lot of people who told us to let it go, to let it be, that the body would eventually come out on its own. That wasn't good enough. We called in the Park Service who had management of the river. They said, "We're just going to have to wait for the water to drop." Senator Thurmond said, "No, we're not going to do that. What else can we do?"

It just so happened that the father from Pennsylvania found a company that could actually divert the water temporarily so they could get in there and get his daughter's body out. But to do that, the company had to drive iron bars into the bed of the river. Well, there are aspects of the Wild and Scenic River Act which say you can't do that. We briefed the Senator on this predicament. He thought about it for a minute and said, "I will personally see to it that we amend that law if we can't figure out how to make this happen."

The environmentalists were going nuts. We got so many nasty calls saying that we hated the environment. Of course, it had nothing to do with that. It was all about the fact that this man's daughter was pinned at the bottom of that river, and he wanted her out so he could bury her. That was it. And Senator Thurmond, because he'd lost his own daughter, could relate to that. I remember the moment when the Senator told the man, "We're going to get your daughter out of that river. We're going to help you."

And ultimately we did. We cleared the way to have the temporary dam installed and diverted the water; and we got the remains of that young girl out and the family finally put her to rest. The dad came in to see the Senator after it was all done. It was naturally a very emotional meeting. He broke into tears. He was crying, saying, "Thank you, thanks for caring." I remember the Senator just kind of took his hands and said something like, "It's okay. I'm glad we could help."

We got lots of negative mail and phone calls over that case. We took a whole bunch of grief from rafting companies and from environmentalists — people who are nothing but extremists when it comes to this kind of thing. They don't like anybody messing with the river. But we got calls and letters from other people thanking us for what we did, and saying that's why Strom Thurmond matters.

It was pretty incredible if you think about it. He had all that crap arrayed against him: all those people were against him doing anything to help that family; politics would have said don't touch it, don't make all those environmentalists mad because they can create more grief for you than it's worth. But the Senator said no, we're not going to let all that stand in the way of doing the right thing here. And the right thing is letting these people get their daughter out of that river so they can bury her and put this behind them.

I know we did the right thing there. And that family knows we did the right thing. You should have seen the Senator's reaction when I first told him about that young girl stuck in the river. You could see it in his face: he was going to fix this; he was going to help that family. But we got calls every day from the extremists, from people who called us devils for messing with that river. And you know, that river was back to normal an hour after we got the girl out.

Duke Short, Dennis Shedd,
and Strom Thurmond. September 1987.

U.S. SENATE PHOTO

All of a sudden the applause stopped. Every jaw dropped.
And there was dead silence in the room.

– Dennis W. Shedd –

The Menachem Schneerson Story

DENNIS W. SHEDD

There's a conservative orthodox Jewish movement based in New York City that's called the Lubavitcher. The leader of their group is called the Rebbe; it's the equivalent, I guess, of the Catholic Pope. Now this is a very orthodox, very conservative group. On alternating years they attempted to get either Senator Thurmond or Senator Helms to sponsor a resolution honoring their spiritual leader, the Rebbe, Menachem Schneerson.

At the time I was the Chief Staffer of the Judiciary Committee. I got a call one day, and the receptionist said, "Mr. Shedd, there's a man here to talk to you. He said Senator Thurmond sent him to you." The man turned out to be a very conservative Rabbi from New York City. He had on the full length coat with the curls on the corner of his head, the hat with the fur trim. He said, "Mr. Shedd, Senator Thurmond sent me to you to do a resolution to honor Menachem Schneerson."

I checked with the Senator, and he said go ahead and handle that for them. Since the Judiciary Committee had changed its rules and no longer honored individuals, we put together a resolution called National Education Day, which would coincide with Menachem Schneerson's birthday. It passed the Committee. The Lubavitchers were just thrilled to death about it. They wrote a letter thanking Senator Thurmond profusely for doing what he'd done. And they asked him, could he get them a room in the Capitol so they could have a celebration on National Education Day, which of course was actually Menachem Schneerson's birthday.

So Holly Richardson, the Senator's Personal Secretary, called me when she got that letter. She said, "Dennis, do I need to take this to the Senator?" I said, "No Holly, don't worry him with it. Go ahead and get them a room in the Capitol; that'll be fine." So we lined them up with a room in the Capitol under Senator Thurmond's name, which we had permission to do. Well, they were so excited that Senator Thurmond had gotten the resolution passed, and then gotten a room in the Capitol for them to celebrate the resolution, they wrote another letter and asked him to be their keynote speaker at their celebration. Are you with me so far? It's now escalated beyond anything Senator Thurmond had any idea about.

Holly again called me when she received this second letter with the request that he be their keynote speaker. I told Holly absolutely not; we got lots of requests like that. I said, "Senator Thurmond does not need to be their keynote speaker. Just tell them he has a conflict, but thank them very much." So Holly politely turned down their invitation, and everything went along fine; that is, until the day of the celebration at the Capitol. Now, let me tell you what happened then.

Senator Thurmond was walking through the Capitol one afternoon, and he just happened to look in that room. He asked the staffer with him, "Who are all those people in that room with those funny hats on?" The staffer said, "Senator Thurmond, you don't need to go in there. That looks like some kind of private event." But of course now his curiosity had been peaked. He said to the staffer, "Well, I think I better go in there. There could be some people from South Carolina in there that might need to talk to me." So Senator Thurmond went in the room.

Now get the picture. Senator Thurmond has arranged for the room for this group, but doesn't know it. Senator Thurmond has been asked to be the keynote speaker for this event and has declined, but doesn't know it. So when he walked in the room, the crowd just erupted with a thunderous ovation because lo and behold, miracle of miracles, the keynote speaker who declined has shown up!

So imagine a room full of orthodox Jewish Rabbis cheering at the top of their lungs, "Senator Thurmond! Senator Thurmond! Senator Thurmond!"

Senator Thurmond had no idea who they were. But he knew, for some apparent reason, they were very glad that he was there. He had his hand over his head waving at everybody while they whisked him up to the podium. They were still chanting, "Senator Thurmond, Senator Thurmond!"

Of course, like any politician, here was a crowd who loved him and they wanted him to say a few words, so he's naturally going to say something. But remember, he had no idea what this group was or what they were there for.

As he looked out across the crowd, he spied a banner on the back wall, and on the banner were written the words, "Happy Birthday Menachem Schneerson!" Senator Thurmond looked at that sign and said, "The first thing I'd like to say is Happy Birthday Ma-nee-kim Schlakem! Ah....Happy Birthday Ma-nye-kem Schleekim!" He couldn't get it quite right, so finally he says, "Ah, Happy Birthday to the man whose name is written on the wall back there!" And the crowd erupted again with applause.

Now it started to dawn on Senator Thurmond, looking out at the crowd, that this might be some kind of a religious group. So he said, "Now, I've got to get back to work. I appreciate being with you all on this auspicious occasion. But as I go, I want to leave you with the words of Jesus Christ."

All of a sudden the applause stopped. Every jaw dropped. And there was dead silence in the room.

The Eddie Murphy Story

MARK GOODIN

Here's one story I will never, ever forget. Mrs. Thurmond had arranged to have comedian Eddie Murphy perform at a fund raiser for Children's Hospital. I found out about it and asked the Senator. He said, "Now you stay out of this. This is her thing. She doesn't want you and Mr. Shedd messing around in it." I said, "Okay Senator, but I think I owe it to you to tell you that Eddie Murphy's kind of profane. I'm not so sure if he would be a good pick for that event."

Well, he evidently mentioned that to Mrs. Thurmond because she called me on the phone and said, "You stay out of this! I don't want your involvement. I don't want Dennis Shedd in this either. This is my thing! You have anything to say about it, you say it to me!"

Not too long after that, Senator Thurmond came around and asked me, "You told me this fellow was profane. Is he kind of risqué?" I said, "No Senator, not kind of risqué. He's kind of profane." He thought about that and said, "What does he say, hell and damn?" I said, "No sir." "Well, what does he say?" I said, "Sir, I'd rather not say." He goes, "I said, WHAT DOES HE SAY!" I said, "Well sir, it's more like mother f— and c—sucker."

"Mother f—! C—sucker! Oh my God! We can't have that now! We can't have that!" He was getting very upset. I said, "Yes sir, Senator. I was watching him the other night on TV. Some people don't like him, but I think he's kind of funny. He was doing a sketch where he was a reggae singer at a VFW Hall singing a song about *Kill All the White People*."

"KILL ALL THE WHITE PEOPLE! KILL ALL THE WHITE PEOPLE! Get her on the

Strom Thurmond, Duke Short, and Mark Goodin watch the returns during the Senator's final election on the evening of November 5, 1996 in Columbia, South Carolina.

phone right now! GET HER ON THE PHONE!" He started acting like Fred Sanford where Fred is grabbing his heart and stumbling around saying, "I'm coming to see you Elizabeth!" The Senator then yelled, "My career is over! Oh my God! Get her on the phone!"

After he got Mrs. Thurmond on the phone he handed the receiver to me and said, "You tell her what you told me!" I said, "Sir, I'd rather not." "YOU TELL HER RIGHT NOW!" And he made me say mother f— and c—sucker right there on the phone to Mrs. Thurmond. She started crying.

He got on the phone with her and yelled, "This thing is over! It's over right now! This is not happening! You almost cost me my career Nancy!" She hung up.

He goes, "You call this Murphy fellow and tell him this thing's off!" I said, "But Senator, the event is tomorrow!" He yelled, "It's over right now, you hear me!" I said, "Well, yes sir."

So I called Eddie Murphy's agent, a guy named Bob Wachs, and told him the publicity was out of control and that we couldn't go through with it. He blasted me. He said, "Let me tell you something. Don't you think I know what's going on here?!" He cussed me out. It was a bad scene.

But I'll never forget that as long as I live; watching Senator Thurmond stumble around yelling, "Mother f—! C—sucker! Kill all the white people! Oh my God! She's ruined me! It's over; my career is over!"

Congressman John Napier (center) and his wife Pam Napier with Strom Thurmond.

*Before we left, the Senator walked down to the gate and apologized to the guard
for being in such a hurry. He said, "The President was waiting on me.
I appreciate you doing your duty."*

– John L. Napier –

"You're With Me"

CRASHING THE WHITE HOUSE AND MORE

Strom Thurmond had a tremendous sense of loyalty to his friends, staff members, and constituents, and he had little regard for formalities based on social or economic hierarchies. To him, everyone deserved respect, attention, and opportunity. For this reason he always tried to include aides or interns in Capitol Hill events to which they would not normally have been invited.

The Senator also had immense respect for the law and for officers charged with enforcing it. Countless times, I heard him sincerely thanking state patrol officers, sheriff's deputies, and police officers for their efforts in upholding laws and regulations.

These two qualities — Senator Thurmond's inclusiveness and his belief in deferring to law-enforcement personnel — sometimes conflicted when he tried to bring "non-VIP's" to VIP events. While these confrontations were probably nerve-wracking or exasperating to some of the people involved, they were (and are) hilarious to others. In addition to being entertaining, these incidents provide marvelous insights into the ways that Senator Thurmond handled obstacles.

JOHN L. NAPIER

The Senator asked me to pick him up one Saturday morning to go to the White House for a bill singing ceremony. President Ford was President at the time. When we got down to the White House gates, the guard came out and walked up to the car. Of course, my name was not on the list of guests. The Senator leaned over and said to me, "Just tell him you're with Senator Thurmond. We've got to go in." So I rolled the window down. I said, "I have Senator Thurmond here. We are going in." He said, "Where's your clearance?" Senator Thurmond said, "We're in a hurry! Move forward, John!" The guard said, "Let me see your identification." The Senator said, "Move forward, John!" I said, "Senator —" "Move!" I said, "But Senator —"He yelled, Move!"

I was caught between the White House guard and my boss, who was a United States Senator. So I moved on up and parked right in front of the West Wing. The Senator jumped out of the car and quickly walked back to the guard. He said, "I'm Senator Thurmond. I've got an appointment with the President of the United States. I don't have time for all this stuff. You call him if you don't believe it! Come on John!"

We turned around and walked right into the White House. As we're walking through the door, he turned to me and said, "I hated to do that, but you weren't on the clearance list." We went into the ceremony. When it was over, we came back out to the car. It was still right there in front of the West Wing. Before we left, the Senator walked down to the gate and apologized to the guard for being in such a hurry. He said, "The President was waiting on me. I appreciate you doing your duty."

HENRY MCMASTER

is the South Carolina Attorney General and a former U.S. Attorney, having been appointed by President Reagan. He also worked as a Legislative Assistant for Senator Thurmond in the 1970s. He and his family have been good friends of the Senator's for many years.

When I was a staffer up there in Washington we went to the White House to watch President Nixon promote an Admiral. This was back in the early '70s. The Senator always had a practice of taking a staff member somewhere with him so they could have the experience of going to wherever that place was. He would never let an invitation go by without somebody in the office taking advantage of it.

The Senator's secretary Miss Neighbors had called back one afternoon to see who in the Legislative Office hadn't been to the White House yet. Myself and a young man named David Tompkins were new. So Miss Neighbors said, "Tomorrow morning at 10:30 y'all be ready and go with the Senator to the White House."

At the appointed time we went down to his office. As we were leaving Miss Neighbors said to him, "Now Senator, you know they only invited you. They specifically said no staff." He said, "Fine. Come on men." We went down and got in that blue and white banged-up Maverick. It must have hit every post in the parking lot. David was driving, and I was in the backseat. The Senator was riding shotgun, which he usually did.

We pulled up to the White House gate, and the Secret Service police officer came out with the clipboard. The Senator said, "I'm here to see the President." The officer said, "That's fine, Senator. You're here for the 10:45 ceremony. But who are these gentlemen?" He said, "This is Henry McMaster, and this is David Tompkins. They're staff members. They work for me." The officer replied, "Senator, I'm sorry but I don't see them on the list." He said, "But they work for me." And the officer said, "Excuse me sir." He went into the guard shack and got on the telephone.

About thirty seconds later he came out and said, "Senator, I'm sorry; I don't have these gentlemen's names on the list as being admitted to the White House for the ceremony." Senator said, "Oh, well. This is Henry McMaster, and this is David Tompkins. They work for me. You go ahead and put their names on the list." The officer said, "Ah, one moment, Senator." He went back into the shack again and got on the phone. He went back three times! And every time he'd come back to the car, the Senator would tell him the same thing.

The third or fourth time the police officer finally said, "Okay Senator Thurmond, just go ahead." He opened the gate; we drove in and parked right there in front of the West Wing. As we got out of the car, David and I were both shaking because we knew we weren't supposed to be there. As we went past more officers through the door, Senator Thurmond turned over his shoulder and whispered, "Y'all stick close to me and act like you know what you're doing."

When we got inside they took us to the Roosevelt Room. There were several high-ranking Senators and members of the military present. There were probably only about twelve people there, plus David and me! We sat there and drank coffee and tried not to shake too much. About that time a door opened and someone motioned for us to go on into the Oval Office. We thought for sure we'd have to wait there in the Roosevelt Room. But someone motioned everyone in, so we went in. And there we were, standing in the Oval Office for the ceremony. I'll never forget that.

DOUG JENNINGS

The story goes like this. Gene Morehead, a family court judge from Florence, had been one of thousands of young South Carolinians who spent a month interning in Senator Thurmond's office. Later in life he was up in Washington for a conference, and he decided he would go by and pay his respects to his old boss. While he was visiting with the Senator, the bells and lights went off signaling a vote over on the Senate floor. Senator Thurmond asked, "Gene, you want to go over to the Senate with me?" Gene said sure. The Senator said, "Well, come on."

As the story goes, they were walking down the hall. Gene was following along behind the Senator, who was busy talking to an aide about the vote he was going to make. They went down the elevator, got off, and headed down a narrow corridor towards the little subway that goes over to the Capitol.

Up ahead of them, coming towards them, they see a large entourage of people. There's a lot of Capitol policemen, security, and Secret Service. Senator Thurmond was craning his neck trying to see. "Who's that up there?" he said. He politely moved people to the side, trying to get through the crowd to see who it was: "Excuse me, excuse me, Senator Thurmond coming through. Excuse me, President Pro Tem, excuse me." And he turned behind him and said, "Gene, you follow me!"

They walked through three or four levels of police and security until they are right in the middle of the crowd. And there dressed in all his regalia is King Hussein of Jordan, who was on an official trip to Washington that day. They got up there and Senator Thurmond said, "Why King, how do you do? I'm Strom Thurmond, President Pro Tem of the United States Senate. Welcome to the Capitol. Glad to have you here today. King, I want you to meet a good friend of mine. This is Gene Morehead from Florence." Then he made the introductions like this: "Gene, King. King, Gene."

The great part of that story is that it shows how Senator Thurmond treated everybody the same. It mattered not to him that here one man was a head of state, the leader of his country, and the other man was a family court judge from Florence. To him they were like two old friends saying hello: "Gene, King. King, Gene." The Senator made sure that nobody was left out, and he wanted everybody to be treated the same.

TERRY L. WOOTEN

I was riding back to the office with the Senator following a speech he'd given somewhere. He had to go to the White House. He said, "I'm not going to have time to take you back to the office and drop you off. We're going to stop by the White House for a swearing in." There was a new secretary of some kind they were swearing in at a private ceremony. The Senator said, "I don't believe you're on the guest list. When we get there, I'm going to walk straight through the door. They won't stop me. You get right behind me. You don't look right, and you don't look left. You just keep right on walking."

We got up to the White House. The Senator started on in, and I walked right behind him. We walked right through the metal detector and on into the ceremony. I didn't look left or right, just as he said. The Senator always took care of his staff people. It would have been fine with me if he'd asked me to wait in the car. I wouldn't care. But he treated us all with great respect, and he wanted to give us opportunities to go and see things in Washington we wouldn't otherwise get to see. It was important to him that we did things like that.

DAVID T. BEST

served as Senator Thurmond's Legislative Director and Counsel, 1993-2003.

The Department of Veterans Affairs hosted a commemorative event one morning in 1994 in honor of the 50th anniversary of the passage of the GI Bill. President Clinton was going to speak. I went with the Senator to the event, as I was the staff representative to the Veteran's Affairs Committee. There was a special entrance that we were supposed to use at the event. There were metal detectors and all sorts of security because the President was going to be there. But we didn't get dropped off in front of that entrance. Senator Thurmond's driver dropped us off on a side road.

So we started walking across the grass and stepped over the yellow tape that the Secret Service had put up. Well, all of a sudden a bunch of Secret Service agents ran out to meet us. They said, "Senator, we'd like people to go in that entrance over there." He said, "Well, I'm not walking all the way back there." So they told me I had to go back. The Senator said, "He's with me! Do whatever you need to do, but we're not walking all the way back there." They got their hand wands and did the check on us and said, "Go ahead."

This was an outdoor event, so it was under a big tent. The first row of chairs were all marked VIP. The Senator sat down and told me to sit down next to him. The Secret Service said, "Senator, these are reserved for VIPs and dignitaries." He pointed to me and said, "Well, he's with me! He's a VIP today!" They finally quit arguing with him. Of course, Senator Thurmond was right on time for the event; in fact, we were early. But President Clinton's time was not quite Senator Thurmond's time. The President was running late. It got later and later.

In the meantime that front row filled up with Senators. I remember Warner, Robb, and Rockefeller. I think Frank Murkowski was there, and Senator Jeffords came up. He was still a Republican. He had a staff aide with him, a fairly attractive young lady. She naturally caught Senator Thurmond's eye. He patted the chair next to him and said to her, "You sit here by me."

At the end of the President's speech he went down the front row shaking hands. He's saying hello to all these Senators, and then he got to Jefford's aide. He kind of stopped and looked at her. You could just see him thinking: who are these people with Senator Thurmond? There we were sitting in the VIP section. You could just tell President Clinton thought he was supposed to know who we were. It was really funny.

Howard Baker, President Ronald Reagan,
Strom Thurmond, and John Tower.

Having a direct hand in helping his constituents is what made
Strom Thurmond most happy.
– R.J. Duke Short –

"Mr. President, When You've Been Around as Long as I Have..."

STROM THURMOND THE LEGISLATOR

Senator Thurmond relished the effectiveness of constituent service. He liked knowing he could get the secretary of some department or agency on the phone and make something happen immediately that would help someone. And he didn't mind picking up the phone to call the President or a member of the Cabinet either. Then he'd get back on the phone with a constituent down in Chesnee, Columbia, or Charleston and say, "Hey, I've taken care of that problem for you." Having a direct hand in helping his constituents is what made Strom Thurmond most happy.

Because the Senator enjoyed helping people, he was usually back in his office working on constituent service projects while other Senators might be on the Floor trying to push through a giant, bipartisan bill that had their names on it. When it got right down to it, Strom Thurmond didn't enjoy legislating, but he was very good at it and had real talent for engineering support for his bills.

While the Senator's constituent service is the stuff of legend, his reputation as a great legislator has been very much underestimated. It's true that he did not go to the Senate with a big bill every session and grab headlines in the process. But nonetheless, he did achieve significant success as a legislator, as this and the next two chapters will attest.

DAN QUAYLE

*was Vice President of the United States, 1989-1993. He is now
the Chairman of Cerberus Global Investments.*

On a professional basis Senator Thurmond was the best vote counter and vote get-ter in the Senate. One reason I think he was so good at getting votes is because he would twist your arm, and I mean that literally not figuratively. We did more things and voted for more projects for South Carolina than we probably ever should have. It's primarily because of Strom Thurmond. He always knew how to get things done for his state.

BOB DOLE

I remember when the Martin Luther King Holiday Bill came to the Floor. Senator Thurmond asked me if I would manage the bill on the Floor. He wasn't opposed to it, but he wanted me to take care of it. He said, "You manage this bill, and I'll be back after awhile." Well, he didn't come back for two days! But he knew I was the Majority Leader and it was a very major piece of legislation; he just thought I should do it.

I'll always remember when he said, "I'll be right back." Two days later I said, "Strom, where have you been?" He said, "Oh, I've been watching you. I've been sitting right back here. Just let me know if you need any help."

STEPHEN L. JONES

*was the Executive Assistant to Senator Thurmond, 1974-81.
He is now the Principal Deputy Assistant Secretary of Defense
(Health Affairs).*

I remember a time that we were eating in the Senate Dining Room with a delegation that had come up to visit from the state. Senator Hubert Humphrey was still alive then, and he was there in the Dining Room. Senator Humphrey came over and shook hands with Senator Thurmond's guests. Thurmond and Humphrey always got along well, laughed and joked, even though they were totally opposite on the political spectrum.

I'll never forget Senator Humphrey said, "Gentlemen, you have a fine elected official in Senator Thurmond. He doesn't want to waste a vote with us when we're cooking up the cake, but when it comes to the cutting, he sure knows how to get his fair share!"

DENNIS DECONCINI
was a United States Senator from Arizona, 1977-1995.

When I served on the Judiciary Committee with Senator Thurmond, he and I kind of bonded together. A few times I was the swing Democrat that voted with Republicans -- not all the time, but every now and then. Senator Thurmond respected that. He liked the fact that even though I was a Democrat, he knew I was going to do what I thought was right. When I would vote against him or the Republicans, he would say to me, "I know you're doing what you believe is right." He had tremendous respect for that.

DAVID T. BEST
In the mid to late '90s we were in a battle with the wine industry over alcohol labeling. The wine industry was trying to get authority to put labels on bottles claiming health benefits. The Senator thought that was bad policy. We fought very vigorously against that, and we were successful. It got to the point where *Wine Spectator Magazine* even put Senator Thurmond on the cover as Public Enemy Number One. Of course, that did nothing but energize him even more. I remember he said, "That's just great!" He loved it.

During all of this, I went to a reception with the Senator. I asked him if he wanted anything to drink. He said, "I think I'll have a little wine." I said, "Senator, I don't think that's a good idea." And I reminded him about the public policy battle he was engaged in. He looked right at me and said, "Why not? A little wine now and then is good for you." I just sunk. I thought, oh my God, I hope there are no reporters around here.

I said, "Senator, remember the magazine? Public Enemy Number One? We're fighting their claim that wine is healthy." He said, "I know that! But it's a separate thing." In his mind, it was a separate matter altogether. We were fighting the wine industry's efforts to permit labeling that drinking wine is beneficial. With all the negative things associated with alcohol use, why should we do anything to encourage drinking? That's what the Senator's efforts were all about.

There were some in the press who attributed his position to his daughter being killed by a drunk driver. But four or five years before his daughter was killed, he had been the author of the original alcohol labeling act with Joe Kennedy, a liberal Democrat in the House. So Senator Thurmond had been involved in this issue for a long time.

ARNOLD PUNARO,

Major General, United States Marine Corps (ret). He served as the Staff Director for the U.S. Senate Armed Services Committee and worked on Capitol Hill from 1973 to 1997. He is now the Executive Vice President of Science Applications International Corporation.

Let me give you an example of what Senator Thurmond was like behind the scenes when it came to taking care of things he believed were important. At the time, this would have been back in the early '80s, I was the Minority Staff Director for the Armed Services Committee. Jim McGovern was the Staff Director for the Majority. Senator Tower was Chairman and Senator Nunn was the Ranking Member. Jim McGovern and Carl Smith, another great Armed Services Committee staffer, a super guy, had not always liked the National Guard and Army Reserve add-on. The Pentagon had never asked for it, and yet the Congress was always adding things in the budget for the Guard and Reserve. It was seen by some as a pork barrel add-on rather than something that was necessary. Senator Glenn and Senator McCain tended to have that view back then as well.

Historically, the Pentagon did not budget for new or cutting-edge equipment for the Guard and Reserve. Most everybody figured that they were not the first to deploy, so they didn't need the newer stuff. Of course, this was back before our current situation. Senator Thurmond and Senator Stennis usually worked together and developed a bipartisan Guard and Reserve add-on to the budget package. They both agreed that the Guard and Reserve were becoming more important, and that they should have the same modern equipment and advanced training as the active forces. That just shows you how far-thinking they were. So that was the way it had usually worked. The Guard and Reserve add-on averaged about $700 million a year.

Like I said, Jim and Carl had this idea to leave the Guard and Reserve add-on out of the mark-up package. It was one way to compel the Pentagon to budget better for what they needed. They figured Senator Tower and Senator Nunn basically weren't going to support the add-on, and they had Glenn and McCain, another bipartisan duo, that weren't going to support it either. Even though Senator Thurmond and Senator Stennis wouldn't be wild about leaving it out, they figured they'd just read the writing on the wall.

So we came to the end of the mark-up. Just as Senator Tower was getting ready to lock everything up, Senator Thurmond asked to be recognized. He said something like, "Mr. Chairman, what about the Guard and Reserve? Are we going to forget about them?"

Tower then launched into some explanation about why he and the others didn't think it was appropriate that we add money for the Guard and Reserve into the package. Senator Nunn chimed in. Senator Glenn chimed in. Senator McCain chimed in.

Senator Thurmond listened to everyone very patiently. When they were all done, and

Senator Tower was again getting ready to end the meeting, Senator Thurmond said, "Mr. Chairman! I have an amendment!" Senator Tower said, "An amendment?!" Senator Thurmond said, "Yes, I have an amendment to add money in for the Guard and Reserve."

Everything that had just been said didn't count much to Senator Thurmond. He wanted that money for the Guard and Reserve. He put his amendment down on the table and said, "Here's $700 million for the Guard and Reserve." He explained what it was for, new equipment, training: all a part of his philosophy that the Guard and Reserve were going to be more important to us in the future and we better get them ready.

Then, before anybody could even respond, Senator Stennis said, "Mr. Chairman! Senator Thurmond is making a real good point, and I'm supporting his amendment. By the way, I've got my own amendment." He reached into his coat pocket and slowly pulled out a piece of paper. He said, "Here's my amendment too. I've got $700 million more for the Guard and Reserve. I'd like to amend that to Senator Thurmond's amendment."

Senator Thurmond said, "Well, I'd welcome that amendment Senator Stennis! Set your amendment to my amendment there." So there we had pending in the Committee a $1.4 billion add-on for the Guard and Reserve. A few other Senators start chiming in now about their support for the add-on. Senator Thurmond and Senator Stennis obviously had this prepared. They knew what was going on, and they had everything lined up ahead of time.

Senator Tower said, "Well, I didn't think this was the way to go, but I sense the sentiment on the Committee. We'll just take it to Conference. Without objection —"

Senator Thurmond said, "No Mr. Chairman! I insist on a roll call vote!" Senator Stennis said, "Yes! We need a roll call vote. It will give us a stronger position when we take it to Conference."

So Senator Tower had no choice but to call a roll call vote. The vote was unanimous in support of the add-on. Not only did we not have zero, like they had tried to do, we had double what we usually had! That was another lesson from Senator Thurmond.

DIRK KEMPTHORNE

was a United States Senator from Idaho, 1993-1999.
He served as Governor of Idaho from 1999-2006. Since May
of 2006 he has served as U.S. Secretary of the Interior.

On one occasion the Armed Services Committee was dealing with spent nuclear fuel rods from submarines and aircraft carriers. The ultimate repository was the state of Idaho, but because of different issues raised, we had a situation that Idaho was not receiving any. So we began to see a stockpile of these fuel rods at shipyards in different states, causing a great deal of concern and uproar.

Senator Nunn was Chairman of the Armed Services Committee at the time. We were having a debate about the issue. It was indeed a political minefield. In the course of the discussion, Senator Nunn offered a potential solution. Right at that point, Senator Thurmond called for a recess. It was something of a surprise, because that didn't happen very often. He signaled that he'd like me and a few other Senators to step out into the hall.

John Warner and I and a few others were out in the hall with Senator Thurmond. Now it was not unusual for Senator Thurmond to kind of tap you on the chest when he spoke to you. So he started tapping me on the chest saying, "Senator Kempthorne, this is a tough issue. But I'm going to do everything you want to do. I support you. I think Senator Nunn has offered you a viable solution. He's an honorable man." The whole time he kept thumping my chest while he made his points. He finally said, "So Senator Kempthorne, what do you want me to do?" I thought for a moment and said, "Well, can you stop thumping my chest?" We all broke out laughing.

We agreed we had a solution and went back in the hearing room. But for Senator Thurmond to call a recess like that and take a moment to pull me aside just to say he supported me, I'll never forget that. I was a freshman Senator, and he knew I was in a political predicament. He was going to back me no matter what I chose to do, and that meant the world to me. I had a great affection for the man.

MIKE TONGOUR

is a former Legislative Director for Senator Thurmond, 1985-97.
He is now a Government Relations Consultant with Tongour,
Simpson, Holsclaw.

To use a basketball expression, Senator Thurmond loved putting points on the board. He loved getting legislation done. He wanted to make sure that as his Legislative Director you were on top of everything he had going. One of the things I initiated was a Legislative Status Report in which we looked at everything he was trying to do legislatively, outside the Judiciary and Armed Services Committees: who was the staffer assigned to it, where we were in the process, what was the next thing that we could do as staff to move the process along, and what was the next thing he could do as a Senator to move the process along. We would often go over that Report and discuss things. He was very engaged in the process and very goal oriented.

One issue in particular I remember was his legislation to require warning labels on alcohol. One of the first things I did as Senator Thurmond's Legislative Director was to research all the various issues in the health and labor areas that he was interested in. I noticed that many years ago he had offered amendments to the tobacco warning label legislation which would have required warning labels on alcohol. I approached him to see if that was something that still interested him. He was very willing to work hard on that issue, and went after it quite diligently. Ultimately, Senator Thurmond was able to accomplish his goal. That is certainly on the list of his major legislative accomplishments during the course of his career in the Senate.

As I recall, it would have been easy for the alcohol beverage industry to kill this legislation because it came up sort of late in the year. And that is exactly what they wanted to do at first. But Senator Thurmond wanted it done. In the end, the legislation passed unanimously. Nobody would have predicted that he would have gotten that passed over the initial objections of the alcohol beverage industry. But thanks to his negotiating skills, he was able to accomplish his goal. Look on any beer or wine bottle and you'll see the warning label he drafted.

GARRY D. MALPHRUS

was appointed an Immigration Judge for the Arlington, Virginia Immigration Court in 2005. From 2001 to 2004 he served President George W. Bush as Associate Director of the White House Domestic Policy Council. Judge Malphrus served as Senator Thurmond's Chief Counsel on the Senate Judiciary Committee from 1997 to 2001.

Senator Thurmond's commitment to constituent service is legendary. His love for the people of his state and his desire to help them was clear to anyone who knew him. No project was too big or too small for him to help with, and no one was more dedicated to constituent service and to getting things done for people than Senator Thurmond. Even newly elected Senators knew about Senator Thurmond's effectiveness in constituent service and would seek out his expertise when they were organizing their offices. In his final years in office, Senator Thurmond often said he wanted to be remembered for helping people and would deflect questions about his legislative record to talk about constituent service.

However, it is Senator Thurmond's legislative achievements that are too often overlooked in any discussions of his Senate career. News articles and books about Senator Thurmond written during his latter years in the Senate make little note if any of his accomplishments as a legislator. It is particularly striking given his years as Chairman and Ranking Member of the Senate Judiciary Committee.

This book is certainly not the place to recount the Senator's legislative accomplishments. However, I would like to talk about just one example of a major bill called the Sentencing Reform Act of 1984 that Senator Thurmond got enacted while he was

Senator Thurmond, Duke Short, and Senator Joseph Biden at a Judiciary Committee Hearing.

Chairman of the Senate Judiciary Committee.

Senator Thurmond, along with Senator Ted Kennedy, the ranking Democrat on the Committee at the time, fundamentally changed the way that all criminals were sentenced in all Federal courts through the Sentencing Reform Act. The legislation for the first time established ranges in which Federal judges could sentence criminals based on the crime and the characteristics of the offender, such as his prior record. Before this law, two criminals who had committed the same crime and were just alike in every respect could get dramatically different punishment simply based on which Federal judge they happened to appear before, even within the same courthouse. One defendant might get probation while the other might get many, many years behind bars. Moreover, even once a judge imposed a sentence, there was no way to know how long the person would actually serve in jail because of parole and other factors.

This bill changed all that by establishing a specific, narrow range in which judges could sentence an offender based on this crime and on a host of other facts, such as whether he had committed other crimes in the past and whether a gun was used to commit this crime, for example. Also, the bill established truth in sentencing in the Federal system, something that is routine in the criminal justice system throughout the country today.

The bill was a radical departure for the criminal justice system then and a major change to the power of individual Federal judges. Critics said it would never pass and if it did, it would never work. They said that no one could create a guidelines system that could take into account the huge number of facts and circumstances that judges consider in sentencing a defendant. However, Senator Thurmond, with help from Senator Kennedy, proved the critics wrong.

Not only was Senator Thurmond able to get the bill passed; he was able to get the President to appoint a Federal judge from South Carolina, Judge William Wilkins, to lead the effort in creating the Sentencing Guidelines for judges to follow, and getting them implemented throughout the country.

A couple of years before he retired, Senator Thurmond held hearings in the Judiciary Committee on the Sentencing Guidelines and issues regarding their implementation. More recently, the Supreme Court has changed the mandatory nature of the Sentencing Guidelines, and the Congress has been responding to that decision. Of course, Senator Thurmond is no longer in the Senate to deal with these issues. However, he is the primary architect of the way that all Federal criminals are sentenced in Federal court today. It is something he does not get enough credit for.

Through this and many other bills, Senator Thurmond also increased penalties for serious violent criminals. He also worked with President Ronald Reagan to confirm a record number of Federal judges to the Federal courts up until that time. And much more could be said.

Senator Thurmond wanted to be remembered for constituent service, and it is fitting that he is. However, he should also be remembered for his legislative accomplishments, particularly his work on the Senate Judiciary Committee.

ORRIN HATCH

is a United States Senator from Utah, 1977-present.

For years I had led the fight against unfair Civil Rights legislation sponsored by Senator Kennedy. It was unfair. It was always too extreme. But in 1988 Kennedy agreed to my amendments on the Fair Housing Bill thanks in part to a phone call from Muhammad Ali, who was a friend of mine. When the bill reached the Floor, many conservatives, including Senator Thurmond, intended to filibuster the bill. But when I announced that I supported the amended version, Senator Thurmond changed his vote in support of it. The bill sailed through, 94 to 3. Strom did that because he knew that I would not have supported it had it not been right. And he basically was a strong supporter of honest Civil Rights legislation.

Soon after the vote Kennedy came to me and said in a low tone, "I have really done you a favor. The *New York Times* wants a picture of us in the President's Room. I suggested you should be there, rather than Strom, because you were the one who made it possible to pass this bill." So I left with Kennedy and Senator Specter.

When I entered the President's Room, there was 85-year-old Senator Thurmond. Kennedy had arranged the group. He was a little taken aback, but he couldn't do anything about it. Kennedy put me on his right, Specter on his left, and Thurmond on the other side of Specter. Just as the *New York Times* photographer started to snap the picture, Thurmond's face suddenly appeared between Kennedy and Specter. Kennedy said, "Strom, what are you doing?" Strom said, "I'm the Ranking Minority Floor Manager of the Bill. I thought I ought to be able to stand next to the Majority Floor Manager." Thurmond had in fact deferred to me to manage the Bill on the Floor.

With that, Thurmond put his shoulder into Specter and muscled him out of position. Kennedy and I burst out laughing, but Specter muscled his way back in. The tussle between Thurmond and Specter continued until Thurmond stopped and looked at Kennedy. "Well," Strom said, "then I'll get on the other side of you." So Thurmond started to nudge me, and I good naturedly stepped aside. The next morning the *New York Times* carried an article of four Senators laughing, from left to right, Hatch, Thurmond, Kennedy, and Specter. I'll never forget that. It was one of the funniest things. Strom wasn't about to be pushed out as being the Ranking Member on that Bill.

JOSEPH R. BIDEN, JR.
is a United States Senator from Delaware, 1972-present.

Of all the labels that are placed on Strom, the one that wasn't often placed on him that I most remembered him for was "legislator." If there was ever anyone in the Senate who knew how to get things done, it was Strom Thurmond. He understood people. He knew how to read them, how to move them, how to make things happen. The most vivid example of that for me was a time we went down to see President Reagan.

We sat in the Treaty Room in the White House. President Reagan came in with William French Smith, Howard Baker, his Chief of Staff, and Ed Meese. We all sat at a long table. Smith, Baker, and Meese were on one side. Strom and I sat on the left and right of the President on the other side of the table. We were there to try and get the President to sign on to the Thurmond-Biden Crime Bill.

We started out by listening to the President. And then at one point Strom said, "Joe, you tell him." I was on the President's left. He turned to me, and I started making our case for the bill. The President listened, and he started nodding his head and saying "Yeah, yeah, yeah." It was clear to Ed Meese and his staff that we were convincing the President.

Suddenly Ed Meese jumped to his feet, looked at his watch, and said "Mr. President, it's time to go! Time to go Mr. President!" Just as Strom and I both thought President Reagan was about to agree to our bill. The President said, "Well, I'm sorry gentlemen, but I have to go."

The President put his hands down on the table to lift himself to stand up. As he started up, Strom put his left hand firmly on the President's forearm and literally pulled him back down to his seat. I mean, literally! The President gave him a glare. Strom said, "Mr. President, when you've been around as long as I have and you get as old as I am, you learn that you've got to compromise if you ever want to get anything done."

The President was furious. Strom didn't budge; he still had his hand on the President's arm. President Reagan moved his arm away and said, "Well, I'll think about it." President Reagan ended up signing on to the legislation. Strom had convinced him. Can you imagine that? There he was talking to a nearly 80-year-old President, telling him, "When you get as old as I am, you've got to compromise." It was an unforgettable moment.

John Walsh and Strom Thurmond at the 1997 Boys and
Girls Clubs of America Congressional Breakfast.

Strom Thurmond was the true champion of the Missing Children's Bill.
He was right there with us from the beginning.

– John Walsh –

The Missing Children's Act of 1982

JOHN WALSH,

founder of the National Center for Missing and Exploited Children,
is a globally recognized advocate for children's and victims' rights.
He is the host of the television program America's Most Wanted,
which has helped law enforcement capture well over 900 fugitives.

Before I became well known on television, my son Adam was murdered. He went missing on July 27, 1981. His remains were found two weeks later. In those days the FBI didn't get involved in missing children's cases. They had this bizarre criterion left over from J. Edgar Hoover's policy that said there had to be proof for crossing a state line before they would get involved. But nobody that kidnaps a child is going to tell you where they are. So I tried to direct my heartache and bitterness and anger after Adam's murder toward a piece of legislation called the Missing Children's Bill.

The bill was introduced in the Senate by Republican Paula Hawkins, a friend of Strom's, and in the House by Democratic Congressman Paul Simon. They were kind of strange bedfellows, but it was a good bill. It would simply mandate that the parents of a missing child could go to their FBI Field Office and get their child listed in the National Crime Information Computer. The FBI already kept information there about stolen boats, planes, and cars, but had so far refused to get involved in missing children. They saw it strictly as a local law enforcement affair. Because the FBI refused to get involved, your child could possibly be found dead in another state and you would never know. We found out that the FBI had spent hundreds of thousands of dollars looking for a stolen racehorse, but it wouldn't look for missing kids.

Don Edwards was a Congressman from Northern California and a former FBI agent. He was vehemently opposed to the Missing Children's Bill. He chaired this now famous Committee hearing in the House that my wife Reve and I went to. The FBI testified at the hearing, as did a representative from the Justice Department. They were full of BS, saying that dealing with missing kids would clog their computers. They said anything they could to convince Congress because they simply didn't want to get involved in missing children. But of course, I had learned first hand that local cops didn't have the resources, didn't have the training, and didn't have the manpower. We needed the FBI to get involved.

When it came time for Reve and me to testify, everybody at the Committee table got up and walked out. I'm talking about Pat Schroeder, Harold Washington: they all just left. The only person left up there was Don Edwards. The first thing I said when I got a chance to speak is how my wife and I were absolutely appalled. I said, "We paid our own way up here. We're the parents of Adam Walsh, a murdered child. And these Congressmen and women don't even have the common decency to listen to the parents of a murdered child from Florida. Where are they going – to have lunch with a lobbyist?" I was outraged. In spite of Congressman's Edwards efforts to stop the legislation in Committee, the bill was forced out by the general public because I started a big campaign. It went out to the House Floor and it passed.

On the Senate side, Paula Hawkins and Strom had formed a kind of swat team to support the bill. Strom was President Pro Tem at the time, and he had the power to get the bill through the Senate. The bill went to a Conference Committee and passed. And President Reagan signed it into law in the Rose Garden. Reve and I were there with our baby daughter Megan, who was born after Adam.

A couple of years later we got the Missing Children's Assistance Bill passed, which created the National Center for Missing and Exploited Children. There are FBI agents who work there now; how ironic is that? The FBI had told the *New York Times* that the Missing Children's Bill would never pass, and that the couple from Florida can go pound salt. Now here we are, years later, and I've caught fifteen guys off the FBI's Ten Most Wanted and have been honored as the FBI's Man of the Year. Only in America.

The Missing Children's Bill was a defining piece of legislation in our nation's history. It changed the way our country deals with missing children. It forced the FBI to get involved. As a country, we have been able to help so many children and families because of it. I'll never forget sitting there in the Conference Room when Strom called for the vote.

I had tears in my eyes. I was thinking about Adam, and I was thinking about what a lonely, tough battle it had been for Reve and me.

Strom Thurmond was the true champion of the Missing Children's Bill. He was right there with us from the beginning. This bill was a political hot potato. It would have been so easy to bury. Nobody took on the FBI and the Justice Department in those days. But Strom had the guts to go against them. This country will always be grateful to him for that.

ROBBIE CALLAWAY

The Missing Children's Act changed America. It's that simple. It was the single most important piece of child protection legislation that had passed in this country's history. And Strom Thurmond's role in making it happen cannot be understated. Strom Thurmond made it happen.

He was up against a lot of folks who didn't want it to happen, including the FBI and a lot of people in law enforcement. Some folks perceived it as causing turf problems. But Senator Thurmond understood this legislation was needed, that it would help children and families, and he fought to make it happen. Thank goodness he won that battle. America is a better place for it, and kids are safer because of it.

I got involved because John Walsh turned to me to help lobby the original bill. We went to meet a young staffer in Senator Thurmond's office. The guy really blew us off, really badly as a matter of fact. I kind of had to hold John back from punching the guy. But then we got to sit down and talk about it with Duke. And Duke sat with the Senator and explained it to him. Next thing you know, bam! We're off to the races.

Senator Thurmond told Senator Hawkins that he would support the bill, and that's what really made it happen. Senator Hawkins was the original sponsor because she was from Florida and that's where John Walsh was from. Senator Thurmond had the power at that point to either make it happen or not. Only Senator Thurmond had the power to stand up to the FBI and all the organizations who fought this legislation.

So Senator Thurmond got the legislation passed. The Missing Children's Act dramatically changed the way America deals with missing kids, abducted kids, and runaway kids. There's nothing like it. This law led to the creation of the National Center for Missing and Exploited Children, which has led to the recovery of tens of thousands of kids. All of that came from this bill that Senator Thurmond got signed into law.

Of course, those of us close to the action knew that Duke was working behind the scenes to make it happen. When the Senator said he was going to make something happen, he'd turn to Duke and say, "Okay, let's make it happen." And Duke would get to work. If the Senator made a promise, Duke was the one who made sure they delivered on it. You could always count on them. They were a fantastic team, and did so much good for this country. We should all be so lucky to have a Duke Short in our life.

Strom Thurmond speaks at the Congressional Breakfast for the Boys and Girls Clubs of America on September 26, 2001. Senator Thurmond was a staunch supporter and ally for the BGCA for many years. He was proud to receive their Man and Youth Award as well as their Outreach Partner Award. Thanks to the Senator's efforts, millions of at-risk kids have benefited from the work of the Clubs.

BOYS AND GIRLS CLUB OF AMERICA

He got them all to stop for a moment and realize hey, we're not against prevention that actually works, and the Boys and Girls Clubs really works.

– Robbie Callaway –

The Boys and Girls Clubs of America

For many years Strom Thurmond led the way on Capitol Hill in his enthusiastic support for the Boys and Girls Clubs of America. He often used to tell me, "Duke, these Clubs are one of the reasons America is a great country. We need to do all we can to help them." I couldn't agree with him more. This amazing organization provides a positive, nurturing environment for millions of at-risk children in a variety of communities in every state in America. Countless Club alumni have gone on to beat the odds, to overcome challenges, and to set examples of achievement and accomplishment of which they, their families, and the nation can be most proud.

The success story that is the Boys and Girls Clubs of America, now in its second century helping kids, is a testament to the passion and dedication of the Clubs' volunteers and employees. Every day they reach out and make a child's life better. In so doing, they make a neighborhood better, and we all ultimately benefit from their efforts. Boys and Girls Clubs are located across America, in big cities like Atlanta, Georgia and in small towns like Chesnee, South Carolina, where the "Gertrude Robinson Powers Club" is located. I'm proud to say that this club was named after my wife's mother and is doing a great service for the children of Chesnee. Senator Thurmond was deeply proud to advocate for the Boys and Girls Clubs in the U.S. Senate.

The Senator was also proud, as am I, to call Robbie Callaway a friend. Robbie is the former Senior Vice President of the Boys and Girls Clubs of America. If there is any one person that deserves to be recognized for his tireless efforts in championing the mission of the BGCA, it is Robbie Callaway. I first met Robbie when he was a young man working for the Clubs about twenty-five years ago. I've had the great privilege of watching him mature into a superb leader. His passion for helping the underprivileged children of this country is infectious. Robbie has personally made a tremendously positive difference in the lives of so many children and their families. It is rare that a man creates, by his unselfish efforts, as powerful a legacy as this at such a young age. Robbie is that rare and special person.

Strom Thurmond did his best when he was alive to see to it that the Boys and Girls Clubs received the support they deserved. That mantle has since been passed to others in Washington, like Congressman Steny Hoyer and Senators Judd Gregg, Orrin Hatch, and Joe Biden — all of whom are to be commended for working so diligently to expand and strengthen the Boys and Girls Clubs of America.

ROBBIE CALLAWAY

Perhaps my most unforgettable memory of Strom Thurmond is at a Congressional Breakfast in September of 1995. We were grateful that the Senator and Congressman Steny Hoyer of Maryland regularly co-hosted our BGCA Congressional Breakfasts. We had a number of Congressional leaders there that morning. At that time we were in the process of trying to secure a multi-million-dollar authorization. As I recall, things weren't exactly tilting our way. We had some powerful friends trying to help us, like Joe Biden. But by and large, Congress was shying away from allocating money to prevention efforts for at-risk children. The Republicans were speaking out against "midnight basketball." Newt Gingrich and other conservatives were being very vocal about shutting down any kind of prevention efforts. So things didn't look great for us back then.

But then came that Congressional Breakfast. I had no idea that Senator Thurmond was going to make the statement he did. We hadn't even discussed it. He caught us totally by surprise. During the breakfast, Senator Thurmond literally slammed his fist down on the table and told everybody there that he wanted the Boys and Girls Clubs to receive full support. He said something like, "This is a good way to spend money. This authorization should happen. I want it to happen. This is prevention that works, and it's going to save the taxpayers money in the long run."

Quite honestly, there was stunned silence in the room. It was definitely not a party line statement. There were conservatives in the room who just the day before had spoken out on the Senate Floor against any more money going to prevention efforts for children. They didn't want to have anything to do with it. They saw it as a waste of money. But Senator Thurmond wanted it done. And thanks to the statement he made that morning, Newt Gingrich came on board. Bob Dole came on board. All those guys eventually came on board to help us. Senator Thurmond did it. He got them all to stop for a moment and realize hey, we're not against prevention that actually works, and the Boys and Girls Clubs really work.

Congressman Steny Hoyer, Robbie Callaway, Sue Callaway,
and Senator Thurmond on September 18, 1998 at the Boys
and Girls Clubs of America Congressional Breakfast.

That was an historic moment. Senator Thurmond turned the tide with that one state-ment. I don't know if any of them would have supported us like they have if he had not stepped up and done that. He was adamant. I mean, his fist hit that table hard. Everybody knew he wasn't going to rest until Congress had thrown its support behind the Boys and Girls Clubs. I will never forget that moment.

Thanks to the Senator we have since helped millions of children, and these are some of the poorest, most disadvantaged kids in the country. We're talking about kids who live in neighborhoods where the strongest role models are drug dealers and gang leaders. There is a war going on in some of these communities. We're fighting the dealers and the gang leaders for these kids. We're fighting to bring these kids into our Clubs and get them involved in positive things.

Many studies have since been done that show without any doubt that the Clubs work. Wherever we open a Boys and Girls Club the crime rates go down, delinquency rates go down, school attendance and grades go up. Senator Thurmond's strong advo-cacy made it all possible.

President Ronald Reagan, Senator Strom Thurmond,
and Duke Short discussing Judge Billy Wilkins
as a potential Supreme Court nominee.

*There is a kind of patriotism in any public official that the public doesn't understand. ...
He was an excellent example of that sincere and profound sense of patriotism.*

– Stephen Breyer –

Strom Thurmond and the Judiciary

S enator Thurmond had a tremendous impact on the U.S. courts through his long tenure and influence on the Senate Judiciary Committee. I can remember one incident, however, when that influence was not enough to get what he wanted.

When Lewis Powell resigned from the Supreme Court in 1987, President Reagan nominated Judge Bork to fill the vacancy. Despite being one of the best candidates to ever be nominated to the high court and a man with a brilliant mind, Bork was not ratified by the Senate. Judge Douglas Ginsburg got an even cooler reception when he admitted to occasional marijuana use years before. That's when Senator Thurmond and I went to the White House to meet with the President.

At that point, given two failed nominations to the Supreme Court, President Reagan and his staff were looking for a sure thing: a judge who had the highest qualifications and the appeal to meet with a quick confirmation in the Senate. Senator Thurmond believed that Judge Billy Wilkins was the right man for the job. So the Senator and I went to the White House to make a strong case for Billy's nomination.

We met in the Oval Office — President Reagan, the Senator, Reagan's then Chief of Staff Howard Baker, and myself. Senator Thurmond talked directly to the President, laying out all of Billy's superb qualifications. Then he turned to me. "Duke, you have anything you want to say to the President?" I told the President that I had checked with a number of key Senators on the Judiciary Committee and Billy could be approved by the Committee. It was also more than likely that he would be confirmed by the full Senate. Howard Baker added, "Duke's right, Mr.

President. Billy could get confirmed." President Reagan sounded very positive when he said that he would confer with his advisors and get back to us. When we left the White House that day, the Senator and I were both confident that Billy would be at the top of a short list of potential nominees.

A few days later Holly called me into the Senator's office. President Reagan was scheduled to phone, and the Senator wanted me in on the conversation. So I picked up the extension in his office. He picked up the phone on his desk. "Mr. President!" "Strom, how are you?" They chatted for awhile, and then President Reagan said, "Well Strom, I've got some good news and some bad news. The bad news is that I'm going to appoint someone else to the Supreme Court. I know you wanted Billy, but I've got a man from my state that I'm going to appoint instead. I've selected another man for the job. The good news is that I'm going to offer Billy Wilkins the job of FBI Director."

I was looking right at the Senator during the call. I could see he wasn't really pleased. That's not what he wanted. Billy was offered the job of FBI Director but did not ultimately take it. He was already Chairman of the U.S. Sentencing Commission and a Judge on the Fourth Circuit Court of Appeals, for which he now serves as Chief Judge. The Senator and I were both tremendously disappointed when we hung up the phone, but the President had made up his mind.

I went back to my office, called Billy, and broke the bad news. I then put him through to the Senator so he could tell him how sorry he was it didn't work out. Very few people know how close Billy Wilkins actually came to being a Supreme Court Justice. As it happened, President Reagan appointed Judge Anthony Kennedy of California to the Court. He was unanimously confirmed by the Senate in February of 1988.

ROBERT H. BORK

was a Judge on the United States Court of Appeals for the District of Columbia Circuit, 1982-88. He was nominated to the Supreme Court of the United States in 1987 but not confirmed by the Senate. He is now a Distinguished Fellow with the Hudson Institute, a legal consultant, teacher, and author.

I recall that a clergyman, clearly a left winger, testified that I had said that the courts should reinstitute school prayer. I certainly did not get into that topic. Strom listened to him for awhile and said simply, "I don't believe you." Senators don't usually say that. I kind of enjoyed it.

C. BRUCE LITTLEJOHN

was the former Chief Justice of the Supreme Court of South Carolina and a former Speaker of the South Carolina House of Representatives. Judge Littlejohn was a close friend of Strom Thurmond's for well over sixty years.

I've always said, except for Strom Thurmond's help, I probably wouldn't have been elected Speaker. If I hadn't been elected Speaker, I probably wouldn't have been elected Circuit Judge. If I hadn't been a Circuit Judge, I wouldn't have gone to the Supreme Court. If I hadn't gone to the Supreme Court, I wouldn't have been elected Chief Justice. Strom had a profound impact on my life. He really did.

STEPHEN BREYER

is an Associate Justice on the United States Supreme Court, 1994-present. He formerly served as Chief Counsel to the U.S. Senate Judiciary Committee.

There is a kind of patriotism in any public official that the public doesn't understand. They think it's all superficial. It isn't. That was the lesson I drew from working with Senator Thurmond. He was an excellent example of that sincere and profound sense of patriotism.

KAREN HENDERSON

is a Judge on the United States Court of Appeals for the District of Columbia Circuit.

Whenever I talked with Senator Thurmond he was always careful to emphasize the limits of judicial power. He often discussed the struggle between power and duty. Given his long and successful career, he certainly knew more about that than most people. To me, he saw his influential position not as one of power but as one of duty. That was one thing he tried to impress on the people whose careers he helped and whose candidacies he supported. He always taught, and his life was a testament to this lesson, that we must never forget we are public servants. That was very important to him. He made such a change in my life, and all for the good. He was a wonderful mentor and patron of mine.

Senator Strom Thurmond and Federal District Judge and former staff member Terry Wooten.

DENNIS DECONCINI

When it came to the nomination of judges before the Judiciary Committee, Strom would never fail to impress upon the nominee the importance of judicial temperament. He had been a judge himself, so I believe he had a deep understanding of the challenges a judge can face. He thought it was very important to get on the record that the nominee was not going to be changed when he or she put on those robes. So he always asked this question: "You seem to have a lot of respect; a lot of friends support you, and you have a nice temperament when you sit here in front of us. Are you going to have that after you're sworn in and you sit on the bench?" Of course, no judge is going to say "No, I'm not."

I picked that up from Senator Thurmond and used to ask every judge that same type of question: "Will you have respect for the defense counsel, the plaintiff's counsel, the witnesses, and the experts that come in, treat them all fairly and impartially as Courts do?" Of course, they all said yes. But I always made sure we put that on the record. Strom Thurmond was the one who set that standard for me.

JUDITH RICHARDS HOPE

is a Senior Advisor to Paul, Hastings, Janofsky & Walker, Adjunct
Professor of Law at Georgetown University Law School, and
President and CEO of Oncovir, a biotechnology company.

I came to know Senator Thurmond well when President Reagan nominated me in 1988 to be Judge of the United States Court of Appeals for the D.C. Circuit. The Senator was on the Judiciary Committee, of course, and Duke Short was his most senior aide. The thing that I remember most is that Senator Thurmond and Duke Short were a team. Because it was an election year, and because battles over judgeships are usually difficult, Senator Thurmond and Duke took a particular interest in trying to guide me through the Senate confirmation process. I never had a hearing as a result of my nomination.

The majority on the Senate Judiciary Committee, then the Democrats, wanted to make an election year issue out of Judge Bork. And I had been nominated to be Judge Bork's successor. So they blocked my hearing and thus my nomination, despite having promised Duke and Senator Thurmond that I would go through in a breeze. Well, it wasn't very breezy. And that's all right. It worked out fine in the long run. But from that moment on until the last time I saw him, Senator Thurmond would always greet me by saying, "You should have been a judge. I wish you'd been a judge." He had a clear memory and a clear devotion to his duty.

J. HARVIE WILKINSON III

is a Judge on the United States Court of Appeals for the Fourth Circuit.

I was nominated to the Court in 1984. Senator Thurmond was the Chairman of the Senate Judiciary Committee at the time. The nomination was pending before the Senate for about a year and a half. There were multiple hearings and cloture votes and filibusters. It was quite an eventful nomination. I had need of a strong supporter to boost my confidence going through the process. Senator Thurmond was just that kind of person. He was always on an even keel. He never wavered in his support. He was optimistic that patience would get the job done.

When people talk about Senator Thurmond having been a person of conviction and rock solid in his loyalties, that was really proven to me. He was a great man to be in a fight with. Believe me, there was nobody you'd rather have on your side. He saw things through; he persevered, and if he gave you his word, you could take it to the bank. I was well aware that my nomination was outside his home state and a whole lot more trouble for him than a usual nomination for a lower court judgeship, particularly at that time. But he went through it all with the greatest patience and humor. I have a lot to thank him for. I think those of us on the Federal bench never relinquish our sense of gratitude for the people who helped us get there.

ANTONIN SCALIA

is an Associate Justice on the United States Supreme Court, 1986-present.

For me the most unforgettable Strom Thurmond moment was the time he was chairing the Judiciary Committee when I was nominated to the Court by President Reagan. That was simultaneous with the nomination of William Rehnquist to be Chief. There were, of course, many members of the committee opposed to my nomination although ultimately nobody voted against it. But they were giving me a hard time during the hearings, as is the Washington game. I will always remember what a wonderful, big fat softball Senator Thurmond served up to me as my first question. He said, "Judge Scalia, what do you think about judicial activism?" I thought, let me answer that one! It was nice to have someone who was friendly to you chairing the proceedings.

JOHN PAUL STEVENS

is an Associate Justice on the United States Supreme Court, 1975-present.

When I went through the confirmation process, I paid a visit to Senator Thurmond. He was very courteous to me and introduced me to his staff and so forth. And he then asked me to come into his private office for a conversation. At that time the death penalty was very much at issue. The constitutionality of the death penalty had not been resolved.

After we sat down and had a pleasant conversation, he said to me, "Judge Stevens, I want to talk to you about the death penalty." I thought to myself: well, I'm not sure I should engage in this conversation. And he said, "I'm not going to ask you how you feel about it, because that would be highly improper as a candidate being considered for a judgeship. But I want to tell you how I feel about it." Then he told me all the reasons why he thought it was a very important matter of law.

I thought it was very interesting the way he got me in his private office and made it clear he was interested in the death penalty, but he didn't ask me a single question about what I thought about it because he thought very strongly that that went beyond the bounds of what a judicial nominee should be asked to discuss. It was very pointed because there was a great interest in what a candidate's reaction to an issue that might

U.S. Supreme Court Justice Antonin Scalia, Strom Thurmond, and the Senator's former Personal Assistant of many years, the late Holly Richardson.

come before the Court might be.

Most of us have felt we shouldn't talk about things that might be a subject of litigation. I thought it was quite interesting because that went beyond the bounds of proper inquiry, but then he went ahead and explained how he felt about it, which is entirely proper for him to do.

The reason I remember it so well is that I was very much concerned as I went through the process that I might have to discuss an issue that I thought I should not discuss. Senator Thurmond was very respectful of that. When there was nobody listening in on us or anything else, he treated me just as he would have in open court. I really had a lot of respect for the way he handled that.

SANDRA DAY O'CONNOR
was the first woman to ever serve as an Associate Justice on the United States Supreme Court, 1981-2006.

I first met Senator Thurmond when I was nominated by President Reagan for the Supreme Court. The Senator was Chairman of the Judiciary Committee at the time. I went over to his office where I first met Duke Short, who then introduced me to Senator

Thurmond. The Senator was a very polite and gracious man. He told me it was nice to meet me and then he said, frankly, that he knew very little about me. He had actually called President Reagan and asked him, "Are you serious about this nominee? Do you really want me to do all I can to help make this happen?" President Reagan told him, "Yes Senator, I think she is an excellent candidate."

So Senator Thurmond said he would do everything he could to help confirm my nomination to the Supreme Court. The first thing he had me do was to call on a few key Senators that he wanted me to meet. Throughout the process, Senator Thurmond was a master politician. He had an incredible knowledge of how things worked in the Senate and how to effectively get things done. It was a thrill and an honor to have known him.

After my confirmation to the Supreme Court, Senator Thurmond arranged for me to speak at the University of South Carolina in Columbia. We traveled down there together, so for the first time I got a chance to see him in a public setting in the airports and around people in his state. He was amazing to watch, the way he interacted with people. He seemed to personally know everybody who came up to him. It was remarkable.

ANTHONY KENNEDY

is an Associate Justice on the United States Supreme Court, 1988-present.

I first met the Senator in 1975, the year in which I was confirmed as a Judge for the U.S. Court of Appeals in the 9th Circuit. My wife and I and our three children traveled to Washington from Sacramento for the confirmation hearing. It was of course a great thrill for us to come to the Capitol. It had been arranged that, following my hearing, I would go to one of the very elegant Senate offices and see if any of the Senators wanted to come and meet me. It being St. Patrick's Day, everyone agreed that it seemed like a good time for people to come greet each other. One of the first Senators to come through to say hello was Senator Thurmond. He was so gracious, cordial, and warm to my wife and me, and later to my children. This was not political, though it certainly helps to have that quality in a politician. It was natural to Senator Thurmond. I was quite impressed with that.

The Senator then acted as one of the co-hosts that afternoon as people came to meet me. He kept saying, "Now Judge, there's some other Senator I want you to meet." And he would go out and bring in one of his other colleagues. I met over fifty Senators that day. Perhaps I was a mild curiosity in that I was one of the youngest judges ever appointed to the Court of Appeals. So that might have caused some interest. In any event, Senator Thurmond thought this was such a wonderful occasion. He really took me under his wing, and I will never forget that.

Whenever I saw the Senator after that he was always immediately solicitous of my family and remembered the St. Patrick's Day event. I thought I would mention it for this reason. The Senate had the reputation as a club. This was a disparaging remark or perhaps a patronizing remark in the view of some. But there were some very real advantages to having an organization that had that feeling about itself. The Republic functions best if there is a high degree of cordiality and collegiality among its officials. This is the essence of democracy. Democracy depends on civility, decency, and conversations in which both participants are trying to find a common answer. Senator Thurmond was one of the great defenders of that idea of the Senate.

Senator Thurmond remained most courteous and gracious to me. If I happened to be in the Senate Dining Room, he would come over to greet me. If I saw him at the airport, he would rush over to say hello. He was always quick to show the cordiality, warmth, and the affection that he had for me and for the Judiciary and for all of those who serve in the government of the United States.

When I came to the confirmation hearings for my nomination to this Court, my children were of course older. Once again Senator Thurmond rushed to meet them and my wife. He wanted to make very sure that they had seats towards the front. The confirmation hearings went on for about three days. As I recall, I was there for only one full day. After the excitement of the morning, the afternoon session for the visitors and spectators was growing somewhat tedious. It was not tedious for me, of course, because I was at the witness table and taking questions from the Senators.

My son tells the story that he had a big lunch that day and had begun to nod a little. Then he brought himself up. There looking him straight in the eye with this intense look of determination was Senator Strom Thurmond. The message was clear: "Look son, I'm an elderly man and I can stay awake for this. It's your duty to do the same!" That has become a great story in our family.

CLARENCE THOMAS
is an Associate Justice on the United States Supreme Court,
1991-present. He is also the former Director of the Equal
Employment Opportunity Commission (1982-1990),
having been appointed by President Reagan.

One of the most moving moments for me during my confirmation to this Court was to see how adamantly Strom Thurmond defended me, not just as a nominee but as a person he had known and dealt with for a decade, as someone he had watched grow up in these governmental positions. At every meeting, confirmation hearing, or event of any consequence, he passionately defended me.

When you're being beaten pretty soundly and someone in the midst of all that stands up and defends you against a mob, it really makes a lasting impression on you. Of course,

I could mention Senator Danforth, Senator Simpson, Senator Hatch, and many others. But the one that I looked to on the Floor most was really Senator Thurmond. At the time he was just short of his 90th birthday. He stood up there without notes and defended me with amazing energy and passion. I deeply appreciated that.

KAREN J. WILLIAMS

is a Judge on the United States Court of Appeals for the Fourth Circuit.

Senator Thurmond and my late father-in-law, Marshall B. Williams, enjoyed a great friendship. The two of them were fairly close contemporaries. They even used to double date. My father-in-law had the good sense to drive and give the Senator the backseat. I tell people that's how I came to the attention of the Senator and probably to what I owe my judgeship! In all seriousness, Senator Thurmond was so helpful to me throughout the confirmation process. He would always say to me, "Don't you worry honey, we've got it all taken care of." That's quite a process, to be interviewed by the members of the Judiciary Committee and the Justice Department. The Senator was most encouraging, as was Duke Short. They were both so supportive. You will probably hear that from every federal judge. They all loved Senator Thurmond, and knew how helpful he was.

When I completed the process, the Senator gave me a copy of the Constitution which he signed, "To my pretty judge; you'll be a great judge." And I've still got my Strom Thurmond letter opener and my Strom Thurmond key chain. He was always so generous, and he gave you something to remember him by in addition to his wisdom. I recall that following my confirmation, he said to me with a smile, "You know, you're going to make a lot of money as a federal judge. I want you to make sure you don't go spending everything you make. You've got to put at least half of it aside and save." He was a wonderful man, and we miss him very much.

Elbow Jabs from the Amazing Strombolini

STORIES FROM THE FLOOR OF THE U.S. SENATE

*I*t didn't matter how often I went to the Floor of the U.S. Senate with Senator Thurmond, which I did countless times over three decades; it never stopped being a terrific thrill. Going through the "Senators Only" doors with him, listening to the debates, watching the rituals, just being there in that "great deliberative body" at the heart of our democracy — it was, of course, an honor and a privilege, but also genuinely exciting each and every time.

The C-SPAN cameras couldn't catch, however, all the little things that made the U.S. Senate so particularly memorable for me personally. You never got to see Senator Thurmond get upset when he discovered there were no more sweets in his desk drawer. Watching the Senate from home, you wouldn't know that one of the staffers rushing off the Floor was actually running down to a gift shop to get a bag of candy. You never heard Senator Thurmond nudge someone sitting next to him and whisper, "Who do you think is the best looking female Senator?" Or, practically yelling because he had his hearing aid turned off, "What are they talking about over there?!"

One of the most unforgettable moments I witnessed on the Floor of the U.S. Senate came during President Clinton's impeachment trial in 1999, when Senator Thurmond was almost 100-years old. David Kendall, Clinton's attorney, had a young lady on his staff who came to the Senate each day for the trial. I was alerted to a situation when a staff member came to me and said, "Duke, the Senator's making goo goo eyes at one of Clinton's lawyers!" Sure enough, he was waving and winking and flirting just like a school boy. Senator Thurmond flirted with that young woman throughout the entire proceedings. I think he had more fun during Clinton's

Strom Thurmond, Duke Short, and Jesse Helms in the President's Room in the U.S. Capitol, October, 2002.

impeachment trial than anyone else in the Senate.

At one point during the trial the young woman even showed up with home-baked cookies she'd prepared for the Senator. Senator Thurmond passed most of them out to the staff. But I do remember him eating one of the cookies back in his office. He had a mouth full when he said, "You know, that man, President Clinton, doesn't seem like such a bad man. He's just made some big mistakes." Despite his love of sweets and his affection for young ladies, Senator Thurmond never lost focus on the duties before him. He voted to impeach.

HOWARD METZENBAUM

was a United States Senator from Ohio, 1976-1995.

Strom and I didn't agree very often, but in spite of that we got along very well. I had a lot of respect for him. I thought he was a tiger on the Floor of the Senate and considered him one of the great Senators that I had the privilege of serving with.

I remember one occasion he was speaking. I got up to speak against it. But I didn't know exactly what he was saying because he was speaking Southernese. I knew whatever he was saying though, I'd be against it. So I spoke the opposite of his side.

We used to call him Strombolini. I don't know how he got that nickname. Saying Strom just wasn't enough, so we added a little extra. We all really liked him quite a lot.

SCOTT FRICK

I always enjoyed watching Senator Thurmond interact with the other Senators down on the Floor. Every time Senator DeWine of Ohio walked by, Senator Thurmond would say, "How's that boy at Clemson?" because Senator DeWine had a son who went to Clemson. Senator Kohl of Wisconsin owned the Kohls Department Stores. Whenever he walked by, Senator Thurmond would yell, "There's the richest man in the Senate! How many stores you got now?" Senator Kohl would always laugh and give him a number. Senator Bunning was a former professional baseball player. Senator Thurmond always referred to him as "the strongest man in the Senate," and Bunning would say, "No, you are!" Senator Campbell was "the King of Colorado." Later Senator Thurmond promoted him to "the King of the West." He had little nicknames for nearly everyone he saw down there. It was very entertaining.

Now, Senator Thurmond's hearing wasn't the best. And he didn't like using a hearing aid. I remember one time when there was a colloquy on the Floor between Senator Daschle and Senator Lott. Other than those two talking to each other, the entire Senate was dead quiet. Except for Senator Thurmond. He wanted to know what they were talking about, so he kept saying to me rather loudly, "What are they saying?! What are they saying?!" I was trying to whisper in his ear in response, but he kept yelling, "You got to speak up! I can't hear you!" I had to really project for him to hear me, which meant I had to be loud while Daschle and Lott were trying to talk. I kept waiting for the Presiding Officer to tell the Senator from South Carolina and his staffer to leave the Floor.

If you were sitting next to Senator Thurmond down on the Floor, he would frequently pop you with his elbow whenever he asked you a question. I can't tell you how many of those elbow jabs I got. It was funny. You're down there trying to pay attention to the debate, and he's kind of hitting you with his elbow, asking you questions: "What did they say? Who's the girl? Where's my candy?" And every question it's elbow, elbow, elbow right to the ribs.

The Senator was always handing out candy to the female Senators, to the pages, and to the ladies who worked up at the front desk. There was one particular lady who worked up there, I recall; the Senator really liked her. He was always asking pages to take candy up to her. He'd wait to see her get it. She would acknowledge it and wave. Sometimes he would wink at her. He was so funny. He's almost 100-years old and he's flirting during debates.

MICHAEL MISHOE

I was standing on the Senate Floor with the Senator one time. He was preparing to offer an amendment that I had responsibility for. Senator Humphrey came walking by in front of his desk. Senator Thurmond got up; they exchanged pleasantries, and he introduced me to Senator Humphrey.

Then Senator Thurmond jokingly said, "Hubert, you know, I'm up for reelection next year. I'd like you to come down and campaign for me." Senator Humphrey said, "Ah Strom, you know if I go down there I'd do you more harm than I would good." They both laughed. As I understood it, on a personal level, they were actually good friends.

GEORGE LAUFFER

I was sitting with the Senator during a Floor debate one time. He saw the Senator from Oregon walking by and asked me, "George, what's the population of Oregon?" I said, "Senator, I don't know but I can find out." He said, "Do it right now. Get one of the pages to find out what the population of Oregon is." And the next time he went up to talk to the Senator from Oregon, he just happened to mention the population of the man's state. He liked doing things like that. He was always interested in knowing trivia like that so he could drop it into conversation.

JAMES D. GALYEAN

is a former Legislative Assistant to Senator Thurmond. He worked for the Senator from 2001 until the day he left office in January of 2003.

I can never forget the first time I was down on the Senate Floor with Senator Thurmond by myself. I had only been down there a few times before that with our Legislative Director. But the first time by myself I was quite nervous. It was supposed to have been a very simple bill they would be working on that night. It wasn't supposed to be anything complicated.

All of a sudden the bill blows up and people start adding amendments and everything. I'm at a total loss. Things in the Senate can move pretty quickly. You really have to pay attention. Now, generally speaking, when you're trying to get rid of an amendment you don't like, you move to table it. I walked into the Cloak Room to find out from someone exactly what was going on. While I was in there, a Senator on the floor had moved to table the amendment. So when I came back, they had just called a vote. I mistakenly thought it was a straight up or down vote on the amendment.

Well, the Senator started asking me about some of the details on the bill. Then he said, "What's your recommendation?" I said, "Senator I think you ought to vote yes." He looked at me kind of funny and said, "Are you sure about that?" I told him I was. Then Senator Thad Cochran from Mississippi walked by. Senator Thurmond said, "Thad, how are you voting?" Senator Cochran said, "Well Strom, we're all voting no." The Senator turned and looked at me and said, "This fellow here is telling me I got to vote yes!" Senator Cochran looked at me like, what are you thinking? So Senator Thurmond ended up voting no against the motion to table the amendment and yes on the bill. I was terribly chagrined to know the first advice I'd given the Senator was incorrect. To his credit, he had sensed something wasn't quite right, and he called me on it.

You know, I'd heard all the stories about him being too old to know what was going on. Not true. Believe me, he could have done that kind of stuff in his sleep.

DAVID T. BEST

Senator Thurmond was always asking me questions when I sat with him down on the Senate Floor. I think sometimes he was just trying to test me, make sure I was paying attention as well as he was. Other times I think he was just making small talk. And of course, every time he asked you a question he gave you that elbow jab of his. Bang, in the ribs! "Who's the Presiding Officer? Who's that up in the gallery?" Whatever it was, a jab every time.

So one time we were sitting down there and he jabbed me with his elbow and said, "Who do you think is the best-looking female Senator?" Then he started to answer his own question, "I think the Republican female Senators are better looking than the Democrats." I said, "I'd probably agree with you Senator." He asked again, "So who do you think is the best looking?" I wasn't in the mindset of eyeing up the Senators, but I said, "I guess Kay Bailey Hutchison."

All of a sudden Senator Thurmond said, "Kay! Kay! Come 'ere!" This was during a vote on the Floor so she was most likely standing nearby. She walked over and he pointed to me and said, "He thinks you're the best looking Senator!" Of course, I was totally embarrassed. But then he added, "And I happen to agree with him." That was typical of the kind of things he did. Without even knowing it was coming, he could really embarrass you.

ERNIE COGGINS

Let me tell you about the first time I was with the Senator on the Floor of the Senate. We were talking about a bill before the Senate. He was always very interested in discussing both sides of the issue. The Senator looked at me and said, "How would you vote?" I explained to him, given the issues at hand, that it was in the best interests of South Carolina that he vote a certain way. He looked at me again. I never will forget this as long as I live. He stared right at me and said, "I asked you how you would vote!"

I realized that he was asking me if I were him and I were casting the vote, how would I vote. I broke out in a cold sweat. It was an emotional moment. I really gave it some thought. I told him I would vote this way, which was the same as my earlier counsel. He said. "Good. Then I'll vote that way."

He stood up and said, "Mr. President!" Of course he was immediately recognized. He voted right then. The Senator never questioned my counsel again. He would always listen to what I had to say and would sometimes ask for additional information. But he never questioned again what I was telling him.

BILL TUTEN

I was with him on the Floor when Senator Max Cleland was giving his final speech. When it was over, Senator Thurmond wanted to go over and talk to him. But all the Democrats had gone over to shake his hand so he was surrounded by people. We finally started heading over there. Senator Thurmond was nearly 100-years old, but he walked down the aisle, through the Well, and up through the Democratic side to say goodbye to Senator Cleland. You could tell Cleland couldn't believe that Senator Thurmond had made such an effort on his behalf.

I was standing by the door as Senator Carl Levin was walking off the Floor. He couldn't believe it either. He said something like, "That's one of the greatest sights I've ever seen: the most Senior Republican coming over, up the Democratic aisle, just to say goodbye to a colleague."

MICHAEL BOZZELLI

is a former Staff Assistant to Senator Thurmond. He worked from 1999 until the Senator's retirement.

Whenever we went to the Floor, Senator Thurmond always checked his desk to see if there was any candy. He liked to have some on hand to give out to the pages or to his fellow Senators, especially the women. If there wasn't any in the desk, he'd send me to get some. And he would insist on it. "Find me some candy!" Sometimes we'd be down there on the Floor at nine o'clock at night when the dining rooms were closed. So I'd have to run back to my office and look through my stuff. Sometimes all I could dig up was a pack of gum. That would be okay; as long as he had something to give out. He never wanted to be empty handed.

Senator Thurmond was always a gentleman on the Floor of the Senate. He would always make an effort to greet every one of his colleagues. I remember one time Senator Hollings made some criticisms about the Senator that were totally unwarranted. This fact was brought to Senator Thurmond's attention. Nonetheless, I remember that very day Senator Thurmond pulled Senator Hollings over and said, "I don't think two Senators have ever gotten along better than we have."

He was a true gentleman, just totally above the fray. I was really in awe of that. Even when people made remarks about him being too old and not up for the job anymore. That kind of thing was just trivial to him. He always took the high road.

U.S. SENATE PHOTO

To my good friend and
capable ~~Senate~~ office page
Coy Short.
Strom Thurmond, U.S. Senator- S.C.

Many of [the interns] were high school students from small, country towns back home
who'd never been out of South Carolina. It was always a joy to see them experience the
excitement of the nation's Capitol.

– R.J. Duke Short

Classic Thurmond

THE PAGE AND INTERN PROGRAM

*S*trom Thurmond had the largest, most successful page and intern program in the history of the Senate. He recruited over 150 interns a year for well over 30 years. There was quite a competition among college students to see who would get to spend an unforgettable summer in Washington. Our office was inundated with more applications every year.

Instead of hosting just a few pages a year, as is common among a select group of senior Senators, Senator Thurmond welcomed new pages every month, both to work on the Senate Floor and in the office. Many of them were high school students from small, country towns back home who'd never been out of South Carolina. It was always a joy to see them experience the excitement of the nation's Capitol.

In rare circumstances, some of those pages fell short of being a joy. I recall a few over the years who bought fake IDs so they could go to bars. There was one who got caught climbing the fence at the White House. One was caught shoplifting in the Senate cafeteria. And we discovered that one office page, instead of opening the mail, was secretly dumping unopened letters into the trash so he wouldn't have to work. Needless to say, I personally called all their mothers and fathers and sent them home — but not before they'd given me a few more gray hairs.

The vast majority of pages and interns who came to Washington to work for the Senator were well-behaved young men and women who understood and appreciated the honor they'd been given. We were lucky to have them with us, and I know they all have fond memories of their time with Senator Thurmond.

MARY CHAPMAN WEBSTER

worked as an intern in the Senator's office in the summer of 1968.
She and her parents were dear friends of the Senator's for many
years.

I worked as an intern in Senator Thurmond's office in the summer of 1968. Back in those days, the Senator didn't have dozens of interns like he later did. I was one of only three that whole summer. It was a wild time to be in Washington. I arrived literally the day that Bobby Kennedy was shot, and Bobby Kennedy's office had been right next door to Thurmond's. That was the summer of the Abe Fortas hearings for the Supreme Court; Resurrection City was set up on the Mall; Nixon was running for President, and there was big gun control legislation they were trying to get through because of Bobby Kennedy and Martin Luther King. There was a lot going on. It was a busy, busy time.

I was supposed to go with the Senator to the Republican Convention in Miami that year. I'll never forget it. The Senator came up to my desk and said, "Miss Chapman, I've got you a reservation at the Hotel Verse-a-lee!" Having taken a little French, I said, "Would that be Versailles?" He just cracked me up. I ended up not going because of what happened with the Democratic Convention in Chicago. I was too afraid something like that would happen in Miami.

Another day I was at my desk, and he walked up and said, "Get your coat! We're going to lunch!" The other two interns came along. We all piled into his car, and the next thing I know we're going through the gate up to the White House. He took us to General Westmoreland's swearing in as the Army Chief of Staff. After that we went to a private reception. There were only twenty or thirty people there. We all got to meet President Johnson.

Johnson was so funny. Instead of saying hello, nice to meet you, he looked me straight in the eye and said, "How tall are you?" I wanted to answer, "How big are your ears?" But I said, "I'm tall enough to look you in the eye, Mr. President." He smiled and said, "Well said." Lady Byrd was just mortified. She said, "Oh Lyndon, don't talk like that!" Senator Thurmond gave me the experience of a lifetime. I was only 21-years old. I had more fun that summer than I've had in my entire life. I will never forget it.

ELIZA EDGAR

Of all the Senators, Senator Thurmond was known as being particularly supportive of the Page Program. He used to speak at most of the Page School graduations. And he often took the pages down to the Senate Dining Room for ice cream. That was a big day

Strom Thurmond hosts Senate Pages for ice cream in the Senators' Private Dining Room.

they all looked forward to. Senator Thurmond usually hosted about 75 pages a year. With all the interns, the numbers go into the hundreds. He really believed in the program, and thought it was a great way for kids to broaden their horizons and learn more about the world outside South Carolina. Whenever we took the kids in to meet him for the first time, he always had some advice: "I want y'all to take advantage of all you can learn about Washington. Go to the museums; see the monuments. There's a whole lot going on here. And remember, if someone wants to fight you, just walk away."

BECKY FLEMING

Every month the Senator would have a different group of high school pages come up to Washington. They were from all over South Carolina. Some of those children had never even been out of whatever county they were from. It was neat to watch them encounter new things and realize for the first time how big the world really is. I distinctly remember this one little girl from Edgefield; she actually went to Strom Thurmond High. I recall the day when she discovered Godiva Chocolate — only she pronounced it "Gordeeva." She was totally astonished by the Metro. Everything about Washington amazed her. And there were so many children like her. Back in South Carolina, I run into some of those kids occasionally. To a person, they all have such wonderful things to say about the time they were in Washington. It really was an important part of all their lives. And Senator Thurmond made that possible for so many, many people.

TRENT LOTT

is a United States Senator from Mississippi, 1989-present,
and served as Majority Leader from '96-02.

When I got to the Senate, from the very beginning, Senator Thurmond was always so kind and generous. I'd watch him talk to the elevator operators and take the pages down to the Senate Dining Room for ice cream. No other Senators really took the time to talk to and get to know the pages. But it was classic Thurmond.

MARIE BOYLE BUCKLER

served as a Personal Assistant to Senator Thurmond and was a
Director of his Page and Intern Program. She worked for the
Senator from 1988 to 1999.

When I worked in Washington with the pages and interns, I could see that a lot of them were in awe of and often intimidated by the Senator. Before I took them in to meet him for the first time, I made a point to tell them, "He doesn't want you to be intimidated. He doesn't see himself as any more important than your father. He's just a man out there trying to make a living for his family." The Senator was always so great with those kids. Often times he knew their grandfathers or uncles or daddies. Sometimes they would pronounce their own name a certain way and he would correct them. Or he would tell them facts about their own family history that they didn't know. It was so neat to witness that.

CHRISTIE DENISE HUMPHRIES

was a Page for Senator Thurmond in 1995 and 1997, an Intern at
his Columbia, South Carolina office during her college years, and
later worked full-time in the Columbia office. She is the niece of
Duke and Dee Short.

I was a Senate Floor Page in October of '95. I remember that month specifically because it's when they had the Million Man March. I was down on the Floor during a vote when Senator Thurmond motioned for me to come over. So I walked up and said, "Yes, Senator?" He said, "Go get your friends; we're going to get ice cream in the

Senators' Dining Room." Well, this was right in the middle of a vote, which is a very busy time in the Senate. Pages are often needed at that time. But I was not about to tell Senator Thurmond no. I said to myself, "He's the boss. I'm from South Carolina. He's my Senator. I'm going to get ice cream."

Now, you have to be with a Senator to get into the Senators' Dining Room. You can't just walk in and eat. It's a real treat to go there. It was after hours, though, and I think it was closed. But he just barged on in and said, "We're here for ice cream!" So we all sat down and he said, "What flavor do y'all want?" The Senator paid for it and everything. He got ice cream too. I was the only page there from South Carolina. Everybody else was from somewhere different in the country: Wisconsin, Texas, Rhode Island, you name it. He was asking everybody where they were from, how old they were, things they'd learned about Washington. It was a real experience I'll never forget.

JACK DANFORTH

*was a United States Senator from Missouri, 1976 to 1995, and is a
former Ambassador to the United Nations. He is now a partner
with the law firm of Bryan Cave.*

Outside the Senators' Dining Room was a little bowl full of mints. I remember one night Strom went up to the pages down on the Senate Floor, reached into his pocket, pulled out a handful of these mints, and held them out for the pages. You could tell from the looks on the pages' faces that it was not an appetizing presentation, to say the least. But they of course dutifully accepted the gift.

ERNIE COGGINS

Down on the Senate Floor, the Senator would often motion for one of the pages to come over. You could always tell a new page from the ones that had been around a while, because the new ones didn't know what the Senator wanted. They'd come over and say, "Yes sir?" And he would say, "Now, how many of you are there?" And the page would count how many pages were working the Floor that night. Then Senator would count out pieces of candy and give it to the page to hand out. The Senator could get pretty fussy if his desk wasn't stocked with candy. Only after he made sure all the pages had some candy would he turn to us and ask if we wanted any. I still have the last piece of candy he gave me.

Senator Mac Mathias of Maryland, Duke Short, Senator Dennis DeConcini of Arizona, Senator Thurmond, and Senator Joseph Biden of Delaware at a Judiciary Committee Hearing.

With the cameras rolling, he presented the bill to the other Senators that were there, and he used that opportunity to sign them all up for his bill. It was brilliant politics.

– Stephen Breyer –

From Frog Jumping Festivals to the U.S. Senate:

STROM THURMOND THE POLITICIAN

One of Senator Thurmond's most remarkable characteristics was how easily he related to people from all walks of life. Whether chatting with constituents at South Carolina frog-jumping festivals or negotiating legislation with Senate colleagues, he knew how to hit the right notes.

Senator Thurmond's genuine affection for people, his willingness to extend the hand of friendship, and his determination to affect positive changes at the state, national, and international levels all made him an unparalleled politician.

CLARENCE THOMAS

My years at the EEOC were a bit contentious. There were only a few people I could count on in the Senate. One of them was Strom Thurmond. I could always count on him and Duke Short to make sure I was treated fairly. They were always there for me. The Senator never backed down; he was never absent, and he was never too busy to help. God only knows what would have happened to me had people like Strom Thurmond and Orrin Hatch not been there to defend me.

Senator Thurmond was one of those people who really helped me in this town when I needed help the most. It's easy for people to forget the seven years and ten months I spent at EEOC, right in the eye of the storm. I was really getting hammered. But I could always count on him to defend me. I'll never forget it. And he defended me to the bitter end, and aided me whenever he could.

You're going to see it in your life. If you don't tow the line, and you don't do what you're told, people feel that they have license to do bad things to you. In a sense, I am at peace now because I know who my friends are. When the chips are really down in your life, that's when you find out who your friends really are. I'm fortunate that I know who mine are. When the chips were really down, Strom Thurmond stood up and defended me against the mob. The same can be said for Duke Short. And I will go to my grave appreciating that. They never stopped fighting. They were always there. They were always moving, always working. You can't forget that. You don't forget your friends.

STEPHEN BREYER

I will always remember what a good politician Strom Thurmond was. When I worked in the Judiciary Committee with Duke Short and the others, I recall when Senator Kennedy was running for President. Steve Smith, his brother-in-law, wanted to shoot a commercial with different Senators from the Judiciary Committee talking to Kennedy, who was Chairman at the time. But that was a problem. Who would actually like to do that commercial with Senator Kennedy? I called around, and met with reluctance from some on the Democratic side.

One of the first people to agree to do the commercial for Senator Kennedy was Senator Thurmond. When he came in, he used the opportunity to discuss a bill that he was sponsoring to help some policemen and firemen who'd been hurt in the line of duty. With the cameras rolling, he presented the bill to the other Senators that were there, and he used that opportunity to sign them all up for his bill. It was brilliant politics.

He and Senator Kennedy always got along very well personally. Their politics were different, but they got along very well. I always thought in those ancient days when Duke Short and Emory Sneeden and I were there working for the Judiciary Committee, that all the elected officials on the Committee, whether they were Republicans or Democrats, deep down wanted to accomplish something good for the country. Very often their politics were different, but the merits of a particular issue would be the same. They wanted to avoid contention, and they wanted the staff to try to work together.

BAKTYBEK ABDRISAEV

is Former Ambassador of the Kyrgyz Republic, which won its independence from the former Soviet Union in 1991.

Senator Thurmond was a great friend. He was there for us in 1999 when we received threats from the Al Qaeda network. The Islamic Movement of Uzbekistan made the first attempts to attack our territory in the southern part of Kyrgyzstan. Senator Thurmond was among the first in a group of seven or eight Senators who wrote a letter to Defense Secretary Cohen demanding that the Pentagon expedite military assistance to Kyrgyzstan. Thanks to that letter, the Pentagon did everything very quickly to help. Senator Thurmond was one of the driving forces behind that. That was two years before the September 11 attacks. But we were already suffering from attacks by Bin Laden and his terrorist network. Senator Thurmond was right there ready to help us fight.

Senator Thurmond never traveled to the Kyrgyz Republic, but his Chief of Staff Duke Short has been there on several occasions. Duke is a strong supporter of our country and is admired by all. He was responsible for providing Senator Thurmond with first-hand reports of what was happening in Kyrgyzstan, which I am confident resulted in the great support we received from the Senator.

Senator Thurmond pushed for legislation for permanent normal trade relations with Kyrgyzstan. We became a member of the World Trade Organization in 1998. After that, a group of Senators initiated legislation in Congress to grant us most favored nation status. And again, Senator Thurmond was among the first to push for that. We really appreciated the Senator's warm hospitality and his strong personal involvement at improving relations with our country.

Two years ago when our President was here on a state visit, Senator Thurmond organized a special reception at his room in the Capitol. It was an unbelievable gala. There were many of our friends from Capitol Hill who were there. Our President Akaev awarded Senator Thurmond a medal we call "Glory" to commemorate the significant assistance in developing the reforms in our country and strengthening our sovereignty.

He was there at a critical time for our country. We considered Senator Thurmond as one of our greatest friends and supporters in the United States. When he passed away, it was a very sad period of time. For us, it was a great loss.

Senator Hatch, Strom Thurmond, and Duke Short
at a White House ceremony, 2002

ORRIN HATCH

About three months into my first session of Congress after my election to the Senate,
I wrote the following about Senator Thurmond: "A straight-backed elderly gentleman
and one of the truly great men in the Senate. He never fails to stand up and be counted
on some of the most important issues facing this country. He has painted himself into a
right-wing corner however, and is predictable on every issue. That seems to be a draw-
back here. I have great love and respect for him." I wrote that way early in the game
before I really got to know him very well.

HALEY BARBOUR

is the Governor of Mississippi, 2004-present, and a former
Chairman of the Republican National Committee, 1993-97.

Strom was one of a kind, a remarkable politician. His great political attribute was that he was a friend to everybody. His personal style, which spilled over to his staff, was to consider everybody important. I remember I'd be in the Capitol, and I'd run into him. He might have some working-class, rural constituents with him, and he introduced them to me like they were Roger Milliken. He treated every constituent with tremendous respect. That's a great trait for a politician.

PAUL LAXALT

was a United States Senator from Nevada, 1974-1987.

I don't know anybody I've respected more than Strom Thurmond, politically or otherwise. From the first time I came to the Senate as a rookie he befriended me, looked after me, took care of me. He was one of my political godfathers.

I remember full well, particularly, how he wondered about my politics at times. When Ronald Reagan was considering running against the incumbent Republican President Gerald Ford, the announcement came that I was going to Chair Ronald Reagan's campaign. Strom came up to me and said, "Paul, I thought I knew you. But I think you're a political radical!"

SAM NUNN

was a United States Senator from Georgia, 1972-1996. He now
serves as Co-Chairman and Chief Executive Officer of the Nuclear
Threat Initiative which works to increase global security by
reducing the threat of nuclear, chemical, and biological weapons.

Strom was a very effective combination of a man of principle, very firm in his views, and a man who understood the nature and necessity of compromise. He stuck to his principles, but he was also very good about making compromises that were essential to move the process forward.

I remember one time when he was chairing the Committee and I was Ranking

Minority. We were in conference. Somehow or another his staff had not kept our staff informed, so there were a couple of deals made in the conference that I did not agree with and that we had not been consulted on. I got real steamed up, in a nice way because I always loved Strom. We never had a cross word. We had disagreements, but never anything personal.

I said, "Strom, I just have to tell you, you're my friend. But if we get blind-sided again like this I'm not going to sign the conference report, and we'll oppose it on the Floor." I told him that in front of his staff. He looked right at his staff and said, "We did not blind side them with my approval. Staff, I'm going to tell you one time. Whatever we're doing, we want Senator Nunn and his staff to know about." He understood the need to work together. He was very good at that. He could do that even if he had fundamental disagreements with your position. And that's what it takes to be a good Senator and a real leader.

ALAN SIMPSON

was a United States Senator from Wyoming, 1979–1997.

I recall Ted Kennedy got irritated at Strom one day. But an hour later, Ted said, "I can't leave any bitterness with that dear old man." And he went and apologized. Strom said, "Ah, you probably didn't get enough sleep last night. No need to apologize!"

Then there was that now well-known day that Strom supposedly took a punch at Ralph Yarborough of Texas. At the time, my father was a Senator and had his office right across the hall. Yarborough was trying to drag Strom into the Judiciary meeting for a quorum. My dad was there. He was an eye witness. He said old Strom took a kind of wrestler's spin on Yarborough and just spun him to the ground. I don't think he actually hit him. But Strom was powerful. Dad went over. Dad was about 67-years old then. Strom said, "You stand back Millard! I don't want you to get hurt. I'll handle this." My old man said, "Boy, I wouldn't have wanted to tangle with old Strom. He exercised and ran all the time."

There's another story that took place when Joe Biden was Chair of the Judiciary Committee and Strom was the Ranking Member. Biden was running for President of the United States of America. They'd just rained it down on him that he'd plagiarized a speech. They said he'd taken a speech from a British Parliamentarian. The staff apparently had done that, but Joe didn't know it. The staff guy had put together a beautiful speech. And somebody said, "Hey, that was said by so-and-so in England." Well, they just crucified Joe. I mean they just crucified him. The cry went up, resign! Quit the race! Well, he later did quit the race.

Joe called an Executive Meeting of the Judiciary Committee. No staff. Joe got us all together and said, "This has been a terribly embarrassing thing for me. And I've embarrassed you. I've embarrassed my Committee. I care about you all. And I want to tell you that I'm ready to resign as Chairman of the Committee."

When he finished talking there was complete silence in the room. And then Strom reached over and put his hand on Joe's knee and said, "Oh Joe, forget that. We've all done things we've regretted. And here we are. This makes no sense. You're not going to resign."

Then it was fascinating. All of us chipped in. I said, "Hell, I was on probation for shooting mailboxes and even punched a cop when I was in college." Metzenbaum chipped in with something. Ted Kennedy chipped in with something. All of us had something to say. And then we just all started to laugh. We told Joe he was not going to resign. We said, "You're our Chairman." Strom set the tone. It was an amazing moment. Strom said, "You get back out there and grab that gavel! We love ya." That's Strom.

JACK DANFORTH

Strom would always be called on to speak at our Tuesday lunches because he was the President Pro Tem. He would always stand up and harangue us about how we all had to stick together no matter what the proposition was. "We've all got to stick together on this!" He was such an unusual and unique character. It was so enjoyable to see him in action. And of course Duke was always there at his side.

JAMES A. BAKER III

served as Secretary of State under President George Bush (1989-1992), as Secretary of the Treasury under President Reagan (1985-1988), and was Chief of Staff to President Reagan (1981-85).

Senator Thurmond was an extraordinarily good politician of the Old School. He understood how important it was to maintain your base, stay in touch with the folks back home, and to do the best you could to further their interests. There were any number of times that Senator Thurmond would call me when I was Chief of Staff and say, "We have a wonderful person for this or that position." He was not the least bit embarrassed or hesitant to pick up the phone and really lobby for people he wanted appointed to governmental positions; or for that matter, to pick up the phone and talk directly to the President or the Chief of Staff about policy matters that were coming before the Congress. I just remember him as being very prepared and aggressive in the way he lobbied the White House.

I recall one time I was in the transition office, and I got a message that Senator Thurmond wanted to speak to me. I went right to the phone. He said, "I want to recommend for your consideration a very fine young political operative who worked on the campaign and would do a good job for you in the White House. His name is Lee Atwater." I thanked the Senator very much for calling. I had not known Lee well during the campaign. I brought him in and interviewed him, and the rest is history. We put him in the political office as Deputy to Lyn Nofsinger and then Ed Rollins. Lee was the person on whom we relied in the '84 reelect. We ran that campaign out of the Chief of Staff's office in the White House. It was a resounding success. We won 49 states. Lee was the guy we relied on as the liaison between the White House and the campaign.

MATTHEW J. MARTIN

Everyone had great respect and admiration for Senator Thurmond, even the people who disagreed with him most politically. I had some friends in Senator Kennedy's office. I was at an event one night with them. They warned me not to let Senator Kennedy find out that I worked for Senator Thurmond. But somehow he did find out. And the next thing I know, Senator Kennedy walked right over to me and started talking about how much he admired Senator Thurmond. The folks who worked for Kennedy didn't even realize how much he respected Thurmond. It was an eye opener. I thought that was so great of Kennedy to take the time to personally tell me that.

KATHRYN HOOK

worked as Chief Receptionist in Senator Thurmond's Washington office from 1967 to 1997. Senator Thurmond gave her the title "Dean of Women."

I'll never forget that one afternoon when the White House called. President Nixon wanted to talk to the Senator. I put the call through. A few minutes later the Senator buzzed us and told everyone to come to his office. We all went right in. I remember the Senator was standing up there behind his desk. He said, "I just talked to the President. He told me he's resigning the Presidency." Oh God, it was just horrible. You could see the Senator was really shaken up. He really liked President Nixon and his policies. I think we were all shocked to some degree. It wasn't officially announced until the next day.

I remember sitting out on my balcony after work later that day. I lived over in southwest Washington on Tiber Island, overlooking the Potomac River. I saw the Presidential Yacht heading down the river. I got out my binoculars and saw the Nixons, the whole family, going down the river. I guess it was their last hurrah on the yacht.

Senator Thurmond was never one of the very social Senators. He went to the events, but he was never a best friend. In the early years he was friends with Senators Eastland, Irwin, and Dirksen. In the later years, he and Biden were good friends. He got along well with everybody, and people respected him. But I don't think you could characterize him as being particularly sociable with the other Senators. He wasn't a hail-fellow-well-met by any stretch of the imagination. That was just not his bag. He was more worried about his constituents and the state of South Carolina, and that meant more to him than being a popular Senator. He was popular on his home ground, and tremendously so.

DENNIS DECONCINI

On occasion Strom used to reminisce with me about how the Senate used to be in the old days. When I came to the Senate in the late '70s it had changed. By then, you didn't have to have permission from the leader of your party to get up and offer an amendment. You just did it. Somebody didn't like it, hey that's tough. I don't know if Thurmond had a problem adjusting to it. I don't think he did. But he remembered how things used to be. He remembered how important it was to work hard, keep quiet, earn the respect of your fellow members, then participate in the heavy duty law making.

He used to say that when he was young, new Senators just didn't get up and speak whenever they wanted to. And when you did make your first speech as a Senator, the Majority Leader or Minority Leader would come out and sit on the Floor to show his support. And half a dozen other Senators would come out to listen to your speech as well. When I made my first speech on the Floor, there was only one other Senator on the Floor, and nobody cared. I didn't have to get permission from anybody.

We always called Strom the Old Man, but it was with respect, like you'd refer to your father.

BUTLER DERRICK

was a United States Congressman representing South Carolina's
Third District from 1975 to 1995.

When I ran for Congress, Senator Thurmond had, of course, switched to the Republican Party by that time. So he endorsed my Republican opponent, Marshall Parker. I remember my mother commented to me, "I'll never vote for him again. He had no business doing that." I said, "Mama, he is the top Republican in the state. He has no alternative. Strom Thurmond will never do me any harm or say anything unkind about me, and

I know he will be as helpful to me as he can." She said, "I don't care. I'm never going to vote for him."

My father died in 1977, which was a couple of years after I was elected to Congress. Strom came by the house and brought Nancy and the children. He made a contribution to a fund on behalf of my father. When he left my mother said, "You know, Strom isn't a bad sort after all, is he?"

MELINDA KOUTSOUMPAS

I remember back in the mid '80s Senator Howard Metzenbaum, a very liberal Democrat from Ohio, held what we call a mini filibuster against the death penalty. During a regular Thursday morning business meeting of the Judiciary Committee, Senator Thurmond said to him, "I know what you're doing. You're filibustering this bill!" Senator Metzenbaum said he wasn't. They bantered back and forth. Finally Senator Thurmond interrupted him. Metzenbaum said he couldn't do that. Senator Thurmond said, "I'm the Chairman! I can do anything I want, and I want you to get out of here and don't you ever come back!" He gaveled the meeting to a close and left the room.

Well, I stepped out into the hall. Senator Thurmond and Senator Metzenbaum were out there. They had their arms around each other as they were walking down the hall. I will never forget that. They were laughing and smiling. One of Senator Thurmond's interns said to me, "I don't understand. They were really mad at each other." I had to explain to the young man that they still understood the good old days of the Senate, when Senators left their politics in the hearing room. They had their debates and they argued, but it never got personal. Senator Thurmond understood that better than anyone in Washington.

JOHN L. NAPIER

I remember a conversation I had with Senator Thurmond in 1987 or '88. I asked him to name the five best Senators with whom he had served. And as a prerequisite to the answer, I asked him to exclude any that were still serving in the government at the time. That, of course, excluded Senator Baker, Senator Dole, Senator Helms, Senator Tower, Senator Biden, Senator Byrd of West Virginia and Senator Hollings, plus a number of others. We did not define the term "best," but we both know what it meant. Generally, it would have meant those with whom he got along with best and admired most.

He was quick and emphatic in his response. He said "Harry Byrd, Senior" of Virginia. He then quickly added parenthetically, "And Harry Byrd Jr. is a good man, too." His next response, and he was specific that this was in no particular order, was Senator John

L. McClellan of Arkansas, whom he described as "the most fearless man I have ever known." Senator McClellan was the Chair of the Senate Permanent Investigations Subcommittee which investigated the mafia in the 1950s. He later chaired the Appropriations Committee. The other three were Frank Lausche of Ohio, "a man of courage and principle;" Millard Simpson of Wyoming and father to Alan Simpson; and Paul Laxalt of Nevada. Except for Senator Laxalt, they were all senior to him and members of the Senate when he first arrived in Washington.

He then discussed several other Senators most favorably: Jim Allen of Alabama, Richard Russell of Georgia, Willis Robertson of Virginia and father of Pat Robertson, Price Daniel of Texas, Herman Talmadge of Georgia, Cliff Hansen of Wyoming, Russell Long of Louisiana, Allen Ellender of Louisiana, Jim Eastland of Mississippi, and Spessard Holland of Florida. There were several others that he obviously had reservations about. He called them "slick." The word "slick" was about the worst I ever heard him use to characterize another Senator.

As an aside he also told me that night that Senator Robert Kerr of Oklahoma, formerly President of Kerr-McGee Oil Company and a close associate of Senator Lyndon Johnson, was the most skilled and "incisive" he had ever observed in debate. He admired his skills greatly, but he said Senator Kerr's shortcoming was taking his debate skills to the point of intimidating people.

Senator Thurmond was very decisive and knew what he wanted. He was very tough politically, but he always opened the door for a political opponent to one day become a political ally. I thought that was one of the great things that will be a part of his legacy. He never closed the door on potential political friendships. He always had the door open to come in and be an ally on a particular subject.

RON KAUFMAN

is a former Deputy Assistant and Political Advisor to President George H.W. Bush.

One of my responsibilities when we first took over the White House was the regional jobs: jobs in the states and regional centers like U.S. Marshals, U.S. Attorneys, Judges, those kind of jobs. I remember it like it was yesterday: Lee Atwater called up one day and said, "Ron, why don't you come up for lunch tomorrow in Senator Thurmond's office? The Southern states are getting together, and it would be a good idea for you to get to know these guys." I said, "Thanks Lee, that's a great idea."

I was a little bit late for the lunch. Something was going on at the White House, and so I was a little bit late getting over there. But I figured no one's going to care because I'll just be sitting in the back of the room listening anyway. So I walked in to the office and there was every Republican Senator from the South, one per state, whoever the ranking Republican Senator was. And Newt Gingrich was there as well, representing Georgia. That's when I realized I wasn't late for lunch — I was lunch!

I died a thousand deaths because one thing the former President always teaches is never to make anyone wait, particularly a member of Congress. I sat down, and Senator Thurmond in his fine, gentlemanly way said, "Nice of you to join us. Ron, we're here to talk about our regional jobs. What is the White House position on our regional jobs?"

Traditionally, the patronage had gone to the Senators. The ranking Senator from each state got to name his or her buddy as U.S. Marshal or as U.S. Attorney. They traditionally had a big say as to who got the regional jobs. I felt it was important that we laid down a marker; to say, listen, I'm going to work with you but the bottom line is, this is important to the President and his people.

I looked around. Of course, Atwater was hiding under the table! I said, "Senator, first of all, I can't apologize enough for being late. There's no excuse. But second of all Senator, to be honest with you, they're not your regional jobs. They're President Bush's regional jobs. Those are jobs for the foot soldiers of the election. Once we get through the first term, you can have them all in the second term. But in the first term, they're really President Bush's regional jobs to give out."

Boy you could have heard a pin drop. I mean, I thought they were going to kill me. Literally, Lee was hiding. Senator Thurmond, God bless him, saved my life. He said, "Well Ron, I really appreciate your honesty. You're the first guy who didn't try to BS us. But these jobs are really important to us." I said, "Well Senator, having said what I said, there are plenty of people out there who are Bush people and Thurmond people. Let's just find people who can do these jobs who are Bush and Thurmond people together." So instead of having big political wars, we had big victories. I'll always remember that.

Senator Thurmond was always so gracious to me. That very day we actually cemented what I considered to be a very good relationship over the years. He always used to introduce me to people, "Here's the man who runs the White House!" He was a terrific man.

DAVID T. BEST

When Senator Hillary Clinton was sworn in, Senator Thurmond gave her a big bear hug to welcome her to the Senate. One of the New York publications ran a cartoon of that. Senator Clinton got a copy and wanted Senator Thurmond to sign that for her. She brought it over to me when we were down on the Floor one time. She said, "Can you please get this signed?" She asked me for days after that, "Do you have it? Did he sign it yet?" Finally I had a chance to get it taken care of. We were taking the subway back from the Capitol to the office, and I happened to see Senator Clinton. I gave her a sign that I had what she'd been waiting for. She literally broke out in a run to where the train stopped so she could get it. She was very happy to get that signed cartoon of Senator Thurmond giving her a big hug.

Senator Thurmond had a friendship with most every Senator on the Hill, even Senator Clinton. You would think, after voting to impeach her husband, that there might be some strain there. But he put aside political and personal differences. Senator Thurmond showed me by his example that the Senate was a very friendship-based institution. While there are political and policy differences, the Senators still are very civil to each other and always looking for friendships and bonding to whatever degree they can.

But I know Senator Thurmond had some frustrations with that. He was disappointed when the camaraderie was lacking and the animosity carried over. He commented at times that Senators didn't socialize as much as they used to, that everybody just ran off in their own direction. He used to comment about how things used to be in the old days, when the Senators weren't in Washington year-round. The Senators tended to do things together more. They stayed at the same hotels and boarding houses, ate dinners in the same dining rooms. I know he missed that. It really changed the tone of the Senate.

WILLIAM W. WILKINS

Senator Thurmond had been unable to obtain a favorable response from the Administration concerning a textile issue. So he invited the Assistant Secretary of the agency involved over to his office. After pleasantries were exchanged, the Senator, the Assistant Secretary, and I walked into a small anteroom where Senator Thurmond had a bunch of peaches stored.

Senator Thurmond started to peel some peaches and offered them to the Assistant Secretary. Then he started to explain what he thought needed to be done to help the textile industry in South Carolina. Every time the Assistant Secretary tried to explain why he couldn't help, Senator Thurmond handed him another peach slice. With his mouth full of peaches, and juice running down his chin, the Assistant Secretary couldn't get a word in edgewise. Senator Thurmond just kept talking and handing him peaches until the Assistant Secretary finally nodded in agreement and said, "Anything you want, Senator."

JOHN WALSH

He was quite a character. He was really something. You can say what you want about Strom, but in my mind he always had his priorities in order. If you talked to him about children or about victims, he was right there. He'd listen to you. He'd say, "We'll do something about this." And he always would. He always followed through. Strom kept his word every time.

Over the years I've heard more bull from more people in Washington. I mean, I met with Bill Clinton nine zillion times in eight years. And he was always gracious and we took pictures. But he never came through. With Strom, you only had to sit down with him once. He would say, "We'll get this done." Then Duke would work out all the legislative details, and it would get done. I always called Duke the "Secret Senator."

PHIL JONES

Strom Thurmond absolutely had politics figured out. But I don't think what he did would work today. The electorate is too disinterested, turned off, jaded, cynical. I don't think Strom would make it today. It's all about TV. It's just too blow-dried for him to make it now. While he figured it out back then, he had the luxury of maturing with his constituency. He was a legend. The next generation would vote for him because Mom and Dad had talked about him. You can count on ol' Strom. And he managed to keep himself clean. There were some things, though. His personal life was sort of messy at times, thanks to Nancy. She probably did more to try and do him in than anybody I know of. In the later years, she was constantly trying to undermine him for her own benefit.

HENRY MCMASTER

The Senator never held a grudge. It was just business, the people's business. You could disagree on the issues, but there was no point in getting personal and impugning the integrity of people just because they disagree with you. It always surprised me how friendly he was with other Senators whom he never agreed with on hardly anything. But they'd treat each other very cordially, and you could tell they were good friends. A perfect example is Thurmond and Joe Biden. They got to be friends real quick. But I never heard the Senator impugn anyone's integrity on these matters. He presumed that they were saying what they said because they believed it. That's all that counted for him. He was never ugly with anybody, never called anybody a name.

STEPHEN L. JONES

I remember one time we were dealing with an Army Corps of Engineers project. If I recall, it had something to do with Charleston Harbor. We had a meeting with a Colonel about the project. The Senator said to him, "Colonel, we've made our case and I think it's a good one. Now if you could get back to us by this afternoon, I'd appreciate it. If not, we can call the White House and see if we can't arrange a meeting down there for tomorrow."

Of course, the Colonel kind of gulped. The Senator walked him out. I'll never forget this. The Senator shook the Colonel's hand then dusted the Colonel's Eagle on his shoulder, just dusted it a little with his fingertip. He looked at the Colonel and said, "Colonel, a star really would look nice up there, wouldn't it?" The Colonel said, "Senator, it sure would." About two or three hours later that Colonel was on the phone. He said, "Steve, that Senator really knows how to twist somebody's arm, doesn't he?" I said, "He sure does!"

ARNOLD PUNARO

Let me tell you about my first real experience with Senator Thurmond. I was working on the military bases in Georgia. There was an issue where the Army wanted to beef up training at both Fort Gordon in Augusta and Fort Benning in Columbus. Being good Georgians, we were very excited about that. We did a lot of work to support the Army's position on that. Unbeknownst to me, one of the ways that the Army was going to beef up training at Fort Gordon was to reduce training at Fort Jackson in South Carolina.

One day I got a call from Mr. Ed Kenney, who was the Senior Staffer on the Senate Armed Services Committee. He summoned me to come visit with him on the Armed Services Committee to talk a little bit about how things worked. Senator Stennis was the Chairman at the time. I think Senator Tower might have been the ranking member. But of course, Senator Thurmond was a pretty prominent presence under any circumstance.

So I went over to see Ed Kenney. The next thing I know, I'm being marched right into Senator Thurmond's office for a lecture on how things work. Senator Thurmond was always the gentleman and always very polite. We talked a little bit about my relatives in Augusta, Georgia. After the pleasantries were over he said, "Now son, I need to explain to you how things work. Georgia and South Carolina, we're in this together. We rise and fall together. I'm all for improving things at Fort Gordon, but you've got to be all for improving things at Fort Jackson." The way he explained it, it made a lot of sense to me!

From then on out Ed Kenney and I, and then Senator Thurmond and Senator Nunn, had a very good strategic working alliance for our two states. We actually ended up working on a tremendous number of activities jointly to benefit both states. We kind of nipped that competition in the bud, and it proved to be a wise way to go. I learned a very important lesson at a very early age as a young staffer. That was my first interaction with Senator Thurmond.

He was a very savvy guy. He also believed in the Committee process and in the art of compromise. Senator Thurmond was not one of these Senators who said my way or the highway. He was always looking for a bipartisan approach and always looking for a way to make things work. You don't see enough of that anymore.

COY JOHNSTON II

was a long-time friend of Senator Thurmond's and the father of
Holly Johnston Richardson, Senator Thurmond's Personal
Secretary. Holly worked for the Senator from 1979 until her death
in September of 2002.

We had an event down here dealing with the Southeastern Wildlife Expo, where we were featuring the ACE Basin — Ashepoo, Combahee, and Edisto Rivers Basin Initiative, protecting land and all. The Senator had done quite a bit to make this program effective. We really wanted the Secretary of the Interior to come to our event. Secretary Lujan was the Secretary at that time.

I'm told that Senator Thurmond called him up and said, "Mr. Secretary, I want you to go with me to South Carolina tonight. I sent you a note about it." Lujan replied and said, "No Senator, I can't go because I've got something else I've got to do." The Senator said, "Well, you put that off. You need to go with me." Lujan said, "No, I can't." The Senator said, "Well, I'll tell you what. James is coming by to pick you up. He'll be there in about twenty minutes. Be ready." Secretary Lujan told us that story that night at the event. He said, "I didn't plan on coming here. Senator Thurmond said the excuse I gave wasn't acceptable. So he sent James by to pick me up, and here we are."

I remember another time we were dealing with a mitigation situation having to do with Lake Russell. The Corps of Engineers had taken land when they dammed Lake Russell. Half of the land that went under water was in Georgia, and half was in South Carolina. We had a mitigation of some 20 or 30,000 acres of South Carolina. By that I mean that the Corps of Engineers had to buy equal land of the same nature in South Carolina and Georgia for mitigating the land that they had flooded. But they were dragging their feet, and there was a lot of red tape. So of course we brought it to Senator Thurmond's attention.

We ended up with a meeting in the Senator's office with the Colonel who was head of the Corps of Engineers. He made a few remarks to the Senator about procedures. Senator Thurmond cut right to the chase. He told that Colonel, "Well, we're going to cut out this bureaucracy. We're going to cut out all that red tape. We just have to get it done. Now if I have to call you in again, you will come in with the Secretary of the Army. And by the way, do you have aspirations of continuing your career in the military?" Then right towards the end of the conversation the Senator said, "You know Colonel, I'm a man of action. And I'm sure you're a man of action too." With that he motioned over to Holly and said, "How about getting him some peanuts out of the refrigerator." Holly got them and gave them to the Senator. The Senator handed them to the Colonel and said, "Colonel, you better take these. You're going to need some energy to get this done."

MARK GOODIN

A country music singer I knew told me that the hardest thing for him to do once he obtained stardom was to continue to write great music because he lived in a mansion. All the songs that had made him famous were about his lean years when he was poor and struggling. When he didn't have to struggle any more, he forgot what it was like. And he couldn't tap into that reservoir that had made him famous, and he couldn't write those songs anymore.

I believe something like that inevitably happens to elected officials as they become career politicians. They lose the ability to know what the common man is thinking because they don't move in the common man's circles anymore. They travel by limousine. They have drivers. They have people who do everything for them and tell them how great they are. There are a million of those guys.

But Strom Thurmond was different. He always had a cadre of people around him who would walk over, shut the door, and tell him exactly what they thought. But even more important than that, Strom Thurmond kept moving in the common man's circles. He was never too big for the frog jump. He was never too big for the watermelon festival. He was never too big for the peach festival or the Rotary Club luncheon. All the things you would think a man of his stature would pass on, he would go to.

He didn't just do it for constituent service. I think he did it for the same reason that Abraham Lincoln would open the doors of the White House once a week and let anybody come in. Lincoln called them his public opinion baths. It was his way of finding out what people thought beyond his little group of advisors that ultimately told him what he wanted to hear. Thurmond took these public opinion baths as well by constantly going back to South Carolina every week. He'd go the Rotary Clubs, the Ruritan Clubs, the peach festivals, the watermelon festivals, and the frog jumping festivals. He put himself right out there in those crowds every chance he got.

I never knew anyone in Washington who could use a phone as well as Strom Thurmond. He was the master. Once he actually got on the line with someone, the magic would start.

– R.J. Duke Short –

Strom Thurmond Calling

Kathryn Hook, Senator Thurmond's chief receptionist for thirty years, was once asked if the Senator used a computer. She laughed and said, "Hell, he doesn't even know how to use a phone!" That statement had some truth to it. The Senator certainly never used a computer, to my knowledge, and he never quite had phones figured out either.

Senator Thurmond believed that no matter what might be wrong with a phone — no dial tone or a bad connection, for example — all you had to do was press on the numbered buttons a little harder. So he pushed and jammed those buttons down as hard as he could all day long. As you can guess, we had to have the phones in his office repaired quite often. It's a good thing that Holly was there to place the calls for him, because I'm not so sure he could have figured it out.

His technical limitations aside, I never knew anyone in Washington who could use a phone as well as Strom Thurmond. He was the master. Once he actually got on the line with someone, the magic would start. Whether it was the caring condolence calls he made every evening to families in South Carolina, the insistent calls he sometimes made to the White House over a federal judge, or the calls he made to request assistance from the secretary of an agency, the phone was one of Senator Thurmond's greatest political tools.

ELIZABETH MCFARLAND

was the Office Manager at Senator Thurmond's Aiken, South Carolina office from 1986 until his retirement.

The Senator frequently called me at home. I never got over that. Here I was at home, washing dishes or something, and this powerful U.S. Senator calls me on the telephone to check and see if there's anything he needs to know. That was another great thing about him. He always kept in touch with his staff to stay informed.

JASON ROSSBACH

Everyone talks about how the Senator would call the old widows and widowers. I've heard people say that's just old politics. But hey, it's great old politics! People need that in their lives. He knew it was important to reach out to people who were going through a hard time. It seems like an easy gesture, but no one did it every day like he did. It means a great deal more to people than you might realize.

DONALD BALDWIN

I got a hold of one of the books that had been written about Senator Thurmond and left it at his office for him to autograph for me. Well, at the time my daughter Elizabeth was Secretary of the Majority. When he sat down to sign the book to me, he decided to call up my daughter just to let her know he was doing that. She was out cleaning her pool at the time. She said she dropped everything and ran into the house when she heard Senator Thurmond was on the phone. She said, "I thought it was some business about a vote or something. No, he just wanted to say, 'Elizabeth, I'm writing a little note to your father here. I want you to know he's a fine man and you can be proud of him.'" That was the way he did things. He could have just signed the book. But he took that extra step to call my daughter and share those kind thoughts with her. He was a wonderful man.

DEE SHORT

Many times the Senator would telephone Duke at home just to see what was going on or if there was anything he needed to know about. He would call on weekends to let us know that Lawrence Welk was on television. He was so funny. Sometimes when he'd call, I would pick up the phone and say hello. I'd hear this voice say, "Lawrence Welk is on television!" And then click, he would just hang up. I would have to call him back to find out what channel it was on.

On my birthday, our wedding anniversary, and many other occasions, he would call with greetings. The most memorable and closest to my heart were the times he called when I was sick or not feeling well. Sometimes when I was sick with a migraine, he would call me, and in his softest and gentlest voice would ask if there was anything he could do for me. How we miss this giant of a man, Strom Thurmond, and his very personal and caring touch.

DENNIS W. SHEDD

When Joseph Kennedy, who was Robert Kennedy's son, was elected to Congress, he called our office and asked if he could come over to personally thank Senator Thurmond. He told us that the night he got elected, the only person of any national prominence from either party to call him was Strom Thurmond. Senator Thurmond told him, "I worked with your daddy and your two uncles in the Senate, and I look forward to serving with you." Joseph Kennedy wanted to come over and thank the Senator face to face.

I knew a person whose son was killed in a go-cart accident. The boy was only ten- or eleven-years old. The daddy was just inconsolable. It was a terrible situation. The daddy was put on Senator Thurmond's obituary list to call. The Senator got on the phone with this father to make a regular, two-minute condolence call. The next thing I knew, he'd been on the phone for 45 minutes.

I later talked to the family, and they told me that the only person who could in any way console this father during that awful time was Strom Thurmond. That phone call from the Senator was the only time during that terrible period that he had any peace of mind. That's another side of Senator Thurmond most people don't know about. Even over the phone, he could talk to anybody and make them feel better no matter how tragic the situation.

DON FOWLER

This is very personal. When my father died, when my mother died, and when my wife died — one happened in the early '80s, one in the early '90s, one in the mid '90s — in each one of those three cases, Senator Thurmond was the first one to call me to express his sympathy.

WILLIAM SCHACHTE,
Rear Admiral, U.S. Navy (ret.)

I was in the Senator's office one day and the staff was going crazy. Somebody had died, and they were trying to find the man's brother so the Senator could call him and convey his condolences. They finally found the guy in a barbershop in Pelzer, South Carolina. They got the guy out of the barber chair to hear from the Senator. And of course, that was the talk of Pelzer for at least a year.

GLADYS V. MOSS
*is the wife of the late Thomas Moss, Senator Thurmond's Field
Representative for South Carolina from 1971 to 2001. Mr. Moss
was Director of the South Carolina Voter Education Project and a
veteran of the Korean War. He was the first African-American
staff member to be hired by any U.S. Southern Senator.*

The Senator often said that he had the best staff God could provide. And he would pick up the telephone on several occasions to call and tell me how much he appreciated Thomas. Sometimes he would call me on Mother's Day or my birthday or just to check on the children and see how they were doing. We all worked together as a family. That's what I enjoyed about the Senator most; he was a family person. He genuinely cared about the families of his staff members. It wasn't just about working all the time. It was also about giving time to your families. That was something I really appreciated about him.

JOHN F. HAY,
*Lieutenant Colonel, U.S. Army (ret.) is also the former Vice
President of Government and International Affairs for
Westinghouse Electric Corporation. He is currently a partner
with P3 Consulting, LLC*

I was down in South Carolina to close on a house, sort of a get-away, weekend place. While I was down there, my brother called on the cell phone. I pulled off to the side of the road. I knew why he was calling. I sort of expected the call. He called to tell me our mom had died. She was in her late 80s. I hadn't hung up from my brother ten or fifteen minutes at the most when the phone rang again. I picked it up. "Colonel?! This is Senator Thurmond. I just wanted to track you down. I just got the terrible news about your momma. I am so sorry. I feel so badly about this."

He asked about the service and asked about my mom. "She had a bunch of kids, didn't she?" I said, "Yes sir, there are eight of us, Senator." He said, "You know, she had to be a good woman to have so many children. I just wish I'd had the opportunity to meet her. Now when you get home, you do me a favor and tell all your brothers and sisters that Strom Thurmond sends his deepest sympathies. And if there's anything I can do for you or any of them, you know my door's always open. You just call me."

Even now as I tell that story it's hard not to choke up. How many Senators would do something like that? That's the kind of man he was, and I'll never forget that. He was a great person and a great leader. My family and I held him in high esteem and always will.

BILL TRAXLER
*is a Judge on the United States Court of Appeals
for the Fourth Circuit.*

The thoughtfulness he exhibited to me and my family was unbelievable. The night I was elected a State Circuit Judge in 1985, he called to congratulate me. It must have been about 9:30 at night. He said, "You know, I was a State Circuit Judge. That was one of the best jobs I ever had."

MELINDA KOUTSOUMPAS
We had a woman who worked on the staff, Patty Vaughan. She was our antitrust counsel. Of course, she handled all the telecommunications issues. One afternoon Holly called her and said the Senator wanted to talk to her right away about a telephone issue. Well, Patty gathered up all of her telecommunications issues. About an hour later she came to the office just dying of laughter.

She said when she got to the Senator's office that he had his telephone bills spread all out on his desk. Patty pulled up her chair thinking that she was going to have to explain the legalities of some telephone issue before the Senate. But you know what? The Senator wanted her to explain every charge that was on his phone bill! He kept pointing at charges. "What's this one for? What's that one for?" She was there trying to explain those bills to him for a solid hour.

WALKER CLARKSON

worked for Senator Thurmond from January of 2001
until his retirement.

The Senator read the obituary notices from the South Carolina newspapers every day and marked off the ones he wanted us to call or ones he wanted to call personally. I remember there was a young man from South Carolina who was attending the Air Force Academy in Colorado. He had a tragic accident trying to help somebody else on the side of the road. He stopped to help someone else that had broken down, and he got killed. He was 18- or 19-years old, and the Senator took the time to call the parents. He did that for so many people. It meant so much to them. It's a very Old School thing, but it meant so much to people. And you know, the Senator lost his daughter, so he understood what parents were going through.

BO BLUDWORTH,

Lieutenant Colonel, U.S. Army (ret.), was with the Army
Legislative Liaison Office assigned to the United States Senate,
1984-89.

When my mother passed away the funeral home director came up and said, "Bo, can I talk to you for a second? I got a phone call back here for you. Guy on the phone says he's Strom Thurmond." The Senator had called me at the funeral home to express his sympathies about my mom. This funeral home director was about to faint. That's just the type of person the Senator was. He had a big heart.

GEORGE LAUFFER

The Senator really took an interest in the staff's children. He had met my son Michael probably after he came back from his junior year at the London School of Economics. That had to be about 1992. I brought my son in to talk to the Senator. They had a nice conversation. My son had focused on South America and had studied some of the regimes down there. He and the Senator enjoyed a very interesting discussion.

In 1995 my son got married out in Santa Cruz, California, which is probably one of the most liberal cities in the country. The ceremony had concluded, and we were having dinner at a private house on the bluffs above Santa Cruz. My son's mother-in-law calls out,

"There's a guy named Thurmond on the phone." Of course, I immediately knew that was the Senator. He wanted to speak to Michael.

He spoke to Michael for about ten minutes, congratulating him on his wedding, wishing him the best, and just chit chatting. This was on a Saturday, you know, when he wasn't even at work. He called from his house, and took the time to congratulate my son and my daughter-in-law. The folks out there in Santa Cruz just went crazy. They couldn't believe that Senator Thurmond would call just to congratulate him. Now, for folks in South Carolina that's probably routine. But folks in California, they're not used to that. It was a very touching moment for the whole family.

PHIL JONES

Do you know about Bride's Day? Every Wednesday or Thursday at a prescribed time when they were in session, come hell or high water, Senator Thurmond would return to his office to get on the phone. Holly and some other staff people would have called all the state offices and gotten the information on who was going to be married over the weekend. The state offices would have gone through all the newspapers to read all the marriage announcements.

So the Senator would sit down at his desk, and Holly would make the first call. She'd say, "Mary? It's Senator Thurmond calling, just a moment." And he'd pick it up: "Mary! This is Strom Thurmond. I just wanted to call you and congratulate you on getting married this weekend. You know, Nancy and I had planned on coming, but we had something come up. We're so disappointed we weren't able to make it. But I just wanted you to know we were thinking about you, and I'm going to be sending you a little something. I wish you the best. God Bless You." He'd go through eight or ten calls every week. They called it Bride's Day. Only Senator Thurmond!

PATRICIA RONES SYKES

I don't even remember when it was, but I know it was a Saturday night. I was at home with my husband Paul. The phone rang. Paul answered it. He's a Lieutenant Colonel in the Air Force. He came into the room saluting. I said, "Paul what's wrong?" He said, "It's the Senator." On a Saturday night, Senator Thurmond just called to say hello. And he did that from time to time. Now and then he would pick up the phone on a weekend and just call, "How's it going? What's new? Can I do anything for you?" And he would quickly say "bye-bye" and hang up. That was his famous ending to a phone call, just a very quick "bye-bye" and then he was gone.

Senator Thurmond and Duke Short at a hearing
on a nominee to the Supreme Court.

*I saw a leader who was doing his best to understand something that genuinely
confounded him. So he did what a good leader does: he asked questions of someone
who could answer them.*

– R.J. Duke Short –

"Speak Into The Machine!"

UNFORGETTABLE MOMENTS FROM COMMITTEE HEARINGS

*I*t was a well-worn phrase of Strom Thurmond's I will never forget. During Committee Hearings, when he had trouble discerning what a witness was saying, he would lean forward across the dais and yell, "Speak into the machine! Speak into your machine!" which was his unique way of saying, I can't hear you; use your microphone. To this day, whenever former Thurmond staffers get together, one of them will invariably say in their best Thurmond impersonation, "Speak into the machine!" It is always greeted with much heart-felt laughter.

Perhaps one of the most memorable of Senator Thurmond's moments from our countless committee hearings over the years took place in 1986 during the testimony regarding the nomination of William Rehnquist to be Chief Justice of the Supreme Court. I usually scheduled the lesser-known witnesses for late in the afternoon. At this hearing there was a young man testifying who represented the Gay and Lesbian Task Force. He commented at one point that 25 million Americans were homosexual. Senator Thurmond leaned over to Senator Biden — they were the only two on the Committee who were present that late in the day — and asked something like, "Joe, what did he say? Where does he get that number?" Senator Biden put his hand over the microphones and whispered back, "Strom, some people think that ten percent of humanity is gay." Senator Thurmond asked, "Is that right?" Biden said, "Most scientists think it's more like one or two percent."

You could really see that Senator Thurmond was perplexed over the issue, and understandably so. The man was born in 1902. To expect a man nearly 90-years old to be totally up on the current notions of homosexuality was most unreasonable. Culturally, Strom Thurmond could not wrap his mind around this issue at all. At that point I was afraid Senator Thurmond might say something he would regret. So I leaned forward from my seat behind him and whispered to Senator Biden, "Senator, don't let him embarrass himself." But Senator Thurmond couldn't contain himself. He wasn't being mean. He honestly didn't understand.

Senator Thurmond asked Senator Biden, "Joe, do you think he's one of them? Ask him." Senator Biden said, "Strom, you ask him." Senator Thurmond interrupted the witness. "Excuse me, young man. How did you arrive at the figure of 25 million?" The witness explained how they arrived at that number. Then Senator Thurmond said, "Well, what are you doing to help your people become more normal?" The witness answered, "Senator, we think we are normal with one small exception." At that, Senator Thurmond hit the table in front of him and exclaimed, "That's a mighty big exception!"

The conversation went on for a bit longer as Senator Thurmond made a sincere effort to understand. But it was simply too foreign to him. His questions generated a lot of laughter among the audience present. Many people saw it as a sign of just how out of touch Strom Thurmond was with what was going on in the world. I guess that could have been one way to look at it. But then and now, I saw a leader who was doing his best to understand something that genuinely confounded him. So he did what a good leader does: he asked questions of someone who could answer them.

DENNIS DECONCINI

In Committee Strom was either 110 percent or not paying attention at all. He usually showed up, but lots of times he wasn't there. I don't mean there was anything mentally wrong with him. He was usually just working on something else, talking to his staff, or conferring with Duke.

When it came to Committee meetings when he knew he was going to participate, you couldn't beat him back. I don't care who you were. If Strom Thurmond wanted to get a point across, he didn't take no for an answer. You just couldn't stop him from pursuing wherever he wanted to go. That was a great technique of his. If you had Strom Thurmond on your side, you had a great voice of determination on whatever the legislation happened to be. Of course, if he wasn't on your side, you had a great voice of determination against your position.

Sometimes he would get right up in your face about why he needed to have this or that amendment passed. He didn't always win, but boy you knew where he stood. Even before he went in, he knew what he wanted to accomplish from a meeting. He was totally focused on that goal completely, almost to the degree that if the subject changed, sometimes he didn't.

MARY CHAPMAN WEBSTER

I remember when Abe Fortas was being interrogated by the Judiciary Committee. I was sitting there listening to Senator Thurmond question Fortas about his stand on pornography. It got kind of embarrassing. At one point somebody tapped me on the shoulder. It was one of the other interns. He said, "Come on; we've got to run an errand." Senator Thurmond's driver took us to a magazine store. I said, "What are we doing?" The intern said, "The Senator wants us to buy him some pornographic magazines." I said, "What?!" He said, "No really, he wants us to buy him some pornographic magazines." I said, "You're going to go buy them! I'm not!" I stayed in the car while this guy went in the store and bought four or five porn magazines. Then we headed back to the hearing. I went back and took my seat back in the audience.

This guy went around the back and came up behind Senator Thurmond, tapped him on the shoulder, and put these porn magazines in a plain brown paper bag in front of him. While another Senator was questioning Abe Fortas, Senator Thurmond proceeded to look at these porn magazines. And he turned them so the public could see what he was looking at! I thought to myself, oh my God, where is he going with this?

DAVID LYLES

is the former Democratic Staff Director on the Senate Armed Services Committee. He is now the Chief of Staff to Senator Carl Levin.

When Senator Thurmond stepped down as Chairman of the Armed Services Committee, Senator Warner became Chairman. I remember we were having a full Committee hearing in Hart 216, the large Central Hearing Room. It's the biggest hearing room in the Senate. Of course, after Senator Thurmond stepped down, he sat one place to the left of Senator Warner. At this hearing, Senator Levin was sitting on the other side of Warner. At one point, Senator Warner got up to take a phone call or something.

Senator Thurmond kind of turned his head, put his hand over his mouth so the audience wouldn't hear him, and said in a stage whisper to Senator Levin, "You know, I miss working with you." Senator Levin looked up, smiled, and reached out to Senator Thurmond. They kind of took each other's hand and shook for a moment. It was really nice. That was an indication of the respectful relationship they had. I don't want to minimize the fact that they disagreed on a lot of things. But both of them understood the importance of the Committee working as a group for the national security of the country.

NADINE COHODAS

is a former reporter for Congressional Quarterly *and the author of* Strom Thurmond and the Politics of Southern Change.

Senator Thurmond served right with Senator Helms. People often wanted to lump them together. Their voting records may be quite similar, but I found them to be very different kinds of politicians. Watching Thurmond run the Judiciary Committee, when he had the gavel in his hand, he really was listening to the debate that went on around him. I remember an argument between Howard Metzenbaum and Orrin Hatch. Senator Thurmond finally banged the gavel and said, "Listen! You two aren't that far apart. I want you to work together and figure something out!"

Senator Thurmond was always interested in moving things along. I don't think he would consciously tell you that he wanted to shed the reputation of being an obstructionist, because I don't think he thought about life that way. Also, when I talked to people that worked on the Democratic staff, they felt that he was indeed a man of his word. That said, it was also made clear to me that he understood the power of the Chairmanship. A piece of legislation was only going to come up on his time table. And Judicial nominations were going to come up on his time table. He was going to set the agenda. There's nothing wrong with that. He fully understood the prerogatives of being a Chairman.

ALAN SIMPSON

I'll never forget the time we had the feminists before us at the Judiciary Committee. Strom looked down at Molly Yard, the leader of NOW. She could swear a stevedore off a ship. She was a tough old bird. Strom looked down and said, "It's good to see you ladies this afternoon." They looked back up at him like, you ornery old kook. And they kind of huffed. I said, "Just a second there ladies." I explained to them that he was just being cordial. I said, "It's called chivalry. You wouldn't understand that while you're burning bras." Oh gosh! They went crazy at that one. I said, "For a courteous gentleman of the South to be assailed by a couple of people who don't appreciate a gentleman or chivalry, even if it's old fashioned, that's very offensive to me." They just absolutely snorted. They didn't like that at all.

I saw Molly Yard two or three days after that. I really let her have it. She swore at me. Boy, she could match every word of mine. She just stalked away. But she had a cameraman there. So I walked over in front of her camera. I said, "Now isn't that childish of her? Here we are trying to have a good hearing, and she's just like a little child running around." She heard me and ran around and said, "I didn't say that!" Oh, then the fight was on.

Senator Thurmond at a Senate
Judiciary Committee Hearing.

U.S. SENATE PHOTO

Senator Strom Thurmond is honored on the 75th
anniversary of his being commissioned an Officer in
the United States Army, summer 1999.

U.S. ARMY PHOTO, JEROME ROBERTS

*I always enjoyed seeing the Senator with soldiers. They flocked to get around him and meet
him. They all knew the devotion and appreciation he had shown the military over the years.
They had tremendous respect for him.*

– Eliza Edgar –

One of Their Own

STROM THURMOND AND THE U.S. ARMED FORCES

*T*he American military has never had, in all its magnificent history, a greater advocate in the U.S. Senate than J. Strom Thurmond. I believe that very strongly. A soldier never had a better friend in Washington. Senator Thurmond was one of a now rare breed: a soldier and a statesman. I agree with others who have pointed out the dwindling numbers of veterans who take seats in the U.S. Congress. Too few of our politicians know what it is really like to fight for your country. Strom Thurmond knew what it was like. He truly understood the sacrifice soldiers make when they leave home and enter the battlefields of war.

Strom Thurmond was commissioned as a Second Lieutenant in the Army Reserve (1924) after he graduated from Clemson University in 1923. He volunteered for service in the wake of Pearl Harbor and left his post as a Circuit Court Judge to serve on active duty with the U.S. Army. He was 39-years old. Lieutenant Colonel Thurmond was a Civil Affairs Officer attached to the 82nd Airborne during Operation Overlord, or D-Day. On the night of June 6, 1944, he was a passenger on Glider 34 as it crossed the English Channel into France. He would later say that he "had so many narrow escapes that it is a miracle to me that any of us who landed by glider are still alive." His experiences during World War II had a deeply profound impact on his life. Though he seldom reminisced about the war, he never hesitated to say that each day he lived since June 6, 1944 was a gift from God.

He was not able to be there in Normandy for the 50th anniversary of D-Day. His son Paul was graduating from high school, and he didn't want to miss that. You could tell it bothered him to miss the anniversary, but as many people told him, he needn't worry. He had been there when it really counted.

Senator Thurmond received eighteen separate decorations, medals, and awards for his service, including the Legion of Merit with Oak Leaf Cluster, the Bronze Star for Valor, and a Purple Heart. He retired from the U.S. Army Reserves as a Major General.

He fought hard in the Congress to generously fund the military. "If ever you get weak," he used to say, "there will be someone waiting to take advantage of you. The military must remain strong." He was also the leading advocate for the Guard and Reserve. Some of his colleagues believed that they weren't very important. But Senator Thurmond lived long enough to understand that it was only a matter of time before they would be called to serve on the battlefield. And as we have seen with the Guard and Reserve's brilliant displays of courage and devotion to duty in the War Against Terror, he was absolutely right.

In the wake of September 11, 2001, Senator Thurmond made a special trip to the Pentagon that most people never heard about. He went over there to show his support. The Senator asked us not to contact any press. It was not a publicity event. It was very low-key. He simply wanted to go and let the people there know he was thinking about them.

The devastation was even more horrific in person. The Senator said that as he stood there at the scene, not really believing what he was seeing, people began coming up to him. They thanked him for being there, and he told everyone how sorry he was and that he was going to do whatever he could to help. In only a few minutes he was completely surrounded by people, all of whom either worked at the Pentagon, were part of the rescue effort, or knew a loved one who had been killed. One young woman whose husband was still missing wrapped herself in the Senator's arms and cried. She looked up at him with tears pouring down her face and told him how much it meant to her to see him standing there that day.

Strom Thurmond was a symbol of strength, courage, compassion, and resolute determination for many in this country and around the world.

ELAINE ROGERS

has been President of the United Service Organizations (USO),
Metropolitan Washington, for nearly thirty years.

The military truly loved him. He was one of them. And that's exactly how they treated him. They all knew his story: leaving his judgeship to volunteer in World War II, flying in a glider on D-Day, crashing behind enemy lines. I think, truth be told, the military was always his true love. He had such patriotism and pride in the service he gave his country and tremendous admiration for the men and women who did the same.

Senator Thurmond leads an Army unit in PT run.

DEE SHORT

Strom Thurmond was the most patriotic man I have ever known. We were with him at a number of military parades. He would stand there so tall and proud with that straight back, his hand over his heart. The look on his face was always so powerful — pure patriotism. He believed in this country, and he believed in the men and women who fight for it. They held a special place in his heart.

TOGO D. WEST, JR.

was Secretary of Veterans Affairs, 1998-2000, and Secretary of the Army, 1993-97. He also served as General Counsel of the Department of Defense under President Jimmy Carter.

One of the most memorable things about Senator Thurmond was his courtliness and thoughtfulness. It was not surprising to see him in the corridor or at a reception and have him respond with such sincere interest and kindness. He was that kind of a person. It wasn't like the rather brusque, good-to-see-you-but-I-got-to-rush-off greetings you got from others in Washington. Senator Thurmond always took time to stop and talk. He was a good man.

Senator Thurmond was one of only a handful of members in Congress who'd actually had active duty. That number continues to dwindle. His impact in Washington was larger than most because he knew what it was like to be in combat; he knew what it was like to put his life on the line in one of the riskiest endeavors of all. He knew what it was like to have been in the greatest war ever fought on the planet, and he knew what it was like to be a veteran. He knew what it was like to be in the Reserves, which is not that easily understood. Most people think of the Reserves and the Guard as, you're there but you'll probably never be used. Well, Senator Thurmond knew they'd be used. And he knew it was important to keep an eye on how they were maintained, sustained, and supported.

On a number of occasions I had the honor of speaking with Senator Thurmond, typically to an audience of men and women in uniform. Even though he was quite senior, he had a way of speaking that really endeared himself to any audience, especially those in uniform. One never forgets that the Senator crash-landed behind enemy lines in a glider during D-Day. His service and dedication to the military mattered a great deal to all of us.

The Senator truly cared for those in uniform and as well for veterans. He had first-hand knowledge of both experiences. That allowed him to be a much more perceptive advocate in the Senate as well as a better communicator when he was with them. Men and women in uniform and veterans alike recognized Senator Thurmond as one of their own.

DON FOWLER

My first acquaintance with Senator Thurmond came through my involvement with the United States Army Reserves. The Senator served in World War II, as we all know. He maintained a keen interest in the military after that, and was active in the Army Reserves. Immediately after the Second World War, the Reserves were much less formally organized and there was uncertainty about how the command structure was developed. During his last year as Governor of South Carolina, Senator Thurmond personally organized a unit that is currently known as the 360th Civil Affairs Brigade. I think it was originally called the 360th Military Government Group. When I moved back to South Carolina from graduate school and active duty in the mid 60s, I joined the 412th Civil Affairs Group which was a subordinate unit to the 360th Civil Affairs Brigade. It was through that connection that I got to know Senator Thurmond personally.

In the mid 1980s we had a big celebration to commemorate the founding of the 360th. I was Commander at the time. We renamed it the Thurmond Brigade because he had literally founded it. A lot of people, many of them with political backgrounds, have served in that unit. Senator Thurmond came and spoke at the celebration. Of course it was a great speech.

ELIZA EDGAR

In 1997 when Senator Thurmond broke the record for the longest-serving Senator, it seemed every branch of the military did something to honor him. The Army had the Olde Guard; we went to a Twilight Tattoo on the Elipse; they did something out at Fort Meyer's; we went to something at the Marine Barracks; they did a sunset parade at 8th and I in his honor. Everyone in the military wanted to take a moment and recognize the Senator for his service.

I always enjoyed seeing the Senator with soldiers. They flocked to get around him and meet him. They all knew the devotion and appreciation he had shown the military over the years. They had tremendous respect for him.

JOHN F. HAY

The Senator had a special relationship with the U.S. Military. He was a soldier until the day he died. And he was an airborne soldier. There's a place down at Fort Bragg in North Carolina out at Pope Airfield that I used to know as the Green Ramp. It's where we used to suit up and hang around for hours waiting to deploy, waiting in the rain, snow, mud, whatever, laying out there with our parachutes strapped up so tight you could hardly bend over. Well, they dedicated that whole Green Ramp as the Senator Strom Thurmond Deployment Center.

There are buildings there now. The troops can go inside and get their briefings and suit. They've got air conditioning if it's hot and heat if it's cold. They may have to wait two or three hours to take off to Iraq or some place else in the world, prepared to give their lives. The first time I saw it I thought, there's ol' Senator Thurmond again, getting the troops out of the snow and the rain. Right up until the day he left office, I know he was thinking, what else can I do to help these soldiers, sailors, marines, and airmen?

ARNOLD PUNARO

Senator Thurmond had a number of far-sighted initiatives that we are only today beginning to realize the true impact and importance of, particularly as they relate to the Guard and Reserve. I'd say he has an unparalleled record of service in uniform as well as a record of service on the Armed Services Committee in promoting and maintaining a strong national defense.

He never wavered in his support of the military. He was always concerned about the men and women in the Armed Forces and their families. He had been in combat himself, so he understood. He knew what it was like to be overseas, far from home, not sure if you're going to see your family again. He had a way about him. He was a down-to-earth person. He was able to talk to the troops. He had an empathy for the troops and their families that they understood, and it came through in everything he did.

RICHARD QUICK,

Brigadier General, U.S. Army (ret.), is President of the United States/Asia Foundation.

In the early '90s Senator Thurmond came to speak to a group I belong to, the Senior Army Reserve Commanders' Association. Before it took place, I happened to be in the office talking with Duke and he said, "Hey, why don't you come in and talk to the Senator and tell him about the event?" So I went in and told the Senator how we were going to be giving him an award at his talk. He was looking forward to it.

Then I said, "By the way, Senator, you've had such a distinguished career: you were Governor, you were a Judge, a United States Senator, and of course you retired as a Major General in the U.S. Army. Of all those achievements, what would you prefer to be referred to as?" He thought about it for a minute and said, "I really liked Major General Strom Thurmond."

NEWT GINGRICH

served as a U.S. Congressman from Georgia, 1979-99 and as Speaker of the United States House of Representatives, 1995-99.

It really tells you something about how the Senate viewed Strom Thurmond by making him the leader of the Armed Services Committee. It is a very powerful position. And I think it's quite clear that we are a stronger country because of Strom Thurmond's leadership on that Committee. He served his country very well.

MATTHEW J. MARTIN

The men and women in the Armed Forces know the history of the man. He was almost in his 40s when he volunteered to go into combat in World War II. You can't help but admire the man for that. The soldiers knew he was a man of honor, and that he was a man of his word. They didn't always agree with what he did, but they saw him as a soldier's soldier. He was much more than just one of their supporters in the Senate. He'd been on the field of battle. He'd risked his life for his country. From the young, new private to the 80-year old veteran, they all had great respect for him.

GEORGE LAUFFER

Senator Thurmond was perhaps the last in a long line of Southern senators who had a strong military background. I'm thinking of Senators Russell, Goldwater, Baker, Stennis, men like that. That background made him a dedicated leader in support of the military. There was one thing that was true about Senator Thurmond: he never failed to look out for the individual soldier. He was always there to support pay raises, construction of new barracks, improving hospital care, you name it. He didn't put forth big bills like the Goldwater Nichols Act of '86. It's the little things that he added to these big bills that made them better. He was the champion of those kind of amendments that improved or fixed things.

I think the admiration from the military begins with what he did during World War II, as well as the fact that he was a retired Major General. He knew what the soldiers were all about. The series of awards and honors that he received during his tenure show the great respect the military had for him. Right before he retired, they even named a C17 Aircraft after him.

DENNIS W. SHEDD

Jan Scruggs, who was the leading force behind the building of the Vietnam Veterans Memorial, told me this story. He said that he was going around talking to people about the Vietnam Veterans Memorial, and that a lot of people were supportive of it. But he said once he told Senator Thurmond what he wanted to do, that Senator Thurmond stood up right then and there and took money out of his wallet and gave it to Jan Scruggs. Jan Scruggs told me that Senator Thurmond was the very first public official to give him money for the Vietnam Veterans Memorial.

JOHN DALTON
was Secretary of the U.S. Navy, 1993-98.

When I came in as Secretary, the Democrats had control of the Senate. Senator Thurmond was the Ranking Member of the Senate Armed Services, and Sam Nunn was the Chairman. I got to know Senator Thurmond in that capacity. He was always very gracious and supportive of the Navy, and very interested in doing things for South Carolina. Before I came in as Secretary, much of the Charleston Navy Base and the shipyard had been shut down. So he was very concerned about building things back up in Charleston. Every time we were together he talked about things that could be done for Charleston. He was a very strong and able advocate for his state.

ALFONSE D'AMATO
was a United States Senator from New York, 1981-1999.

Strom held very strong opinions, but you could still get him to listen. He was always willing to listen to the other side. One thing he would never compromise on however was supporting the defense of this country. He was totally unyielding on that issue. You could always reason and work with him. The only time you couldn't was when it came to national defense. He wouldn't budge. Nobody could budge him. He was totally uncompromising on that one issue.

DAVID G. MCLEOD,
Colonel, Medical Corps, U.S. Army, Walter Reed Army Medical Center. Colonel McLeod is Chief of Urology and Director of the Center for Prostate Disease Research at the Uniformed Services University.

Senator Thurmond was a stalwart when it came to defending people in the military from erosive cuts to save money. He was always rightly proud of his military service. People in uniform saw in Senator Thurmond a politician, a decorated veteran, and a true hero. He was a man who absolutely understood and appreciated our mission, our sense of duty, and our sacrifices. The military respected him enormously for everything he did for us and for the country. He always stood by us, without fail. We could always count on him.

BO BLUDWORTH

He loved the military and we loved him. Not only did he support the military; he understood the military. He volunteered and served in open combat. He loved the constitution of the United States and the freedom that we enjoy here. But he understood the price that is paid for that. That was his motivation to support the military. His great value is that he was a soldier. He could articulate that from the heart.

ELIZABETH DOLE

is a United States Senator from North Carolina, 2003-present. Her career includes her service as the Secretary of Transportation under President Reagan, as Secretary of Labor under President George H.W. Bush, and as President of the American Red Cross.

Bob and I were in Europe for the 50th anniversary of D-Day. We talked a lot then about Strom and his historic place in the Normandy invasion. That was another very important part of his public service, the work he did for the military both as a soldier and as an elected official. He was absolutely dedicated to the men and women in uniform, and I believe they knew he was there for them. Strom's tremendous military record was one to be greatly admired. He was a genuine American hero and a great servant of the public.

FRANK NORTON,

Colonel, U.S. Army (ret.), was former Army Legislative Liaison to the United States Senate and later served on the staff of the Senate Armed Services Committee. Colonel Norton was a great friend and supporter of Senator Thurmond's.

Senator Thurmond was the epitome of an American soldier. When he graduated from Clemson he was still too young to be commissioned, so he actually had to wait a while before he could serve. But when he did, he served for decades, retiring as a Major General in the Army Reserves. When I joined the Army Liaison office in 1980, he and I really hit it off. I started traveling with him quite a bit to visit various bases. We literally traveled all over the world. I've got to say, he took wonderful care of me. He treated me like I was on his own staff, and to a great extent his staff was like family to him.

I'll never forget one Christmas and New Year's we went to Wildflecken, Germany. It was a very cold and wet winter there. The battalion commander was Lieutenant Colonel Ron Odom, a West Point graduate, a super guy. I happened to mention to him that the Senator liked to run and do PT. Odom asked the Senator if he wanted to join the troops. So at the age of 82, in borrowed boots, Senator Thurmond was out running with the soldiers at 6:30 in the morning. He ran at the front of that formation for over two miles.

It's very hard to describe the affection that American soldiers and their families had for him. It didn't matter: black, white, Hispanic, they all really admired the Senator. I saw it everywhere we went anywhere in the world. They knew he truly cared about them, and not only them, but their spouses and their children.

I remember after Desert Storm, Senator Thurmond led one of the largest delegations of Senators overseas to Saudi Arabia and Iraq. He must have been in his early 90s at the time. It was a tough, grueling trip. But Senator Thurmond never faltered, never missed a step or anything else. He was very well received, and I know Americans were proud to have him representing us at that time.

P.X. KELLEY,

General, U.S. Marine Corps (ret.), was Commandant of the Marine Corps, 1983-87, and a member of the Joint Chiefs of Staff. He is currently the Chairman of the American Battle Monuments Commission.

The Senator and I go back in a personal way to when I was appointed by President Carter as the First Commander of the Rapid Deployment Joint Task Force, which ultimately became the Central Command which now is so engaged in Iraq and other places. During that period we also had a fairly significant problem with budgetary matters in the Congress. When you take a fairly sizeable cut out of the budget, the Marine Corps, being the smallest of all the services, suffers across the board. I had many meetings with Senator Thurmond over these issues. He was a stalwart supporter and always fought to make sure the Marine Corps had its fair share of the appropriations and authorizations that were necessary to keep us a viable military force.

I remember Senator Thurmond frequently asked me, "General Kelley, have you ever served at Paris Island, South Carolina?" To which I always replied, and this happened probably a dozen times, "No, Senator, and it's amazing that I should ever be the Commandant of the Marine Corps not having done so." To which he would say, "Thank you; I'm glad you recognize that."

The period 1983 to '87 during which I was Commandant is recognized by a lot of people as a period of resurrection of the Marine Corps in terms of our budgetary matters and the modernization that we went through. We literally replaced almost every single item of hardware within our Marine divisions and the bulk of the aircraft within our Marine aircraft wings. That was in no small measure due to Senator Strom Thurmond and his understanding not only of the Marine Corps as an institution but also of where the Marine Corps fit in to an overall national strategy. So we can thank him today for where the Marine Corps really is, in terms of its structure and in terms of its equipment.

When it came to creating a World War II memorial, Strom Thurmond was a very strong force in the Congress supporting the process since the beginning. As we all know, he was one of the great heroes during World War II. The things he has done for the country, for South Carolina, and for the military put him at the top of a very special list of patriots in our nation's history.

ANTHONY PRINCIPI

was Secretary of the United States Department of Veterans'
Affairs during the George W. Bush administration. He formerly
served as the Staff Director on the Senate Armed Services
Committee.

Strom Thurmond truly was one of the great advocates for the men and women serving today and those who served in the past. This dedication stemmed from his great military career in World War II, his bravery and patriotism, which I think transcended everything he did in the Senate. His true love was the men and women who served in the wars of our nation. He was a real champion. He always attended Armed Services Committee meetings. Every time we had a hearing, he was there. And with any legislation on the Floor of the Senate that impacted veterans, his voice would be heard. When you think of the great advocates for veterans' causes in the United States, Strom Thurmond has to be right at the top of that list.

There was no base we could travel to together where he wasn't revered. They just loved him. He was the Dean of Veterans' Causes. It transcended political parties. I mean, on both sides of the aisle he was held in that kind of esteem. Indeed there was no one quite like him in my view in the annals of the United States Senate. He was very proud of his service. It was like he never left uniform. I remember visiting him up at Walter Reed. I think if he could be at any place in his last days, he'd have wanted to be at a military hospital. That's the kind of man he was until the very end. You don't find people like that anymore.

CLAUDE M. "MICK" KICKLIGHTER,
Lieutenant General, U.S. Army (ret.), is Director, Department of State and Defense, Iraq/Afghanistan Joint Transition Planning Group.

Senator Thurmond was a great soldier, veteran, patriot, and statesman. He was a charter member of the greatest generation: the World War II generation. I first met him in person in 1985 when he visited the 25th Infantry Division in Hawaii, which I was commanding. He came and spent an afternoon with the Division. The troops enjoyed being with him because they knew that he genuinely cared about the welfare of the soldiers and their families. The troops also were aware that he was a World War II military hero having landed in a glider on D-Day, 6 June 1944, in Normandy, France. His visit to the Division was a very memorable experience for all. We knew he had been a Major General in the U.S. Army Reserve, so when he departed I offered him my fatigue cap which had two stars. He proudly accepted that cap and was wearing it when he departed the Division by helicopter. That was a great visit which will never be forgotten by any of us who were honored to have spent time with him on that occasion.

Some years later when I was selected to head up the 50th Anniversary of World War II Commemoration Committee, the support of the Senate and the House was essential. So we turned to Senator Thurmond. He was one of the strongest supporters we had, and his support was instrumental in getting Congress behind the 50th Anniversary of World War II. He continually supported and personally participated in many events of the Anniversary. He very much wanted to attend the 50th Anniversary of the Normandy landing, but was unable to do so because one of his children was graduating from high school. Naturally, knowing the Senator, his family came first. So he missed an event that would have been very special for him, but we knew he was there in spirit. He helped a great deal in the planning of the 50th Anniversary of World War II and set the example in Congress to ensure that the support we needed throughout the almost four years of the commemoration was available.

Senator Thurmond always made time for his friends. At the very end of his time in the Senate I was nominated by President Bush to be the Assistant Secretary at the Department of Veterans' Affairs. Senator Thurmond found the time to come to my hearing and testify on my behalf and recommended that I be confirmed quickly by the Senate. He stated at the hearing that I was needed to assist in taking care of the veterans and their families.

Until the very end of his service to our nation as a U.S. Senator, he never ceased caring for our soldiers and their families, as well as for veterans and their families. I will always miss him and respect his service to our nation.

General Shelton, Colonel Will Webb and Strom
Thurmond at a ceremony honoring the Chairman of
the Joint Chiefs of Staff, Ft Meyer, Virginia. Sept. 1999.

THE STROM THURMOND INSTITUTE, CLEMSON UNIVERSITY

Lt. Col. J. Strom Thurmond, Governor's Island, New York - September, 1943.

He said, "I expected to die that day. I should have died that day. Every day since then has been a gift to me, and I've tried to use what I've been given to help somebody else."

– David T. Best –

Every Day a Gift

MEMORIES OF WORLD WAR II

*I*n 1941, Strom Thurmond was enjoying his third year as a circuit court judge in South Carolina. He was 39-years old and had already spent four years as a State Senator representing Edgefield County. Probably no one expected that he would request a leave of absence from his judgeship to volunteer for service in the U.S. Army. No one would have thought less of him for sitting out the war on the bench in South Carolina. But Strom Thurmond was deeply patriotic. He knew that his country needed him. Having received his commission as a Second Lieutenant in 1924, he sent a telegram to President Roosevelt and volunteered for active duty on the day of the attack on Pearl Harbor. Although he wasn't activated until April 17, 1942, he was now ready for action.

Between 1942 and 1946 Strom Thurmond saw action in the European and Pacific Theatres. Perhaps his most memorable moment was crash-landing in a glider with the 82nd Airborne Division well behind enemy lines in Normandy on D-Day. With all the human carnage he saw during his time in Europe during World War II, he never forgot that he was fortunate to be alive. For the rest of his long life, Strom Thurmond saw every day as a gift, and he tried each day to do all he could to help others.

RON KAUFMAN

You had to be in awe of a guy like the Senator who could wax eloquently about history because not only was he there; he was part of it.

DEE SHORT

I never grew tired of listening to the Senator tell stories. On more than one occasion he told me what it was like in Europe during the Second World War. I remember him saying that during the Battle of the Bulge was the coldest he had ever been in his life. He talked about Buchenwald and how the bodies were stacked like cordwood. He said that he had never witnessed such inhumane acts. He talked about the effect that had on him and how he appreciated life and freedom so much more than he ever had before. He never failed to mention how important it is that we keep the strongest military defense possible. We will forever be indebted to Senator Thurmond and the thousands of other heroes for their sacrifices so that we are able to enjoy the freedom we have today.

NEWT GINGRICH

We were having a joint meeting for the purpose of hearing the head of state of a foreign country. Senator Thurmond came over as President Pro Tem to join me at this meeting. As we were standing there waiting, we started talking about his experiences in 1944 going into Europe. The patriotism, the sincerity, and the courage were overwhelming.

FRANK NORTON

I remember being with Senator Thurmond in Normandy in 1983. We literally walked in the area where his glider had gone down. He told me the most amazing story.

The Senator said, "When we took off, it was very, very quiet. All you could hear was the airplane in front of us. The tow rope the plane used to pull us was not that long, so the glider just kind of bounced back and forth. It was a very rough ride. When they unhooked us, all of a sudden it got stable, and the plane pulled away. Then the pilot said, 'I see a field! I see a field!'" So they started their descent to land in the field. But as they got closer, Senator Thurmond said, "The pilot started yelling, 'It's not a field! It's an orchard! It's trees!'"

So they literally flew the glider into an apple orchard. The Senator said the wings came off right away. Those trees just stripped the canvas right off the glider, and the whole thing broke apart. They had been carrying a Jeep, which went right out the back end as they hit the trees. Senator Thurmond said they walked out a big hole in the side of the glider and started to fight.

He showed me where he spent the first night, in a little depression next to a hedgerow. The hedgerows in Normandy along in there vary in height, but can be as tall as eight feet. And they are the thickest things you've ever seen in your life. If you're a soldier with a pack on your back, you've really got to fight your way to get through them. The Senator told me that their first night, they heard a German unit marching within a couple of hundred yards on the other side of a hedgerow. I remember him saying, "Thank God for the hedgerow!" They knew that no matter how close that unit was, they probably weren't going to try to get through that hedgerow. You know, he had volunteered to go on that mission. He did not have to go, as I understand it, but he felt he should go in on D-Day with his unit. Strom Thurmond was a true American hero.

CRAIG METZ

I was so impressed, as we all are, with his experiences in World War II. I asked him once, "Senator, that was so amazing what you did. What was going through your mind then?" I thought he'd tell me something like: well we were scared or we were doing it all for freedom or we looked death in the face or something about the military tactics. He said, "Well, we were there to liberate the French. I have never in my life seen women who wanted to be liberated so much!"

MARK IVANY

is a former Special Assistant to Senator Thurmond. He worked
for the Senator from 2000 until January of 2003.

This story I'm going to tell you took place about a month or two before the Senator retired. I was 25-years old at the time. As far as I know, I was his youngest Special Assistant. On top of that I was handling all of his scheduling responsibilities. The term "scheduler" does not do any justice to what Holly Richardson did for Senator Thurmond. She served the Senator so well for so many years, and though I could never do it like she did, I certainly tried my best. I was extremely stressed and very exhausted in trying to do both jobs, especially at a very important time in his career with things winding down. I was also, at the same time, trying to find another job for when the Senator finally retired.

The week or two before this story took place, Senator Thurmond was awarded the

THE STROM THURMOND INSTITUTE, CLEMSON UNIVERSITY

Lt. Col. Strom Thurmond
drives a captured German vehicle.

2002 All-American of the Year Award by the 82nd Airborne Division Association. They gave him a very nice plaque. I put it up there on one of his cabinets for him, but it wasn't in a place where he could see it from his desk. I don't think he ever really noticed it was there. That plaque sat there for a couple of weeks. He never mentioned it.

One day he and I were in the office watching TV. The plaque caught his eye, and he asked me about it. I reminded him about the award. And then, well, he just got this look in his eye. I could tell that he was thinking back about his days during World War II. He and I had never spoken about that. So I asked him, "Senator, what was that like, being in that glider?"

We were both quiet, just thinking about it. And then he told me the story. He said he was in the glider and it was being pulled by another plane in the middle of the night, not having really any idea where they were going to land for sure, or what would happen.

The attrition rate for those gliders was like 40 or 50 percent, and he volunteered for that mission! I asked him, "Senator, were you nervous?" I had never seen him nervous. I'd never seen him not fully in control of every situation. I figured if he ever was nervous, that surely must have been the time. I expected him to say yes.

He looked over at me with all seriousness and said, "No, I wasn't." I kind of chuckled, because I thought he must have been kidding. But he never laughed. I said, "Senator, are you serious?" He said, "There are some things in life that you can't change, and so there's no sense in worrying about it."

That statement really hit home with me, given what I was dealing with in my own life at the time. I was so stressed and had so much anxiety about my future. From that point on, when things got tough for me, I always thought back to that moment with the Senator — with him looking over with complete calmness and complete assurance, and saying, "There are some things in life that you can't change, and so there's no sense in worrying about it." I've thought about that moment many, many times since then.

DAVID T. BEST

Senator Thurmond was not the kind of man to sit around and tell war stories. The only time I heard him share his memories of the war was during the 50th anniversary. We were down in the Senate Dining Room. It was late at night. We were waiting for votes on the Floor. Frequently on those occasions, we'd go down for soup; that's almost always what we had. He'd invite his driver to come over and join us, or whoever was still working back in the office. We'd all meet over there at night and have soup.

I remember one night we were there, and he started to tell the story about going in on the glider. He told us about the crash landing, about the person next to him being killed by a German artillery shell. It was kind of a gruesome story. That person right next to him was basically cut in half. The crash landing was way behind enemy lines. He told us how they managed to regroup, capture a German motorcycle, and get back to their operations base at St. Mere Eglise.

At the end of the story he said, "I expected to die that day. I should have died that day. Every day since then has been a gift to me, and I've tried to use what I've been given to help somebody else." That was the point that he was making to us. He was there working late, trying to help people back in South Carolina and around the country. That really stayed with me. But as I said, he did not reminisce frequently. He didn't just share his memories to tell stories. It was always to illustrate some principle that he stood by.

SUSAN PELTER

A lot of people think that older people live in the past — but not Senator Thurmond. I really think one of the secrets of his longevity and success is that he rarely looked back. He always looked forward. I don't think that he was a particularly introspective person. He always made an effort to move ahead, to press on. Whatever happens today is today and we're moving ahead!

But occasionally I'd be there at night when there were late votes on the Floor or something. I'd be in the office working with him, and he would sometimes get reflective. He would let some little tidbit drop about an historical event. He'd say something like, "Well, I told Eisenhower not to do that."

I had been there for quite some time before I knew he had actually helped to liberate a concentration camp. He told a reporter about the experience. It clearly had etched itself in his memory in a horrible way. He talked about seeing "bodies stacked up like cordwood all over the place." The very words he used expressed the horror of it. But his face had this almost detached expression. I don't think that he could bring himself to relive it. It was like he was recounting a memory of a memory rather than going back there.

ROBIN ROBERTS

is a former Thurmond staffer and the Co-founder and President of
National Media Inc., a leading political/advocacy media planning
and placement firm. He knew and worked with Senator
Thurmond for many years.

I was with him one day when I was on the staff in 1979. We were walking over to the Capitol. It was a bitter cold January day. I remember we were crossing the street. I was just making conversation, and I said, "Senator, it sure is cold today." He said, "Yes, it is. The last time I was this cold I was at the Battle of the Bulge."

JAMES B. EDWARDS

The Senator wasn't afraid of anything. I think he proved that in his active duty in World War II. I've talked to him several times about his flight behind enemy lines the night of D-Day. He told me about flying in the glider. That in itself is almost impossible to do. I remember he said he had a person hurt in his glider, and he sent somebody back to get the doctor who was in another glider behind them. But the doctor was beheaded by the crash. You want to talk about courage!

I was also fortunate to have been with Strom the time that President Reagan asked him to represent this country at the Paris Air Show. On that same trip we took a train down to Normandy Beach where the invasion took place. We were there at that beautiful overlook and that green space with the thousands upon thousands of crosses. It was a spiritual experience for me. One of the moments I will never forget is how Senator Thurmond stood there and told this crowd about his experiences during D-Day. It was like a spiritual experience to hear Senator Thurmond tell about the way it was on that bloody day when they made history. He was truly a courageous man.

DAVID WILKINS

I got on a small plane in Clemson one night with the Senator. We were flying to Lancaster for a fish fry. We had been at a big rally that night. We got up in the clouds. The Senator and I were in the backseat. Nobody else was on the plane except the pilot. Somehow we got to talking about D-Day. He started describing what happened on that glider. He spoke in such rich detail, I thought I was in the glider there with him. He talked about somebody getting killed, about crashing into the apple orchard, and then being in pitch black darkness and not being able to find anybody. They had no idea where they were.

The way he recalled the experience, in vivid detail, you would have thought it happened that very morning. That night on that plane was just one of countless times that I learned to really appreciate that man. He was a genuine war hero, a real patriot. He didn't have to put his life on the line for his country. But he did.

KATHRYN HOOK

One year President Reagan asked Senator Thurmond to represent him at the Paris Air Show at Le Bourget in France. While he was there, the Senator wanted to go out and visit Normandy. We got on the train and went out to Caen, which is the capital of Normandy. It is a beautiful place. Everyone with us knew the Senator was a hero from the war, and had come in on a glider on D-Day. He was a passenger on that glider, not the pilot. As I understand it, the Senator's glider landed in a grove of apple trees.

In Normandy, they took us to a beautiful luncheon at the city hall, which looked like a castle. They served Calvados, which is a very mild apple wine. The French made toast after toast, one accolade after another about the Senator. It was all in French, so of course we didn't know exactly what they were saying. We were all waiting anxiously to see how the Senator would respond to all those accolades. He didn't know what had been said. Everybody was speaking French! When the time came for him to say something, bless his heart, he was always up to the occasion. The Senator stood up, raised his glass of Calvados apple wine, and said, "Viva La France!" It brought the house down! One thing about the Senator, he always knew how to win over a crowd, even in France!

JOHN WARNER

is a United States Senator from Virginia, 1978-present.

Tom Brokaw has written about the greatest generation, those who served in World War II. Strom Thurmond has had the most extraordinary of service. I remember one time he called me up and he said, "John, the President has invited me to go with him to the D-Day beaches." It was the 40th anniversary. It was the thinking of President Reagan at that time, very wisely, that many of those veterans would not live to see the 50th anniversary. So Strom embarked for the beaches of Normandy on the 40th.

Howard Cannon, Democrat from Nevada, went with us. Howard had gone in on D-Day in a glider. Lowell Weicker went with us. I remember his father had been Chief of the Air Force Intelligence, 8th Air Force, Army Air Corps. So there were just the four of us who went.

Strom Thurmond was assigned a helicopter right behind the President's helicopter and perhaps one with the Secret Service. We traveled up and down the Normandy beaches for two days, visiting almost every single site where our troops were involved. I just remember it so well. I remember a Congressman from Florida who joined us and beckoned to Senator Thurmond to come over. He said, "Look Strom, I can see the indentation where I dug my foxhole." Sure enough, there was the beach and an indentation was there. He was consumed with emotion; Strom likewise. I remember these two men embraced on that spot.

JOHN DRUMMOND

*is President Pro Tempore of the South Carolina State Senate, a
highly decorated veteran of World War II, and was a life-long
friend of Strom Thurmond's.*

Senator Thurmond was a paratrooper in World War II, and I flew cover for them on D-Day. He and I had been very good friends before the war. I was probably the first one who introduced him in the Piedmont when he ran for Governor. I introduced him at the Lion's Club in Ninety Six, South Carolina.

When I got home from the war, I called on Holly Self. She had been in the ninth grade when I was in the tenth grade. She played basketball. I was always in love with her, but I'd never dated her. When I was in the prison camp in the war, I prayed about her. I said Lord, "If Holly Self is not married, the first thing I'm going to do when I get home is call on her."

Sure enough, when I got home as a war hero in 1946, just out of prison camp, I called on Holly Self. I asked her if she would go out with me. She said yes! Now, there was nothing moving in that little town of Ninety Six. So I got my daddy's old '36 Chevrolet and went around the hill and up to her house for the date. Holly's father had died when she was five. Her Uncle Bubba had pretty well taken care of all the family. She lived with her mother and her mother's sister, an old maid aunt they called Mamie.

When I got to the house, Mamie came out on the side porch of that big, old, rambling house. She said, "John Willie!" — everybody in town called me John Willie. She said, "John Willie! Holly said she's going out with you. But you should know that Strom Thurmond's up there in the parlor talking with Holly's mother." I couldn't believe it! I believed Strom was actually there calling on Holly! Mamie said, "John Willie, you stay out here on the side porch. Holly's going out with you, so don't you worry."

I used to tease Strom about that. He'd insist he was really there to visit with Holly's mother. And I used to tease Holly, who became my wife, that if she hadn't gone out with me, she might have been the first Mrs. Strom Thurmond! That's a true story.

THE STROM THURMOND INSTITUTE, CLEMSON UNIVERSITY

"His face would always light up when he talked about her. ... Often he would tear up when he spoke of her, especially in the latter years. He never failed to mention how beautiful her eyes were."

– Dee Short –

If Ever a Man Loved a Woman

STROM THURMOND AND MISS JEAN

Those of us who knew Strom Thurmond well knew that Jean Crouch was the love of his life. They were married on November 7, 1947. He was then Governor of South Carolina and just shy of his 45th birthday. She was 21, the youngest first lady of South Carolina since 1789.

Jean was at his side when he made an unsuccessful bid for the Presidency in 1948. And she was there in 1954 when he became the only person in our nation's history to win a seat in the United States Senate as a write-in candidate.

Jean was just 33 when she succumbed to a malignant brain tumor in early January, 1960. Of course, Strom Thurmond was devastated. He would remember her with great love and affection, often with tears, for the rest of his life.

C. BRUCE LITTLEJOHN

I knew Jean well. My wife and I got to know her before she and Strom were married. She was a delightful person and played the part of the Governor's wife rather well. She was very gracious. I was disappointed that no children came of that union. About eleven years later, she died of a brain tumor. She was only about 33-years old. She was a great wife and quite beautiful.

MARY CHAPMAN WEBSTER

I don't remember ever *not* knowing Senator Thurmond. He was a very good friend of my grandfather's and a good friend of my dad's. I even remember Jean, his first wife. She was absolutely delightful. I think I was all of eight or nine when he and Jean got married. But I do remember it, because Mother and Dad were friends of his and we used to see quite a bit of him. Jean was twenty years younger than he was. He didn't get married until he was in his 40s, when he was Governor. Everybody said he was too old for her. To prove that he wasn't, he called the press and with all of them watching, he walked on his hands across the front yard of the Governor's mansion. We all just hooted and hollered.

ELIZA EDGAR

The Senator would sometimes intercom us to come to his office and make copies of various articles that he thought we should have or that he wanted us to send to his sisters, his children, or whomever. One of those times I went back, and he asked me to make a copy of the *Life Magazine* article about his proposal to Miss Jean. He told me to be sure and make a copy for myself and for the other girl who worked up front. I said, "Yes sir, got it." Later he asked me, "Did you read it yet? I was quite the Romeo, wasn't I?"

DEE SHORT

Often, I would ask the Senator to tell me stories about when he was Governor and about Jean. His face would always light up when he talked about her. With a chuckle, he told me how Jean would slide down the banister at the Governor's mansion whenever she came down to greet their guests. He always said she was so fun-loving and down-to-earth. Often he would tear up when he spoke of her, especially in the latter years. He never failed to mention how beautiful her eyes were.

CHRIS KELLEY CIMKO

In the nook of the Senator's office where he had his desk, both sides were lined with filing cabinets. I think a significant portion of his life was in those filing cabinets. I remember one year when Congress was in recess, the Senator called me at my desk and said, "Miss Cimko, come here." I went to his office, and there he was with some of the file cabinets open and all these large manila envelopes open on his desk. He looked up at me and

Miss Jean and Governor Thurmond on their wedding day, November 7, 1947.

THE STROM THURMOND INSTITUTE, CLEMSON UNIVERSITY

said, "Have you ever seen photos of Miss Jean?"

We sat there and looked through all the wonderful old photographs of him and Miss Jean, from their wedding and even their honeymoon in Havana. It was very unusual that he had that private, quiet time. It was not like him to stroll down memory lane like that. But about once a year after that we would pull out all the photos of Miss Jean and look at them together. I was always so honored and pleased that he wanted to share that with me.

When Senator Thurmond broke the record for longevity in the Senate, we did a number of interviews. It really was a big moment in his life. The *New York Times* did a front-page story. One of the people who came to interview the Senator was Steve Piacente who at that time was the Washington reporter for the Charleston *Post and Courier*.

Steve had covered the Senator for many years and was deeply fond of him. Sometimes he had to write things the Senator didn't like because after all, he was a reporter. But I knew how very fond of the Senator he was, and how really taken he was by the Senator's strength and ability to carry on despite his age and all the things that life had thrown at him. Steve started the interview with some questions. Then the subject of Miss Jean came up, the Senator's first wife. I believe the question that he asked was, "Senator, how did you meet her, and what did you think of her the first time you met her?"

The Senator had a habit of putting both of his hands over his face, very flat, to rub his eyes. When Steve asked the question, the Senator put both of his hands up to his face as if he was going to rub his eyes. But they stayed there on his face a little bit too long. I looked over at Duke Short as if to say, oh my God, what's going to happen now? In between his hands, I could see the Senator's mouth. His lips began to quiver.

By the time he pulled his hands down from over his eyes, his eyes were all teared up. He looked at Steve and he said, "She had the prettiest eyes I'd ever seen." He went on to describe how he met her at her high school graduation where he spoke and handed out diplomas. He was Governor at the time. By the time he was done talking about her, there wasn't a dry eye in the room. If ever a man loved a woman, Strom Thurmond loved his Miss Jean.

WARREN ABERNATHY

served as Senator Thurmond's State Manager throughout the Senator's career in Washington as well as working with him when he was Governor.

When Strom Thurmond was Governor of South Carolina, his office had thirteen employees and two prisoners. If we got in a rush and needed more help, we called down to the prison and ordered more prisoners. Most of them were life termers. They were hard workers. Of course, the Governor's Mansion was also run by prisoners. I think we had five up there. They did all the housework, the yard work, and all the cooking.

    Strom Thurmond liked to clean his desk before he left the office for the day. He wanted to make sure everything was done. But it got so the girls that worked for him didn't want to stay late at night. They wanted to go home right at 5 o'clock. But Strom Thurmond wanted to work until about 9:30 or 10 at night. So he hired a male secretary that came in about 1:30 in the afternoon and stayed as long into the night as the Governor wanted him to stay.

    I'll never forget the time Governor Thurmond invited 6,000 boy scouts to a football game at Carolina. Then he told them all to come by the mansion and get a little box lunch. By the time all those kids left, most of the flowers were gone.

ALAN SIMPSON

was a United States Senator from Wyoming, 1979–1997.

Here's a great story that Strom loved to tell. Truman had been elected President of the United States in 1948. Alben Barkley was the Vice President. Alben and Strom were great friends. Of course, Strom had run as a Dixiecrat in that race and had picked up a lot of votes against Harry Truman. I think Strom managed to carry four states in the election.

    Anyway, at the inaugural parade Strom walked with the South Carolina delegation. As they passed the reviewing stands, Vice President Barkley raised his hand to wave at Strom. But Harry Truman reached over and grabbed Barkley's arm and pulled it down. Later that night Strom saw Barkley at one of the inaugural balls. He said, "Alben, when we went by the reviewing stand, I saw the President grab your arm and pull it down and say something. What did he say?" Alben said, "He told me to keep my arm down. He said, 'That son of a bitch nearly lost me the election!'" Strom always loved to tell that story.

"He'd fire them up and then let them go."

– *Warren Abernathy* –

Fire Them Up
and Then Let Them Go!

THE ORATORICAL STYLE OF STROM THURMOND

Senator Thurmond was rarely "out of his element"; he was confident and gentlemanly in every situation. There were few contexts, however, in which he came alive more than in front of a crowd.

The Senator was a natural orator, sensing the mood of an audience and finding exactly the right words to connect with them. He was a persuasive, energetic, and eloquent speaker. He could make beautiful speeches off the cuff, but he and his staff also worked diligently to insure that his written remarks were impeccably prepared. The Senator recognized his speeches as an important part of his legacy and, as with other aspects of his life in service, he was committed to doing them right. After he finished reviewing and editing a speech, Senator Thurmond would put a little check mark in the upper right-hand corner of the first page. This was to show that the document had his stamp of approval.

WILLIAM REHNQUIST

was the Chief Justice of the United States Supreme Court. He served on the Court from 1972 until 2005.

Over thirty years ago, shortly after I was confirmed as an Associate Justice of the Supreme Court of the United States, I attended the dedication of a new courthouse in South Carolina. As I listened to the string of speakers, I began to look around at the others seated on the small stage. I could not help but

Former U.S. Supreme Court Justice Sandra Day O'Connor, Senator Thurmond, former Chief Justice William Rehnquist.

notice that Senator Thurmond appeared rather listless, as if he was not at all following the goings-on. But when the Senator was called to speak, I realized I could not have been more wrong. He fairly bounded up to the podium, raring to go, and gave a rousing speech. Senator Thurmond had a very long career of service to the State of South Carolina and to his country. One of his secrets may have been the ease with which he came to life in the public eye.

MELINDA KOUTSOUMPAS

Whenever the Senator gave a speech, we always made a number of copies. One we labeled an original that would go to his library. Then we'd have the Senator's copy, the AA's copy, the Press copy, all this. And they would each have to be stapled a certain way according to the Senator's instructions. The staple always had to be in the upper left hand corner, horizontally rather than vertically.

Well, the Senator had been a schoolteacher. So he was very good about going through the speeches, checking them over, and marking them up so he knew what phrases to emphasize and where to pause. The first time I went in with a speech for him to look over, I guess the staple was crooked. He looked down at it. It must have taken him five minutes, but he explained to me, in no uncertain terms, how this was to be. He proceeded to pick out the staple and redo it. Then he took out every one of the other staples in all the other copies so he could show me how to do it properly.

JOHN R. STEER

One of my jobs was writing drafts of a lot of the Senator's speeches. When I took them in for his review, I had to make sure that the copies that were supposed to be stapled, were stapled! And the staple had to be in the right place: one half inch down from the left corner and one half inch in. That was as important as the content of the speech. And God forbid if I ever made a spelling error. He never missed a spelling error. There was never a time when I got back to my desk and found a spelling error that he had missed. If I had an error in there, he would find it. In part, I think he did that with an eye towards history. It would show that he had personally examined and corrected this speech, which he did do.

DENNIS W. SHEDD

There are a lot of things that people don't know about the Senator. First of all, he knew more about vocabulary, grammar, syntax, and spelling than anybody I've ever known. I've been through college. I've got two law degrees; I made well over 700 on the verbal section of the College Boards. But the Senator surpassed my knowledge or that of anyone else in any situation. It was astounding. He was just that smart.

When the Senator and I worked on speeches together, we would often disagree on how to pronounce a word or what a word meant. He would say, "Holly, get out the dictionary!" He'd look up the word and more often than not he was exactly right. One time we were editing a speech that included the word "capacity." Someone had hyphenated the word at the end of a line as "capa-city." The Senator said, "That's wrong. It's not capa-city; it's capac-ity." I said to myself: that old codger, he doesn't know what he's talking about. But I got the dictionary, looked it up, and he was exactly right.

MIKE DEWINE

is a United States Senator from Ohio, 1995-present.

When I came to the Senate in 1995, Senator Thurmond still had the ability to go into a room without any notes and speak eloquently before any group. We had a fund raiser one time, and Strom came as one of the guests. We'd asked him to say a few words. He stood up, no notes, and spoke quite beautifully. No matter how old he got, he was still perfectly comfortable in front of a crowd. That was a remarkable thing to see.

ALFONSE D'AMATO

When I was reelected in 1986, we had an informal swearing-in ceremony at the Russell Senate Office Building. Senator Thurmond came to the event. He was absolutely spell-binding. He got up there with his accent and said, "I'm so glad you sent this little eye-talian boy to the Senate of the United States. And I know how he got here. Look at his beautiful mama! She did all those ads for him!" My mama lit up. There was a local TV crew there, and when they turned on the camera, Senator Thurmond was at his very best. He stirred up that crowd. That very day Mama D'Amato became a Strom Thurmond fan.

TRENT LOTT

We had a crime law up before the Senate. In those days, Senator Thurmond was Chairman of the Judiciary Committee. He got in the center well on the Senate Floor; he must have been in his late 80s at the time, and he gave a stem-winding speech about the horrors and victims of crime. It was magnificent. I really was so impressed with it.

He was nothing but a pleasure to work with — a typical Southern gentleman, courteous to a fault; sympathetic when you had difficulties; helpful when you were working on an amendment or an issue on the Floor; ran a meeting totally fair to everybody there, but he wouldn't be pushed around by liberal Democrats either. He was just a classic gentleman of the Old School, which is a beautiful school. I dearly loved him. In the Senate, he was like a father figure to me. He was an important part of my being elected to the leadership. I view him as one of the finest gentlemen I've ever known, regardless of his age or his politics. He was just a fine, fine man.

MARK GOODIN

The Senator had a sixth, seventh, or eighth sense about what people wanted at a particular moment. It was just primordial. It was instinctive. We were at the Southern 500 in Darlington two days after the Soviets had shot down Korean Airlines 007. Senator Thurmond was the Grand Marshal of the Southern 500. The Senator pulled me aside and said, "Now, should I say anything about this airliner?" It seemed a little raw to me. There we were at a race. It just didn't seem right. I said, "Senator, I think feelings are a little raw. I wouldn't do it." He kind of nodded okay. So I went to go get myself something to eat as they led him to the box to make his introductory remarks.

I heard him on the loudspeaker saying, "Ladies and Gentlemen, welcome to the

Governor J. Strom Thurmond making his Inaugural
address on January 21, 1947.

granddaddy of all stock car races!" Everyone cheered. And he said, "It's a great day to
be alive! And it's a great to be an American! And I'll tell you one reason it's a great day
to be an American: because in America, we don't shoot down civilian airliners!"

And 50,000 people jumped to their feet and for five minutes cheered as loudly as I've
ever heard a crowd cheer. It went on and on. People waved flags. He just sat there and
soaked it up. He came back to me later and said, "I hated to go against you on that one,
but after doing this awhile, you kind'a get a feeling for these things."

WARREN ABERNATHY

He loved a crowd. He'd work any crowd he could find, the bigger the better. He'd go
into a restaurant and shake hands with everybody in there. Then he'd go back into the
kitchen and shake everybody's hand back there. It took us a couple of years to get him to
shorten his speeches. He always spoke for 35 minutes. I told him, "Senator, you lose them
at about 18 or 20 minutes." He said, "Abernathy, your problem is that you've heard it

before." But he finally cut them down to about 18 to 20 minutes. And then in the latter years the speeches were less than 10 minutes. He'd fire them up and then let them go.

STEPHEN BREYER

I remember one of the first times I heard Senator Thurmond speak. We were in Williamsburg for a judicial meeting. Justice Douglas had died. Warren Burger gave a kind of eulogy which was not really very much about Douglas. It went on for quite a long time. At the end of his talk Senator Thurmond stood up, and he said the following: "As a Justice, I disagreed completely with almost everything Justice Douglas said. But as a man, I admired him. I admired him because he was a fighter, and I always admire a fighter. And I admired him because he loved the environment. He loved the outdoors. And any man that loves the outdoors is okay with me. I'm sorry he died." Then he sat down. It was fabulous. He was straight, to the point, and it was an absolutely decent thing to say.

COY JOHNSTON II

When Senator Thurmond went to a speaking engagement, he always had a little card with him that had the names of some of the people who were at the event so he could recognize them. The first thing he would do when he got to the event was to go to the men's room to memorize the names on the card. When he came in and sat down at the table, he'd show me the card and ask me if any names were left off, and to confirm that all those people were actually there. People were always so surprised that he knew who was there in the audience. But he prepared for that every time, and worked hard to make it look easy.

DON FOWLER

People would often ask me why Senator Thurmond always got elected by such big margins and why he has such an enduring popularity. I told them he had a greater ability to sense what people want and what they respond positively to than anybody I've ever seen.

We all remember, not very pleasantly, the Watergate matters. I remember hearing Senator Thurmond make a speech at the Watermelon Festival at Estill. The Senator got up in the back of a flatbed truck. The essence of what he said was that the administration was not handling the situation properly. "Unless they are frank and honest about these matters," he said, "it will spell the end of the Nixon administration." And that was almost a full year before Nixon resigned. We all knew that Senator Thurmond had actively supported Nixon in '68 and '72. It was very surprising to hear one of Nixon's most vocal supporters say something like that. But the Senator was absolutely right about it.

HENRY MCMASTER

Back in the early 1970s there was an education program in Washington for graduate students to meet the Senators. I recall a particular group came from a northeastern Ivy League university. They were very bright people, very interested in government. Senator Thurmond had agreed to be one of the speakers to address the group and answer questions.

Well, the Senator got tied up in a committee meeting, so they asked me to go. I had only been there about two months at the time, so I really knew nothing. Fortunately, I went with Stanley Hackett, who was what they would now call the Chief Legislative Assistant. We both headed over to talk to this group.

Stanley had done this kind of thing before, so he wasn't particularly concerned. But I was. The idea of going before a bunch of highly motivated, educated graduate students from a very liberal Ivy League school was pretty daunting. There were about 30 of them in the room. Stanley and I walked in and explained that the Senator wasn't available. Just as the first hand went up for a question, we heard Senator Thurmond's voice out in the hall. You can just imagine how good it felt to hear his voice!

The Senator walked in the room. Body language experts could have told you that not a soul in that audience had any use for this conservative Senator from the South. They were all sitting there with their legs crossed and their arms folded high on their chests. They knew they didn't agree with him on anything. Stanley and I stood over on the edge of the room, and the Senator took over.

As I remember, the first question was something about foreign policy and war. Vietnam was very much of a hot subject at that time. The Senator's answer was, "Well, when I was in World War II and flew into France on a glider, this is what I discovered." He shared those personal experiences and used them to support his belief in a strong defense of our country. The crowd lightened up a little bit.

The next question was something about how he could be in favor of the death penalty. The Senator said, "Well, when I was a judge I had to impose the death penalty, and I did. Let me tell you how I formed my beliefs based on my direct experience as an attorney and judge." As he spoke, heads started nodding in agreement. Then they asked him something about the federal government's role in education. He said, "When I was Superintendent of Education and then Governor, this is what I learned about that." More heads started to nod. There were even a few smiles.

Questions went on like that for maybe another 45 minutes. But every time they asked him a fairly hostile question, knowing that his views were going to be contrary to theirs, he explained his position based not on political theory but on his actual real-life experiences. When he finished that group of students jumped to their feet and gave the man a standing ovation. It was amazing. Strom Thurmond had a remarkable talent when he spoke in front of a crowd, even a hostile crowd.

BUTLER DERRICK

I remember one morning we had to go down to Barnwell to make a speech at 11 o'clock. It got to be about 10 o'clock, and then 10:30. I said, "Strom, we're already late. Let's go." He said, "Butler, don't you worry about that. If you don't get there late and leave early, they think you got nothing else to do."

ROBERT MCNAIR

was Governor of South Carolina, 1965-71.

One thing I will always remember about the Senator is that he loved to wear a highway patrolman's hat. I saw him at a lot of parades and festivals. He always had that hat on. He usually arrived late and rolled right to the head of the parade. He would frequently be asked to speak. The Senator had a reputation for fiery, long speeches. I always made arrangements with the folks in charge to let me speak first, because by the time the Senator finished, the sun was hot and the crowd was thin.

SUSAN PELTER

Senator Thurmond was one of the last of the great sort of 19th- and early 20th-century orators. He had a very full blown, eloquent style. He liked to explore things in a certain measured way. It was very colorful. I have thought many times, here is a person who first heard public speakers at stump meetings where there really was a stump. We have pictures of him in the buggy with his dad going to an actual stump meeting.

It was unfortunate that he was not always the most technologically savvy speaker. He didn't do well with microphones. But when he was interested and moved by a topic, like military or children's issues, he was a terrific speaker. And it was a real pleasure to hear him. It was like a moment out of time — like going back and hearing what great speakers of the past sounded like.

"How Y'all Doin'?
I'm Strom Thurmond!"

ON THE CAMPAIGN TRAIL

Strom Thurmond first ran for public office in 1928. He was elected to the post of Edgefield County Superintendent of Education. He was 25. By every account, he was a progressive, compassionate leader. Teachers, students, and parents were pleased with his reforms. He campaigned for public office for the last time 68 years later. He was victorious in that race as well, winning his ninth election to the United States Senate.

The Senator spent his entire adult life campaigning for office. As stories from this chapter will reveal, he didn't just enjoy it — he loved it. He loved everything about it: working the crowds, riding in the parades, shaking hands, talking with reporters, traveling through the night, racing to the next event. If ever a man was born for the campaign trail, it was Strom Thurmond. Generations of South Carolinians responded in kind. When Pug Ravenel lost to Senator Thurmond in 1978, he commented that "asking people to vote against Strom Thurmond is like asking them to cut down a palmetto tree."

JOHN DRUMMOND

Any time we were going somewhere, he'd stop at every corner, at every house. He knew everybody and he wanted to stay and talk. But he spent too much time talking with people. I'd say "Strom, you can't just stay all the time with one person." I used to have to almost drag him away. Nine times out of ten we'd wind up late wherever we had to go.

Duke Short's mother Eloise Strom, Strom Thurmond, and Dee Short.

I remember when we were campaigning against Pug Ravenel. Strom was 78-years old. That was when he said, "If I win this one, this will be my last campaign." Well, we beat Pug and boy, the Democrats got mad. I had cut some tapes as a Democrat for Strom. The Democrats threatened me. But not the big boys in the Senate. They said, "Drummond, don't you worry; they're not going to do anything with you." Because they were supporting Strom also! The big boys, the ones in the know, have always supported Strom.

MARY CHAPMAN WEBSTER

Of course I invited the Senator to my wedding. It turned out he had a speaking engagement at the University of South Carolina graduation the same day, but he told them he couldn't do it because he had to go to a wedding. There were a thousand people at this wedding. It was a typical, insane, Southern wedding. Every textile executive in the Southeast was there because they were all friends of my father's.

I thought, oh, the Senator's coming to my wedding because he loves me so much because I used to work for him! My father said, "The Senator's coming to your wedding because every textile executive in the Southeast is going to be there and he's running for reelection! He can raise more money there than he can speaking at a commencement!" The Senator not only stayed for the reception; he stayed for the party at the house. I think he was one of the last people to leave! It was absolutely hysterical. That man was no dummy.

GEORGE ALLEN

was a United States Senator from Virginia, 2001-2007, and served as the Governor of Virginia 1994-98.

Without a doubt, Strom was ever resourceful and always campaigning. I sat beside Senator Fritz Hollings and his wife Peatsy at Senator Thurmond's funeral. Fritz and Peatsy remembered that Strom attended their wedding in 1971. While everyone else was throwing rice outside the Citadel Chapel, Strom was handing out pencils for his re-election.

DAVID WILKINS

During the Senator's 1972 campaign, my brother Billy was the state-wide Chairman. I was helping out by running the Senator and his wife Nancy around Greenville. They came in one Saturday. We went to church the next morning. Then he said, "Let's go to lunch." I suggested the Greenville Country Club. He immediately came up with a better idea: the S&W Cafeteria at a big shopping center. So we headed over there.

There was a long line for lunch, which is of course just what the Senator was hoping for. As Susan and Nancy stood in line, he and I walked up and down the line. There wasn't a person he didn't greet. I handed everybody a brochure, and he would shake hands and talk. We did that until it was time to go in and get our own trays and go through the line.

So we sat down to eat. And it just happened that we got a seat right up front. He made sure he sat right where he could look at everybody as they walked by. He ate pretty quickly, then he got up and started working the cafeteria. Being a novice, just about a year out of the Army, I didn't have a clue who we'd already met and who we hadn't. Remarkably, the Senator knew. He remembered everybody. So he hopped, skipped, and jumped from one table to the next, making sure he said hello to whomever he hadn't spoken to yet. He was really something to watch.

R.C. PREACHER WHITNER

is the Founder and President of R.C. Whitner & Associates.
He and his family were long-time friends and supporters of
Senator Thurmond's.

In 1972 I agreed wholeheartedly to work on the campaign for the Senator. During that period, I had gotten to know some of the nationalist Chinese in the Military Attaché Office. The Senator was always very open and vocal about his support for Chiang Kai-Shek and what he was doing with the democracy movement within that part of China. They called me one day and said hey, we have $2000 we want to give Senator Thurmond. I told them that was great; let me tell the Senator.

The Senator thought about it, and he looked at me and said, "No. Please go back and thank them. But I want no one, myself included, to ever think that I would stand up and speak on behalf of General Chiang Kai-Shek because they contributed money to my campaign. I will do that out of the heart, from my belief in the country and the man, and not for any campaign contributions." So I went back and told them. They were very impressed with that. They thanked the Senator profusely. And we went about the campaign. As everyone knows, it was successful like all his Senate campaigns.

The funny thing I remember about that election year was that the Senator's opponent was making a splash about him getting too old. That was in 1972! Right after all that talk about him being too old, we announced the fact that Mrs. Thurmond was pregnant with their first child. That kind of shut them up a little bit.

WILLIAM W. WILKINS

During the 1972 campaign we were in Greenville for a dedication, and then the Senator was to attend an event that night in Columbia. In the meantime, he wanted to go to a funeral in Saluda County. So we drove to Saluda and went to the funeral. The cemetery was surrounded by a wrought-iron fence that had just one gate. After the service was over, Senator Thurmond walked over to the gate and stood there as everybody came through the gate. He shook everybody's hand at that service.

After everyone left, there were two fellows back at the grave site shoveling dirt into the grave. Senator Thurmond walked back across that cemetery and shook hands with both of them. He made a point to let them know he appreciated the job they were doing. Those two men were just as important to him as all the people who had attended the service.

There was not a person with whom he didn't shake hands. When we were in a restaurant, Senator Thurmond would typically go around and shake hands before he left. He wouldn't shake hands with a few people just for the cameras. Whether there was a camera there or not, he shook hands with every single person. And then he'd go back in the kitchen and shake hands with the cooks and tell them how good the food was. He didn't want anybody to think that they weren't important enough to be thanked.

WILLIAM C. PLOWDEN, JR.

was the Assistant Secretary of Labor for Veterans' Employment under President Reagan. He was a close friend of Senator Thurmond's for over fifty years and served as Chairman for three of his Senatorial campaigns. Mr. Plowden now holds the position of State Director of Veterans' Employment Training for South Carolina, under the U.S. Department of Labor.

During the '72 campaign, Harry Dent was Chairman of the Republican Party of South Carolina. The Saturday night before the election on the following Tuesday, we had a big party out at the fairgrounds. Harry came down from Washington. He saw my wife and me slipping out of the party, and he came rushing up and said, "Bill Plowden! You're losing this election! You're going to lose! Nixon sent me down here to tell y'all you got to do something real quick or you're going to lose the election!"

I said, "Harry, where'd you get your figures from?" He said, "We got the right figures in Washington." I said, "Well I don't think we're going to lose the election. I think we got it made." He said, "Well, we got to do something. What can I do?" I said, "I don't know of anything you can do. Go ask the Senator. I'm going home."

A few days later I bumped into Harry, and I asked him what the Senator had told him to do. He said, "The Senator asked me, 'What did Bill Plowden say to do?' I told him, Bill Plowden said there's nothing left to do; we're going to win.' So the Senator said, 'You take that back to Nixon and tell him to relax.'" Senator Thurmond won by well over 50,000 votes.

The night of the election in '72, we were down at the headquarters here in Columbia. The Senator was back there in the office. I happened to see his sister, Miss Gertrude, drive up in a taxi. She had a little brown bag with her, bringing him something to eat. She always wanted to take care of him. I went out to meet her and took her back to the office. I said, "Senator, not many people have sisters that love them like yours, and your sister wants to take care of you. Now, she brought you something to eat." I handed him the bag. In the bag was an apple, an orange, and a banana.

The Senator said, "Bill Plowden, you and Gertrude sit down." And he proceeded to give us a lecture on green-tipped bananas. He said, "You should never eat green-tipped

Senator Thurmond waving in a parade.

bananas. Remember this Gertrude. And you shouldn't drink orange juice on an empty stomach. Remember that Bill Plowden." We got a good lecture right there on election night. Everybody else was out there all excited, counting the returns, and there he was lecturing us about green-tipped bananas.

BUD ALBRIGHT
is the Staff Director for the Energy and Commerce Committee of the U.S. House of Representatives and a former Thurmond staffer. His father "Icky" Albright was one of the Senator's oldest and closest friends.

We were working a crowd one time. I don't recall the exact event, but there was a South Carolina, North Carolina, and Virginia delegation all mixed in together. The Senator had been working his way through the South Carolina delegation shaking hands. As he got over into the North Carolina crowd, I tapped him on the shoulder and said, "Senator, we need to turn around. You're in the North Carolina crowd now." He stopped and said to me, "Well, you never know when they might move!"

ROBIN ROBERTS

I recall in the '78 campaign we would go all day long from event to event to event, then finally drop the Senator off at midnight at a little house he was renting on Waccamaw Avenue up there in Five Points. The next morning we'd pick him up at seven o'clock and go again all day long. There we were, a couple of us in our mid twenties, young guys in good shape, and he was just wearing us out. Day in and day out, going all over the state.

I remember that whenever we got near Columbia we'd have to stop by Cromers so he could get himself a big ol' bag of Spanish Reds. He'd eat them as we went down the road. The Senator loved his Spanish Reds peanuts.

I really got to know him on those trips in the campaign. We'd be out there driving across the state in the middle of the night, God knows where. In those days I had a larger car with a big backseat, and I always kept a pillow in the trunk. There were many nights I'd get the pillow out for him. He'd lay down in the back seat and get a couple hours of sleep as we went up and down the interstate. Later on I traded that car in. The guy gave me about $100 less than I thought it was worth. I asked him why. He said, "Because you've got two bushels of peanut hulls underneath the passenger seat."

DAN QUAYLE

I campaigned for Senator Thurmond down there in South Carolina. He had a great memory of names. You could line up a couple hundred people at these receptions, and he knew 90 percent of them by name. He knew their first names and their children. That's the reason he never had any competition down there. He knew everybody.

JESSE HELMS

Senator J. Strom Thurmond will forever be prominent in the memories of hundreds of thousands of Americans, and indeed people all over the world who knew of this legendary gentleman. People who personally knew this great American will forever carry vivid memories of this unique man.

For me it is the memory of a tireless and selfless campaigner who wore me out on those days he would come to North Carolina and speak to one gathering after another about why they should vote for me.

I shall never forget one particularly long and warm day when we had traveled many miles and shaken hundreds and hundreds of hands. As we were finally headed to our motel all I wanted was to be able to lay my head on a pillow and get some sleep. Not Senator Thurmond. He was planning to go jogging, and asked if I wanted to run to the center of town and back along with him! I was humbled by this legend's vigor and by his interest in my success. I am honored to have been his friend.

TUCKER ESKEW

served as the Deputy Assistant to the President and Director of the White House Office of Global Communications under President George W. Bush and prior to that, as Press Secretary and Communications Director to South Carolina Governor Carroll Campbell. Mr. Eskew served as a Page for Senator Thurmond in the summer of 1978.

I came to Washington after graduating from the University of the South. I worked for President Reagan's reelection campaign. Eventually I went back to South Carolina and helped Carroll Campbell run for Governor. I got to spend a good deal of time with Senator Thurmond during that campaign. I remember traveling around the state with him when Carroll Campbell and Tommy Hartnett were running for the top two offices in the state in 1986. The Senator really wanted to make sure we were covering all our bases. He made sure that Congressman Campbell was hitting the right precincts and going to where the votes were. He also helped to make sure we went over to Aiken and Edgefield, his home turf.

You get to see the character of a man when you're flying around the state in a little airplane. He was just so generous with anecdotes and friendly advice. But I'll tell you what, you get him in a car driving to an event, and that advice gets kind of sharp. He'd tell the driver, "Just step on it! Come on! We got to get there!" He didn't want to keep people waiting. He didn't like to waste time getting to the next event. That was a window on a man's character. He didn't want to waste time. He wasn't there to mark time. He was there to see people and listen to them and talk about what he believed in. He wasn't one for wasting a lot of down time. He was in his 80s then, but he wore us all out. He worked longer into the night than any of us. He got up fresh and ready to go the next morning with that big old brown satchel in his hand and that straw hat. He was always raring to go.

LINDSEY GRAHAM

My first real exposure to Senator Thurmond was when I ran for Congress. I was the first Republican elected since 1877 from the Third Congressional District, which includes Edgefield, his hometown, and Aiken, where he was living. He helped me tremendously during that campaign. He spent three days campaigning with me. I was very worried about this 90-something-year-old man being pushed too hard.

The first day he got there he landed in a private two-seater plane. We went to Westminster in the middle of August, hot as it could be, where we rode in the Apple Festival Parade. He was in a suit and wearing a hat. Once that was over, he got out of the car and said, "Let's walk through the crowd." It took us about an hour to get down the street. He was treated like a rock star. Then he wanted to go visit the man who owned the funeral home, because he remembered he used to give him apples. So we walked into the funeral home unannounced. The guy was sitting in the corner asleep. Senator Thurmond said, "You still got them apples?" I thought the guy was going to be his own customer, he was so surprised to wake up and see Strom Thurmond standing there. They scrambled around and got some apples for me and Senator Thurmond.

That same day, Senator Thurmond had a cousin who was in the Oconee County Hospital. She was about 90-years old, and she'd hurt herself out in the garden. She'd fallen and broken her hip. So we went over to see his cousin. He talked to every doctor and nurse in the hospital and about half the patients.

That night we had a fund raiser in Anderson. He started to put all the food in his pockets to eat later on that evening. At one point he got up on a diving board, had everybody gather around the pool, and made a speech on my behalf. It was a barn burner of a speech and really helped my fund raising. Then he said, "Is there any place else we can go?" We'd been doing this all day, and I was tired. But I said, "Well, there's a high school football game." He said, "Let's go up there!" So we went to the Daniel High School football game where I went to high school. At halftime the stands emptied as everybody came down to meet Senator Thurmond. It was quite something to witness people from 10-years old to 80-years old wanting to say hey to him.

After that we were headed back to the hotel when he spotted a sign for a rodeo. So we stopped at the rodeo. The crowd went nuts when he walked in unannounced. The ringmaster was on a horse with a microphone. They took him out into the ring and put him up on a barrel, and he give a speech on my behalf to the rodeo crowd. Everybody just went crazy. At that point it was about 10 or 10:30 at night. I said, "Senator, the mill is about to change to third shift. You can go if you want to. I'm going home."

So we finally got back to the hotel in Clemson. We're all dead tired. But we had one more thing left to do that night. He was going to sign a fund-raising letter for me. So he read the letter. Then he corrected it! We had accidentally put down the First

Congressional District. He said, "You're not in the first; you're in the third!" So we had to rewrite the letter before he could sign it. The moral of this story is this: in 1994, when Senator Thurmond was 92, he was hell on wheels as a campaigner. I've never seen anything like it before or since.

ROBERT R. SMITH

During his last Senate campaign in 1996 there was a lot of talk about his age and his health. I think he summed it up pretty good when a very attractive reporter asked him a question. She said, "Senator, how do you feel?" She did not even have the words yet out of her mouth before he said, "As good as you look!" That said it all. He was ready to roll. It was so amazing to watch him out among the people. He could really work a crowd. He'd put his hand out and say, "How you doin'?! Good to see ya!" Quite often he would tell people about their father or their grandfather; chances are he knew both of them.

Still, there would be news reports saying he was too old or that he wasn't all there, which was ridiculous. It was very disheartening to me when people said that. Because I had spent time with him, I knew first hand those stories weren't true. People would point out that he had to read his remarks when he spoke. But he always did that throughout his career, even before he was Governor. I remember during the campaign that he was always wanting to know what was going on, asking how he could help, wanting to know if there was anything he needed to do. It was such an honor to work on that last campaign with him and watch him work. He was an incredible man.

BILL TUTEN

During his reelection campaign in '96 we went down for a fund raiser with President George H.W. Bush and Mrs. Bush. It was at the BMW plant in South Carolina. Everybody who had paid the high dollars got to come up on the stage and have their picture taken with Senator Thurmond and President and Mrs. Bush. They all had nametags and the Senator was asking everybody something about themselves. "Good to see ya! Didn't your boy go to Clemson? Wasn't your daddy from Edgefield?"

That was the first time I actually got to watch him work a room. He worked the entire line, never even stopped to get anything to drink. He was on the whole time. It was amazing. He knew something about every single person that he shook hands with, or their family or where they were from. And not once was there anyone standing beside him giving him cues or whispering in his ear or anything like that. He just knew everybody. That's what made him so good.

DAVID WILKINS

There were obviously some people in '96 who doubted whether Senator Thurmond ought to run. But I don't think he ever doubted it. I'll tell you what, when I was out on that campaign trail with him in '96, I saw a man running as strong as anybody I've ever seen. He wore me out every day. And he was in his mid 90s! I was half his age, and he still wore us all out. Once he got out there on the trail, I didn't notice any difference from any of his other campaigns. He ran just as strong.

I never heard him say anything like, "Man, I'm tired" or "Good, we only have one more stop." You never heard anything like that from Strom Thurmond. It was always, "I think we've got time to run by one more place," or "So and so said they were having a football game; let's drive by and see that for awhile." It was just constant. He never let up. He had to know that he was going to win that election. He wasn't running that hard because he was scared of losing. He just honestly wanted to get out there and meet and greet as many people as he could. He had a genuine love of mingling with the people. I'm not sure every politician has that, but Strom Thurmond genuinely loved doing it.

As a result of that, there's a great love affair that always existed between the people of South Carolina and Strom Thurmond, a relationship that other people never could understand. During the '96 campaign, I remember some people would ask me, "How in the world can people vote for somebody that old?" I told them, "You don't understand. As long as Strom Thurmond's alive and as long as he wants to serve in the United States Senate, people of this state will send him there." There's a love affair that's been going on for decades between the two that will never end. It stems from him helping people, one generation of a family after another. When you spend your lifetime helping people like he did, it creates a bond between you and the people that can never be broken. It didn't matter who ran against him. It didn't matter what the issue was. It didn't matter what the state of the economy was. Strom Thurmond on a ballot meant Strom Thurmond was going to be reelected.

GEDNEY HOWE III

Senator Thurmond was always on his game. I remember one time we were having lunch in a restaurant. There were four or five of us there. After we ate, the Senator quietly got up and went around to every table in the restaurant. "Hi, how y'all doin? I'm Strom Thurmond! I just wanted to say hello." He eased around the room, looked everybody in the eye, and shook hands with every single person.

Another time we were at a cocktail party. Of course he worked that crowd, shaking hands and saying hello. About twenty minutes before we were supposed to leave, he headed back to the kitchen. He went back there and introduced himself to everybody who was working that party. "I'm Senator Strom Thurmond. I just wanted to say what a good time we had and how much I enjoyed the food. And we appreciate all your hard work." And he shook everybody's hand back in the kitchen. I remember him saying to me, with a twinkle in his eye, "You know Gedney, there's a lot of voters in the kitchen." I said, "And you want every one." He laughed, "That's exactly right. I want every one."

Most politicians have this talent to some degree, but not nearly to the extent that Senator Thurmond demonstrated: that talent was his ability to retain personal information about people so that when he saw them there was never a blank look. He not only knew their names but he remembered something about them. It might be their mother's name or where their brother went to school. A few years back, when he must have been in his 80s, we were in Charleston. I was driving him from one event to another, and we had a two-hour break. I suggested lunch. He said, "I'll just have a light sandwich and then let's go walk Broad Street." I knew that meant he wanted to go see people.

We walked from one end of Broad Street to another. And we walked into the law offices so he could say hello to people. I remember him visiting with J.C. Hare and Alan Legare. I know he hadn't seen J.C. Hare in forty years. But he didn't just know J.C.'s name; he knew his wife's name and he asked about the children. I was amazed and totally flabbergasted with the depth of his knowledge. It was like, if you'd ever been in the circle of his life, you never left the circle. You might have had an inactive role for twenty years, but you were never out of the circle because when he saw you, he made that eye contact and he knew who you were. The power of that is something to behold.

He had this remarkable gift. When you get right down to it, he really did like people, and he really did love the politics of what he was doing, so that when he met people and said, "I'm glad to meet you," he meant it. It made him a very powerful campaigner, because it was all real. As we walked down Broad Street I said, "Senator, I guess there's some votes up and down Broad Street too. We want them all?" He said, "Yes son, we want them all."

Tales from the Sky

FLYING WITH STROM THURMOND

*I*n early April, 1991 the Senator and I were in California to attend a dedication for the U.S. Marshal Service. That weekend the Senator went to Los Angeles to visit with his daughter, Essie Mae Washington. I did not go with him to her house. I knew where he was going, but I did not accompany him. He went alone to that meeting.

We flew back from California on one of those small private planes. At one point we landed in Kansas to refuel. While we were on the ground, we got word that Senator John Heinz had just died in a plane crash in Pennsylvania. It was very tragic.

We got on the plane and kept going. We were headed to South Carolina to drop off Senator Thurmond, and then on to Washington. The weather was horrendous. That small plane was jumping all over the sky. When we finally landed and got off the plane in South Carolina, we learned that Senator John Tower had just died in a plane crash in Georgia. It was getting pretty weird.

During that whole trip, no matter how rough the plane ride was, Senator Thurmond was not at all concerned. The rest of us were pretty nervous, especially when we kept hearing the terrible news about other plane crashes. But Senator Thurmond wasn't bothered one bit.

Then the pilots couldn't get our plane started! It just wouldn't start, no matter what they did. Finally, somebody in our group suggested we take a commercial plane back to D.C. We all quickly agreed.

It was much the same thing on another occasion when we flew back from the Middle East, where the Senator had visited with troops of Desert Storm. It was a real white-knuckle flight for

Strom Thurmond, President Bush, Senator John Warner of Virginia, and Secretary Anthony Principi aboard Air Force One on the way to visit the National D-Day Memorial. June 6, 2001.

most of us. A lot of people got pretty scared because it was so rough. Senator Thurmond slept through it all. He finally woke up at one point, very well-rested, and said, "Ah! That was a real nice trip!"

BUTLER DERRICK

When Carroll Campbell was Governor he loaned Strom a state jet to go down to Aiken to make an announcement. Senator Thurmond asked me if I wanted to fly down with him. We were making a joint announcement at the Savannah River Site. On the way back, we were both sitting on a bench seat, just talking. He put his arm around me and said, "Butler, how'd you like to be my successor?" My first thought was that he'd probably asked many other politicians the same thing. I said, "Strom, you know I am honored that you would ask me that. But I think you need to get somebody younger than me. I'm not sure I can outlast you!" He laughed real hard at that one.

WILLIAM C. PLOWDEN, JR.

In 1972 the Senator and I were flying out of Charleston on a private plane. After we got up in the air he said to me, "Bill Plowden, I need to have a conference with you." I said, "Senator, I don't know any better time than right now. We're going to be on this plane for about forty-five minutes. What's on your mind?" He said, "You have been wasting my time." I said, "Sir? Wasting your time? What do you mean?" He said, "Well, why don't you have these airplanes warmed up before I get in them? We go out to the airstrip and have to sit and wait while the engines are warming up. I could be shaking hands all that time!"

BILL TUTEN

We went to the airport one time. Senator Thurmond was going down to South Carolina for a monument dedication. As we went through the airport, everyone was saying hello to him. "Hi Senator! Hey Senator Thurmond! Senator, it's so good to see you!" We got up to the counter and the woman said, "Hi Senator, where are you going today?" He said, "I'm going down to Columbia. They're giving me a statue." And then all of a sudden the woman says, "Okay Senator, I need to see a picture ID." I thought he was going to pitch a fit. He didn't. He pulled out an old military ID card and showed it to her.

When we got up to the metal detector, the Senator just walked on through ahead of me. I put his briefcase up on the X-ray. Well, Senator Thurmond never traveled without a bunch of letter openers, which he gave out as gifts. You can imagine what all those letter openers looked like in the X-ray. They stopped and looked at it. Then they said they wanted to open the bag. About that time the Senator realized I wasn't right behind him. He turned around and started walking back. Next thing I know they called the supervisor over.

The Senator got there, and they started pulling all the letter openers out of the briefcase. One of the security people said, "We don't think you can take these on the plane Senator." He didn't know what to do with them. He said to me, "You want them?" At that point they called the supervisor's supervisor over. He turned the corner, saw who it was, and just waved us on. So Senator Thurmond got on the plane with a briefcase full of letter openers. Every single one of them ended up as a gift to somebody in South Carolina.

DENNIS DECONCINI

I traveled with Strom Thurmond two times on overseas trips known as CoDels, Congressional Delegations. I remember one in particular. Strom was in his 80s at the time and was the Ranking Member of the delegation. There were about eight or nine of us Senators, and we had our wives with us. We had a long haul of twelve hours flying to Moscow. Some of us were drinking, eating, sleeping. Bob Byrd was reading Socrates. And Strom Thurmond was exercising, almost the entire way to Moscow.

I sat with Strom for part of that trip. He told me about his career, about being a Judge and a General. And then about every two hours, he'd get up and exercise for twenty or thirty minutes. He did push-ups in the aisle. And he pulled on these springs in his hands as he walked up and down the plane. When we first got to Moscow, he immediately went out jogging.

JAMES B. EDWARDS

I was Chairman of the Republican Party in Charleston. Senator Thurmond was always campaigning. He would call me to meet him at the airport and take him around. I was flattered to do that. He would frequently arrange for flights from a friend of mine who owned an airplane. He had all sorts of courage. He didn't care what airplane he got into or who was flying it. He'd get in it and fly anywhere around the state in all sorts of weather. I honestly didn't know whether it was raw courage or poor judgment that made him get into some of those planes.

HENRY MCMASTER

In the 1986 race for the Senate, I won the primary but lost against Fritz Hollings in the general election. It was an uphill battle. After the election, I had a campaign debt. So we had a fund raiser in February of 1987 out at Seawell's Fairgrounds. Senator Thurmond was one of the special guests, along with Tommy Hartnett, Arthur Ravenel, and Jack Kemp. Arthur and Tommy were in Congress at the time. I had to get a plane to go up to Washington and pick up the Senator, Jack Kemp, and Arthur.

So I arranged to borrow a plane, a big King Air two-engine plane. It was a big plane, but it was not a jet. Kemp rarely flew on anything other than a jet because he was afraid that the propeller planes were not as safe as jets. Well, we couldn't get a jet. That was the best we could do. So I flew up in the empty plane with the two very experienced pilots. We got up there and met the Senator, Kemp, and Arthur at the airport. Then we

Strom Thurmond campaigning by "air".

THE STROM THURMOND INSTITUTE, CLEMSON UNIVERSITY

got on the plane to fly back.

We ran into some very stormy weather. It was a real rough and bumpy flight. Somewhere over North Carolina the motor on the right-hand side of the plane started acting up. Then the pilots started talking to each other. We could tell they were getting a little nervous. Finally they turned to us and said that they may have to feather the engine. We didn't know what that meant. It got to be a semi-frantic sort of a situation.

I was sitting on the right side of the plane, facing Arthur Ravenel. Jack Kemp was sitting on the left side of the plane, facing the Senator. Everybody's eyes were wide open. Kemp's eyes were as big as saucers. I'll tell you, I was pretty worried. Arthur Ravenel looked out the window and then pulled down the little window shade. He told us later he looked out and saw the propeller just sitting up there dead in the air not even budging. All he could think about was who's going to be running for ol' Arthur's seat after this plane crashes!

The plane veered to the right. Then it leveled out. Then it veered to the right again, then leveled out. Arthur was sweating. I was nervous. Kemp was nervous. And then with all that frantic motion going on, Senator Thurmond put down his newspaper he was reading and looked at all of us and said, "Boys, there's no point in getting excited. There's not a thing in the world you can do about it." Then he pulled his newspaper back up just as calm as if he was sitting on a park bench. I remember sitting there looking at that man wondering, how in the world can he be so calm? How can he do it?

We ended up circling around and making an emergency landing in Raleigh. There were fire trucks and ambulances chasing us down the runway. When we finally got off, everybody was very relieved but still shaking. They took us over to the airport, where we got some water. We were all standing around shaking. And then I looked up and there was Strom Thurmond, going around shaking hands with people, introducing himself!

Everybody, including the pilots, had been really scared, except Strom Thurmond. It was just another day in the park for him. That's how you are when you're at peace with God and your life and you've seen it all.

JACK KEMP

is the Co-Director of Empower America. He was the Republican
Nominee for Vice President in 1996. He was Secretary of Housing
and Urban Development under President George H.W. Bush, and
served nine consecutive terms in the U.S. Congress.

I remember that plane ride very well. We were flying that King Air down to South Carolina. Senator Thurmond and I were sitting right across from each other. He was reading the *Wall Street Journal*. That right engine went out over North Carolina. I just about had a fit. I said, "Strom, aren't you concerned?" He said, "No, young man. This has happened to me many times." And he kept on reading that newspaper.

I was saying the Lord's Prayer, absolutely convinced that we were going to end up in the drink. Strom Thurmond read the *Wall Street Journal* all the way down. He didn't blink an eye. And that's the way he lived his life.

STEPHEN L. JONES

I remember one time we were flying back to Washington from the Hampton Watermelon Festival. The Senator had notes stuffed into his pockets that people had given him to follow up on. I had a briefcase. And we each had watermelons under our arms. When we got on the plane, the stewardess said, "Senator, you and your staff man want to sit up front? We have some seats in first class that are vacant." Of course, the Senator was a man of the people, and he never wanted to fly first class. He preferred to fly in that bulkhead right behind first class so he could shake everybody's hand as they got off the plane. He said, "No honey, we'll just sit back here where we are." Then he said, "But it would help us if you'd give us some room here. Maybe you could put these watermelons up there." So the watermelons flew first class and we flew coach.

Robbie Callaway, Senator Thurmond, Duke Short, and
Arnie Burns attending a fund raiser
at the Hay Adams hotel, Washington, D.C.

"Now, I don't want to go in any fancy car. I don't want to be seen in a fancy car."
He was very aware of how he wanted to come across to all these farmers.

– Michael Mishoe –

"Step On It!"

BEHIND THE WHEEL WITH SENATOR THURMOND

*I*f backseat driving was an Olympic event, Strom Thurmond would be the world's all-time gold-medal winner. No one else would even come close. He'd tell you to speed up if he thought you were going too slow. He'd tell you to slow down if he thought you were going too fast. In traffic, he'd tell you to change lanes. And then seconds later he'd tell you to change back. He'd tell you to turn on your turn signal then to turn it off. He'd tell you when to brake, when not to brake, and how to brake. He may have been sitting in the passenger seat, which was his preferred spot in every car (even limousines), but that didn't prevent him from doing most of the driving.

While Senator Thurmond could certainly be a source of frustration to anyone behind the wheel — I'm sure James his driver certainly knows that — it was actually one of the things that endeared him to many people who knew him well, as some of the following stories attest.

I recall attending a law enforcement conference in Nashville, Tennessee with the Senator back in the 1980s. We were met at the airport and escorted out to a waiting limousine. An impressive police escort of motorcycles and squad cars stretched out behind and in front of the limo. We got in the limo, the blue lights started flashing, and we took off for the event.

After the event and on the way back out to the limo, Senator Thurmond pointed to the lead police car. "Duke, you think we could ride in that police car?" I said, "Sir, I'm sure we can." We got in the police car. He sat up front with the driver and the shotgun rack between them. I sat in the back. The Senator was sitting tall and proud with his hand on that shotgun the entire time. We raced off into the city with the light flashing and the siren blaring. And the empty limousine following behind.

The Senator was not one to require a fancy car while going about Washington. It did not matter to him if we were going to the White House or to Elsie's Magic Skillet: we often went in my old CJ-7 Jeep. Once while at a major fund raiser which took place at the Hay Adams Hotel, the attendees heard that the Senator was riding in an old jeep, so everyone had to come out and pose for a picture with him. He was just a man of the people, and the car he was in would not change that.

WARREN ABERNATHY

The Senator loved to travel fast. He'd encourage all his drivers to "move on!" If necessary, even to go up on the sidewalks, whatever it takes, to get him to the airport on time. One night we were coming out of Aiken. I was driving. We weren't going that fast, maybe 70 or 75. We met a highway patrol. I looked in the rearview mirror and I said, "Senator, that patrol's turning around to get us." He said, "Pull off up here." So I pulled off on the side of the road. The patrol car pulled in behind me. The Senator jumped out of the car and yelled, "Meet me in Columbia!" Then he went back and got in the patrol car. He told me later that the patrol car could get him to where he wanted to go a whole lot faster than I could.

WILLIAM W. WILKINS

At one point during the 1972 campaign, we were going to a wedding in McCormick. It was a high-noon wedding. I had on my business suit and Senator Thurmond was wearing a tuxedo. The automobile I was driving began to overheat, so we stopped the car and got out. I looked over and saw Senator Thurmond standing there on the side of the road in his tux with his thumb out trying to get a ride.

Well, this big old dilapidated truck stopped, and we climbed in. The driver took us right up to the front of the church. I was a little embarrassed, but not Senator Thurmond. He wasn't embarrassed a bit. He jumped out, thanked the fellow, shook his hand, and we scooted on into the church.

MICHAEL MISHOE

Around 1977 I helped make a recommendation to Senator Thurmond to hire Raleigh Ward to be his representative in the Florence office. Raleigh actually continued to work for the Senator for the remainder of his career. He did a wonderful job for the Senator.

That summer, Senator Thurmond said he wanted to do a tour of the tobacco region of South Carolina. So Raleigh and I put together this day and a half function where we would visit some tobacco farms and markets.

When I went in to talk to the Senator about the tour, he said, "Now, I don't want to go in any fancy car. I don't want to be seen in a fancy car." He was very aware of how he wanted to come across to all these farmers. The Senator didn't want to show up in anything ostentatious like a limousine or something. He knew the farmers would be paying attention. When we went out on the tour, the Senator was dressed in a light blue leisure suit with short sleeves. I'd never seen a leisure suit with short sleeves, but there he was.

And sure enough, when a newspaper article later came out about the Senator's tobacco tour that summer, the first thing it said was something like, "Senator Thurmond arrived in a 1968 Chevrolet Impala." Raleigh Ward's grandmother had just given him her car. So we took the Senator around to all those tobacco farms in Raleigh's grandmother's old Chevy Impala. That car was a big hit with the farmers. Leave it to Senator Thurmond!

STEPHEN L. JONES

This is a story Lew Beasley used to tell. Lew was the Senator's Administrative Assistant for a time. He has since passed away. This was when the Senator was running against Pug Ravenel in 1978. Lew and the Senator were driving from Florence, South Carolina over to Columbia on I-20. Back then we didn't have cell phones and all that. About halfway over, the car broke down. Lew pulled over to the side. The Senator started getting antsy so he said, "Mr. Beasley, I'll go ahead and catch a ride. You get another car and meet me at the next event." He went over and put his thumb out. After about five or ten minutes nobody had stopped. The Senator came back to the car. Lew said he looked kind of perplexed. Lew asked him, "Senator, what's wrong?" The Senator said, "Nobody seems to want to stop. Must be a lot of out-of-staters on the road today."

KEVIN SMITH

My first day on the job, I was standing on the sidewalk with the Senator outside the Russell Building. Jason Rossbach, the Senator's Personal Assistant at the time, was pulling the car around to get us. I figured that the Senator was naturally going to want to ride in the backseat, kind of like having a chauffeur. The car pulled around and all of a sudden the Senator just backhands me across the shoulder and says, "Get in the back!" I was shocked. He came across with that backhand to my shoulder so hard, I almost fell over. I didn't know what to say, so I just jumped in real quick. I guess you could say the Senator liked to ride shotgun.

ROBERT R. SMITH

When you drove for Senator Thurmond, he'd either be reading the newspaper or telling you how to drive. And it was only when you got the car up to a good speed, say around 70 or 80, that he would finally open the paper and start reading. Until you got going that fast, he was busy telling you how to drive. He would often ask, "What's taking so long?" How do you respond to that when you're sitting in traffic?

ELIZABETH MCFARLAND

Whenever I drove the Senator, he was notorious about not wanting to stop for red lights or stop signs. If there was no one coming, he'd say, "Keep going." I'd say, "Senator, that's a red light." He'd always say, "Well, I'm with you; it's okay." He just didn't want to waste any time at all.

JAMES FLOYD GRAHAM

was a close friend of Senator Thurmond's as well as his personal driver
from 1986 until the Senator's last day in office in early January of 2003.

Senator Thurmond and I were in Tyson's Corner, Virginia for a speaking engagement at a hotel. All of a sudden, a fifteen-minute vote was announced over the pager. That meant I had fifteen minutes to get the Senator from the hotel into the car and back to the Senate floor. I must have driven 90 to 100 miles an hour all the way back to the Capitol. We never saw a policeman. And we made it to the Capitol just in time for the vote. The whole way back there, the Senator kept asking me, "James, can't you go any faster?!"

TERRY L. WOOTEN

Senator Thurmond always liked to drive fast. He had a reputation for that. He called my office one afternoon and asked if I would like to go to the French Embassy that night for a dinner. I said, "Senator, that would be fine; yes sir, I'd like to go." He said, "Alright then, why don't you drive and pick me up about six o'clock." So I went over to his personal office at that time. We walked down, got in my car, and drove off. I knew Senator Thurmond liked to go fast. So I decided to see just how fast I could go. I said to myself,

I'm just going to see if I can maybe get him to flinch, because I know he just loves to go fast and he just takes it in stride and seldom flinches at all.

So I started down Constitution Avenue, going pretty darn fast. I was cutting in and out of cars. I was going through some yellow lights. We were going really fast for being in town on Constitution Avenue. I looked over at the Senator, and he was just looking right straight out the window. He didn't flinch in the least. Then I hit the parkway and picked up even more speed. I was really going fast on that parkway. I mean, very, very fast, cutting in and out of heavy traffic. The Senator never said a word. He looked right out that window just as comfortable as can be.

I started coming off the parkway, going much too fast really. As we came up to Massachusetts Avenue the light was red. So I slammed on the brakes and skidded up to the line. The Senator hadn't flinched through the whole ride. We're sitting there at the red light and he leaned over, tapped me on my leg, and said, "Mr. Wooten if you don't work out as my Chief Counsel, I'm going to make you my driver."

FRANKI ROBERTS

Senator Thurmond was quite a driver. Sometimes the staff would drive him to the airport. He always said it was an eight-minute drive. If anybody got in our way, he would yell, "Honk your horn! Honk your horn! Put 'em on notice!"

STEPHEN L. JONES

I used to hate to get on the road with him. You didn't know whether it was worse for him to drive and you'd almost get killed, or for you to drive and have to put up with his backseat driving. At the time, he had an old blue and white Ford; a Falcon I think it was. When he drove he'd always tap your leg and say, "Yep, I'm the best taxi driver in Washington!" I'd roll my eyes and say, "Yes sir."

One time we were going over to some agency. I was driving. Of course, he was backseat driving: "Go here! Go there! Scoot like a rabbit! Scoot like a rabbit!" It would just about drive you crazy. We came up at one point and skidded to a stop at a red light.

By the time I stopped, a blind fellow came out of nowhere and started walking right in front of the car, tapping with his cane, going across the road. I looked at the Senator and he looked at me. I said, "Phew! I'm relieved we didn't try and run that red light. We would have been in trouble, wouldn't we?!" The Senator looked at me; he smiled and said, "Yeah, sure would have been a lot of paperwork, wouldn't it?" He laughed for a bit and said, "Aw, you know I didn't mean that."

BILL TUTEN

This is one of my favorite stories about the Senator. The funniest thing about it, he never said one word when this happened, not one word. I was driving him in to work one morning. Of course, he was in the passenger seat as always. He said he sat up there because that's where the action was. We naturally got caught in D.C. traffic. We were sitting at a stop light at the bottom of Capitol Hill, getting ready to cross Independence Avenue, when the car phone rang. It was Jason Rossbach. He said, "Where the heck are you? We're supposed to walk into the Senate in two minutes!" Senator Thurmond was President Pro Tem at the time, and they were waiting on him to open the Senate that morning. I said, "Jason, I'll have him there."

I could see the light was getting ready to change. I said, "Senator, when this light turns, we're going to take off real fast. And we're going to go around those statues and fountains in front of the Capitol very fast. We've got two minutes to get you to the Senate." He just looked at me. He didn't say a word. Then he very slowly reached up and grabbed the handle to hold on. He never said one word.

When that light turned green, we peeled off. I mean, we were spinning as we went around those circles. I flashed the lights, they opened the gate, and we got him in to open the Senate on time. It was so funny, the way he looked at me and didn't say a word. His arm just went straight up and grabbed a hold of that handle. I bet he wished he could have ridden like that more often.

TERRY L. WOOTEN

On this one occasion I had gone with the Senator to the White House for a swearing-in ceremony. When we got out, there was some type of demonstration or parade going on, so we couldn't get back over to where the car was parked. The Senator said, "I'll never get back to the car! I've got to go!" There were some U.S. Marshals there, and they offered to give us a ride back up to the office. So we got in the car and off we went.

Well, the car came up to a red light. The agent driving the car hit the siren to get us through that red light. The lights were flashing and the siren was going. So the Senator's sitting there in the passenger seat. He looked over and said, "Now, how do you make that siren sound?" The guy said, "You just push this button right here." So the Senator said, "Let me try that." He pushes the button and the siren goes off. He really enjoyed that. When we came up to the next red light, the Senator said, "You go ahead and drive, I'll hit the siren." So the Senator's working the siren as we're driving through D.C. traffic. He hit that siren through every light.

We got to the door of the office building. I got out of the back, and the Senator got out of the front. He leaned into the window and told the agent, "Look here, how about you go to work on this right away. I need one of these sirens for my car. I got to have one right away! Get me one down here and get it put in my car!"

WILLIAM C. PLOWDEN, JR.

One night we were driving from Camden, and the car we were riding in broke down. It just stopped. We couldn't get it started again. I said, "Senator, we'd better do something because we're going to be late for our appointments in Columbia." So he said, "Let's get out here and bum a ride." So we did. The Senator waved his thumb at the first car that came along, but they went right on by. The second car came along, and the same thing happened. He looked at me and said, "Bill Plowden, there's a lot of foreigners passing through South Carolina tonight."

WILLIAM W. WILKINS

Senator Thurmond was so urgent about everything. No matter what it was, everything had to be done right then. I remember one time I was driving him somewhere in Washington. We'd reach a red light and he'd say, "Billy, go ahead and run that light; nobody's coming and we can't waste time!" And of course I'd run it.

We were going to the Department of Justice once to meet with the Attorney General. The Senator said, "Turn right here; it's a shortcut!" I said, "Senator that's a one-way street." He looked and said, "No cars are coming; go ahead!" So I drove down the street, promptly meeting a D.C. patrol car. I stopped and the officer drove up alongside our car. I yelled out the window, "Strom Thurmond!" and the policeman just stuck his hand out and waved us on. I think he was used to that.

BUD ALBRIGHT

We were always late everywhere we went. He always wanted you to drive as fast as possible. For some reason, it seemed like he could never get to the airport on time. One time I picked him up just outside the Capitol. It was summertime, so there were a lot of tours going on with lots of people walking around. The Senator opened the door to the car and stood on the edge there with one hand on the door and the other hand on the roof. And he started screaming at all the tourists in the street, "Get out of the way! Get out of the way! Strom Thurmond, United States Senator, coming through! I got to get to the airport! Get out of the way!"

CRAIG METZ

A former Thurmond staffer, Ken Black, has unfortunately passed away. But Ken used to tell the unforgettable story of having to drive the Senator to the airport one time. Evidently Ken wasn't driving fast enough for Senator Thurmond. So the Senator made Ken pull over and he got behind the wheel instead. Ken said he was driving so fast that he lost control of the car and impaled it on some type of concrete embankment. The Senator supposedly said, "Well, I'm going to have to leave you because I can't miss my plane." So he hopped out, flagged down a car, and hitched a ride to the airport. The Capitol Police handled the accident. I think they told Ken it wasn't the first time that had happened.

JOHN R. STEER

About 1978 the Senator and Mrs. Thurmond went to one of the Carolina home football games. I was driving them in my little car. At halftime we had to leave to get to the airport. But they had all these traffic barriers and police officers out there to control the crowds. Getting through all the barriers was a bit of a challenge. We'd pull up to a traffic barrier and the Senator would stick his head out the window and yell, "Strom Thurmond! Got to get to the airport!" Usually he'd get good cooperation. As we drove through, he'd hand the police officer a pen and say, "I'm running for reelection. Here's a pen; I'd appreciate it if you'd vote for me!"

Well, we came up to one traffic barrier, but the police officer didn't respond. We couldn't get through. So Mrs. Thurmond said, "Strom! Throw him a pen! Throw him a pen!" So the Senator grabbed a pen and threw it at the police officer. The young man was so astounded. He didn't know at first what was being thrown at him from this little car. He tried to duck, but the pen hit him square in the chest. Needless to say that got his attention. He moved the barrier, and we got the Senator to the airport on time.

MICHAEL MISHOE

Senator Thurmond had a unique ability to be one heck of a front-seat driver. I drove him to the airport many times. He'd start out by saying, "Now Mr. Mishoe, be careful changing lanes. Eighty percent of accidents occur when you're changing lanes. So you be careful!" He spent the entire time commenting on your driving. And then if a car got in front of you, he'd say, "Why'd you let him do that?!" He never let up, never. It was amazing.

GEORGE LAUFFER

In 1993 Senator Thurmond and Senator Hollings were very active trying to defend the Charleston Navy Complex. We were in Charleston at the time, where the Base Closing Commission was holding hearings to review the matter. It just so happened that on that particular trip, we had to stay over for the weekend. We had Sunday morning free. So Senator Thurmond called me up and said, "Let's go for a ride."

He had a SLED driver [South Carolina Law Enforcement Division]. They often drove for him when he was in the state. We had just finished eating breakfast at the hotel; it was about nine o'clock in the morning. We went out and jumped in the car and started driving around Charleston. We ended up on Isle of Palms where Senator Hollings lived. The driver pointed out that this was the complex that Senator Hollings lived in. So Senator Thurmond said, "Come on; let's go drive in and see what Fritz's house looks like."

It was a gated community. The security guard said, "What business do you have here?" Senator Thurmond said, "Oh, we just wanted to see Fritz's house." The guard said, "That's not enough business to go in there." So the driver said, "Don't you know who this is? This is Senator Strom Thurmond." The guard said, "Yeah, I know who it is. But he still has no business going in there just to look around." So Senator Thurmond dutifully said, "Let's not cause a fuss. Forget it." So we turned around, went back to Charleston, and did our business that day.

At a reception that afternoon, Senator Hollings and Senator Thurmond got to chatting. Senator Thurmond told him, "You know what happened to me this morning?" And he relayed that particular incident. Senator Hollings without hesitation looked right at Senator Thurmond and said, "I'm going to have to give that security guard a raise for keeping out the riff-raff."

KEVIN SMITH

When I would drive Senator Thurmond in to work in the mornings, most of the time he would just read the paper. He might mention certain articles he came across; he might ask me what I knew about something in the news. Obviously the traffic getting in to Washington in the morning is unbearable. We'd always get caught in it. The Senator would look around at the cars and say, "I can't imagine what all this traffic is for." He said that every day, without fail. I always said, "I don't know Senator; they're going slow today."

He was such a notorious backseat driver. All of a sudden he would say, "Can't you go around them? Let's see if we can't get over here." He'd start looking over his shoulder to see what was coming. He'd tell me, "Get on in that lane over there! We can get around these folks!" The whole time I'm scared to death, thinking, that's all I need to do is cut somebody off with Senator Thurmond in the car with me. Not only is he 98-years old and some sort of big accident could hurt him, but there goes my job too!

Interestingly enough, on the way back home he always said, "Now, don't go too fast out here because the cops are bad." It was always "hurry up" on the way in to work. But then on the way back home, he said, "I don't want you to go over 50; the cops out here are bad. I want you to just keep it around 45 and we'll be okay. And stop for all red lights!"

MARY CHAPMAN WEBSTER

Senator Thurmond drove like a maniac. I was going somewhere with him one night and of course we were late. We were on Connecticut Avenue. The traffic in the right-hand lane going in the direction we wanted to go was bumper to bumper. But there was nothing in the left hand lane coming towards us. The Senator was looking this way and that way. He said, "Miss Chapman, we're going to be late! We're going to be late!" I said, "Senator, if we're late, we're late. We can't help the traffic."

With that, he drove the car into the left-hand lane of oncoming traffic, of which there was none, and he drove on the wrong side of the road! He kept going until this car started coming straight at us and laid on its horn. The Senator just eased to the right to get out of the way, then kept going.

BUD ALBRIGHT

We were campaigning, driving down the road somewhere in the backwoods of South Carolina. It was real late at night. The Senator, of course, liked to go fast. He never wanted to waste any time, so we were zipping along; I must have been going about 90 miles an hour up and down those contoured roads in the back country. The Senator had put his seat back and was kind of dozing off.

I went over one of the hills and there was a policeman sitting right there on the side of the road. I started to slow down. As soon as I took my foot off the gas, the Senator said, "What's happening?" I said, "We're getting pulled." He just said, "Oh."

I stopped and got out of the car. But the Senator didn't get out with me. I kept waiting for him to get out, but he didn't move. So I went ahead and walked on back to the policeman. He asked me, "What are you flying down the road for?" I said, "I'm driving Strom Thurmond, Senator Thurmond, United States Senator." He chuckled, "Yeah right." I said, "I am; I am. He's in the car up there." And I thought to myself, gosh, won't he get out and wave or something? Why doesn't he get out?

Finally, the door opened and out stepped the Senator. He reached in the backseat and got that highway patrolman's hat he always wore when he campaigned. He plopped it on his head and came strolling over. Of course, the policeman immediately recognized him and the hat.

The Senator stuck his hand out and said, "Hello officer, I'm Strom Thurmond, United States Senator, running for reelection! You fellas sure do a fine job patrolling the roads. You put your lives on the line every day to protect us, and we sure appreciate everything." He went on and on. Then he said, "I really would appreciate your vote for reelection." With that, he kind of stretched and looked at his wristwatch and said, "Good gracious look at what time it is! We got to go!" And he slapped me on the back and pushed me back towards the car. He said to the policeman, "Officer, it's so good to see you; you take care and keep the roads safe!"

The highway patrolman was still standing there with his pad trying to write me a ticket as we got back in the car. He didn't know what to do. He kind of waved us on and said, "Uh, okay." The Senator tossed his hat in the backseat; he leaned his seat back and closed his eyes. We pulled back out on the road. I was just astounded. The Senator finally rolled his head over and looked at me and said, "You thought I was going to leave you out there, didn't you?"

Duke Short and Senator Thurmond "Born to be Wild".

TOM WOLFF 11-16-99

Duke, you and I were "Born to be wild"
Good to have you at my side
Strom Thurmond
November 15, 2001

When you travel with some Senators, there could be a lot of wasted motion. Put it this way:
Senator Thurmond was not the kind of person who was in favor of wasted motion.
– Arnold Punaro –

On the Road

TRAVELS WITH STROM

For most people, getting to know Senator Thurmond meant letting go of assumptions and impressions they'd previously had about him. Time and again, the Senator surprised new staff and new colleagues with his commitment to frugality, his enthusiasm for exercise, and his bold but caring ways of interacting with others.

If new colleagues did not discover these features of Senator Thurmond's personality in other ways, they certainly did so if they traveled with him. Being on the road with the Senator was never a dull occasion, and the people who traveled with him never forgot their experiences.

ARNOLD PUNARO

Back in the '70s I was invited to go on one of the Military Construction Subcommittee, or MilCon, trips overseas. Senator Thurmond was the ranking member on the MilCon Subcommittee. Jim Smith was the great staffer on that Subcommittee. Jim was a retired Army officer, and he had a PhD in civil engineering. So he did all the MilCon work. That was a real honor for a young staffer like me to travel with Jim Smith, who was a legend, and Senator Thurmond, who was an even greater legend. I think Frank Norton was our Army Liaison Escort Officer on that trip.

On the way to Europe we stayed in London at the Grosvenor Hotel. When we got in, I went right to sleep. About 0600 I heard this loud pounding on my door. I opened the door and there's Senator Thurmond in his jogging clothes saying, "Let's go! Let's go! Let's go! Up and out! We got to do our morning PT!" I didn't know I'd even signed up for that. He rousted everybody out of bed: me, Jim Smith, and poor ol' Frank Norton. I was still in the Marine Corps Reserve, and I thought I was in good shape. That is, until I ended up jogging with Senator Thurmond. We got out there, and he pounded us into the dirt. I don't think we had more than a couple of hours rest, but there he was, up and at' em!

Throughout the trip he maintained a furious schedule. We didn't have a minute to rest the entire time. That was my first experience traveling with Senator Thurmond. From then on out whenever they would call and say, "Hey, Senator Thurmond's going on a trip overseas; you want to go?" I'd say, "Well, I'm not sure I can make that!" Of course I'm kidding. The bottom line is that Senator Thurmond was just a pleasure to travel with. He was very engaged, very active, very considerate of the staff, and he always wanted to get things done in a timely fashion. When you travel with some Senators, there could be a lot of wasted motion. Put it this way: Senator Thurmond was not the kind of person who was in favor of wasted motion.

JAMES B. EDWARDS

When Ronald Reagan was President, he asked Strom to represent him at the Paris Air Show. He took a lot of his friends with him on the trip. I was fortunate to go with him. During the flight over, I had to get up at one point, and I stumbled over something in the aisle. I looked down. It was Senator Thurmond sleeping on the floor! It didn't wake him up at all that I stumbled into him. He had given his chair to a lady because her chair didn't recline. He just stretched out and slept on the floor.

In Paris, a translator introduced the French President Mitterrand to Strom Thurmond. Mitterrand didn't pay much attention to him at first. Then the translator told Mitterrand that Senator Thurmond flew a glider in the Normandy invasion the morning before D-Day. With that, Mitterrand turned around and in French said, "Thank you very much." Then he grabbed Strom Thurmond and kissed him on each cheek, as they do in France. I looked at Strom. He seemed to appreciate Mitterrand's thanks, but he didn't appreciate that kiss.

STEVE SALEM

is Executive Director of the Cal Ripken, Sr. Foundation.

In the Spring of 1992 Senator Thurmond received the Ellis Island Medal of Honor in New York City. My boss, Robbie Callaway, asked me to meet the Senator up there at the airport, take him to a reception for the award winners, then get him over to his hotel that evening. Robbie, who was also receiving the award, planned to meet him the next morning and take him to the ceremony.

I was just out of law school at the time. I went with a buddy of mine and we met the Senator at the airport. Someone from the Ellis Island group had sent a limousine for the Senator. But he told the limo driver, in this great southern drawl, "You're here to get me, but I'm going to ride with these young guys." So we drove him on into New York to the reception. He stayed for about an hour and had a good time, then said he was tired and ready to go.

We headed out to the parking garage where we'd left the car, but there was a big argument going on. Somebody had blocked the exit with a car, and we couldn't get out. We waited a little while for the car to move. Finally the Senator got out of our car, walked up to the guys, and asked them what was going on. I think the guy didn't want to pay. He was yelling that he was being charged too much or something like that. Senator Thurmond tried to mediate the problem. He said, "Do you know who I am?" Again, he had that great southern drawl. We're in the middle of New York City at 11 o'clock at night, stuck in a parking garage with these rowdy hoodlums. The Senator said, "Now, the police are going to come. What are you going to accomplish with all this?" The guys yelled, "We don't care! We're not moving!"

He finally comes back to the car and said, "Let's just walk." We grabbed his bags, but he wouldn't let us carry them. I said, "Senator, it's about fifteen blocks to the hotel." He said, "I don't care. I can carry my own bags. You two just try and keep up." So we walked. He told us stories as we went, the whole time carrying these two heavy bags. He absolutely refused to let us help him with them. We went the fifteen blocks at a running pace. It was probably midnight by the time we got to the hotel. We got him checked in and made sure he found his room. That's when he gave us each a Pro Tem key chain.

He later sent me a letter thanking me for helping me get around the city. It was an amazing experience watching a 90-year-old man try and mediate a fight between hoodlums, then grab these two bags and practically run fifteen blocks to his hotel. It was great, a night I'll never forget.

ANTHONY PRINCIPI

Shortly after I arrived to serve as the Staff Director and the Republican Chief Counsel on the Armed Services Committee, I learned that I'd be traveling to South Carolina with the Senator. It would be my first trip with him. I was real excited, thinking about the great inns and restaurants in Charleston. Then I got a call from Holly. She said, "Tony, can you come over? I want to chat with you for a moment." So I went over to see Holly.

She said, "Now Tony, I know this is your first trip with the Senator. I just wanted to apprise you of a couple of things as to the way the Senator travels. Well, he's very fiscally conservative and very conscious of the tax payer's dollar." I said, "Sure, that's fine, Holly." She said, "I don't think you understand. The Senator does not like to spend more than $29 a night on a hotel room." I asked her, "Do they have government rates that low?" Holly said, "No, they don't. So you'll probably be staying outside of town at a motel near the freeway. But don't worry, a state trooper will be picking you up at the airport." "A what?!" She said, "A state trooper will take care of you." Well, I didn't know quite what to expect. From the great inns of Charleston to a motel off the interstate, just like that.

When I got off the plane in South Carolina, sure enough, there was a state trooper waiting for me. He was kind of grumbling. I asked him what was wrong. He said, "I can't believe this. I've got to protect you guys all night." I asked why. He said, "Wait til you see where you're staying." He drove me out to a motel in a drug-ridden area. It was not the kind of motel where you'd want to take your shoes off, put it that way; the kind of place where you'd be more comfortable sleeping in your clothes. Of course, when the Senator got there, he thought it was the greatest place in the world. And all that night we had state troopers right outside our window. We sure saved a lot of money on the hotel room, but I don't know how much the state troopers cost! So that was my introduction to traveling with Senator Thurmond.

ARNOLD PUNARO

I recall on another trip with Senator Thurmond we went to Russia to meet with Gorbachev, right after he had come to power. Senator Nunn was there, as was Senator Robert Byrd, Senator Warner, and a couple of others. The whole purpose of the trip was for this group of high-level Senators to interface with Gorbachev so that they could really take a measure of the man, find out if this guy was as different as everybody thought he was. It was a pretty seminal meeting. In fact it was so important, the President had Senator Thurmond come down and debrief him when we got back. Of course, all the things that people were speculating about Gorbachev we found to be true. That was an important part of our report.

When it came to the meeting with Gorbachev, we sat down and coordinated what each Senator was going to say to him. We scripted the meeting so that each Senator had his own particular thing he was supposed to say; that way they wouldn't duplicate one another and take each other's time. Everyone agreed that this was the most well-orchestrated way to go about it.

So there we were in the meeting with Gorbachev. He understood English, but everything was done through translators so there were delays. It finally rolled around to Senator Thurmond. It had been agreed that because he was a veteran of World War II and the Normandy invasion, and because the Americans and Russians were allies at that time, he would make some very nice comments about the Russian-American relationship during World War II, and tell Gorbachev how we can have that kind of relationship again. We had done some research and had learned that Gorbachev's father had fought in some of the key battles in World War II. We had agreed as well that Senator Thurmond would say something nice about Gorbachev's father's service in the war.

So here it came, time for Senator Thurmond to talk. It had been all smiles up to that point. And then Senator Thurmond got going. He started by talking about South Carolina. Certainly it was important for Gorbachev to understand a little bit about South Carolina. That wasn't in the script, but I think Senator Thurmond felt that was important. Anyway, then he got started on World War II. He talked a little bit about his own service. We were all thinking, okay, he's back on track with what he's supposed to say.

But then he got cranked up and started talking about the Bolsheviks and the Communists. I could tell right then that people were thinking, uh-oh, this may not be going where it's supposed to be going. To make a long story short, he started saying something like: "Well, we could have beat the Ruskies into Berlin. But we got held up, so the Russians could look good. And you guys didn't have a lot of great battles. I understand your father fought in such-a-such a battle. Let me tell you about some real battles."

In any event, needless to say he didn't stay with the script. And he certainly gave his own impression of World War II. But at the end, as Senator Thurmond always did, he brought everything back to an even keel and ended on a high note. When he was done talking, he got up and walked over to Gorbachev and gave him one of his key chains! The U.S. delegation was about to bust a gut over this harangue about the poor Russian fighting performance during World War II. But there he was in a very nice gesture that he did in such a meaningful way. He gave Gorbachev a genuine Strom Thurmond President Pro Tem key chain!

BO BLUDWORTH

Not long after taking over as Majority Leader in the Senate, Senator Dole led a Congressional Delegation on a tour of NATO countries. Senator Thurmond was one of the Senators on that trip. I went along as the Escort Officer. We stopped in London on our way over to Europe. While we were there, we attended Easter Services at Westminster Abbey. At one point during the service we were instructed to kneel. As we were going to kneel, Senator Thurmond leaned over to me and whispered — of course, in the quiet of Westminster Abbey, everyone could hear what he said. The Senator's whisper wasn't exactly quiet. He said, "Bo, I thought this was a Protestant church!" The Senator's voice seemed to echo through the Abbey. Everybody was sort of biting their lip not to laugh.

On another bipartisan Congressional Delegation we went to Russia. I believe we were in Kiev, Russia, which is now the Ukraine. We were getting ready to check out and the Senator came up to me and said, "Bo, I'm going to take a couple of little things home with me. I've picked up a couple of these Communist bath towels. I want to take 'em back and show them to my textile people. Make sure they know that here at the hotel, because I want to pay for them."

So I went up to the Russians and told them we wanted to pay for a couple of these towels. The guy looked at me like I was crazy. The Senator was so insistent about it, I wanted to make sure we handled it properly. So we got the interpreter there who could explain to them exactly what we wanted to do. The whole time the Russians are trying to figure out why Senator Thurmond wants these towels. You could see them asking each other, what is it about the towels?! We didn't want an international incident. The Senator just wanted some of those Communist bath towels. We probably went through ten minutes of this back and forth. They were still trying to figure out whether it was some kind of plot. They kept asking, "Why do you need these towels?"

Finally, after all that, they came up with a figure that we could give them for the towels. But right then the Senator came over and said, "Bo, did you get this all squared away with them?" I said, "Yes sir, we're going to pay them for these two towels just like you wanted." Then he said, "Now, I've got this smaller towel here, but it's so small I don't guess that matters. I'm just going to take this one too, but we won't say anything about this third one." Of course, the Russian guy was standing right there and he heard the whole thing. So I just handed him a bunch of money and told him not to worry about it.

All the Russians were looking around talking, trying their very best to figure out what was so important about these bath towels. The Senator wanted those Communist towels so the folks in the textile industry could see how poor the quality of craftsmanship is in Russia versus America. It was classic Thurmond. He was dead serious about it too. The Russians were trying to figure out if the Senator had discovered some crack in their national security hidden in the bath towels!

From Burgess's Store to the Great Wall of China

THE FAME AND NOTORIETY OF STROM THURMOND

*S*enator Thurmond was a famous man, and he was well aware of it. Like all politicians, he enjoyed the notoriety immensely. No matter where we went around the world, he was not only recognized, but people also wanted to shake his hand and say hello. I'll never forget the moment the Senator climbed to the top of the Great Wall of China only to hear an American tourist yell out, "Look! It's Strom Thurmond! Hey Strom! We're from Charleston!"

I can recall only one time Senator Thurmond confided in me that he wished he wasn't so famous. We were walking through the Capitol one day when a group of very attractive female tourists passed by. Of course they wanted to meet the Senator and have their picture taken with him. He was very happy to oblige them. As we walked away, he said to me, "Duke, wouldn't it be something if you were a bachelor in Washington with all these pretty girls around here? But everybody knows me; I couldn't get away with anything!"

Despite his fame, the Senator — as we say in the South — never got above his raising. He might have been one of the most recognizable, well-known individuals in the entire world, yet there was absolutely nothing pretentious about him. I recall a formal dinner he and I attended in Berlin. Most of the prominent and powerful people from across Germany were there. The table was incredibly long and laid out with all sorts of fancy dishes. Each place setting had the most silverware I'd ever seen in my life. There must have been ten forks, ten knives, and more spoons than I could count. No one seemed to know the proper utensil to use for each course. I glanced over at Senator Thurmond and watched him pick up the first fork he came to. He used that same fork throughout the entire meal. He just wasn't overly concerned about social eti-

ELIZABETH MCFARLAND

Senator Strom Thurmond in the Trenton Peach Festival in 1995, the year before he ran for Senate for the last time. The shirt was a gift from Strom Jr. that very morning. The horse is Lucky Miss Mocha, a Grand Champion Halter Mare.

quette. Those kind of things didn't bother him.

He loved the crowds, loved the attention, and loved being recognized. But he was not a pretentious man. In many respects, until his last breath, he was just a fella from South Carolina. I know that he thought of himself that way. He could meet Kings and Queens, janitors or elevator operators, and he treated them all the same way — with great respect, attention, and compassion.

BUTLER DERRICK

Strom Thurmond covered South Carolina like a blanket. I ran into him all the time at various political things. I remember specifically he always rode a horse in the Trenton Peach Festival Parade. When he was in his mid to late 80s, I said "Strom, I know it's politically desirable to ride that horse. But if that horse throws you off it's going to break every bone in your body; you know you're not 21-years old." He said, "Whoa Butler, don't you worry about that. All you got to do is show those horses who's boss."

ELIZABETH MCFARLAND

The Senator was always a very good equestrian. He grew up with horses, and he really enjoyed riding them, especially in parades. Whenever he went to a parade, they usually had a convertible ready for him to ride in. But if he saw anybody with a horse, he would commandeer the horse for himself to ride.

He called us one morning and said, "I'm going to be up at the Trenton Peach Festival; do you have a horse I could ride?" Well, we do have quarter horses which are good riding horses and pretty sensible and smart. My husband did have this one mare that's just beautiful. She'd been ridden before but never in a parade. We decided that she would probably do okay. So we took her up to Trenton for the Senator.

We got to the parade, and they put that mare right in front of the Marine Corps Band. If you don't know about horses, they do tend to get a little spooked, especially with a marching band right behind them! But the Senator had no qualms about it. When the band started playing that horse started prancing around a little bit. But he took right hold of her and off they went, leading the parade. After a few steps, that mare recognized she had a master horseman on her and she'd better behave. He ended up riding her in several parades. Anybody else that was less of a horseman would have been a little intimidated, but not Strom Thurmond.

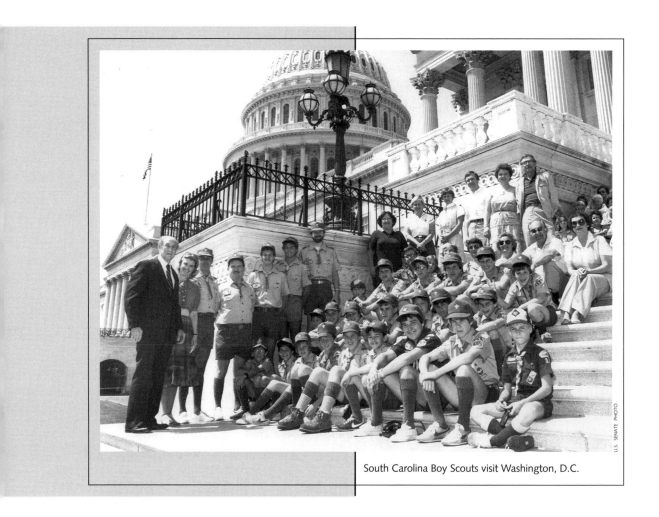

South Carolina Boy Scouts visit Washington, D.C.

SUSAN PELTER

Senator Thurmond liked things to be just so. When I first started out as low person on the totem pole in the press office, one of my responsibilities was to set up the photos with visitors. Everybody wanted to have their picture made with the Senator. And every group that came up from South Carolina — the Future Farmers of America, the 4H, the marching band from the high school — they all wanted to meet Senator Thurmond and have their picture taken.

We'd start by lining everybody up on the steps of the Capitol. The Senator would zoom in and shake every single person's hand in the whole group no matter what kind of hurry he was in. If you didn't have them arranged on the steps to his satisfaction by the time he got there, he would rearrange them all. It didn't matter if he was supposed to meet with the President; by gosh, he was going to make sure they were lined up in an appropriately symmetrical fashion, and he was going to shake everyone's hand.

It was aggravating and endearing at the same time. He'd literally move people around on the steps and set up the shot: "You come over here now!" And he'd say, "You're taller than her; step back a step. How is she going to see over you? You boy with the red hair, get back; get back!" Usually this was happening at the height of summer in Washington, D.C. when it's a million degrees and everyone is sweating. The kids had probably straggled down the mall from the Smithsonian; they were wiped out. But the Senator was fresh as a daisy.

BECKY FLEMING

When I first started in Senator Thurmond's office, I worked as a receptionist in the front office. As a part our duties, every morning we got a list of the obituaries that had run in the South Carolina newspapers that day. The Senator would go through the list name by name to see if there was anyone he had known or a family he knew. We would then send out letters of condolence or in some circumstances he would call the family personally to say how sorry he was.

One morning I went to get the list from him, and he told me there was a name on it who sounded familiar to him. "I think I bought a mattress from that man back in the early '60s." So he asked me to call the man's wife and express his condolences on the death of her husband. He also asked me to check and see if he did buy a mattress from the man. I walked back out to my desk thinking, "Who is going to remember something like that?"

I called the lady and told her how sorry the Senator was to hear about her husband's death. She said, "Do you know, I have not spoken to Strom since he bought a mattress from my husband and me; it must have been back in the early '60s." Senator Thurmond was 95-years old at the time. He had the most amazing memory for little things like that. It didn't matter how old he got; he could remember almost everything.

ALFONSE D'AMATO

I remember one day I had a group of Hasidic Jewish constituents visiting me in Washington. Senator Thurmond came in the room to say hello. He got up there, looked out and saw all these people in black with beards, wearing their black hats. And he said, "Whoa! You've got all these Amish people here!" Of course, he said it like "Aim-ish." The Rabbi and his people were a little taken aback. But they thought it was funny. Senator Thurmond said something like, "You Aim-ish people are hardworking, God-fearing people. I want to commend you. You're hardworking farmers; you have high moral values, and you worship the Lord." He went on and on. Of course, nobody would tell him they weren't "Aim-ish." They got the greatest kick out of that. They fell down laughing, and this is a very serious group. They were absolutely bowled over laughing. They loved Strom. He was so warm and funny. He really helped me earn their support.

MARY CHAPMAN WEBSTER

In the summer of 1960, when I was fourteen, my mother and dad took my sister and me on a family trip to Washington. And of course you just don't go to Washington and not go by to visit Senator Thurmond. Miss Jean, his first wife, had just recently died. He was very shaken up by her death. We went by his office. Mother and Daddy had something else to do on Capitol Hill, and we all decided to meet up for lunch later in the Senate Dining Room. So my sister and I went with Senator Thurmond to see the Capitol.

As we were going to the subway train which is beneath the office building, we saw John F. Kennedy walking our way. At that time he was running for President, and Thurmond was still a Democrat. Once we saw Kennedy coming our jaws dropped. Senator Thurmond said, "Jack! Come over here and meet my pretty little friends!" My sister and I were all of fourteen and twelve. Jack Kennedy shook our hands and gave us each a JFK button, which I don't think we took off for a month!

So in my memory, Kennedy is directly associated with Thurmond because I'll never forget that moment when Strom Thurmond introduced me to Jack Kennedy. I couldn't even eat lunch after that; I was too excited. My parents, who were very strong Republicans, were none too amused when my sister and I showed up for lunch wearing JFK buttons.

WILLIAM C. PLOWDEN, JR.

I remember one trip Senator Thurmond and I took to California. He was retiring as Governor of South Carolina at the time, so this must have been back in the early 1950s. We went out there for a meeting of the Reserve Officers Association. After the meeting, there were some people who wanted to get a picture of him up on the roof of the hotel. So I arranged that for them.

When we got up there, we discovered they wanted him to have his picture taken with a beauty queen who was Miss California at that time. He was very happy to have his picture made with that pretty girl. But when it came time to take the picture, it turned out they wanted him to hand her a mint julep and she was going to be handing him a glass of orange juice. When he saw that mint julep he said, "Bill Plowden! Come get in this picture right now! You've got to hand this girl the whiskey. I can't be seen handing this young girl a whiskey!"

ELAINE ROGERS

I remember the time the USO gave Senator Thurmond the Spirit of Hope Award named in honor of Bob Hope. It was a very emotional event because we brought people he had known throughout his life to the reception on the Hill. There were quite a lot of people there. We also invited an elderly man and woman who had been volunteering for the USO since it formed in 1941. In fact, those two people actually met at a USO dance, later got married, and volunteered for us all those years. At the awards reception, I introduced them to the Senator. He was so wonderful to them.

Everybody at the event was rushing up to meet Senator Thurmond, to say hello and get their picture made with him. He was mobbed by people. I walked up through the crowd and kind of tugged on his sleeve and whispered to him that this elderly couple really wanted to have their picture taken with him if it was possible. The Senator immediately stopped everything. He said, "Everybody else can wait right now. I'm going to go take my picture with these USO volunteers." It was such a touching moment to see how he singled them out and showed them such attention. Later, when he made his remarks to the audience, he talked about that couple and thanked them for all their contributions to the USO. That touched my heart so much.

JOHNNY MACK BROWN

*is the U.S. Marshal for the District of South Carolina. He first met
Senator Thurmond in 1972 when he was asked to represent law
enforcement in the Senator's reelection campaign.*

One of my greatest memories of Senator Thurmond was when I was President of the National Sheriffs' Association in 1993-94. He came to a congressional drop-in we hosted. It seemed like every sheriff there wanted to meet Senator Thurmond and have his picture taken with him. I spent the whole time introducing him to people. He was so gracious and stood there for so long shaking hands. Everywhere I went, people wanted to meet Senator Thurmond. He was not only South Carolina's Senator. He was a well-known and well-liked Senator throughout this country.

KEVIN SMITH

When people came to the office to meet Senator Thurmond, it was really quite something to see their reactions and the looks on their faces. They were just in awe, like they'd never seen such a thing in their life. They couldn't actually believe they were standing there talking with Strom Thurmond. Everybody who walked into that office wanted to have their picture taken with him. And he was happy to do that. He'd shake hands and smile for pictures all day long if somebody asked him to. I felt so lucky to be a part of all that. It's something I will never forget. I thank God I had that opportunity to know him and to work with him.

JOHN DECROSTA

In South Carolina, you are hard-pressed to find someone who hasn't met Strom Thurmond or someone he hasn't done a favor for. Even outside of South Carolina, or even outside of Washington, you can very easily run into people who have a Strom Thurmond anecdote to share with you.

I recall the time a Polish journalist came in to interview the Senator some years ago. I was Press Secretary at the time. I was chatting with him afterwards, and he told me about Strom Thurmond's powerful reputation even among people in the Eastern Bloc. They liked him, and they respected him. Somehow word had gotten through to them that there were people like Strom Thurmond in the government in the United States — people who vehemently opposed Communism, who believed that people should have the right to live in a democratic society and speak for themselves, and who believed that the notion of living in a Communist-governed country was an abhorrent concept.

That journalist from Poland told me that Senator Thurmond was an inspiration and a heroic figure to many people overseas who lived under a Communist regime. So you see, even someone visiting from Poland had a Strom Thurmond story.

ERNIE COGGINS

A young woman from the Department of Health and Environmental Control for the State of South Carolina came up to meet with the Senator one time. It turned out she was from Saluda County. When she met the Senator, they got to talking about her family. The Senator said, "Oh, I knew your great-grandfather." And he went into all these wonderful stories about her family that this woman had never heard before. Then he proceeded to tell her the history of her mother's family, people he had known personally. I literally had to lead the woman out of his office, she was so overwhelmed from the experience of meeting him. And she wasn't the only one. Episodes like that happened pretty often.

HENRY MCMASTER

Senator Thurmond always treated people with dignity and respect. I never saw or heard him belittle anybody. From the lowest to the highest, he treated everybody just alike. It was really remarkable. I'd be with him at events in the state, and people would line up to come speak to him. He was interrupted all the time. I don't know how he ever had time to eat. He'd be sitting at a plate of barbecue and every thirty-five seconds somebody would come to shake his hand. Of course, he'd get up and give everyone of them a gracious hello and spend a little time with them. He was never too busy for anybody.

It is an amazing talent and a rare quality in a man. Most people just will not do that. For some people in that position, it's a burden. They just want to be left alone. But it was a burden Senator Thurmond readily accepted. When it got right down to it, he got pure delight from pleasing and helping people. He hugged babies, had his picture made, signed autographs. Somebody would say, "Senator, will you walk over here and meet this woman? She's in a wheelchair and can't come in." He'd say, "Let's go!" He enjoyed it. He got that kind of joyous reception from people no matter where he went in the country. Everybody wanted to meet the legendary Strom Thurmond.

ARNOLD PUNARO

We got a lot of visitors to the Armed Services Committee. And we were very happy to show people around; we were quite proud of the Committee and all the work we did there. Because Senator Thurmond's office was right across the hall, I frequently called over there to see if we could bring our visitors by to meet the Senator. I'd get Holly or Duke on the phone, tell them we had a really important group of new Marine Corps Generals, for example, and ask if there was any chance we could come over and show them the Senator's office. His office was a whole history lesson in itself.

Every time I asked, Holly or Duke would say, "By all means, come on over!" Many times the Senator would be there, and he'd take the folks around personally to show them his office and to meet the staff. That's one thing I will always remember about him. He was never too busy to take time out of his day to meet with visitors. That was pretty unique on the Hill, because there weren't a lot of Senators who would do that kind of thing.

KAREN J. WILLIAMS

My daughter was married in June of 1991. I had just been seated as the mother of the bride. Now, typically once the mother of the bride is seated, that's the end of seating everybody. But I heard this commotion behind me. I turned around and there was the Senator pushing the grandparents over as he squeezed into the pew right behind me. He gave me a big smile. He was so wonderful. I think more people at the reception preferred to see him than the bride and groom.

DAVID WILKINS

The thing I will remember most is that whenever I was with the Senator, people were constantly coming up to thank him for helping their father or brother or grandmother or whomever. It could have been a military issue, or social security, or getting a passport; whatever the problem was, he solved it for them and they all wanted to thank him for it. I saw that for myself during the 1972, campaign and there was nothing different when we were out campaigning in 1996, except that there were even more people coming up to meet him and thank him. It was a continual theme of his tenure. We could have been in the town square in Laurens or Barnwell or Allendale or wherever; it didn't matter. The reaction from the crowd was the same. Everybody wanted to shake his hand, look him in the eye, and say thank you.

I remember during the '96 campaign we stopped at Clemson. No matter where we went on the campus, there was a mob of people who wanted to meet him. What impressed me most were all the young people. They obviously hadn't grown up with him like I had. And yet wherever we were, there were 20-year-olds who treated him with incredible reverence, like he was a rock star. They wanted nothing more than to shake the hand of Strom Thurmond, the man they'd probably been hearing about from their grandparents as long as they could remember.

COY JOHNSTON II

Here in South Carolina, if somebody names any five names, you either know them, you're kin to them, you know who they work for, or you have some connection. When Senator Thurmond met somebody he usually asked, "Who's your daddy?" And nine times out of ten, he knew their daddy personally or he had some connection there. He'd say, "I know your daddy. Let me tell you about the time your daddy and me…" He was like that all over the state. His roots just kind of seemed to grow everywhere. As we say in the South, he covered South Carolina like the dew covers Dixie. He flat covered it.

There wasn't any little crossroads or anybody he didn't know. And everybody just thought Strom Thurmond was the greatest thing since sliced bread. He knew their way of life. That was important. I mean, he knew how to talk to a farmer; he knew how to talk to a textile worker; he knew how to talk to a financier. He could go to all levels and be at home. Some people are born with it. I think he inherited it from his father. I think it was in the genes. He was a man with a cause to help people, to help South Carolina, to help the nation. You go anywhere in South Carolina and mention the name Strom Thurmond, it's like apple pie and Chevrolet. Democrats and Republicans, rich and poor, young and old, it didn't matter; everybody knew him and everybody respected him.

ROBERT R. SMITH

Some friends and I were walking down Assembly Street in Columbia one time with the Senator. We'd just finished eating, and he had decided we all needed a good walk. So we started heading down the street. Well, we got down to the corner of Assembly and Blossom, which is a pretty busy intersection in Columbia, and the horns started honking. People were driving by, waving, honking, yelling, "Strom!" He was waving back and working the crowd. It was fantastic. When people stopped at the stop light, he would chit chat with them. At one point, I remember he turned to me and said, "I guess I could never do anything wrong here in South Carolina because everybody knows who I am!" We all got such a big kick out of that.

DEE SHORT

Everywhere we went with the Senator, people wanted to come up and meet him. Duke and I took him down to Elsie's Magic Skillet for brunch, which we did every Sunday for many years right up until he left Washington. Once on the way home we stopped by a Lowes Home Improvement Warehouse. I'll never forget when we went in there; he was just mobbed by people. Nobody expected to look up and see Strom Thurmond walking down the aisle at a Lowes. Everybody was doing a double-take. You could see them thinking: is it him? Is it him? It is him! People were so excited to meet him and shake his hand.

Another time I took the Senator out to a Krispy Kreme for doughnuts one night. He really enjoyed that. Every time he ate those doughnuts he'd get this big contented grin on his face and say, "Why Dee, this is like eating hot sugar air!" All of the regulars at the Krispy Kreme took turns coming over to shake his hand and say hello. You could tell they were so proud that Senator Strom Thurmond was eating there with them.

HENRY SACKS

is a dear friend of Duke and Dee Short, and was a close personal friend of Senator Thurmond's.

One time Duke and Dee and her brothers, Rocky and Jordan Robinson, and I took the Senator to a very nice restaurant in Virginia called the Morrison House. We were all sitting there eating when we heard music coming from the piano bar. After dinner, the Senator wanted to see where the music was coming from. As we approached the door, the piano player saw Senator Thurmond and right away started playing "Dixie." He followed that with "Nothing Could be Finer Than to be in Carolina." Old people, young people, they all started lining up to meet him. Of course, he just loved it.

JOHN R. STEER

Driving Senator Thurmond up and down those back country roads across South Carolina was a real experience. I was out with him one time when he said, "Let's pull in here at this country store." I said, "Senator, why in the world would we stop way out here?" He said, "I'm hungry. Let's get something to eat."

I expected the store owners wouldn't know who he was; or if they did know him, I thought they would be shocked to see him walk through the door. I mean, we were out in the middle of nowhere. Well, the minute he comes in the door I heard a voice from behind the front counter say, "Hey Strom! Nice to see you again!" I should have known.

BILL TRAXLER

I was asked one day to pick up Senator Thurmond at the airport in Greenville and take him up to Cedar Mountain to join his family who was vacationing there. Now, I'd always heard that Senator Thurmond liked to stop at these little country stores to visit with his constituents when he was out traveling. He said that the reason he liked to do that was because word of his visit would travel a lot further and a lot faster than it would if had he stopped at a mall in a big city. So as we got to the mountains above River Falls, getting ready to start the trek up Caesar's Head, we came up on a small country store called Burgess's Store. I suggested to Senator Thurmond that we might stop there. He readily agreed.

We stopped in there and talked to the people for awhile. It's just a little one-room store. We got a Coca-Cola, and then we headed on back up towards Cedar Mountain. I dropped him off there and he joined his family. Then I came back to a cabin I had in a small community there. Now, from the time we left Burgess's Store til the time I got back to my cabin was about thirty or forty minutes at the most. When I was getting out of my car, people started coming up to tell me that they'd heard Strom Thurmond was in the area and had just stopped at Burgess's Store!

Two of Strom Thurmond's all time baseball heroes —
Cal Ripken, Sr. (top) and Cal Ripken, Jr.

Duke Short and Strom Thurmond enjoying ice cream, June 19, 1997.

U.S. SENATE PHOTO

One thing I will always remember about Senator Thurmond is how he kept packets of saltine crackers in his pockets. He was all the time handing those out to people saying, "Here you go. You never know when you might get hungry."

– Karen Henderson –

M&Ms, Oysters, and Pockets Full of Food

THE CULINARY STYLINGS OF SENATOR STROM THURMOND

*S*enator Thurmond loved to eat at the 116 Club on Capitol Hill. If he'd had his choice, I believe he could have eaten lunch there every day of the week. We often ate there with Preacher Whitner, President of the prestigious 116 Club, and Ed Kenney, a former staffer. Senator Thurmond enjoyed the people who worked there, Johnny Paleologos (whom the Senator called "the best club manager in the world") and his daughter Stacey (whom he called "D.C.'s greatest waitress"). He especially loved it when they offered the black-eyed peas and collards special. He would eat everything on his plate, sit back, and say, "Now that's what collards are supposed to taste like!" Then he invariably suggested we get some crab cakes to go. "Holly sure would like those. Let's take some of those crab cakes back for Holly."

The Senator would walk back into the office with the crab cakes all wrapped up. Holly, bless her heart, was always so appreciative. "Oh Senator," she would say, "you shouldn't have done that. Here, let me put them in the fridge and I'll eat them later." Well, without fail, when the time came to go home, she'd take them out of the fridge, give them to him, and he'd take the crab cakes home and eat them for dinner. "Holly, you sure you don't want these?" he would ask. "Oh no sir, Senator. I want you to take them home. Go on -- you'll enjoy them!" And that was the 116 Club routine.

On the weekends the Senator made a regular visit to Elsie's Magic Skillet down Route 1 in Alexandria. Dee and I took him there every Sunday for over a decade. Elsie Plues and all the folks down there were so good to him. Elsie specializes in honest-to-goodness down-home cooking, which was, as you might expect, Senator Thurmond's favorite style of cooking. He always ordered a big breakfast and ate every bite. And without fail, he'd even eat some of Dee's breakfast as well. I remember the first time I saw him eat a plate of country ham. He started by cutting off the fat, which I thought was very appropriate, given his strict health habits. But instead of cutting the fat and pushing it to the side, he ate it! He ate all the ham fat first! We got a big kick out of that.

JOHNNY PALEOLOGOS

is the General Manager of The 116 Club on Capitol Hill in Washington, D.C., one of Senator Thurmond's favorite restaurants.

Senator Thurmond came in for lunch maybe once or twice a week for about twenty years. He'd always try to come on Fridays when we had fish. He loved fish, collard greens, and black-eyed peas; those were his favorites. Sometimes he'd even get two orders. Whatever he didn't eat he would say, "Let me take it back to my staff." So we'd pack it up for him, and he'd stick it in his pocket and take it with him. Every time he came in here, people would come up to his table to meet him. He always enjoyed that recognition. He was so friendly to everybody.

WARREN ABERNATHY

When he was Governor, no matter who was around his office at 12 or 12:30, you had to go to the mansion with him and have lunch. It didn't matter who it was; he wanted you to join him for lunch. Usually it was something like chicken salad and asparagus. They usually cooked for five or ten guests every afternoon. If he brought more folks with him, they'd just open some more cans.

MELINDA KOUTSOUMPAS

It was common knowledge in Washington that when Senator Thurmond went to receptions he often ate a lot and even put food in his pockets before he left. Later, he would casually offer the food to people he'd run into. He was really something.

I remember one night after a reception, his pockets were just loaded down with M&Ms and little cheese squares. We were walking down the hall and a page came by, and you know, he was always offering candy to the pages. So he reached into his pocket with both hands. You could hear things rattling around in there. He held out his hands and said, "Here, you want some candy or some cheese?"

Of course the M&Ms had melted some and all the colors were mixed together. What's the page going to do? You can't say no because if you did the Senator would say, "Well, why not?!" So you just take it and smile and then turn around and put it in the wastebasket. He was just trying to be nice.

MARY CHAPMAN WEBSTER

Sometimes he'd call me up on a Sunday morning and say, "Miss Chapman! Get up! We're going to church!" So I'd have to jump out of bed, throw on a dress, and wait out in front of my apartment. Then this big black Cadillac would come flying up. Sometimes he'd be behind the wheel and other times he'd have a driver. We'd go to a Baptist Church somewhere in Washington, and then we'd go to breakfast.

I remember one time I ordered eggs and bacon. I was trying to be proper; I mean, there I am having breakfast with Senator Strom Thurmond. So I was cutting my bacon. But of course it was crisp, so it kept slipping off my plate. Senator Thurmond looked at me and said, "Miss Chapman, why don't you just pick up your bacon like everybody else does in South Carolina?"

KAREN HENDERSON

One thing I will always remember about Senator Thurmond is how he kept packets of saltine crackers in his pockets. He was all the time handing those out to people saying, "Here you go. You never know when you might get hungry."

BILL TUTEN

I went to pick the Senator up for dinner one time. He said he wanted to go to the I-Hop. He was a big fan of the I-Hop. The waitress came over to us and smiled. She kind of leaned over to me and put her hand up to her mouth and said, "You know, he was here for breakfast and lunch." I said, "Hey, he's the boss. I take him wherever he wants to go. I don't ask him when was the last time he was there." We both laughed. The Senator looked over his menu at us and wanted to know what was so funny.

I remember when my dad and I took the Senator to the Officer's Club at Bolling Air Force Base. They had a big brunch set out that day. The Senator started working on those oysters right away. He loved his oysters. He was sucking them down as fast as we could shuck them.

The man liked to eat. We went to a reception one time and there he was, a lamb chop in each hand, saying, "Eat all you want! It's free!" He always wanted to make sure we got plenty to eat. And he never wanted food to go to waste. Let's say he was eating lunch in his office; he would frequently call around to the staff to know if anybody wanted the rest of his french fries or something. "They're real good. Come get you some french fries." You never heard about things like that in the media. But he did that a lot. He was always trying to take care of people.

You'll hear a lot of people talk about how he put food in his pockets, which was true. He did that a lot. I think it had something to do with him not wanting to waste food, but it also had something to do with him being thoughtful of others. On more than one occasion I saw him loading up with food, and I'm sure everybody was thinking: yep, there goes old Strom. Well, I found out later that he was actually taking food out to his driver, James. He knew James was sitting out in the car and he wanted to make sure he got something to eat.

ELSIE PLUES

is the former owner of Elsie's Magic Skillet in Alexandria,
Virginia, where Senator Thurmond and Duke and Dee Short
went for brunch nearly every Sunday for over ten years.

Senator Thurmond loved coming to eat here. We have a family-type restaurant where he could really relax, and everybody knew him. He always extended a handshake to the men and of course gave a hug to the women. And he was never without some candy in his pocket for the children. He loved it when there were babies here. He'd go up to the high chairs and talk with the little ones. He was just such a wonderful, great man.

He loved his country ham. Every Sunday I packed a little lunch for him with some country ham that he could take home with him. And of course he loved the grits. I remember he drank water without ice. And he always wanted a pretty waitress. He seemed to be happier when he got his favorite blonde waitress to wait on him. It was like he and Duke and Dee were part of our little family here. We all miss the Senator so much.

JOSEPH R. BIDEN, JR.

I went with Strom one time to a Veteran of Foreign Wars Dinner. There were about three thousand people there. The Chairman and the Ranking Member sit up on the stage, so we were both sitting up there eating on the stage in front of everybody. They

Craig Metz, Preacher Whitner, Henry Sacks, Strom Thurmond, Dee Short, and Duke Short at the 116 Club celebrating Dee Short's birthday, October 16, 2001.

had just served the meal when along came a vote in the Senate. And of course, we had to get back for that right away. So I walked over to Strom and said, "Should we ride back up together, boss?" He said, "Yeah, yeah." Before he got up to leave, he took the napkin off his lap, put it on the table, and put the filet mignon right there in the middle of the napkin. Then he folded the napkin up and stuck it in his breast pocket! I said, "Strom, what are you doing?" He said, "My driver could use it."

BOB DOLE

We used to tease Strom that he had cellophane lining in his pockets so he could go to these receptions, put fried chicken in there, and it wouldn't get his pants greasy.

MIKE DEWINE

I always loved seeing Strom at receptions. He went to a lot of them, day and night. He worked them hard even into his late 90s. When he got there, he always went straight to the food. And he didn't nibble at the food like most people do at these things. He ate a meal. It was the darndest thing I ever saw. Then invariably, when he was done eating, you'd see him start looking around the room. He would scan the whole entire room until he saw the best-looking woman he could find. Then he'd walk straight over to her, introduce himself, and start talking. The pattern never varied. It was absolutely unbelievable. He was fantastic.

ELIZABETH MCFARLAND

I remember one visit Senator Thurmond and I made to Shoney's together. He loved their breakfast bar. There were a couple of ladies at the table next to us who were very, very overweight. One of them got up and came over and said, "Hey Senator, I'm from Edgefield and my dad is so and so." He said, "Oh yeah, I remember him." They chit chatted a little bit. Then she said, "Senator, I'm trying to get disability. Do you think you can help me with my disability?" He looked at her and said, "Well, first thing you should do is lose a lot of that weight." She said, "Yeah, I guess you're right." You could just see him thinking to himself: well, of course I'm right. The lady slowly turned around and just walked back to her table. I was thinking, only Strom Thurmond could get away with that!

DAVID T. BEST

We were down in the Senate Dining Room, and Senator Thurmond got a bowl of bean soup, cornbread, and a glass of tomato juice, no ice of course. He never wanted ice in his drinks. And he loved that Senate cornbread. Well, he put Tabasco sauce in his bean soup. I mean, he just doused that down with Tabasco sauce, a good eight or ten shakes. Then somebody came into the dining room, perhaps it was another Senator. Anyway, Senator Thurmond went over to their table to say hello. Then he came back and sat down. First thing he did was grab the Tabasco sauce and start putting more into his soup. I said, "Senator, you've already put Tabasco in that. That's got to be pretty hot." He continued shaking the sauce into the soup and said, "Ah! You can never get enough Tabasco." I don't know how he ate that stuff, but he loved it.

TERRY L. WOOTEN

You remember when the fat-free Olestra potato chips came out? There was a question of a patent extension for Olestra. The Senate Judiciary Committee has to approve a patent extension and then the full Senate votes on it. Well the company that developed Olestra wanted to get a patent extension, so they arranged to come in and talk with

Senator Thurmond about it. So while we were all sitting there talking, the Senator was eating some of those Olestra potato chips. In between bites he said, "Gosh, these are really good. I wouldn't know this had no fat. These are really good. This is a good thing. This will stop a lot of heart disease." And so on.

One of the lawyers with the group opened his briefcase and quietly handed me a piece of paper. It was a release form, basically saying that if there's any death or serious bodily harm from eating those potato chips, that you will not hold the company liable. Well, by that point the Senator had already eaten about three quarters of a can of those chips. So I said to the guy, "I'll tell you what. You sat here and watched him eat all these potato chips. If you want me to take this up with him, I'll be happy to do it. But now you're going to have to explain to him why you let him eat three quarters of this can of potato chips if you thought they might kill him. And I don't believe you're going to be able to explain that. We can bring it up if you want, but I'm not putting myself into this mess." The lawyer just looked at me. Then he slowly took the piece of paper back, put it in his briefcase, closed it up, and never said another word.

JOHN F. HAY

I was down on Pawleys Island in South Carolina one time and ate at the Island Café and Deli. They had a sandwich named for Strom Thurmond. The next time I saw him I happened to mention that to him. I told him, "That's exactly what I ordered, the Strom Thurmond sandwich." He was so thrilled at the idea that someone had actually named a sandwich for him. He said, "Was it good?" I said, "Senator, it was great!" He sat there and kind of looked at me and thought about it for a minute. You could see the wheels turning. He had to get used to the idea that there was a sandwich out there with his name on it. He asked me, "Did it have any cheese on it?" I said, "Yes sir, it had cheese on it." He said, "Colonel, I love cheese; do you like cheese?" I said, "Ha, Senator I love cheese!" He said, "A Strom Thurmond sandwich. How about that! Colonel, that sounds real good."

DEE SHORT

A lot of nights when the Senate was in session late, I'd fix dinner for the Senator. James would come by on the way to take the Senator home, and he'd pick up what I'd prepared. The Senator loved chicken, especially the dark meat, and soup and cornbread. And he always wanted lemonade to drink. He couldn't get enough of that lemonade. What was so typical of him, and this was right up until he left to go home to Edgefield in 2003, was that he always made sure I got my containers back. It didn't matter if it was nice china, crystal, or Tupperware; he always wanted to be sure and return them.

There were so many things for him to worry about and do the next day at the office, but his top priority was getting those empty containers back to me. He'd clean them up real good and tell Duke, "Now please make sure Miss Dee gets these back, and you let her know how much I appreciate it." He was the most appreciative, thoughtful man.

JASON ROSSBACH

Senator Thurmond had a voracious appetite for oysters. I remember the first reception I went to with him where they were serving oysters. Right after we got there the guy shucking oysters grabbed me and said, "Your job was to get here early and warn me he was coming!" The Senator just piled them up on his plate and started shoveling them in. He was fast! He stood right next to the garbage can. It was like watching a machine gun. Oysters were going in and any shells would come out the side of his mouth like a casing. I've never seen a man who could put down three dozen oysters in a sitting and not even blink.

He asked me one time if he should stop eating oysters. I think he'd been reading about a lot of the negative health effects from eating too many raw oysters. He was really torn over the issue because he loved them so much. I said, "Senator, you're almost 100-years old. I wouldn't worry too much about it. You just eat what you want to eat."

PAUL LAXALT

For many years I hosted a black-tie, stag event called the Lamb Fry. Boots were optional. The bill of fare consisted of lamb testicles. Strom came for several years, as did President Reagan. I thought Strom was a fan of the dinner until I heard from others that he had said, "I love Paul Laxalt, but I just can't bring myself to eat lamb balls."

COY JOHNSTON II

The Senator enjoyed going out to dinner wherever he could get some soft-shell crabs. That was a real choice meal for him. He liked sweet things too. I make bread and butter pickles, and he'd always say to Holly, "Tell your dad to send me some of those bread and butter pickles." He liked good Southern food like rice, peas, greens, and fried chicken. And oysters, boy, they were his absolute favorite.

I never will forget the night I went with the Senator to an awards event at the National Geographic offices. The reception was well underway by the time we could get there. The Senator went in, spoke to a few people, then he eyed the oysters. There was a whole bunch of them chilled on an ice carving. I think they did those just for him. He headed straight over to them and didn't even pick up a plate. He just took a serving fork and started helping himself. I believe he ate the whole darn thing of oysters. People were trying to talk to him. He just nodded his head and kept eating.

MARY CHAPMAN WEBSTER

One time the Senator invited me to the Chinese Embassy for dinner. But I had nothing to wear, so I called my mother. She said, "Mary, I've got this gorgeous dress I had made in Hong Kong. I'll send it right up to you." Well, back then we didn't have FedEx or Express Mail so Mother put this dress on a bus, and I picked it up at the bus station.

The evening of the dinner, the Senator pulled up in a big car. He had a driver that night so I sat in the backseat with him. Believe me, Senator Thurmond's hands could find their way to your leg so fast! He just cracked me up. I had on this fabulous brocade dress of Mother's and I knew I'd better not even get a wrinkle in it.

A short time later we arrived at the Chinese Embassy. It was probably a dinner party of twelve to fourteen — a very intimate dinner. The table was laid out with some of the most beautiful porcelain I've ever seen in my life. They placed me next to the Senator. I'll never forget the look on his face when he saw that there was no flatware on the table. It was just chopsticks. Now, they were hand-carved ivory chopsticks, the most beautiful chopsticks you've ever seen in your life. But no matter how beautiful they were, he wasn't too happy about using them. Despite his best efforts, he must have flipped half of his plate of food into my lap. The whole time, I was holding up a napkin to try and protect the dress. But the food kept falling on me. It was a mess.

Now, we were drinking wine out of beautiful porcelain cups. After trying so hard to use the chopsticks and spilling most of the food on me, Senator Thurmond finally took his chopsticks and clanged them on his porcelain cup. Clang, clang, clang! And he said to the Ambassador's wife, "Madam! Do you suppose I could have a fork?" And of course, he said it like, "fawk! Do you suppose I could have a fawk?" I was just mortified. But damn if they didn't bring him one! He was a one of a kind.

ROBIN ROBERTS

If we came within fifty miles of Spartanburg, it didn't matter what we were doing, the Senator wanted to stop by the Beacon Drive-in. He always went in and worked the line and talked to people. His good friend, Mr. White, owned the Beacon. We went there for breakfast one time. There was one guy in our group that day who was from upstate New

York. That was his very first time in Spartanburg. The Senator said to him, "Son, you come sit next to me."

Senator Thurmond must have had five or six sausage patties on his plate. He got a stack of napkins and hand squeezed the grease out of the sausages, then handed them around to the other guys who were there. They remarked that they had had hand-squeezed orange juice before but never hand-squeezed sausage! The guy from New York looked at me like, what am I supposed to do? I said, "Eat it and enjoy it. Hand-squeezed sausage patties from the Beacon, compliments of Senator Thurmond! You can't beat it."

CRAIG HELSING

is the Vice President of the BMW (U.S.) Holding Corporation. He previously served as an assistant to Lee Atwater in the Political Affairs Office at the Reagan White House.

Senator Thurmond could really eat. At receptions, most Senators or House members walk around and politely hold something to drink in their hands. I don't ever remember even seeing a Diet Coke in Senator Thurmond's hand, but I do remember he was not at all shy around the food tables. He just seemed to have a tremendous appetite. He held court as you followed him around the buffet table. That is a fond memory, chatting with the Senator at receptions. He was such a wonderful man.

HENRY SACKS

I told the Senator about a favorite little restaurant of mine down on Route 1 in LA, that's Lower Alexandria, called Elsie's Skillet. Well, Duke and Dee and I took him there one time and he ended up going there every Sunday for over ten years! He loved that place. The first time he ordered breakfast there, he got two eggs, two big hotcakes, some good old salty country ham, grits, and homemade biscuits. I was thinking to myself, people talk about how he eats so healthy. I didn't get it. There was nothing on his plate that any doctor would recommend.

He looked at his food and the first thing he did was start cutting the fat off the ham. I thought, well good, at least he's doing that. But he didn't push the fat aside. He ate it first before anything else! No lie, the first thing he did was eat the fat of the ham! Here he was in his 90s eating a mouthful of ham fat! I thought, to hell with all those diets. I'll just eat like the Senator.

From Prune Juice to Push-ups

STROM THURMOND'S FORMULA
FOR A LONG AND HEALTHY LIFE

*T*he fact that Strom Thurmond lived to be 100-years old was no accident. Nor was it simply the work of good genes. He was as committed to his own physical health as he was to helping the people of South Carolina. Months before he returned to South Carolina for the last time, the Senator was still "taking exercise" every morning. His usual routine included stretching, bending, and sit-ups. He often rode a stationary bicycle and went swimming at a local fitness center. Sometimes the Senator and I would ride in to work together in the mornings. He would boast, "I swam a half a mile last night, Duke. What did you do?"

I recall a trip to the Norfolk Naval Base. The Senator and I had a very filling dinner with a number of high-ranking officials. After dinner, the Senator said, "Why don't we all go for a walk?" Of course, everyone agreed. So off we went. There were about a dozen of us. We walked at a steady pace in a big circle around the Bachelor Officers' Quarters. One Admiral who was with us was having a tough time of it. He was rather portly, and it was all he could do to keep up with the Senator. By the time we got back to where we started, that poor Admiral was huffing and puffing. He really dragged himself back. We all stood around for a moment, looking at each other, trying to catch our breath. Then Senator Thurmond piped up, "Hey, that was great! Let's do it again!" That poor Admiral, still panting, tried to be upbeat about it. He said, "Well….sure, Senator. We can try to do that again." And off we went for another lap. The Senator told me later that he thought the Admiral might be consuming "a little too much beer" based on his stomach size.

When I first became a staff member on the Senate Judiciary Committee, I attended a lot of

Senator Thurmond demonstrates his athletic prowess on a stationary bike.

receptions with the Senator. At one point, General Emory Sneeden, a former Judge Advocate General of the Army and Chief Counsel for the Judiciary Committee, said to me, "Duke, you've been going to a lot of receptions with the Senator; has he ever asked you for some 'special orange juice?'" I replied, "No." Emory then told me that at some point he would. He said, "All you have to do is tell the bartender that you want some orange juice with a small shot of rum."

It wasn't too long after receiving those instructions that the Senator did ask me for some "special orange juice," and I did exactly as Emory had told me. The Senator would take one orange juice and that was all. Sometimes he would have a beer or a glass of wine, but only on special occasions. As I spent more time with him, he would ask for an "orange juice," but I knew what he wanted and always had it mixed in a "special" way.

A newspaper reported one time that the Senator had said that he enjoyed a good cold beer. As a result of this article, he was asked to resign from the board of a Christian university in South Carolina. He was told by the President of the university that it would not look good for the university to have someone on the board who admitted to enjoying a beer. The Senator and I both thought this was a bit hypocritical, but he nevertheless gladly submitted his resignation. I often wondered just how many other members of that board might enjoy a good cold beer but would not admit it in public.

Senator Thurmond and I spoke at length one time about his physical fitness. I'll never forget his words to me: "Duke, most everybody could do what I do, but they won't make the sacrifice. I have to sacrifice to do it. It's not easy. But once you start, you never want to stop." He was the most self-disciplined man I have ever met.

BUD ALBRIGHT

When I was a little boy the Senator used to stay with us when he'd come to South Carolina. I always looked forward to those visits. He'd come in and have supper then he'd go out for a jog. My dad used to say that you could always tell exactly where he was by listening to the dogs bark around the neighborhood.

C. BRUCE LITTLEJOHN

I was co-owner of a motel here in Spartanburg from 1956 to 1980. Strom would often come through Spartanburg when he was traveling or campaigning, and he always spent the night in my motel. I remember one night he came in about 11 o'clock. I happened to be there. He said, "Bruce, let's me and you go out here and get a little exercise. We can run down the street here, down Pine Street and back." Well, I was ashamed to admit it, but I certainly wasn't equal to running with Strom Thurmond, so I begged off. A few minutes later he came out of the motel in his shorts and headed down South Pine Street. I headed home. You see, Strom hadn't yet gotten his exercise that day. And he wasn't going to go to bed until he'd run down Pine Street and back. He was a real stickler for exercise.

WILLIAM C. PLOWDEN, JR.

The Senator paid a lot of attention to what he ate. Once when we were eating breakfast at a little hotel in Manhattan, the waiter came up to take our order and the Senator said, "I want a big glass of orange juice, a big glass of warm water, and some prunes. And what kind of cereal do you have?" The waiter said, "Regular cereal, sir." The Senator asked him, "Don't you have any of that new concentrated cereal?" The waiter said, "No sir. I haven't heard of it." The Senator said, "Well, you ought to go tell your chef to get up to date on this cereal business. Bring me a bowl of cereal, a bowl of prunes, a glass of orange juice, and a glass of warm water." Then he said, "Now my friend here, Bill Plowden, he's not going to live very long, so just bring him a regular breakfast."

JAMES B. EDWARDS

Strom Thurmond was one of the most disciplined people I ever knew. His assistant Harry Dent told the story that during the Goldwater campaign, he and Strom traveled together. They'd come back to their hotel room after a hard day campaigning for Goldwater, and Senator Thurmond would get down on the floor and start his pushups. Harry said, "I'd go to sleep and he'd be down there doing his pushups. When the alarm clock would go off the next morning, I'd get up, look down, and there was the Senator on the floor doing his push-ups again!" Harry said it was like the Senator had been doing push-ups all night!

FRANK NORTON

I first met the Senator in 1964 after he'd just moved to the Republican Party. I had what was called a patronage position with Senator Russell, and he and Senator Thurmond were good friends. Senator Russell had an executive assistant at the time, a super young man named Bill Jordan.

On Senator Russell's birthday in 1964, several senators came by late in the afternoon to sip a little bourbon and branch water as they would sometimes do back then, and to wish Senator Russell a happy birthday. Senator Thurmond was among those who stopped by. Now, Bill Jordan was a little full of himself that day, I guess. He said, "Senator

Thurmond, I keep hearing about what good shape you're in and how you can do all these push-ups. Why don't you and I have a little push-up contest in honor of Senator Russell's birthday?" Senator Thurmond said, "Oh no Bill, we don't want to do that." Bill said, "Yeah, come on, let's do it; let's do it. We'll do ten dollars a push-up to go to Senator Russell's favorite charity." So he kept on goading and finally Senator Thurmond said okay.

So Bill Jordan took off his tie, unbuttoned his shirt, and got down. He did maybe thirty good push-ups. Then he did four kind of wobbling, alligator push-ups. He stood up and said, "Thirty four!" You could see he was just whooped. Senator Thurmond stood there the whole time watching very calmly. When Bill was done, Thurmond started to the floor. He didn't take off his tie. He didn't unbutton his shirt, nothing. He just got right down on the floor in a three-position pickup and did sixty-four magnificent push-ups. He never broke a sweat. Every one of them was military perfect. When he was through he said, "And let's do one for Senator Russell's birthday." Boom! He did another perfect one. "And let's do one for the Republican party!" Boom, another! Then he jumped up with a smile on his face. The man wasn't even winded.

Well, Bill Jordan was absolutely beside himself. That was a lot of money back then. He said, "Ah, well, let me write you a check here, Senator." Senator Thurmond said, "No Bill, that's not necessary." And Senator Russell laughed and said, "Oh yes it is! He made a bet!"

I was just a young, 21-year-old kid at the time who happened to sneak into the room and witness this. That was the first time I ever met Senator Thurmond.

MARY CHAPMAN WEBSTER

In the summer of '68 the Senator was not married. A group us went over to his apartment one night for some wine and cheese. Of course, it was non-alcoholic wine. We were horribly disappointed. At one point in the evening I fired up a cigarette. I smoked at the time. The Senator said to me, "Miss Chapman! You're going to an early grave if you keep that up." Back in those days everybody smoked and nobody said a word to you about it, except Strom Thurmond.

CRAIG METZ

I usually didn't see the Senator drink alcohol. Usually he avoided it. But I recall one reception at which he came in, got a glass of beer, and drank it all down in one gulp. Then he said, "Ahh! The yeast in it is good for me!"

Strom Thurmond enjoying a game of tennis.

FRANKI ROBERTS

Senator Thurmond was always ahead of his time when it came to health issues. I remember the windows in his office were lined with bottles of mineral water. And he always kept exercise things in his office, like isometric ropes and barbells. He would take the staff bike riding on the weekends. We'd ride for miles around the monuments and down the Canal in Georgetown. During the week he was busy, running back and forth to the Senate Floor, so you didn't get to see him that much. But on the weekends, we'd all get together.

He was single back then so he took different women on the staff to receptions and dinners with him at night. I'll never forget this fabulous steak dinner he took me to at the Willard Hotel. We were sitting at a table with a whole group of other senators and their wives. After dinner, the waiter came around with dessert. Of course Strom always passed on dessert. Everybody teased him and gave him a hard time about not eating dessert. He said, "That's okay. I'll be here long after you guys are gone." And he was right. He outlived them all.

ED KENNEY

The Senator was taking vitamins regularly back when most people didn't even know what they were and when most doctors didn't even recommend them. I've seen him sit down at a table and take maybe forty vitamins at one time. I think the Senator approached his health very logically. It's no mystery: if you put toxins in your body you're going to get in trouble; if you put good things into your body you're going to live longer and feel better. It's that simple. He understood that. He followed that rule his whole life.

DAVID BLACK

The Senator didn't like to see Cokes or carbonated drinks around the office. If he saw one on your desk, he'd come over and start lecturing you about how bad they are for you. He would say, "You need to be drinking juice or water. Prune juice, that's good for you! Drink your prune juice every day!"

R.C. "PREACHER" WHITNER

I remember back during the Senator's 1972 campaign, I happened to walk into a little room right outside his office where he kept all his vitamins and health supplements. Holy Cow! There were bottles everywhere you looked! Later, I started chatting with him about that. I said, "Senator, why don't we have a Strom Thurmond Multi Vitamin? I'll handle all the marketing for you. We'll make a fortune!" I knew I could sell a million bottles a week. He said, "Nah, we're not here for that." That was so typical of him: we're here to do a job and that's not it.

JOSEPH R. BIDEN, JR.

No one ever doubted Strom Thurmond's physical courage. Not fifteen years ago I was reminded of this. I was coming across to vote in the Senate and going up the escalator, and a fellow who apparently had held a long-time grudge against Senator Thurmond, a tourist, literally interposed himself between me and Strom and said, "If you weren't so old, I would knock you down." I immediately stood between them. Strom took off his coat and said, "Hold my coat, Joe." I looked at him and said, "No! No! No!" With that, Strom went down and did 25 push-ups. He had to be about 88-years old at the time. He stood up, looked at the man, and said, "If you weren't so young I'd knock you down."

ROBERT H. BORK

I rode back to Washington one time from a meeting in Williamsburg with Strom Thurmond and his driver. I was sitting in the backseat and the Senator was in the passenger seat. I was smoking and had the window down so the smoke would go out. Senator Thurmond turned around and admonished me. He really lectured me about how bad it was for me and those around me. So I threw the cigarette out the window and didn't smoke the rest of the ride.

TERRY L. WOOTEN

As most people know, the Senator was very health-oriented. When I got to Washington in 1986, he was still jogging or swimming every day, and he was in his mid-80s then. Then he had that knee problem, so he was not able to run like he used to. But he continued to swim. I remember one night I went down to a fitness club near where I lived, because I was looking for a convenient place to exercise. While I was touring the place I checked out the swimming pool. Guess who was in there swimming? Strom Thurmond! This must have been at 10 o'clock at night.

MARIO D'ANGELO

is the Senior Barber at the U.S. Senate Barber Shop and was Senator Thurmond's Personal Barber for 25 years.

I'll never forget one time I was cutting the Senator's hair; he was sitting right here in my chair, and the whole time he was on the phone chewing out his sister's doctor back in South Carolina. He was so upset because the doctor wasn't making his sister exercise every day. "She needs to be moving!" he said. "She needs to be up and doing things! She needs to take her exercise and I want you to make sure she does it!" He was very adamant that everybody exercise every day. He told me he did 100 sit-ups and push-ups each morning. Plus, he swam up to a mile every other day.

ERNIE COGGINS

One day I was in talking to Duke. At the time I think I weighed around 250 pounds. I'm not a small guy, put it that way. Duke and I were talking and all of a sudden somebody slapped me on my back so hard that I started going across Duke's desk. Duke was backing up, trying to get out of the way. The only reason I didn't go flying across his desk and into his lap is that I caught the lip of his desk with my fingers. So I was laying on his desk and thinking, who in the world?!

I got up and turned around, and there was the Senator with a big smile on his face. He said, "How you doing?" It took me a second or two to get my composure. I said, "Sir, I'm doing fine." By that time Duke was howling. He couldn't stop laughing. I was pretty embarrassed. Senator Thurmond was probably 98-years old at the time. I have never been hit so hard in my life. It literally lifted me right up off the ground. The Senator just smiled and smiled. He thought it was hilarious.

FRANK NORTON

I traveled with the Senator to South Carolina once for the Beaufort Seafood Festival. They had set up a luncheon for us with lots of fried shrimp and oysters. I love fried shrimp and oysters, and these were the best of the best. So I was looking forward to lunch. As I went through the line loading up on that stuff, all of a sudden I felt this strong right hand on my right elbow. It was Senator Thurmond and he said, "You don't want to eat that fried food, Colonel. You know that's just not good for you!" And I'm not kidding: he pushed the shrimp and oysters off my plate and put some baked chicken on there instead! He said, "Here, you'll like this a lot more. It's good for you."

JACK DANFORTH

When Senator Thurmond went to fund-raising receptions he would graze. He would head immediately for the food table and eat everything in sight. What he couldn't fit in his stomach, he'd put in his pocket. He told me once that no matter what time he got home at night he would lift weights. He was in his 90s when he gave me that advice. My wife Sally tells me that a lady once asked Strom, "How do you stay so fit?" He said, "Fibah!" But that wasn't fiber he was stuffing into his pockets at the receptions. It looked more like meatballs and cheese puffs!

JUDITH RICHARDS HOPE

I remember sitting with Senator Thurmond in his office. He had hand weights beside his desk. Even though he was totally focused on the conversation, he would occasionally pick up the weights and pump iron.

BOB DOLE

Quite often I'd look up and see Strom, at age 90-something, running by my office on his way somewhere. I used to say: "I don't know what kind of medical plan they're going to pass in Congress, but I want the Thurmond plan! He eats a banana; I eat a banana. He drinks juice; I drink juice. It's working for him, and it's going to work for me!" Every time I thought I was getting old, I'd see ol' Strom running by my office and I'd think, what the heck am I worrying about?

BIRCH BAYH

was a United States Senator from Indiana, 1963-1981.

Strom Thurmond sure was a health devotee. I remember a trip to Vienna, Austria in particular. Marvella and I had been out to dinner. As we drove back up to the hotel, here comes Senator Thurmond jogging down the road. It must have been 11 o'clock at night. I remember after every meal, too, there he was brushing his teeth. I could see how he lived as long and as healthy as he did because he sure took care of the body God gave him.

LINDSEY GRAHAM

Senator Thurmond had tremendous discipline about exercise and diet. He was constantly telling me, "Watch what you eat and get regular exercise." I went to a breakfast with him one time when we were campaigning. They asked me, "What do you want to eat?" I pointed at the Senator and said, "I'll have whatever he's having!"

Senator Thurmond's ability to do pushups continued
until nearly the end of his life.

TERRY L. WOOTEN

Senator Thurmond was scheduled to speak at a big conference at the University of
Virginia in Charlottesville. Another staffer and I drove down there with him. There was
a dinner and reception the night we got there. About 11 o'clock the Senator told me he
was going back to his room. He said, "Now, I want to make sure I have plenty of time to
take my exercises in the morning before we leave for the conference. Would you give me
a call in the morning to be sure I'm up?" I said, "Senator, I'd be happy to call you. What
time do you want me to call?" He said, "5:30." Now, there it was already 11 o'clock, and

he wanted me to get up and call him at 5:30 in the morning. I stayed down there at the reception and socialized til about midnight. I got to bed somewhere around 12:30 and set my alarm for 5:30 so I could call the Senator.

Well, the alarm went off but I must have hit the snooze. It was about a ten-minute snooze. I might have hit it twice; I don't remember. By the time I looked at the clock, it was 5:45 a.m. I thought, oops. But I was just a little bit late; it probably didn't matter. So I picked up the phone and dialed the Senator's room. The phone rang. All of a sudden somebody picked it up and the first words I heard were, "You're late!" I said, "Well Senator, I overslept." He said, "I wanted you to call me at 5:30. I got up. I'm fine. But you're late making that call!" And he hung up on me. He was mad because if he asked you to do something, he wanted it done. He was already up and doing his exercises.

SUSAN PELTER

If ever the Senator got a chance, he loved to hold forth about his exercise routine. If somebody asked him even the slightest question about health, he'd launch into a whole laundry list of how things should be. "You should eat right and take your exercise every day." Then he would get down on the floor and demonstrate what exercises he did in the mornings. That was fun because he always had on a suit and tie and his polished shoes, and there he is on the floor showing you how to do pelvic lifts and such.

A UPI reporter told me that the first time he met Senator Thurmond, he was nervous and didn't want to embarrass himself in front of this historic figure. He walked into his office and went over with his hand out to shake the Senator's hand and bam! He promptly fell flat on his face. He turned around to see what he had tripped over, and it turned out to be a set of barbells the Senator had been using.

LES BROWNLEE,
Colonel, U.S. Army (ret.) was the Undersecretary of the Army and the Acting Secretary under President George W. Bush. He was also the former Staff Director of the Senate Armed Services Committee. A highly decorated veteran, Colonel Brownlee was a good friend of Senator Thurmond's.

I was honored to attend Senator Thurmond's 95th birthday party. Throughout the party many friends and well-wishers remarked to the Senator that they hoped they could attend his 100th birthday party. The Senator looked at each of them and said, "Well, if you eat right, exercise, and take care of yourself, there's no reason you can't be there."

DAVID T. BEST

There was never a question about the Senator's strength and body tone. His hip and knee were troublesome, and those problems made him look feeble because he shuffled a little. And I know it hurt him to walk. But anybody who took that to mean he was in ill health was totally mistaken.

I remember one time in the office a reporter questioned him about his health. This was probably in 1996 when we were gearing up for his last election. Senator Thurmond immediately got out from behind his desk, dropped down on the floor, and did ten pushups just like that. The man was 94-years old! He challenged the reporter to do the same. Then he said, "Any more questions about my health?"

DIRK KEMPTHORNE

Strom and I often talked about his athletic regimen. He kept physically fit, and of course, it paid off. I remember we were walking back from the Armed Services Committee hearing one day; we were down in the basement between the Russell Building and the Capitol. He was showing me one of the isometric exercises that he did. He stopped and demonstrated how he would tighten all his muscles. I was concerned that some passersby might think something was wrong with him. I said, "Senator, I get the idea, but could you please stop?"

JASON ROSSBACH

The Senator loved being around young people. He had such vitality and loved being alive and doing things, that he was very content to be around twenty-somethings. He loved to go out for lunch or to a ball game with a bunch of young people. He would sit there with a smile on his face and have a good old time.

I recall one morning he came in to the office. He looked exhausted and said, "I stayed up so late last night. I was watching Game Seven of the World Series. It was the Cleveland Indians against the Florida Marlins. It was a great game." Then he thought for a minute and added, "I don't even like baseball. Only problem was, I couldn't decide who to cheer for. Florida was more Southern than Ohio, although Florida's not really a Southern state." You don't picture having that kind of a conversation with a ninety-something-year-old U.S. Senator. But he really enjoyed that kind of thing.

As far as his health and diet were concerned, his self-discipline was amazing. I never saw him drink carbonated drinks. He never ate too much red meat or sugar. Apparently, the Senator's father was a real health and fitness advocate, and of course, the Senator ran track at Clemson. As he got older his limp got more pronounced. That really bothered him. People were like, "Look! Strom Thurmond's limping." He'd been hiding that limp since World War II. He was just too strong-willed and proud to show it.

There were times I would go by and pick the Senator up in the morning and bring him to work. When you walked into his apartment, he was always either lying on the weight bench pumping iron, or stretched out on the floor doing push-ups, or pedaling away on his stationary bike. He worked out like that every morning well into his late nineties.

KEVIN SMITH

When I went to work for the Senator in 2000, he was already 98-years old. So I'd heard all the stories about him being old and out of it. I spent a lot of time with him and I didn't encounter that at all. He was amazing. It was incredible to see at that age how alive he really was and how well he functioned. The man got up every morning, did his workout, push-ups, sit-ups, rode the bike, then put away a big plate of fruit, some water, and a Gatorade. He could exercise circles around me at the time! He constantly told me that his exercising was the reason he lived so long. He would say, "Exercise a little bit every day and you'll live a long, healthy life."

DEE SHORT

Every year Senator Thurmond took me out for my birthday. One year, I think it was 1995, he suggested I invite ten or so of my friends to join us. We went to the Senators' Dining Room in the Capitol. We had a wonderful time. Afterwards, Senator Thurmond took us all on a tour of the Capitol Building. He was the best tour guide the U.S. Capitol ever had. He knew all the stories and could take you to some behind-the-scenes places. It was so interesting.

On our tour we visited the historic Vice President's Office which has a number of treasures in it; there's the Dolly Madison mirror, for one. And the desk in the room was the one that Richard Nixon used in the White House. Before we left, Senator Thurmond pointed up to the grand chandelier that hangs in the room. He told us it used to hang in the White House, but whoever was President or the First Lady at the time didn't like the way the crystal prisms chimed against each other, so they had it taken out and it ended up in the Capitol.

Senator Thurmond said, "Do you want to hear what that sounded like?" Before we could answer he leapt into the air, reached up, and knocked some of the prisms together.

Well, I guess he didn't know his own strength because he hit the prisms of the chandelier so hard that one broke off and cut him right above the eye. Fortunately he had a handkerchief and stopped the bleeding.

Duke gave the broken prism to a Capitol official and told them what had happened, thinking they would have it fixed. But we've checked every time we go by there, and that chandelier is still broken. If you look closely enough, you can see the one broken crystal prism from where Senator Thurmond jumped into the air and hit it. He was in his nineties at the time.

JOHN R. STEER

Senator Thurmond liked to read the newspaper and comment on interesting things he came across. I'll never forget the time he was reading some story about the aging process. The article talked about how, in biblical times, Methuselah was the oldest human being, having lived to be 969-years old. Senator Thurmond looked up and in all seriousness said, "Hmmm. I wonder how he did that." You could see he was figuring out how he was going to try and break that record.

MICHAEL BOZZELLI

Senator Thurmond was health-conscious all the time. If we were eating out somewhere and I ordered a Coke, he would lecture me about how the tomato juice that he was drinking would do me much better than a Coke. And I remember one morning I stopped by his apartment to give him a ride to work. There he was, 99-years old, riding a stationary bike. The man was a machine!

One time we were in his office and he was reading the newspaper. There was an article on some study that showed a correlation between the amount of sleep you get and your life expectancy. According to this study, the fewer hours of sleep you got the longer you lived. The Senator read this article a few times very carefully and intently. He finally sat back and said, "Maybe I'll just skip sleeping tonight."

Dee Short, President and Hillary Clinton,
and Senator Thurmond at the White House;
Congressional Christmas Ball, December 7th, 1993.

WHITE HOUSE PHOTO

*He told me once that dancing was great exercise, and as an added benefit, "You get to put
your arms around some mighty pretty girls."*

– R.J. Duke Short –

The Best Dancer on the Hill

*T*he Senator and I were at a reception some time in the late '80s. He was out there on the dance floor, which he really enjoyed. The women were literally lined up to dance with him. At one point a little lady came up to me and said, "I want to ask you a question." I said, "Yes ma'am?"

She pointed to the Senator and said, "Just look at him out there. He's almost 90-years old and yet he hasn't left the dance floor. He's been out there all night. My husband over there is only 63 and all he does is sit. He hardly gets up for any reason, let alone to dance. What I want to know is this: what is the Senator's secret?" I laughed and told her, "Well, I do know his secret. When I retire, I'm going to bottle it, sell it, and make a fortune."

The truth is, Senator Thurmond simply loved to dance. It was no secret in Washington that he was the best dancer on Capitol Hill. He told me once that dancing was great exercise, and as an added benefit, "You get to put your arms around some mighty pretty girls."

GEORGE ALLEN

For the past thirty years, almost every time I talked about the U.S. Senate with my mother, she would proudly remind me that in the early 1970s she danced with Strom Thurmond who, she allowed, was a very good dancer.

JASON ROSSBACH

Whenever he went out to an evening event, especially an inaugural ball or a wedding, he would just walk in and stand there and the women would start lining up to dance with him. It was amazing.

MARY CHAPMAN WEBSTER

The Senator made sure his staff had a great time when they were in Washington. He took us to everything. One of his favorite things to do was to go dancing. He loved that. And he was a pretty good dancer too. You know, he'd step on your toes a couple of times, but who cared? You were dancing with Strom Thurmond!

VANJEWELL GRAHAM

is the wife of James Floyd Graham, Senator Thurmond's Personal Driver from 1986 to 2003.

I remember the inaugural night for the first Bush administration. I went along with James to ride around in the car with them from one ball to another. I wasn't dressed for a ball. The farthest thing from my mind that night was getting a chance to go to one. Mrs. Thurmond asked me, "Vanjewell, have you ever been to an inaugural ball?" I said, "No, Mrs. Thurmond." She said, "Strom! Vanjewell's never been to an inaugural ball! Can she go with us?" He said, "Sure!" I said, "Senator, I'm not dressed." He looked at me and said, "Mrs. Graham, you're with me, and you're dressed just fine. Don't you be intimidated by anybody. When we go inside, you just say you're with me."

So that's exactly what I did. As long as I was with him, it didn't matter what I had on. We went to the South Carolina Ball and he danced with me. He had me going around that floor; it was so much fun. He was very light on his feet. He was a wonderful ballroom dancer. I said, "Senator, I didn't know you could dance this well." He said, "I'm a great dancer, Mrs. Graham."

CHRISTIE DENISE HUMPHRIES

I was an office page for Senator Thurmond when President Clinton had his second Inauguration. I was lucky enough to go to the South Carolina Inaugural Ball with the

Christie Denise Humphries and Strom Thurmond dancing at the South Carolina Inaugural Ball, January 1997.

CHRISTIE DENISE HUMPHRIES

Senator, Duke, and Dee. I was so excited, not only to go to the Ball but especially to spend time with Senator Thurmond.

I was nervous though because I'd never done any kind of formal dancing before. Before we left to go pick up the Senator, Duke showed me a few dance steps and gave me a few pointers. He said, "You just follow. Just go where I'm going." But it was hard. I couldn't get it down. I didn't know if I could dance or not.

We went to pick up the Senator. That was before he went to live at Walter Reed, when he was living by himself just a couple of blocks from Duke and Dee. The Ball was held at one of the Smithsonians. I walked in on Senator Thurmond's arm. Everybody was like, "Senator Thurmond! Senator Thurmond, so nice to see you!" I was thinking, this has got to be the best thing ever!

When we got to the point where we could hear the music playing, he leaned over to me and whispered, "Now, you're going to dance with me right?" I thought, oh, I hope I can do it! I really had butterflies. Dee had told me what a wonderful dancer he was. The best on Capitol Hill. I remember we danced to two songs I'd never heard before: "Roll With Me Baby" and "Sign, Sealed, and Delivered."

He was twirling me around. I could see flashes of light as people took pictures. I was getting woozy. We were going around and around, and I was following him like Duke had said. I kept thinking, this is really something! Towards the end of the second song, other women started cutting in. They came from everywhere. So I had to step aside. I remember the Senator saying to me, "It was a pleasure; it was a pleasure." It was the best night ever. I will never, ever forget that night.

MIKE TONGOUR

When I married in 1998, Senator Thurmond came to our wedding. He made a beautiful toast to my wife and me, and then he hit the dance floor. He must have spent an hour and a half dancing. He danced with his daughter, my wife, some former staff who were there, you name it. The women were lined up to dance with him.

DEE SHORT

In December of 1993 I accompanied Senator Thurmond to the Congressional Christmas Ball at the White House. I went to a lot of events with the Senator, but I believe that Ball ranks right up there among the most memorable, special evenings I ever had with him. James picked me up and took me over to the office because the Senator and Duke were working late that evening. I walked into his office and he said, "Why, Miss Dee, that's a mighty swanky dress you got on there."

Duke walked us outside. As we got into the car, the Senator grinned at Duke and said, "I'll have her home before morning!" He was so funny and charming the entire evening.

James pulled up to the White House. The Senator and I went in, and he started showing me around. Everything was decorated so beautifully for Christmas. It really was a magical night. We had our picture taken with the President and First Lady. That was the Clintons' first Christmas in the White House.

On the way up the stairs, we bumped into Senator Simpson and his wife Ann. She asked, "Dee, have you ever danced with the Senator?" I said, "No, this will be my first time dancing with him." She replied, "You're in for a real treat. He's the best dancer on the Hill." I had always heard that the Senator was an incredible dancer and had been since his University days at Clemson.

When we arrived in the ballroom, the band was playing but no one was dancing yet. To be honest, I was a little nervous. I'm a little timid on the dance floor. The Senator said, "Miss Dee, can I have this dance?" We were the first couple out on the floor. Then President Clinton and Hillary came out, and then others.

The Senator was a magnificent dancer. Here was this 91-year-old man moving around the dance floor like he was 20-years old. It really was something to be behold. I said to him, "Senator, Fred Astaire would have to take a backseat to you! And you certainly make me feel like Ginger Rogers." He loved that. He laughed and laughed. He told me he taught his sisters how to dance. He was very proud of that fact.

We danced maybe three dances or so, and then the women started lining up to cut in. You wouldn't believe it. It was like every woman there wanted to dance with Strom Thurmond. Of course, he just loved every minute of it. He danced and danced and never broke a sweat. He was so happy out on that dance floor.

About 11:30 or so he said, "Well Dee, I guess we'd better go." As we were leaving the band started playing "New York, New York." By that time I was having so much fun. I said, "Senator! How about one more?" He laughed and said, "Well, it would be my honor." So we turned around and walked back out on the dance floor one more time. That was our last dance for that night, but I was fortunate to have many more. It was an evening I will never forget.

Duke Short, Strom Thurmond, Maureen Callaway, Melissa Penny, and Lauren Garcia .

Senator Thurmond loved the ladies; we all know that. He was a flirt.
There's no other way to put it; he was just a big flirt.

– Judith Richards Hope –

THE CENTENNIAL SENATOR

All the Pretty Ladies

mong the most legendary attributes of Senator Strom Thurmond was his undying affection for pretty ladies. I don't know how to put it any other way: the man was a big flirt. Not a day passed that he didn't wink at, compliment, or delight in having his photo taken with an attractive woman. I have been told that, among women on Capitol Hill, it was understood that you had never "officially made it" in Washington until you had been the recipient of one of Strom Thurmond's infamous bear hugs.

I should add that while the Senator loved pretty ladies, he had an obvious preference for pretty young ladies. No matter how close he got to being 100-years old, his fondness never strayed too far from beautiful young women in their early twenties. The Senator married his first wife, then 21-year-old Jean Crouch, in 1947, just a few weeks shy of his 45th birthday. In December of 1968 he married his second wife, 22-year-old Nancy Moore. Strom Thurmond was 66. He went on to have four children with Nancy, the last when he was 76-years old. In response to questions as to why he preferred marrying women so much younger than himself, the Senator was fond of saying, "In my old age I'd rather smell perfume than liniment."

I remember when the Senator and Nancy's separation was announced to the public. Our office in Washington was immediately deluged with an avalanche of letters, cards, and photographs from women eager to meet the 90-something-year-old new bachelor. (To be perfectly honest, we regularly received letters from female admirers even before they separated, but not in this volume).

I recall one letter in particular from a university professor. She sent us a long letter about herself and enclosed a recent photo. She was an attractive, educated woman in her early fifties. "I can be as charming as needs be," she wrote to the Senator. She also said that she enjoyed dancing, which was a plus, and would like very much to have dinner with the Senator some time. Normally I would have just filed this away. But I thought to myself, it might be nice for the Senator to have someone to go out to dinner and dancing with occasionally. So I showed him the letter. He took one look at her picture, made a face and said, "Ah! She's too old!"

Senator Thurmond not only preferred younger women, but he also advised other men to follow his example. I remember the beautiful autumn weekend in 1991 when Dee and I were engaged to be married. It was one of the most joyous days of my entire life. The following Monday morning I went into the Senator's office to tell him the good news. I said, "Senator, I got engaged this past weekend to a young lady from South Carolina." His first question to me was, "Well Duke, how old is the little girl?" I said, "She's 33." He immediately shot back, "Duke! 33?! That's a little old for you, don't you think?!" I was 57-years old at the time, and thinking that perhaps she might be too young for me.

The Senator continued, "Now, if you'll get you a little girl about 20 or 21, then you can train 'em like you like 'em." Later, after the Senator and Dee had become the best of friends, he pulled me aside and said. "Duke, marrying Dee was the best day's work you've ever done. She's a mighty pretty lady." As usual, the Senator was exactly right. Dee has made my life complete and is the absolute best thing that has ever happened to me. She is the true joy of my life.

FRANKI ROBERTS

I remember back in Hillcrest High School in South Carolina, I had a history teacher who used to tell us how she almost married Strom Thurmond. Later, when I went to work for him and got to know him through the years, I discovered there were a lot of women who said they almost married Strom Thurmond! He must have made all the ladies feel special; that's all I can say.

DR. NED CATHCART

I first met Strom Thurmond on the front porch of our house in Anderson, South Carolina where I grew up. This would have been back in the late 1930s before the War. He was a judge then, and he'd come into town to hold court there in Anderson. He came walking up on the porch because he had a date with my sister Leita. I had seven sisters, but he picked out one that he fancied.

I'd usually be on the front porch just sitting, watching people go by as we did in those days. And Judge Thurmond would drive up, walk up that long walkway, and then up a rather tall set of steps. He was always dressed up, never without a coat and tie. And I

Senator Thurmond and friends celebrating the
engagement of Duke and Dee Short.

remember that he was very cordial to me, a child. I took to him because he was so friendly. Every time he came by our house it was a distinct pleasure because he was so pleasant and thoughtful. Leita was very enamored with him, as was everybody. In fact, all of my sisters sort of envied Lieta for having such a gentleman to call on her.

BUD ALBRIGHT

The Senator didn't get married until he was an older man. I remember my dad told him one day, "Strom, you're a good-looking, successful man; why haven't you gotten married?" The Senator said, "I haven't had time!" And that was absolutely true. He worked that hard. He just never found the time.

ELAINE ROGERS

I remember one night a group of my friends and I accompanied Senator Thurmond to a USO reception. At the event, I'd asked him to please get up and say a few words. We had Miss America there, and we had a number of Miss America contestants who were in town visiting our soldiers. The Senator was so funny. He was always so delightful to women, saying, "Gosh, you are Miss America!" He was so appreciative of Miss America and the other contestants sharing their time with the soldiers and supporting the USO.

After the event was over, he turned to me and said, "You know, you're really my Miss America." And he would call me that from then on, all the years that I've known him. When I got this job I was very young, like 23- or 24-years old. To have Senator Thurmond call me Miss America every time he saw me, wow! He really knew how to make you feel special.

JUDITH RICHARDS HOPE

Senator Thurmond loved the ladies; we all know that. He was a flirt. There's no other way to put it; he was just a big flirt. He would hug you and grab you and occasionally pinch you. That's just how he was. But it wasn't a put-down; it was more like hey, I really like women. He was really something.

MELINDA KOUTSOUMPAS

Most people who knew Senator Thurmond knew he was the epitome of a Southern gentleman. He frequently used the phrase, "lovely ladies," and meant nothing at all negative by it; that was just the way he described women. One time during a hearing for a Supreme Court nominee, there was a panel of witnesses testifying which included several women from the National Organization of Women. Senator Thurmond welcomed them to the hearing and said something like, "I'd like to welcome all you lovely ladies."

Well, those women took offense at that. I mean, they really took offense at it, and even made comments that they didn't like to be called lovely ladies. At our break, Senator Simpson held a news conference and defended Senator Thurmond. When we came back in, Duke had the Senator say something about it, how he didn't mean anything by it. Senator Simpson then spoke for about ten minutes about how Thurmond meant no disrespect and that if we ever get to a place in society where women can't be called lovely ladies without it being a derogatory comment, then we need a little help around here.

KEVIN SMITH

One time the Senator and I popped into the elevator at the Russell Building, heading up to our floor. Some tourists got on the elevator with us, a man, his wife, and their child. They were a young couple, probably early thirties. We all sort of nodded politely to each other. You could tell they knew who Senator Thurmond was. They were kind of in awe.

Now, nearly every time Senator got on an elevator, he'd get in one of those back corners and kind of lean back and relax. He was doing just that. But then he slowly turned to the husband and said, "You sure do have a pretty wife!" I didn't know whether to laugh. I think I held my breath. The man kind of chuckled a little bit. The wife was obviously thrilled.

People had told me when I started working for him, Senator Thurmond loves those pretty ladies, and he always wants to talk to them. That was the first time I'd been with him when it happened. It was great.

WILLIAM SCHACHTE

I recall when Jamie Gorelick was having hearings to be General Counsel for the Department of Defense. I talked to the guy in the office of Legislative Affairs at the Pentagon who had been her escort officer. He came back that day just howling. I asked him what happened. He said, "Well, I was escorting Miss Gorelick around to see the Senators before her confirmation and we went in to see Senator Thurmond." Jamie had a spectacular résumé: Harvard undergrad, Harvard law school, academic honors, very impressive.

The guy told me, "We went into Thurmond's office and he started looking over her résumé. He'd look down at the résumé then look up at her. Then he'd look down at the résumé, then up at her. Then he'd look down at the résumé again, look up at her, turn the page, and look back down at the résumé. Finally he closed the résumé and said, 'Well, I want to tell you one thing. You're just as pretty as you are smart!'" Only Senator Thurmond!

CRAIG METZ

He loved to grab people in a big hug and hold them tight and have his picture made with them. I think that was one of his delights. Even in his old age, he especially enjoyed having his picture taken with all the pretty ladies.

KEVIN SMITH

I'll never forget the time my mom came up to visit me at the office and we got our picture taken with the Senator. My mom had met the Senator many years ago when she was much younger. She was actually in the Miss South Carolina pageant with Nancy when

Nancy won the title. My mom is just a bundle of energy, and she was downright giddy as she could be to get back there and see the Senator. Of course, the Senator always loved the ladies.

We went back to his office, and right away the Senator got that big smile he always had whenever a pretty lady walked in the room. He'd give that infamous squeeze; he'd grab their shoulder and squeeze them in real tight for the picture. The Senator gave her one of those, "You sure are a pretty lady." That was one of his standards. I heard that quite a few times. My mom absolutely loved it.

LESLIE SEALY
served as Senator Thurmond's Office Manager from 1986 until
just prior to the Senator's retirement in January of 2003.

The Senator loved to hug the ladies. I remember one time there were a bunch of interns in the office having their photographs taken with him. As each young lady would come up, he would put his arm around her. Finally, the first young man came up. Having seen the Senator putting his arms around people, he put his arm around Senator Thurmond and smiled for the camera. But the Senator brushed the guy's arm off and said, "No, no, no! I don't hug men. I only hug the ladies." That was very funny.

JOHNNY MACK BROWN
When we were out campaigning, the Senator would always bypass everybody in the crowd to shake hands with the prettiest woman first. If there was a pretty woman close by, you could absolutely guarantee he was going to go right to her, shake her hand, and say hello. He sure liked pretty Southern women. It didn't matter how old he got either. He never lost his affection for the pretty ladies.

MATTHEW J. MARTIN
We had arranged a frocking ceremony for an Admiral in the Senator's private office over at the Capitol. It's a beautiful office that looks out on the Mall towards the Washington Monument. The former Secretary of the Navy was there, plus some other Admirals and guests. The room was packed, but Senator Thurmond hadn't shown up yet. Everybody started looking at me, wondering when he was going to arrive. I said, "He left his office in the Russell Building fifteen minutes ago, so he should be here any minute."

Two pretty ladies and the charming Strom Thurmond
on Myrtle Beach in the summer of 1947.

Fifteen minutes went by, and he still hadn't shown up yet.

We'd set up the room so there was this one chair in front for him to use. But it was so crowded, we wanted to make sure he found his way up to his chair as soon as he got there, since we were already running very late. It just so happened that the Admiral had this very attractive young niece. So we placed the niece right on the other side of that chair. I don't think she realized what we were doing, or anybody else for that matter; we just kind of arranged the family around his chair.

Finally I saw the Senator coming down the hallway. It was one of the last times he was walking, before he got the wheelchair, so it was very laborious for him. As soon as he got to the room and saw everybody, he just snapped up. He looked through the crowd, looked past the chair, and saw the young lady. I'd never seen him move across a room so fast. He went right up to her and said, "Hey, how you doin'? I'm Strom Thurmond." Then he said hello to the Admiral and sat down in his chair.

BO BLUDWORTH

Senator Thurmond liked his orange juice. Every so often he'd like to have what he called his "special orange juice." He wanted you to spike it with a little something, just sort of ease something into it. He'd say, "Bo, go see if they got any of that special orange juice." I remember one night we were at a reception in Washington. I was getting the Senator some of his special orange juice when I saw them bring out a big plate of raw oysters. There were two women standing nearby. I heard one of them say to the other, "If Strom Thurmond comes over here and starts eating these oysters I'm leaving."

TRENT LOTT

One time I went up with Senator Thurmond to Michigan where we both spoke at Hillsdale College. This would have been in the '80s when I was still in the House of Representatives. We experienced some delays on the way to the airport and nearly missed our plane. We finally got to the terminal, but had to run to catch the plane. By the time we got to the gate, I'm huffing and puffing and gasping for air. Senator Thurmond was hardly breathing heavy.

We got on the plane. We sat down. I said, "Now Senator Thurmond, you know, I'm one of your buddies, a fellow Southern Senator. You've got to share with me the secret of your longevity and good health. How do you do that?" He said, "Well, it's pretty simple. I take exercise every morning. I take Metamucil every day too. And I love pretty women." I said, "Senator Thurmond, I believe I can do two out of three; will that do?" He said, "Which two?"

DAVID BLACK

Sometimes older women would visit the office -- say, in their seventies. The Senator could care less. I mean, even if they were there to give him a zillion dollars he wouldn't care. He wanted them gone. He'd kind of look the other way, looked bored. He really could care less what they were talking about. But the minute you bring a pretty little girl in the room, all of a sudden he's very happy.

JASON ROSSBACH

We were reading the newspaper together one morning. There was something in it about a 55-year-old woman marrying a 60-year-old man. He said, "I don't know, that woman seems awfully old." I said, "Well Senator, some people like to date people that are in their same age bracket." He said very emphatically, "Well, I like young women. And I think most men do too."

SAM NUNN

I remember a time when Senator Thurmond and I were getting on an elevator together, on our way over to vote in the Senate. He was probably in his early nineties when this happened. There were a couple of very attractive young ladies on the elevator; they might have been interns. Anyway, I had previously had conversations with both of them, so I knew their names. I said, "Hello Mary; hello Jane. How are you all today?" They said, "Hello Senator Nunn; hello Senator Thurmond."

Later, on our way back over to our offices, he looked at me and said, "Sam, I am really impressed that you knew those young ladies' names. I've got to learn from you on that. That's very impressive." He certainly had a spark in his eye for pretty young ladies; there's no question about that.

BILL TUTEN

Over at the Capitol, the elevators are pretty small. One day Mark Ivany and I were with the Senator. This was when he was in a wheelchair, so it took up a lot of space in the elevator. Senator George Allen of Virginia and one of his staffers got on. We all kind of shoved in; there wasn't much room at all.

Senator Allen joked, "Now Strom, if it gets much tighter in here I think I'm going to have to sit on your lap." Senator Thurmond looked up at him, tapped his hands on his knees, and said, "This lap's reserved for the ladies." Everybody burst out laughing.

BO BLUDWORTH

Whenever the Senator traveled, he always liked to get out for a long walk in the evenings before he went to bed. On one trip I recall we were staying in Rome, and the Senator wanted to get out for a stroll. So, we started out just walking down the street one night, and we happened to run into a couple of ladies of the evening who were out plying their trade.

The Senator sort of zeroed in on them as we approached them, looked real closely as we walked by, and was even looking back after we'd passed them. He said, "Bo, what do you think those nice-looking women are doing out here so late? They ought not to be out here in the dark like that. You think we ought to go check on 'em, make sure they're okay?" I said Senator, "I think we ought to keep walking. I think they're ladies of the evening." He grinned and said, "Nah! You think so?! My goodness gracious, they got some nice looking ladies here in Rome."

BOB DOLE

I remember Strom would always say, "Look at that lady over there! She's quite lovely looking." I'd say, "Yeah, that's my wife!" He'd say, "Ah, yeah, well, er….ah, she's a very nice lady."

BILL TUTEN

I had Senator Thurmond over to my house in 2001 for Thanksgiving Dinner. We picked him up and brought him over. We had all the fixings. We were all sitting around the table talking. The dinner wasn't quite ready yet. I asked the Senator if he'd seen the paper yet; I knew he always enjoyed reading the paper. He said no. So I got it for him. I said, "Senator do you want something to drink? I've got beer, red wine, white wine, lemonade, Gatorade, tea, prune juice, apple juice, tomato juice, milk, you name it." He said, "I believe I'll have a beer." So here's Senator Thurmond sitting at our table on Thanksgiving going through the paper and drinking a beer. It was great.

I went in there a few minutes later and he was looking at one of those full-page ads in the newspaper. There was this tall gorgeous blonde in the ad. I said, "Senator, that's the kind of girl you need to hire at the office. We could just sit around and look at her all day." His eyes shot up at me and he said, "I think she'd be fun to love on too!" And this from a man who was one month shy of his 99th birthday! He was really something.

WALKER CLARKSON

One day we were going over to the Floor for a vote. I was literally running to catch up with the Senator before the elevator door closed. When I got to the elevator, he could tell I'd been running. He said, "If you're tired, you're more than welcome to sit on my lap." He was almost 100-years old! That was typical him. He just loved to flirt.

DENNIS W. SHEDD

I think I was with Senator Thurmond at the point when he came to realize that women needed to be looked at not just for their physical beauty. You know how long it took? It took the time it takes for the Senate elevator to go from the basement to the second floor. The Senator and I were walking to the elevators over in the Capitol. I said, "Senator Thurmond here's Sue Smith; it's her birthday today." The Senator said, "Sue!

Happy Birthday to you!" She said "Well, thank you Senator."

We got on the elevator and he said, "Mr. Shedd, when we go back to the office be sure that we send her a little letter saying 'Happy Birthday to a very pretty staffer.'" I said, "Senator, you know women these days; they don't just want to be known as pretty." He said, "That makes sense. Be sure that letter says, 'To a very competent, pretty staffer.'" It was clear to me that right at that moment he changed in how he saw professional women.

HENRY SACKS

Those last few years he was in Washington, Senator Thurmond's favorite restaurant was Elsie's, down on Route 1 in Alexandria. That last time we all went down there together, I gave him a copy of a Hooter's calendar with photos of all the pretty girls in it. It was still in the plastic wrapper. When I handed it to him, he stopped eating, ripped the plastic off, and started going page by page. I asked him which one he liked best. He got a grin on his face and said, "All of 'em!" The man genuinely had a spark in his heart for the ladies. He was an all-American boy.

ROBBIE CALLAWAY

My wife Sue and I were with Senator Thurmond in New York in the early '90s when he received the Ellis Island Medal of Honor. That was a great trip. At the awards ceremony, there were all these women who were blowing right past the other celebrities and going over to meet the Senator. He loved it.

Later when we dropped him off at the airport, he refused our offer to sit with him until his plane left. He said, "No, you two go on; it's okay." So Sue and I reluctantly left him sitting there alone. We said goodbye and walked away. Not five minutes later I came back and looked around the corner to make sure he was alright. He had five stewardesses sitting around him, and they were all holding Strom Thurmond key chains!

DEE SHORT

Senator Thurmond was at a Judiciary Committee hearing one time. They had all these liberal ladies lined up to testify, including the head of National Organization for Women. He smiled and said to them, "Why, you're all such pretty ladies. If y'all aren't married, you all could be!" Of course he meant it as a compliment, but they weren't happy with that at all. In fact, one of the women went up to Duke after the hearing and said, "Don't scrub the record because I have that on tape." Duke didn't erase the Senator's remarks, and they should still be there for all to see.

Some women like that didn't understand, he was such a Southern gentleman. He was a gentleman in every way. And for him, being a gentleman meant that you held the door for a lady; you pulled out her chair; you complimented her on her beauty. He didn't mean anything negative by it, quite the opposite. He was the epitome of a true Southern gentleman.

SUSAN PELTER

Senator Thurmond would get in trouble sometimes because when he met a woman, he would frequently compliment her on her appearance. Some women took that as an insult. He never really understood that reaction. It was his Southern upbringing. At the time that he was brought up, complimenting a lady on her appearance was the proper thing, the right thing, the nice thing to do. And he always, always tried to be nice. Then there were times when reporters would say to me, "He's sexist; he does such and such." I would have to point out, look at our staff.

There were only about five top positions on the Senator's staff, and two of them were women. Would you rather have him be someone who paid lip service to being politically correct as far as women go, or would you rather have him be someone who actually, substantively trusted women, knew they were smart, and had them in positions of responsibility in his own office? And I can tell you from experience, he listened to them, respected them, and treated them well.

PHIL JONES

was a Correspondent for CBS News for 32 years, which
included his tenure as the Chief Congressional Correspondent
on Capitol Hill.

Senator Thurmond
accepts the infamous
"Thumper" bat from
Senator John Tower.

Do you know about the Tower story? Thumper? As I know it, this was still when Senator Thurmond was in his prime; he was having kids. Little John Tower goes out, and he's kidding Strom back in the Cloak Room as being the stud of the Senate. He says, "You know when you die we're going to need a baseball bat to knock it down." Eventually Tower got a baseball bat and wrote on it, "The Thumper," and left it in the Republican Cloak Room just off the Senate Floor. And the joke was that if anything happened to Strom, they'd have this baseball bat nearby to knock it down so they could get him in the casket.

Senator Jesse Helms, Senator Bob Dole, Senator Strom Thurmond.

THE STROM THURMOND INSTITUTE, CLEMSON UNIVERSITY

The number one pioneer was Senator Thurmond. When he switched parties and became a Republican, boy, that sent a strong message across the country, particularly in the South.

— Bob Dole —

1964

STROM THURMOND SWITCHES PARTIES

Strom Thurmond was elected to the U.S. Senate in 1954 as a Democrat and served as such for a decade. His announcement in 1964 that he was switching to the Republican Party dismayed some people and delighted others.

The decision to change parties was not one the Senator made casually or quickly. The ramifications of his decision were, as he knew, very significant: on a personal level, leaving the Democratic Party could cost him votes, and on a national level, his move to the Republican Party would set a precedent for others. Whatever the negative fallout or positive outcomes might have been, Senator Thurmond made the switch because he believed it was the right thing to do. He felt that the times had changed, and that the views of the Republican Party matched his own — and those of most of his constituents — better than the views of the Democratic Party. For Senator Thurmond, becoming a Republican was a decision based on principle, not on political expedience.

BUD ALBRIGHT

When I was growing up, the Senator used to stay with us when he'd come to South Carolina. I remember when he was talking about changing parties. I was 14-years old at the time. He and my dad sat down in our living room to talk about it. They must have talked for an hour or two.

Dad was discouraging the Senator from switching parties. He said, "No, no, Strom, even you can't get elected as a Republican in South Carolina!" I recall the Senator saying, "Icky, I think I can do it. I think people will follow me." That was the thing about the Senator. He always did what he thought was the right thing to do. Then he would make the best of the politics of it. But the first question he always asked was: what's the right thing to do?

WILLIAM C. PLOWDEN, JR.

Let me tell you how I found out Strom Thurmond was switching parties. I was having an eye operation in Baltimore. I was literally on the operating table when the nurse came in and told the surgeon, "Doctor, somebody's on the telephone and wants to talk to Mr. Plowden. I can't get rid of him. He said he's got to talk to him right now." The doctor said, "You have any idea who that is?" I said, "Sir, it couldn't be anybody but Strom Thurmond."

So I got on the phone. The Senator said, "Bill Plowden! I want you in Washington in two hours!" I said, "Senator, I can't get there in two hours. I'm on the operating table." He said, "Well, how about 10 o'clock tomorrow morning?" I looked at the doctor, "He wants me to be in Washington tomorrow morning. Do you think I can make it?" The doctor said, "It's up to you. You're going to have a tube sticking out of your nose, but if you can stand it, go ahead."

So I went in and met the Senator the next morning. He said, "Bill Plowden, I'm considering switching parties. What do you think about it?" I said, "Senator, you've already made up your mind. It doesn't matter what I think about it." He said, "Well, I want to know if you can help me with the sheriffs in all the counties." That's where the power base was with the Democratic Party. Back in that day, the best political man in every county was the sheriff. They controlled a lot of votes. So it was my job to contact all the sheriffs about him switching parties. Every one of them was ready to go with him. They all loved him, because he'd always supported them.

C. BRUCE LITTLEJOHN

On the night before Strom Thurmond announced he was switching parties in 1964, he came to my house along with Harry Dent. As I recall, it was a little after supper time, and we sat in the living room. I was shocked because switching parties was a brave undertaking. That's not something you did back in 1964.

He appreciated the fact that it was a gamble, but he rationalized that his thinking had become more consistent with Republican views than with Democratic views. So he did it, and it turned the tide in the South. It gave the Republican Party leadership, which it needed badly. Except for Strom Thurmond switching parties, except for his influence, the Republican Party would not be what it is today.

BUTLER DERRICK

I was there at the airport in Spartanburg in 1964 when Senator Thurmond came off the plane and stood there with Goldwater and announced that he was changing parties. It was very dramatic. He tried to get me to switch. He talked to me a long time about it. I didn't do it, but I was complimented that he was interested. You know, South Carolina went for Goldwater. I think the politicians were upset, and there were a lot of people that were upset. But I think Lyndon Johnson was President and was about to sign the 1964 Civil Rights Act, so I can't say that he took a big chance. He was a master at figuring things out. If Strom Thurmond had on a red shirt, you better go buy one because people will be wearing them. He always knew what was coming.

LEE BANDY

I remember the switch. I was told the day before that he was going to do that. Boy, did I want to break that! But it was told to me in confidence, so I couldn't violate the confidence of the individual who told me. That was a major story. It still is. I tried to get the guy to change his mind and let me write it, but he said, "I can't because they'll trace it right back to me." I don't think there was a lot of fallout from it. I don't think it was expected, but people didn't seem to be all that surprised. Strom was an unpredictable, independent-minded kind of person. He was his own man.

JOHN DRUMMOND

I supported Strom since the very beginning. I remember when he tried to get me to switch to the Republican Party. I said, "Strom, I can do more in this party for the causes that you support than if I got into your party." Actually, a lot of Republicans told me at that time that they didn't want me to switch. I was always on his side, on every issue.

Senator Thurmond and one of his favorite
Presidents, Ronald Reagan.

ROGER MILLIKEN

*is the Chief Executive Officer of Milliken & Company and a
longtime friend and supporter of Senator Thurmond's.*

I grew up in Manhattan. I had just moved down to Spartanburg with my family
when Strom showed up at my front door. He was walking the street with a close friend
of his, Walter Brown, who ran the television station here in Spartanburg. That was typical of the way Strom worked the territory. He was knocking on doors and asking for support. That was my first introduction to a legend. He just came up and rang the bell. I
happened to be there and opened the door. I've never forgotten that moment. I was
thrilled when he switched parties.

GERALD R. FORD

was President of the United States, 1974-1977.

When I was in the House of Representatives from 1949 until I became Vice President, most of that time Strom Thurmond was a Democrat. My best recollection was that some time in the early 60s Strom switched from Democrat to Republican. That really pleased me, because ideologically he was a Republican. He grew up as a Democrat because that's what you did coming from that part of the country. But Strom was truthfully a philosophical Republican. I, for one, welcomed him into the Republican fold, and appreciated his willingness to stand up and follow ideology more than just label.

When I first saw him as a Republican, I congratulated him wholeheartedly. He became a leader on the Republican side in the Senate, for which we were most grateful. When he switched, we were in the minority and struggling hard to get a majority. His switch very definitely came at a good time. It encouraged us that this could be the beginning of a revision in numbers based on real ideology. He encouraged others in the South to become Republicans. That was a real shot in the arm.

BOB DOLE

No question about it. Strom helped to change politics in the South. He helped make the South Republican. He was a big help to Nixon. We were opening up the South. If it hadn't been for Watergate, we'd be way ahead right now in the South. That set us back about ten years, but we've been gaining ground. The number one pioneer was Senator Thurmond. When he switched parties and became a Republican, boy, that sent a strong message across the country, particularly in the South.

GEDNEY HOWE III

Because my family was so identified with the Democratic Party, I was head of Democrats for Thurmond. I discussed with the Senator whether or not he wanted me to declare myself a Republican. He said no, he liked me being a Democrat so I could lead the Democrats for Thurmond. He said, "If you were a Republican, you couldn't lead the Democrats for Thurmond. Your daddy was a Democrat; your Momma was a Democrat; you stay a Democrat and be there for me."

JESSE HELMS

Perhaps because he personally worked so hard to make it possible, Strom always referred to me as "Senator Jess Helms"— generally with a postscript about my once having been a great Democrat (when referring to the old days), and later as a great Republican after the skies trembled and brought forth a great change of political arrangement among a great many states. Strom Thurmond, after all, had revised and revamped the political tapestry not merely in his own state of South Carolina but in at least a dozen or more states.

DENNIS DECONCINI

About '81 or close to '82, Strom Thurmond came to see me. Now, that's not something that you'd normally do. Usually the younger Senator goes to see the senior Senator in his office, but he came to see me. He asked me if I would change from a Democrat to a Republican, because it was very close in the Senate then.

He said, "Look, you're more of a Republican anyway, and we'll treat you right. I'll guarantee you, I'll get you the same seniority you've got. I'll get you additional committees, all the perks that Senators like having. We really want you."

I said to him, "Strom, my father is a conservative Democrat. He's been one all his life, though I know he voted for Goldwater once. He's raised me that way. I just can't do that to myself, and I can't do that to my father." He responded to me, "Well, you know, I used to be a Democrat. I was raised with a lot of Democrats. I know they vote Republican. Don't worry. Your dad will get over it."

DAVID T. BEST

We were over at the Capitol one time, and got on the elevator in the basement. It stopped at the first floor and Senator Chris Dodd and Jesse Jackson got on. Jesse turned to Senator Thurmond and said, "Strom! Strom, how you doing?" Then he said to Senator Dodd, "Strom's my Senator. Did you know that? I'm a South Carolinian. Strom's my guy!" There was a little chit chat. Anyway, Jesse then turned to Strom and said, "Strom, why don't you come home to the Democratic Party!"

Without missing a beat Senator Thurmond said, "I'm quite comfortable right where I am. The Democratic Party left me long ago. I'm home where I need to be." We all had a good chuckle. Boy, if the press could have seen that! Jesse Jackson inviting Strom Thurmond to come back to the Democratic Party.

"Miss Chapman, Can You Keep a Secret?"

MARY CHAPMAN WEBSTER

In the summer of 1968 when I was an intern for the Senator, he took me to quite a lot of events and receptions. This was the deal, however: he was engaged to Nancy at the time, but he didn't want anybody to know about it. He wasn't ready to make the engagement public. Remember, Nancy was a heck of a lot younger than he was. He wanted to wait until after the '68 Convention in Miami to announce it so as to avoid any kind of scandal. I didn't know anything about Nancy at the time.

During my third or fourth social function with the Senator, I ran into some friends of my father's. Daddy was very well-connected in Washington. He was sort of an ambassador for the textile industry. His name was James Alfred Chapman, Jr. He had a lot of friends in Washington, so he came up from time to time. One Sunday morning after I'd been out with the Senator the night before, I got a phone call from my father. It was very early in the morning. He said, "Mary, I have a question. If the answer is no, you can go back to bed." I said, "And if the answer is yes?" He said, "Then I'm coming up to get you today." I said, "What's the question?"

He said, "Are you going to marry Senator Thurmond?" I said, "Are you out of your mind?!" He said, "Well, the word around South Carolina is that he's getting ready to marry a girl who is 21 and who was or is an intern in his office. And it's going to happen this fall. That's the rumor. Mary, the only person that fits that description is you." I said, "Daddy, I swear to God I'm not going to marry Strom Thurmond!" He said, "Well, that

Mary Chapman Webster on her wedding day with Strom and Nancy Thurmond, June 6, 1970 in Spartanburg, South Carolina.

makes me feel better, but I hope you're telling me the truth." He was terrified: "Mary! My God in Heaven, he's 20 years older than I am!"

So that was Sunday morning. On Monday morning I walked into the office. Kathryn Hook was out there at the front desk, of course. I said, "Kathryn, where is Senator Thurmond?" She said, "He's in his office Mary. I think he's doing some exercises." I walked right in there. I didn't ask to be seen. I just went right in. His personal secretary said, "Excuse me Mary, the Senator's busy right now." I said, "I don't care if he's busy or not! I have something I need to ask him."

The Senator was down on the floor with his jacket off doing one-arm push-ups. I said, "Senator, could you please get up? I need to talk to you." He kind of rolled over and sat up and said, "What can I do for you, Miss Chapman?" I said, "I just have one question I need to ask you." He said, "What's that?" I said, "Are we getting married?" Well, he threw back his head and laughed so hard. He just howled. I said, "Because my father called me, and he said there's a big rumor going around South Carolina that you're about to get married." I explained to him what my Daddy had said.

He said, "Miss Chapman, can you keep a secret?" I said, "Yes sir." He said, "I am getting married. I'm marrying Nancy Mo." That's exactly how he said "Moore." He told me she was a former Miss South Carolina and went on and on about her. Then he said, "We're getting married in November." I said, "Senator, I promise I won't tell anybody."

News of their engagement was finally announced a few months later after the Convention. There was a lot of talk about it, of course; she was forty years younger than he was!

THE STROM THURMOND INSTITUTE, CLEMSON UNIVERSITY

*If Strom Thurmond hadn't gotten out of Nixon what he wanted, Ronald Reagan would
have been elected President that year. Strom Thurmond made Nixon the President.*

– James B. Edwards –

Miami Beach, Florida

THE REPUBLICAN NATIONAL CONVENTION OF 1968

*I*n 1968, the Republican National Convention was held in Miami Beach, Florida; the front-runners for the Republican nomination for President were Ronald Reagan and Richard Nixon. Few people realize the critical part that Senator Thurmond played in securing Nixon's nomination or know the reasons for his support.

The Senator favored Nixon in large part because of the fair treatment he believed Nixon would extend to the Southern states. Although Strom Thurmond is often best remembered for his service to South Carolinians, his central role in the 1968 convention shows his concern for the South in general and the influence he wielded nationally.

GARRETT CUNEO

is the Executive Vice President of the American Chiropractic Association.

In 1968 I was a member of the California Republican Delegation to the Miami Beach Convention. That was the first time that Ronald Reagan ran for President. In retrospect, of course, part of the problem was that Reagan waited too long to announce his candidacy. He had waited up to about a week and a half before the Convention began to announce. You can't wait that long. Too many people had already committed themselves.

Anyway, I got down to Miami Beach a couple of weeks early. Our plan was to stop Nixon on the first ballot, because most of the delegates that Nixon had were for one ballot only. They would be released on the second ballot. And most of those were the old Goldwater delegates and strong Reaganites. So we had to stop Nixon on the first ballot.

Florida and Mississippi were key to our plan because they each had what was called the Uni-Rule. That meant whichever candidate had the majority at the time of the balloting would get the entire delegation. So if Reagan could get Florida and then Mississippi, and a few other things happened, we could keep Nixon from getting the first ballot victory. That would open it up to the second or third ballot.

My job on the night of the balloting was to monitor the walkie-talkie conversations of the Nixon and Rockefeller people. This was in the pre-Watergate days. They were monitoring our stuff; we were monitoring their stuff. Everybody knew that, so they would try and disguise themselves. But in the excitement you could pick up certain codes. For example, we knew "Leopard" was Mitchell and "Tiger" was Halderman.

At one point in the evening when the balloting had just started, I intercepted a message. I think it was between Halderman and Mitchell saying, "Get Senator Thurmond down to Florida! It looks like Florida is going to go to Reagan! Get Thurmond down here!"

Well, of course I communicated that to F. Clifton White, who was Reagan's campaign manager. He was in one of the trailers outside the convention. I don't know what he did with that information. Obviously he must have been concerned because an hour later when it came time for Florida to vote, they went for Nixon and not Reagan. After that it was a house of cards. Mississippi went for Nixon. Nixon won it on the first ballot.

I've always wanted to know what Thurmond had to say, because I do believe that if Florida had gone for Reagan that night, then Nixon would have been stopped on the first ballot. We very well could have seen Ronald Reagan win the presidency in 1968. It's no secret now that Thurmond helped keep the Southern delegates with Nixon. Senator Thurmond had a great reputation among the Southern delegates. They all trusted him. But I always wanted to find out exactly what he told those guys.

About four years ago, I finally had that chance. I had dinner with Senator Thurmond, Duke, Mark Goodin, and a couple of others. I asked the Senator about that night in Miami. He said he remembered the incident. He said he went down there and basically told those guys that it wasn't Ronald Reagan's time. And more importantly, if the delegates didn't stay with Nixon there was a good chance they would go to Rockefeller, who was anathema to all the conservatives there. Thurmond told them that they needed to support Nixon, that he was a good guy.

Now, there may have been other things he said in addition to that, but in any case, that was in essence what he told them that changed the vote. And who knows: what he said that night may have changed history.

JAMES B. EDWARDS

I was for Reagan at the 1968 Convention. I'd been working for him in the South. Senator Thurmond and his aide Harry Dent were working for Nixon. Harry and I decided that we'd each work for our respective candidates, but that we'd also communicate and work together for the good of the country and South Carolina. I was going to lead the Southern delegates for Reagan. Harry Dent told John Mitchell what was going on. He said, "John, we've got a problem. The Southern delegates are about to break and go with Reagan." Nixon was refusing to meet with anybody, so Harry told John Mitchell he better come with him to a meeting of the Southern delegation to get a feel for what was really happening.

At this meeting, I was chosen to get up there and tell the Southern delegates that they should break and go with Reagan, and that this was the best thing for America. We had an electoral map that showed how Reagan could win in '68 if he was the Republican nominee. Well, Harry Dent had John Mitchell there at that meeting listening to my presentation. I could see them both standing way in the back. The presentation went very well. We had just about done it. The Southern delegation was ready to break with Nixon and go with Reagan. That's when Harry Dent turned to John Mitchell and said, "You know, the only person that can save this for Nixon is Strom Thurmond." Mitchell supposedly said, "We've got to get Strom Thurmond together with Nixon as soon as we can."

When Nixon's plane landed in Miami, the first person that got on that plane was Strom Thurmond. They spent at least a half hour talking. Before Nixon even got off the plane and came to the convention, he'd already met with Strom. As we understand it now, Strom got some commitments out of Nixon for the South, including signing off on Supreme Court nominees and that kind of thing. It was all over after that. When Strom Thurmond endorsed Nixon, it was all over for Reagan in '68.

Many years later I asked Strom what he had said to Nixon on that plane. He said, "Well, I wanted the South to be treated and recognized like the rest of the country. We talked about the Supreme Court and federal judges. We got some significant agreements out of Nixon. Nixon was a good man. He cooperated with us for the South." That's all he could tell me. But Strom was satisfied that he had the commitments he needed to endorse Nixon. When Strom came out with his endorsement for Nixon, all the Southern delegates fell in line behind that. Harry Dent had done his job well for his Nixon.

I'll never forget seeing John Mitchell at that meeting of the Southern delegates. He left out of there, smoking that pipe he always smoked, almost running. He and Harry Dent left that meeting in high gear to go talk to Nixon about what was going on, and to get him together with Strom as fast as they could. Mitchell was running so fast out of the room, Harry could hardly keep up with him. Mitchell saw the writing on the wall. He knew we were ready to go with Reagan. Most people don't realize how close we actually

Strom Thurmond and Richard Nixon at the Republican Convention in Miami, 1968.

THE STROM THURMOND INSTITUTE, CLEMSON UNIVERSITY

came. If Strom Thurmond hadn't gotten out of Nixon what he wanted, Ronald Reagan would have been elected President that year. Strom Thurmond made Nixon the President.

JOHN DALTON

In 1968 I was a young Naval officer, a Lieutenant in the Navy. Senator Thurmond was out campaigning for Richard Nixon. The Senator flew into the southern part of the Battery in Charleston, South Carolina where I was assigned to a submarine. I went to the rally to hear him speak. That's the day I met Strom Thurmond. As a young Naval officer, it was a real treat to meet him.

Of course, George Wallace was also running for President, and a lot of Southerners were voting for him. Senator Thurmond was concerned that those voters were going to drain away votes from Nixon. His message that day was simply this: a vote for Wallace is a vote for Humphrey. I'll never forget that day. He was really hammering that message: a vote for Wallace is a vote for Humphrey. Senator Thurmond worked very hard that year to see Nixon become President.

George Bush, Strom Thurmond,
and peaches from South Carolina.

You never left Thurmond's office empty handed; it didn't matter who you were. He said,
"Holly, give me some of those key chains."

– Phil Jones –

"Take One If You're Single and Two If You're Married"

FROM PEACHES TO KEY CHAINS: LITTLE GIFTS FROM SENATOR THURMOND

*I*f you met Senator Thurmond you were just as likely to receive a firm handshake as you were a keychain — or a letter opener, a peach, a photograph, a book, or any number of other little gifts that he liked to give out to people.

I recall the time I had a new batch of key chains ordered. They were individually wrapped in plastic. It made for a nice little package, and I thought that would make them a better gift. After they were delivered, I walked into the Senator's office to find him hunkered down over the open box of new key chains. He was completely absorbed in the task of taking each key chain out of its plastic wrapper. I said, "Senator! Wait! What are you doing?" He said, "I'm unwrapping these key chains." I said, "But Senator, they're supposed to be wrapped. They came that way. We paid extra for that." He looked up at me with a quizzical expression. "Why would I hand them out like this?"

I think he had opened the box and assumed that the key chains he'd always given out in the past had come wrapped in plastic, but that someone in the office had usually unwrapped them before they got to him. I said, "No Senator, we ordered them wrapped so they'd make a nicer gift." He looked into the box and thought about that for awhile. "Oh," he said. Then he stood up, clapped his hands together a few times, and said, "Okay then, what's next?"

CRAIG HELSING

When you went to see Strom Thurmond in his office, you could never get out of there without him giving you a key chain to remember your visit. He'd call across the room in that southern voice of his and say, "Holly! Get me one of those President Pro Tem key chains for my good friend here." He always made you feel like it was something really special he was giving you. He never wanted anybody to leave empty handed. He wanted to make sure you had something to remember the moment by, whether it was a key chain, a letter opener, or a photograph.

I'll never forget the time my mom was in town, and I took her to meet Strom Thurmond. She got a key chain and had her picture taken with him. He signed the photo, "To Doris, one of the pretty young girls who came to see me in the Senate." He was such a fine southern gentleman. It brings a smile to my face right now to think of that Southern accent of his and the way he would make everybody feel so important, when of course it was him who was important.

ELIZA EDGAR

When I first started working in the summer of 1996, the Senator was busy running for reelection for the last time. He went down to the state nearly every weekend, and most often stayed at the Holiday Inn on Assembly Street in Columbia. When he came back, he always brought the little shampoos and soaps from the hotel. He would bring them out front to us and let each of us pick which "treat" we'd like to have from his trip. I literally had a drawer full of Holiday Inn soap, shampoos, conditioners, and lotions. The Senator was always excited whenever he stayed in a hotel besides the Holiday Inn. He saw it as a new start on the collection.

ASHLEY HURT CALLEN

*worked as a Legislative Assistant in Senator Thurmond's
Washington office from 1999 until January of 2003. She is now
General Counsel to Congressman Gohmert.*

When I was a page for the Senator he gave me a bar of soap. He always brought back soaps and shampoos from his travels. I remember thinking that was so thoughtful of him to remember me like that. I mean, I was just a page. He didn't have to do that.

DEE SHORT

Throughout our home I am constantly seeing reminders of the Senator. Everywhere I look there are little gifts and keepsakes that he gave us. In large part this was due to Holly because she always made sure the Senator remembered us on holidays, anniversaries, and birthdays. Many times at the office the Senator would receive floral arrangements or boxes of candy. Knowing my love for flowers and sweets, he would often send them home with Duke to give to me.

BILL TUTEN

Senator Thurmond was one of the most caring individuals I've ever met. He always wanted to give you something, whether it was a key chain or even part of his lunch. He was always looking for little gifts he could give out to people, especially the staff. He really cared about his staff. When he was on the trip to China in 1997, every morning he went through and picked up all the stuff that they replenished, like shampoos and soap. He brought all that stuff back in a huge bag and put it on the couch in his office. Then he called around to the different sections of the office and had everybody come in and get a souvenir: "Come get you a Communist soap or some Communist shampoo." I still have a comb he gave me that he brought back from China.

GEORGE LAUFFER

Every year the farmers down in South Carolina sent Senator Thurmond loads of fruit. He'd get many cases of peaches, oranges, and grapefruits. After he gave out some fruit to the other Senators and government officials, he always had plenty of boxes left over. So he invited the staff, both the personal staff and the Committee staffers, to come into his office and pick up a piece a fruit.

He oversaw the whole process. There was just one thing to remember. If you were married, you got two pieces of fruit. If you were single, you got one. You would walk into his office with all that fruit laying around. He would say, "Are you married?" No, Senator. "You get one." And he'd watch you just to make sure you didn't take too many.

After doing this for about five or six years, it gets kind of childish walking all the way over there to pick up a piece of fruit. So Les Brownlee, who was the staff director, and I decided we had more important things to do. The next morning we got a call from the Senator's office. Holly said, "The Senator noticed you two guys didn't come over to get your fruit." We told her we were busy. She said, "Well, the Senator wants you to come over right now to get your fruit." So we marched over there and walked into his office. The Senator said, "We missed you yesterday!" Despite all our efforts, he still caught us.

DAVID BLACK

Each year we'd go into the Senator's office to pick up our peaches. He'd always say the same thing: "Take one if you're single and two if you're married." If you picked up two he would add, "Tell your wife to cook y'all a peach cobbler!"

GEORGE ALLEN

Strom's office was across the hall from mine, and I saw a lot of him in the coming and going on our way to meetings in the Capitol and to votes in the Senate. He would bring the best-tasting South Carolina peaches to Washington every summer. On one occasion, my staff took most of Strom's peaches, leaving me only two or three in the bag. I was disappointed not to get more than a couple of peaches. It was something I looked forward to each year. Later that day, I saw Strom and was grousing because I didn't get many peaches. The very next day I had my own bag.

DAVID T. BEST

In most offices you get in to see the staff, but you don't get in to see the Senator. It wasn't that way with Senator Thurmond. He loved to meet with constituents. It didn't matter whether you were a tourist from South Carolina who just happened to wander in or if you were the Secretary of Defense; every meeting was the same. There was a greeting, a welcome, then everyone took a seat. He didn't chit chat. I remember some staffers would come in and chit chat; he didn't like that. He didn't like to waste time. After the greeting you sat down to business. Then came a picture if they wanted that. And then everybody got a key chain. It didn't matter who they were; every single person that visited that office always got a key chain.

MIKE DEWINE

When I first introduced Senator Thurmond to my wife, Fran, I told him, "Now Strom, she's the mother of eight kids." Instantly he looked at her and shook his head and said, "What a woman! What a woman!" He put his arm around her then reached into his pocket and handed her one of his famous key chains. Every time he saw her after that he always greeted her with, "What a woman! What a woman!"

LESLIE SEALY

It was my job to make sure the Senator had enough key chains and letter openers to give out to people. I always got a kick out of how important he made those things. Every time I would go in there, he would give me a key chain or a letter opener. He would say, "Did I ever give you one before?" I would smile and say, "Yes sir, you have." And he would answer, "Well, let me give you another one anyway." Whenever the Senator left his office I would take that key chain or letter opener and put it right back in his desk. Then he would give it to me over again. I thought that was really funny.

RUTH BADER GINSBURG

is an Associate Justice on the United States Supreme Court,
1993-present.

Senator Thurmond was an unforgettable character. Just consider his transformation from what he was to what he became. He had a knack for making people feel that he genuinely cared about them. I still keep my office key on the chain he gave me. When my initial supply ran out, he was good enough to send over more.

ROBIN ROBERTS

It was Christmas time in 1979. A few of us were meeting with the Senator to help him figure out what to give people for Christmas. There were 100 pounds of Young's Pecans that had been shipped up from the state. The deal was that everybody had to submit their list of people that deserved pecans, and the Senator would send out a bag of pecans with a Christmas letter. Of course, there were more names than there were bags of pecans. So everybody had to go through their list and justify why this or that person should get the pecans. It was kind of funny to hear people making a case why someone deserved a bag of pecans for Christmas.

When we finished that, Senator Thurmond asked what was next on the list of gifts after the pecans. We decided it would be a letter opener. I was sitting next to the Senator, keeping a list of who got what. I noticed that Senator Dole's name was on the list to get a letter opener. I leaned over and whispered to the Senator, "Senator Dole is on the letter opener list. He's been here a long time. I'm sure he's already got a letter opener with his name on it." Senator Thurmond reared back in his chair and said, "You know, you're exactly right! But he doesn't have one with my name on it!" So we made sure that Senator Dole got the very first letter opener that Christmas.

STEPHEN L. JONES

Here's a story from back in the mid 1970s. The Secretary of the Navy at the time was a fellow named Middendorf. He was kind of a renaissance man. He played the piano, loved the arts, came from a long prestigious family. He was a super nice guy. We were meeting in the Senator's office about something. At the time, there was a L'eggs factory in the up part of the state. They made the women's stockings and packaged them in those little plastic eggs. They sent them to the Senator as a gift to give out to people.

We finished up the meeting and Middendorf had agreed with the Senator on what he wanted done. Of course, the Senator was always giving out stuff to anybody who came to visit in the office. So he went looking around to find a little gift to give Secretary Middendorf. He came out with a big box of those L'eggs pantyhose that he just happened to have in the office. He loaded up the Secretary with about a dozen of these little eggs. On the way out of the office, Secretary Middendorf said, "Well, I've never been bought before, but if you got to be bought, you might as well be bought by silk stockings!"

STAN SPEARS,

Major General, U.S. Army (ret.), is the Adjutant General of South Carolina, 1995-present.

Every time I went to see the Senator he would give me some trinket that he was giving out that day, whether it was a letter opener or a key chain. I must have pocketfuls of both. Every time he gave me one I always kept it, because I knew one day it would mean a lot to my children and grandchildren.

BUD ALBRIGHT

Senator Thurmond knew me before I knew him. He and his first wife Jean were good friends with my mom and dad. I was born when he was Governor. I have a sterling silver cup that he sent to celebrate my birth. It's a real treasure for me. So he and I go way back.

ARNOLD PUNARO,

Major General, United States Marine Corps (ret) served as the Staff Director for the U.S. Senate Armed Services Committee and worked on Capitol Hill from 1973 to 1997. He is now the Executive Vice President of Science Applications International Corporation.

This story is probably apocryphal, but I'm told on one of his trips overseas that Senator Thurmond gave the Pope one of his President Pro Tem key chains. After he did that, the Senator said, "Well, you got all these important people around you, all these Cardinals; let me give you a few more key chains for each of them." And he gave the Pope a whole big stack of his key chains to share with the Cardinals.

PHIL JONES

This is a story I heard from one of Thurmond's staffers who was there at the time. The Senator had some of these super rich textile people up from South Carolina visiting him in Washington. At the end of the meeting, he wanted to give them something. You never left Thurmond's office empty handed; it didn't matter who you were. He said, "Holly, give me some of those key chains."

Thurmond said, "Gentlemen, before you go I want to give you something." And he held up the key chain. "Now you see on this side here, it's got the South Carolina flag. You turn it over here and it says President Pro Tempore." Then he took the key chain and slammed it down on his desk as hard as he could. He said, "Now this is no ordinary key chain. Normally when you hit a key chain on the desk like that, it would break. But this one didn't." Then he hands a key chain to each person. "Now gentlemen, don't tell everybody, because everybody wants one."

He knew it was just a cheap little thing, but by God he was going to make it sound important to those rich people.

MICHAEL MISHOE

Senator Thurmond was not the kind of person to just sit around and talk. He was all the time working or doing something. If he did have any free time, he'd clean out his desk. One time I got a call to come into his office. I got in there, and he looked up and said, "Why Mr. Mishoe, do you wear cuff links?" I said, "Yes sir, I do." He said, "I found a pair of cuff links here in my desk that I thought you might like to have." I said, "Thank you, Senator." Then he said, "They don't really match, but people only look at one arm at a time anyway." Both of them had T on them for Thurmond, but they were totally different cuff links. I don't think I've ever worn them, but I definitely appreciated the gift.

CLARENCE THOMAS

Whenever I went over to see Senator Thurmond, he was always gracious. The first thing he did every time I went to see him was to take me around and introduce me to every staffer and intern in the office. And he'd always give me a book of matches and key chains. I'm sure if I look in my basement I'd find a bunch of matches and key chains from Strom Thurmond.

KEVIN WILKINSON

is a Senior Congressional Affairs Specialist with the Federal Bureau of Investigation. He has been with the FBI's Congressional Affairs Office since 1980.

Ken Black was a former Thurmond staffer who had a long career on the Hill. When he retired, he had a party out at his house to celebrate his birthday. Senator Thurmond was there with Duke and Dee. The Senator was of course working the crowd. He went from room to room, and every time he came across a pretty lady, he would introduce himself and give her one of the coveted President Pro Tempore key chains. I was in the den chatting with Kenny when my wife walked up with a big grin on her face. I said, "What's the matter, honey?" She laughed and handed me about six Strom Thurmond key chains!

The Senator was going from room to room, but he was actually walking in a circle through the house — from the foyer, into the kitchen, out to the dining room, the living room, and then the foyer again. He was working the crowd and just kept going, handing out key chains as he went.

DAVID LYLES

I remember a night down on the Senate Floor back in the mid 1980s. Senator Goldwater was Chairman of the Armed Services Committee at the time. Senator Thurmond was President Pro Tem. It was about eight o'clock at night, and a few Senators were having a big squabble over a particular issue. The leadership got kind of fed up with what was essentially an internal debate between the Appropriations Committee and the Armed Services Committee. So they suggested the Senators involved take their staff, go off the floor, and come back when they had solved the issue. So Senator Thurmond said, "Let's all go over to the Pro Tem's office to solve this. Come on!"

Senator Thurmond marched out the door to the Pro Tem's office, and all the staff followed him over there. But all the other Senators who were involved went downstairs to get something to eat. Senator Thurmond walked into the office, turned around, and he had about ten staff people with him — but no Senators! We all kind of looked at each other for a few minutes. We didn't know what to do. Senator Thurmond seized the moment.

He started by telling everybody about the history of the Pro Tem's office. He knew it all. Then he came to a framed map on the wall about the Battle of Cowpens. So he launched into this long lecture about the Battle of Cowpens and how that turned the tide in the American Revolution. When he finished, he walked around the room and gave everybody a key chain as a memento for their evening there in the President Pro Tem's office.

Senator Thurmond spoke for about forty-five minutes. By the time he was done, five or six of the other Senators had finally arrived. Since those Senators were not there when he started, Senator Thurmond shared with them a little history of the Pro Tem's office. Then he came to that map of the Battle of Cowpens, and I'll be damned if he didn't give those Senators the same lecture that he'd just given all the staff. He repeated the entire lecture.

Then he walked around the room and gave out Strom Thurmond key chains again! So in the space of an hour I got two introductions to the President Pro Tem's office, two lectures on the Battle of Cowpens, and two Strom Thurmond key chains! And to this day I still have those key chains.

I remember that as Senator Thurmond was handing out the key chains, Senator Levin said, "Strom, I've already got a key chain. Can I have a car this time?"

An Unexpected Gift

THE FREDERICK HART BUST OF SENATOR THURMOND

Most of the time it was Senator Thurmond who did kind things for others, but sometimes he was on the receiving end of good deeds. I recall an unexpected and amazing gift the Senator received in 1997 from the world-famous sculptor, Frederick Hart. Two years before, in 1995, our good friend Henry Sacks had arranged for us to meet Rick Hart. Henry and Rick were also close friends.

Rick and his lovely wife Lindy invited a group of us out to their house for an afternoon. Dee and I took the Senator, Henry, Dee's brother Rocky Robinson, and a small group of good friends to the Harts' residence in Hume, Virginia. Rick gave us a tour of his beautiful home and then took us to his studio, where he was working on statues of former President Jimmy Carter and Senator Richard Russell. We were all naturally impressed with Rick's talent and skill.

On the way home that evening Dee told the Senator that she was going to commission Rick to create a bust of him. "That would be nice," the Senator said, quite flattered. I thought it was a kind gesture, but believed it to be an incredibly expensive proposition. However, Dee was absolutely committed to making the project happen.

She formed the Strom Thurmond Statue Committee and recruited close friends of the Senator to donate $1000 each towards the bust. In a brief period of time, Dee had collected donations from five people (Warren Abernathy, John Campbell, John Napier, Willie Valentine, and Preacher Whitner). What came next was a wonderful surprise to us all.

Rick Hart called Dee to say that if she would hire the artist Willa Shalit to create a life mask, he would donate the bust to the Senate. Willa completed the life mask, and Rick used it to

Rick Hart, Senator Thurmond, and Dee Short at the
dedication of the Senator's bust, June 5, 1997.

determine most of the facial features. Needless to say, what Rick Hart did was a most unexpected and appreciated gift. It was one of the kindest gestures that anyone has ever made to Senator Thurmond.

On June 5, 1997 the United States Senate accepted the bust at a ceremony honoring Senator Thurmond as the longest-serving member of the Senate. The Senator was, as one could imagine, so very pleased and proud of Rick's creation.

The bust was placed in room S238 in the Capitol. This room was officially named the "Strom Thurmond Room." At that time the room served as the Senator's personal room in the Capitol. These rooms are generally referred to as "hideaways" by others, but Senator Thurmond always said that he did not hide from anyone and refused that name.

The Strom Thurmond Room is occupied today by the President Pro Tempore of the Senate, Ted Stevens of Alaska. Rick Hart's bust of Senator Thurmond remains on display in the room.

President Gorbachev of Russia and Senator
Thurmond.

*He never put on airs. He never insisted on star treatment. And he never pushed himself to
the head of any line. He was a principled, humble, Southern gentleman.*

– R.J. Duke Short –

Thurmond the Man

*P*erhaps the most often asked question that I get about Senator Thurmond is this: what was he really like? Behind the image and icon that was Strom Thurmond, there was a very real man. A man, like everyone, with faults and weaknesses, but there was also a man of unparalleled heroism. The stories in this chapter are a window on what this man was like up close, in relationships, behind the public image.

Strom Thurmond was the most down-to-earth, unpretentious individual I've known in my life. As famous and as powerful as he was, you wouldn't expect that to be the case. But if you didn't know that he was a U.S. Senator, you might just as well have thought he was Joe Jones from down the street. He never put on airs. He never insisted on star treatment. And he never pushed himself to the head of any line. He was a principled, humble, Southern gentleman.

On the other hand, he was demanding, impatient, meticulous to a fault, and could embarrass the hell out of you without even realizing it. He was also the most frugal, tight-fisted man I believe that has ever been a member of the United States Senate.

I'll never forget being with him one time during the holidays in Atlanta. We were on a bus during a tour of an airbase. He was talking about getting gifts for his children for Christmas. He said, "Nancy just spends so much money on these children! Five dollars is enough to spend on each of them!" I said, "Senator, you can't even go to McDonald's on five dollars!" He said, "Ah! Five dollars should be enough!" He was always in a time warp when it came to money.

But Senator Thurmond also had more than his share of courage, generosity, optimism, and compassion — all of which he graciously shared with the people of South Carolina. That's what Strom Thurmond was really like.

JACK DANFORTH

When I went to the Senate as young man, all I knew about Strom Thurmond was just 1948 and the Dixiecrats. I thought he was going to be some kind of a mean, hard-edged person. But he was the absolute opposite of that. Strom Thurmond was a good soul. He was just a good human being. He was positive and had great instincts. It's so unusual to be around somebody that old who's in that kind of form for so darn long. When I left the Senate at the end of '94, he was still going full blast.

ALFONSE D'AMATO

Strom had a great way of making people feel comfortable. And he was always building people up. When he ran into other Senators, even Democrats, who might be walking with some constituents, Strom never failed to come say hello and tell them, "You have a great Senator!" There was never a time — if we were on the subway together or we were coming up the elevator together and I had a constituent with me — he never failed to tell that constituent what a good Senator I was. He was always reaching out, trying to make people feel comfortable. He didn't care if they were Democrats or Republicans.

JOHN R. STEER

I can't resist stating how much the Senator always cared about people as individuals. When I got married, I married a woman that I'd met here in Washington. We got married in Northern Virginia, and he came to the wedding. He didn't have to. This was not a group of South Carolinians with whom he could drum up votes. But he came anyway, because he cared.

In 1985 I had a serious leg operation, and he came to see me in the hospital. He helped me with my career. Little things like that. And I am by no means unique. But that was so typical of Strom Thurmond. He honestly cared about people, and not because of any political advantage that might accrue to him. That was his nature. He was very compassionate and unselfish. South Carolina is full of people with those kind of stories.

BUD ALBRIGHT

When I was working for the Senator, I happened to mention that I wanted to get contact lenses one day, whenever I could afford them. They were too expensive for me at the time. I simply said it in passing, in conversation about something else. The next day Sylvia, the Senator's secretary, called me in and said, "Here's an appointment to go have your eyes examined. The Senator wants to give you those contact lenses." That's the kind of guy he was. He was always doing for other people.

BILL TRAXLER

We were riding somewhere one time, and Senator Thurmond asked me how my family was doing. Everybody was doing fine, except I did have one child at the time who was sick. Right then and there he wrote out a short note to my son saying, "I hope you get well soon." He didn't have to do that. It was a simple act of kindness that you don't soon forget. We still have that note, and we'll always have it in the family.

CLARENCE THOMAS

After I was confirmed for the second time at EEOC, Armstrong Williams was working on my staff. He invited Senator Thurmond over to swear me in. I thought that was great because the Senator had always been a defender and had always been there for me. When he swore me in, Senator Thurmond looked around and said, "Who's going to hold the Bible? Where's your wife?" I said, "Well, I don't have a wife." He said, "You don't have a wife?! You need to get you a wife!" Even afterwards, before he left, he came up to me and said, "A young man like you, you need to get a wife!"

ROBERT MCNAIR

The Senator was always very personable, very warm, very friendly, regardless of who you were. That was one of his strengths. And he had a history of having very strong staff people, people who were committed to looking out for the Senator's interests. They were very responsive to people who would call or write in about problems, whether it was Social Security or a travel visa. With a strong staff in place to help him, the Senator always served his constituency well.

KAREN J. WILLIAMS

Senator Thurmond had a great sense of humor. He was warm, generous, uplifting, and always positive. And he was very insightful. He could pare right down to the core of an issue.

JUDAH BEST

was Senator Thurmond's personal attorney. Mr. Best is of Counsel with the law firm of Debevoise & Plimpton.

There was a certain old-fashioned civility in the way the Senator addressed and dealt with people. It was a civility that you don't usually expect these days. He would listen to people, nod gravely and courteously. He was always courteous to people, even when they made the most preposterous of comments. He would simply say, "Well, that is certainly a point of view."

I thought that he was extremely well served between Holly Richardson and Duke Short. He had people who guarded him, protected him, and made sure he was briefed for all assignments. When you met with the Senator, he was always very focused on the matters at hand and would always listen attentively to what was said.

JASON ROSSBACH

The most surprising thing about the Senator was how nice, approachable, and easy-going he was about everything. He was in public service, in some position of power, his entire adult life. Yet he was still so down to earth, so laid back. And he treated everybody the same, regardless of their station in life. If you were a foreign leader he treated you with respect and dignity. If you were a tourist stopping by for a photograph, he treated you with the same degree of respect and dignity.

I was very privileged to enjoy a unique perspective of him, being that I spent all day with him. Never once did I see him refuse to stop and talk with someone or refuse a picture or an autograph. He made time for everybody. I asked him one time how, after all these years, he still had the patience to stop and chat with the tourists. He said, "It's very easy for me. These are the people who live in this country, whether they vote for me or not. And when they come to D.C. it's an important event for them. It may not seem like a big deal to you, but people save their time, their money, whatever it is, and they come here to see us. It's my job to be here for them. I work for them."

But it wasn't like an obligation for him. He actually enjoyed talking with people. I can't say the same thing about most of the Senators and Congressmen I observed in Washington. With very few exceptions, there was no one else like Senator Thurmond who sincerely enjoyed talking with people, hearing where they were from, and listening to them talk about their vacation.

DAVID T. BEST

I remember one evening we were celebrating the Senator's birthday. It must have been December of 1993 or '94. We were at the Retired Officers' Association building. They threw a big party for him. The Joint Chiefs and all the Service Secretaries were there. Charles Barkley was there as well. Senator Thurmond was over at the oyster bar by himself. The poor guy working the event didn't have the right shucking knife, and he was doing his best to keep up with the Senator.

Everybody gravitated to Barkley, getting his autograph and saying hello. When he left, I went over to the Senator and said, "Did you know who that was?" He said, "Well, I think it was a ballplayer or something. He's a big fella. He looks like a ballplayer." I said, "Yes sir Senator, that was Charles Barkley. He's one of the most famous, well-regarded, and talented basketball players in the world." The Senator kept eating his oysters. In between bites he said, "Yeah, he looked big."

Everybody was on the same level for Senator Thurmond. There was no celebrity mystique with him. Whether it was a Senate page or the President of the United States or a famous basketball player, he treated every person with the same degree of respect and regard. Everybody at that event was like: hey! It's Charles Barkley! Senator Thurmond was like: hey, nice to meet ya, back to the oyster bar.

MARY CHAPMAN WEBSTER

I never saw Senator Thurmond lose his temper. He could be short in terms of talking fast. If he had something he wanted to say, he'd say it quickly. I never saw him insult anybody either, not once, even though I gave him plenty of reason to!

One afternoon Kathryn Hook was out to lunch, and I was asked to sit at her desk. Well, my God, there must have been a million phone calls a minute that used to come into that office. At one point my father walked into the office. I said, "Daddy! What are you doing in town?" He said, "I have a meeting with the Senator." I said, "Well, let me ring him." So I rang the Senator. He picked up the phone and answered, "Dick?" I thought, who? What is he thinking? I said, "No Senator, it's Mary. My father, James Chapman, is here to see you." So he told me to send him on back.

The next time the phone rang I picked it up, "Senator Thurmond's office." A voice said, "This is Dick Nixon calling." I said, "Yeah right." And I put him on hold. Right then somebody walked through the office and I said, "It sounds like Rich Little is on the phone. Some jerk is on the phone saying he's Dick Nixon." They said, "The Senator's expecting that call!" I said, "You're kidding!" They said, "No! That's Vice President Nixon calling for the Senator!" Then it hit me how the Senator had answered the phone earlier. So I said, "Oh s—!" I grabbed the phone. It was dead. He had hung up. I couldn't believe it.

Then the phone rang again. "Ah, hello, this is Dick Nixon. I'm calling from California. Is the Senator in?" I said, "Oh Vice President Nixon, I am so sorry; I'll put you right through." You know, the Senator never got upset with me about that. He teased me about it, but he never got upset about it.

MARK GOODIN

Senator Thurmond was a complicated, very complex man. I don't think a lot of people understood the complexity of Thurmond. He was larger than life in so many ways, and yet he could do things that were so incredibly small sometimes. But he was a confluence of very conflicting currents. He was deep cold water; he was shallow warm water; he was clear water; he was all those things. He was an amazingly complicated and complex human being.

Interestingly enough, he had a very soft heart, and it broke very, very easily. You could say things about him that would cut very deeply. You'd think somebody that had been in public life as long as he had, and had been called so many names by so many people, that he'd be immune to it. But he had a soft heart, and a very thin skin sometimes.

I saw him cry three times: the day his brother died; the day his daughter Nancy Moore died; and I saw him cry the night I think he became convinced, for the first time, that his wife Nancy had an alcohol and drug problem that needed attention. That was the night before Jim Eastland's funeral, and there had been some incidents at the house that made it pretty apparent that Nancy had a problem.

SUSAN PELTER

What made Senator Thurmond angry? He'd get angry if he thought that South Carolina was getting short shrift in any way. And he'd get angry if someone broke their word to him. That would really make him angry. And he despised shoddy work, and didn't have a lot of tolerance if things weren't done right. He always paid attention to details, and expected everyone around him to do that as well.

ALAN SIMPSON

Strom was not the kind of man to swear. But I do recall one time. Jack Anderson had written a piece on him alleging that somebody had passed him a brown envelope, implying that he had accepted some money for something. It was a total fabrication, totally phony. I was in the Chair in the Senate the day the column came out. Strom came up and said, "Look at this article. That man is a son of a bitch!" I never heard Strom use that word before or since. Of course, it was all later proved to be false. I never saw Strom more steamed than I did that day.

JASON ROSSBACH

Senator Thurmond seldom got mad, but if he did, it was gone in five minutes. He just moved on and forgot about it. It wasn't because he didn't remember it; he just chose not to live with that anger. I asked him about that once. He said, "I don't live in the past, even in the recent past. We got to keep moving forward!" I think that was one of the reasons he lived as long as he did and was as successful as he was.

I remember one time he got real mad at me. I think he was upset with Holly about something. The Senator wouldn't really argue directly with you. He'd call somebody else in and ask them what they thought. Because my desk was exactly between Holly Richardson and Duke Short, I spent a lot of my time trying to think of how not to say anything at all.

He called me that time and said, "What do you think of this?" I said, "Well sir, I agree with Holly." He said, "Well that's just ridiculous! Are you sure?" I said, "Yes sir." Then he got mad and said, "Well, you're just an ass!" It's really funny when I think about it now.

JUDITH RICHARDS HOPE

The thing I remember most is that Senator Thurmond and Duke Short were a team. Duke always knew what the Senator wanted and was able to implement his polices. They were a great team, devoted to each other professionally and I'm sure personally. And from time to time one or the other would call up and say, "Let's have lunch and talk." That was when I was out of contention for a big high-power job. They both expressed a sense of loyalty and interest I found very surprising in the Senate where, normally, you're only as good as your latest appointment. But that wasn't true for Senator Thurmond or for Duke Short either. Once you were a friend, that was it. They were committed to you.

TERRY L. WOOTEN

The Senator had an extraordinary work ethic. Senator Thurmond went over to meet the troops sometime during the Gulf War. He stopped over in England on the way back, spoke to some more troops there, then flew back home. It was an all-night flight. He came to the office directly from the airport at Andrews Air Force Base. It must have been about 5:30 in the morning when he got there. There was a Judiciary Committee hearing that morning and he wanted to make sure he was there.

He'd flown all night coming back from the Gulf. He was near 90 at the time. I went over to talk to him. I said, "Senator, if you need to get some rest we'd be happy to arrange that. I know you've been flying all night." He said, "No, I'm fine. It's no problem." He came to the hearing at nine o'clock that morning. Then he worked all day after that. I went back over to his office that night about nine o'clock at night to brief him on the Judiciary Committee meeting that was going to happen the next day. This was a man who was nearly 90-years old; he'd flown all night from overseas; then he worked a full 12-hour day before he finally got home.

That's just one example of the kind of dedication he had. The Senator never left the office until he felt like that day's work was done. It didn't matter how long it took; he would stay until it was done. There were many nights when I was there until two or three in the morning, and he was right there too, working away.

MARIE BOYLE BUCKLER

There was one experience I had with Senator Thurmond that really made me appreciate the man, not the Senator, that he was. We were working on the first campaign for George Bush, Senior. He was coming down through the state for a number of appearances with the Senator, and Mr. Abernathy had hired a young man as an aide to go with them.

So the Senator came in one weekend, and the young man was going to meet him for the first time. I told the Senator, "I think this young man is a bit intimidated by you." Senator Thurmond was really taken aback by that. "Intimidated by me?!" He couldn't believe it. "Why would he be intimidated by me?" I said, "Well, you are a United States Senator."

He looked at me and said, "Let me tell you something. I put my pants on just like your father does. I'm no more important than your father is. It doesn't matter if your father is a truck driver, a garbage collector, or President of the United States. We men get up, go out, and make a living for our families. That's what we do. The fact that I'm a United States Senator doesn't make any difference. Nobody should be intimidated by me." He honestly believed he was simply a regular man, just someone's dad, who just happened to be a United States Senator.

DENNIS W. SHEDD

Senator Thurmond was a very demanding person. People didn't see that in his public persona. But I will tell you, he was very demanding. He let me be completely honest with him about everything. I always tried to be respectful. But he would listen to what I said, and he would never say, "I've been elected six times; how many times have you ever been elected?" He never did that kind of stuff. He always listened.

I think he was a great person for testing your metal, throwing you in the fire, seeing how you produced. He started by doing for me what he did for a lot of South Carolinians. He took them and gave them the opportunity to let whatever merits they might have take them as far as they can go. That's what he did for me, and that's what he did for thousands and thousands of people. And in all those people, I think he instilled a great respect for the right way to do things.

JOHN L. NAPIER

We all know that he was a unique man. He was also a very decisive man. Once he made up his mind on something, he didn't turn back. And he never looked back with recrimination or regret. He told me one time that when he was a young man he lost his temper. His father called him aside and told him, "When you lose your temper, you lose control of the situation. You must never lose your temper because that hurts you and no one else." So he learned at an early age that losing his temper wasn't going to do anybody any good. Since 1972 when I entered the practice of law and started working for Senator Thurmond, I never once saw him hold a personal grudge against someone or lose his temper.

DARYL JONES,

Colonel, U.S. Air Force Reserve, served in the Florida State Senate from 1992 to 2002. Colonel Jones was nominated by President Clinton to be Secretary of the U.S. Air Force but was not confirmed by the Senate. He is now an Attorney with Adorno & Yoss.

When I became the nominee for Secretary of the Air Force, I met with Senator Thurmond. He said that he would support me. In fact, all of the Senators, Republicans and Democrats, initially said they would support me. Unfortunately, when it came time for my nomination hearing at which I was to testify, President Clinton was going through the Monica Lewinsky issue. I was ultimately not confirmed. I always felt that my timing had a lot to do with not being confirmed. It seemed that they were actually after President Clinton more than me. In the end, Senator Thurmond was the only Republican who supported me. He was the only one who kept his word.

WILLIAM W. WILKINS

Senator Thurmond was a great man to work with. He was a man of high character and integrity. His word was his bond. He believed that integrity, honesty, and forth-rightness really do count. They were very real things to him that I'm sure he learned from his father. Everybody on the Hill knew that if Senator Thurmond told you something, you might not agree with it, but you could rely on it.

JIM DEMINT

Before I ran for Congress, I recall being at the airport one time and seeing Senator Thurmond. He was walking off a plane, all alone. There was no escort and no staff. I was just amazed that someone of his stature was just walking around, chatting with people at the airport. You'd expect to see an historic figure like that flanked by security and staff. But there he was, just walking along with a smile on his face, all by himself. The man had absolutely no pretensions.

DENNIS W. SHEDD

During all the years that I worked for the Senator, I don't think anybody spent more time right at his elbow than I did. And in all that time, I never heard Strom Thurmond say a bad thing about anybody --- not one negative word. People might not believe it, but that's the truth. He just didn't do it. He had many opportunities to say negative things. I never heard it. Nor did he ever use any kind of racial language. He didn't do any of that.

The Senator was not the type of man to worry about things. He told me once, he said, "Dennis, you know, worrying is a waste of time. You can't do anything about it. Just move on to the next thing." In Senator Thurmond's life, everything was just as important as everything else. Nothing was critically important, and nothing was unimportant. The question about what vegetable he was going to have for lunch was just as important to him as what he was going to do on the next Senate vote. He kept an absolute even keel on most things.

He was a frugal man. I'm sure there are a lot of stories about that. One time he asked me to drive a staffer out to the airport. It so happened that I had to drive out to her house to pick her up, then over to Andrews Air Force Base to catch a military flight. But the flight was canceled. So I had to drive her back around the beltway to her house, then back into D.C. to the office. I must have spent five or six hours that day riding around and sitting in traffic. At one point I had to stop and fill up my 1977 Oldsmobile Cutlass with gas. I must have used up about $20 worth of gas.

The next day Senator Thurmond calls me into his office and says, "Mr. Shedd, thanks for your help with that staffer. I want to pay you for your gas." I told him he didn't have to worry about it, but he insisted. So he pulled out his wallet, licked his thumb and started going through his bills. He went through the twenties; he went through the tens; then he stopped and pulled out a five dollar bill. He even popped it to make sure it was just one five. I was thinking to myself, well, that's not all I spent on the gas but it's better than nothing. The Senator handed me the five dollar bill and said, "Now bring me back three ones."

SONIA HOLMES PRICE

I learned so much about patience from observing the Senator. He was a very patient, quiet man. I loved his disposition. If he got angry, I didn't see it. I just loved that about him. And his work ethic was unparalleled. He had energy to work from sun up to sun down. But he always took time to do things that you wouldn't expect. He would take time out of his incredibly busy schedule to talk with the staff, ask how we were doing. He let each of us know that he cared about us. Certainly that's one of the reasons why I hold him so dear to my heart. He always took the time to show he cared. In a world where there are so many powerful people who are at times condescending and not as accessible, it's just refreshing to know that I worked for a man that many people would have loved to have just said, "I walked into his office." I'm privileged and proud to say that I knew the man.

LES BROWNLEE

Senator Thurmond was extremely frugal. Some people might even refer to it as tight. It was like he still viewed things in economic terms maybe from a 1920s or '30s perspective. Discussing salaries with him was always an interesting conversation. When you described the salary that you believed somebody should get so you could keep them on the committee, he would always be flabbergasted and say, "That's a lot of money!" I'd say, "Well yes sir, but they were drawing this before, and we're going to have to pay them this to keep them." Again, Duke Short was always very helpful in those kind of sessions, and I relied on him greatly. The Senator was actually most tight-fisted with the taxpayers' dollars. He wanted to be sure that they were all spent wisely and that the government got its money's worth.

CRAIG METZ

I went into the Senator's office one time to brief him on something, and he was there at his desk with three stacks of money in front of him: fives, tens, and twenties. He was busy counting them. As I approached the desk, he kind of leaned forward and covered up the money with his arms and gave me a look like I shouldn't come too close. Then he said, "Oh, excuse me Mr. Metz; that's fine, have a seat." I sat down, and he went back to counting the money. He said, "Why, there's three hundred dollars here! Three hundred dollars! Holly, what did you give me this much money for?!"

Holly had given the Senator spending money for his trip to the Republican National Convention in New Orleans. Senator Thurmond was going to be there with Mrs. Thurmond and their four children for a week. Holly said, "Senator, you go ahead and take that money with you and if you don't use it all, you bring it back and I'll deposit it." He said okay. Then he took out a stapler and stapled all the five dollar bills together, the ten dollars bills together, then the twenty dollar bills together. Then he took out this wallet that had several rubber bands around it. He took the rubber bands off and put those three different stacks in his wallet, then put the rubber bands back around it and put it in his pocket. Then he looked at me and said, "Now Mr. Metz, what you got for me?"

JAMES B. EDWARDS

When you think of Strom, you think of courage. He had political courage. He bucked the Barnwell Ring. He went head to head with them. He couldn't get any support out of them when he was running for Governor. So he used the Barnwell Ring as an instrument to talk about. He had the courage to do that kind of thing. He did in fact beat the Barnwell Ring and became Governor.

He went out and ran as a write-in candidate. That in itself shows the courage the man had. He went around and gave out pencils with his name printed on the side so everybody would know how to spell his name. He also had the courage to support Barry Goldwater, the Republican nominee. He had the courage to walk out of the Democratic Convention over the States' Rights issue. The Democratic Party tried to reprimand him for that. He had the courage to switch to the Republican Party.

His whole life is one of dedication to the people of South Carolina in so many ways, and of courage to get things done. He never lacked for courage in anything he has ever done. When I think of him, I think of a courageous man. I think of a judge who stepped down from his post to volunteer for the Army. That took incredible courage. And all his political life, he did the courageous thing and never shirked his duty. He was a disciplined, courageous, fearless sort of guy.

MARIE BOYLE BUCKLER

I had a brother Michael who worked for the Senator for several years. He became terminally ill. It was public knowledge that Michael was gay, and he had AIDS. When he was diagnosed with AIDS he came to the Senator. He no longer worked for the Senator at that time, but I did. Michael told the Senator that he was going public with his AIDS, because he wanted to help other people not make the same kind of mistakes he had made. He wanted the Senator to know this ahead of time, because he didn't want it to hurt the Senator's reputation in any way, and he also didn't want it to hurt me in my job. I was told much later that they had a staff meeting one day when I was away, and the Senator told everyone that he was not to hear anything at all derogatory about Michael or myself, that it was not going to be tolerated in that office.

So we went through nineteen months of Michael's illness. Any time I needed to be off with Michael, the Senator always said, "Go; don't worry about your job. Go be with your brother." But the most touching thing was this: when Senator Thurmond's daughter, Nancy Moore, was killed, he buried her on a Friday. Saturday a week later he was there sitting by himself on the row behind the pallbearers at my brother Michael's funeral. I couldn't believe it. I thought it was such a tribute to his respect for my brother and our family. What an awesome heart he had. Remember, this was just a week after his daughter was unexpectedly killed. He wasn't even seeing anyone in public at this point. They had canceled all his meetings. But there he was at my brother's funeral. That's the kind of person Senator Thurmond was. He always put others first. At the cemetery he hugged my parents and said, "You keep Marie here in South Carolina as long as you need her." Then he hugged me and said, "You need to get back to work; that's the best thing for you."

Before he died, Michael traveled quite a bit, speaking out about AIDS and encouraging young people not to make the mistakes he had made. It was not easy to go public like that. It took a great deal of courage. But if Michael could do anything to make one person's life better, he was going to do it. If he prevented one person from contracting the disease by making a foolish mistake, then it was all worth it. Michael knew he didn't have long to live. But he was going to take whatever time he had left to try and help people. Michael learned that lesson from Senator Thurmond.

DEE SHORT

All my life I thought I knew Strom Thurmond. After all, I was born and raised in upstate South Carolina, studied about him in school, and along with my entire family, was a staunch supporter of his. I recall in fifth grade government class, we were assigned to write a paper about our favorite statesman. I chose Strom Thurmond. Little did I know, twenty-five years later, I would be sharing that paper with him. The Senator was very pleased that he had made a favorable impression on such a young child.

Each time I saw the Senator, he would ask how my family was getting along. He was particularly fond of my brother Rocky, whom he often referred to as one of South Carolina's most successful businessmen. When our brother James, who lived in Spartanburg, South Carolina, passed away in January 1999, the Senator not only called the family to express his condolences, but also sent a personal check in James's memory to Beaumont Baptist Church in Spartanburg. Senator Thurmond had a huge heart and was a man of great compassion. I will never forget his many acts of kindness.

The Strom Thurmond I personally grew to know was more than one of the greatest statesmen this country will ever have; more than the best friend our military, law enforcement, and education system will ever know; and more than the greatest politician South Carolina will ever produce — he was like family to us. I experienced his genuineness, sincerity, caring and concern. I witnessed his love for God, country, family and friends. I am so blessed to have known Strom Thurmond the man.

Strom Thurmond as Daddy

*S*trom and Nancy Thurmond had four children together: Nancy Moore, James Strom II, Julie, and Paul. Like any dad, he absolutely adored his children. He was incredibly proud of each of them. He did everything in his power to see to it that they were well cared for, had opportunities, and knew that they were loved. Having children so late in life (he was nearly 70 when Nancy Moore was born) was not easy on him or the family. His Senate duties kept him away from home a great deal. It was very challenging for him to balance being a father and a public servant.

Those challenges were made all the worse when Nancy Moore was killed in 1993. She was hit by a drunk driver while crossing the street at Five Points in Columbia. She died the next morning. Nancy Moore Thurmond was only 22-years old, and just a few weeks shy of graduating from the University of South Carolina. It has been said in the press that the Senator threw himself into his work as a way of mourning. That was accurate. He seemed to want to work around the clock, always asking us for something else to do. Losing himself in work helped him cope with sadness, which is something I believe he first learned in the wake of Jean's death in 1960.

The death of Nancy Moore was a tragic loss for her entire family and for her friends. It was of course particularly difficult for Mrs. Thurmond. My heart really went out to her. I know she was incredibly distraught and had a very hard time. Dee and I shed our own tears, but I believe in my heart Nancy Moore's passing was a loss for South Carolina as well. She was very much like her father: smart, good-looking, compassionate. Had she chosen to do so, she could have been a real political force in the state and in the nation. It's quite probable that Strom Jr. has that future now. I know he has the natural talents and abilities to do great things for the people of South Carolina. His heart is in the right place, and he will do what his father before him did: help people, all the people. I know the Senator would be very proud.

U.S. SENATE PHOTO

Nancy Moore, Julie, Senator Thurmond, Paul
and Strom Jr.

JACK BALLARD

is a 20-year veteran with the Capitol Hill Police Department, 1974 to 1994.

One day Senator Thurmond asked if I had a family. I told him I had gotten married late in life. With a twinkle in his eye he said, "When an older man wants children, he needs a young wife."

JACK DANFORTH

I remember back in 1970s, my wife and I took our young children to the circus. During the circus I turned around and looked up. There in the stands sat Strom Thurmond, watching the circus with his children. You just never knew where he was going to pop up.

WILLIAM SCHACHTE

I was at a soccer game where my youngest son was playing. We were standing around, and all of a sudden I heard somebody yelling, "Kick the ball Strom!" I recognized it immediately as that unmistakable Senator Thurmond voice. I looked over and yes, there he was: wearing a hat, an overcoat, and brogans. He sure was giving his son hell.

KEVIN WILKINSON

Holly called me one day. This had to be back in the mid 1980s. You could tell there was some commotion going on in the background. Holly said, "Hold on a second!" Next thing I know Senator Thurmond is on the line and he's screaming, "These kids are driving me crazy! Can't they come down to the FBI and see some guns or something?!" Evidently the Senator's wife was in South Carolina, and the two boys were in the office that week. I think the constant interaction was a little stressful for him. Of course we were more than happy to make arrangements to bring the boys down.

The Senator's driver showed up a few hours later and deposited the two boys at the FBI. We took them up to the Laboratory and showed them our firearms. We essentially kept them occupied for a few hours down here before we returned them to their father. Like I said, we were very happy to help. In all my years of service here, we could always count on Senator Thurmond for a fair hearing. He was absolutely a joy to work with.

MARIE BOYLE BUCKLER

When I worked for the Senator in South Carolina, Mrs. Thurmond was still traveling back and forth to Washington, D.C. That was right after they had relocated the family to South Carolina. So she was back and forth quite a bit. The Senator would come in on Friday nights and would be there for the weekends. He was very strict with the children about their diets. He didn't like them going out to fast food restaurants and stuff like that. And Mrs. Thurmond was very strict about what they watched on television and what kind of movies they went to.

I remember one time when the children had all gotten really good report cards. So it was decided to let them have a night out as a treat. Nancy Moore, the oldest, went on a date, and the other three kids picked a movie that they were all going to go to together. They were also going to get to go to McDonald's, which was a grand treat for them. Strom was like 16, Paul the youngest was 13, and Julie was 14. Mrs. Thurmond was traveling, so she told me to get the money from the Senator for the children. She wasn't to come back in until Saturday morning.

So the Senator came in Friday evening, and the kids were all ready to go. I told the Senator, "Mrs. Thurmond left word for you to give the children some money to go to the movies and out to dinner. We're going to let them have a treat this weekend because they got their report cards and they all did very good." The Senator pulled out a five-dollar bill and handed it to them. The kids, they all just looked at him and didn't know what to say. They looked at me. Then he looked at me and said, "What? Doesn't it cost a quarter to go to the movies?"

He was holding a handful of bills. So I proceeded to take two more five-dollar bills and gave it to them. I said, "Senator, that's for dinner at McDonald's." Then I took three more five-dollar bills out of his hand, gave them each one, and said, "And that's to pay to get into the movie." Then I took three more five-dollar bills and gave one to each child and said, "And Senator, that's for popcorn and a drink while they're at the movies." His jaw dropped. He shook his head and said in total disbelief, "It costs that much money?!" So Julie collected all the money. He very sweetly hugged her and said, "Honey, bring me back the change."

On Saturday morning, Julie came down for breakfast. Of course, by that time the Senator had already been up for awhile and done his exercises. Julie plopped sixty-seven cents down on the counter. He said, "Where's my change?" She said, "Daddy, that's it." For the rest of the day, all he could talk about was how when he was a child and went to the movies, it cost a quarter and you could go all day long, and that would buy you a box of popcorn and a Coke as well. The kids laughed and joked about that for several weeks. He never fussed about giving them money. He just had a hard time wrapping his mind around the fact that things don't cost what they used to.

DAVID T. BEST

We were working another late night. Paul and Strom Jr. were in Washington, and they came down to join the Senator for dinner in the private dining room. He invited me to join them. I recall they had a choice menu. It was a buffet, a salad, or you could order off the menu. The two boys ordered the buffet. They ate pretty well. But they didn't clean their plates, because it was a buffet.

Senator Thurmond looked at them and said, "Why'd you take that food if you're not going to eat it?" They said, "Dad, we ate what we wanted." He said, "Well, you should-n't take food if you're not going to eat it. Now I remember World War I and Victory Gardens." And he started going on about rationing during World War I. The boys were typical teenagers: "Oh Dad! You weren't in World War I." He said, "But I remember Victory Gardens. We struggled for food." And he gave them the father-and-son talk about not wasting food.

I just kind of eased myself back and took in the scene. It was really something to sit there and see Senator Thurmond as a father. It was just a great experience, because it sounded like a conversation that could have gone on between any dad and his boys. And their responses were very typical.

I know he always thought about his kids. We'd be down on the Senate Floor voting, and he'd get up and walk back to the Cloak Room and have somebody get one of the kids on the phone. He just wanted to hear their voice and find out how they were doing.

GEDNEY HOWE III

Both Strom Jr. and Paul worked for me for a whole summer while they were in law school. The Senator called them every day, talked to them about what was going on, what they were learning, that sort of thing. So I had a chance to see first-hand his parenting and see how very involved he was in the boys' lives. I remember when Strom Jr. first came to the office the Senator said, "Gedney, I want you to teach him how to practice law." I smiled and joked, "Don't worry, Senator. I'll teach him how to charge a fee." He laughed and said, "Don't just teach him how to charge a fee; teach him how to collect one!"

I know some people had the sense that because the Senator was in Washington and was so involved in the public business, that his children must have suffered as a result. But I watched those calls come in. I watched the kids come back to me with new ques-tions about the law that they had gleaned from conversations with their dad. The Senator was actively parenting those boys. He was very involved in their growing process, all the way up to their adulthood. It was a side of him that I didn't realize was there. I'm sure many people never saw that side of him. I'm honestly surprised that he was able to do it all. In addition to everything he did for South Carolina and the country, I think he was a really good daddy.

I recall one story Paul told about making his bed. His daddy came in and said, "No, you have to do it like this." Paul said, "Daddy, everything doesn't have to be perfect." Senator said, "Well son, everything that can be, should be."

There's another story that shows what a detail-oriented guy the Senator was. They had gotten this tremendous bag of nuts and bolts. They spent two hours sorting them out. It was sort of valueless as a mass, but if you separated them out you could see what you had. The Senator was right in there with them, showing them how to follow through and get the job done. This is what the boys told me: that their basic principles, work ethic, reliability, and attention to detail all came from the old man.

CRAIG METZ

We were riding somewhere one time, and I commented to the Senator, "It's so great that you have two boys and two girls. It seems like such a nice family." He said, "Yes, the boys are nice. But the girls, they just wind themselves right around your heart strings."

MELINDA KOUTSOUMPAS

During our trip to China in '97, we were all out eating dinner somewhere. The Senator's daughter, Julie, and some of the younger people left after dinner to go out to a party. A little while later, somebody mentioned something about the shirt the Senator was wearing. It was a polo shirt. He looked at it and said, "Well, I've never liked this shirt, but I thought I should wear it tonight because Julie gave it to me."

JAMES FLOYD GRAHAM

One Saturday Senator Thurmond, his daughter Julie, her friend, as well as myself went on a White House tour. This was during the Clinton administration. Julie wanted to see the Ford bedroom, but we were told by a Secret Service agent that no one was allowed upstairs. The Senator intervened and stated to the agent, "Get me your boss." The agent in charge arrived and told the Senator that he would have to talk to the President first. After consulting with the President, an agent returned and said, "Let's go upstairs."

We visited all of the bedrooms except the President's private bedroom. We couldn't

The Thurmond family.

go in there because the First Lady was taking a shower. Shortly, the President of the United States, Bill Clinton, came walking down the hall by himself. He greeted the Senator by saying, "Hi, friend."

MICHAEL BOZZELLI

I was with the Senator the night Strom Jr. was officially confirmed as U.S. Attorney for South Carolina. We were driving home, and someone called from the Senate

Nancy Moore Thurmond and her daddy.

Republican Cloak Room to say that they were going to take that issue up and try to pass it that night. I said to the Senator, "It's on the Senate's agenda for tonight. It looks like it's a done deal." The Senator said, "It's not official yet." I think the Democrats were in control at that time, and they were pulling out all the stops. They weren't conceding anything for nothing. They wanted something in return, given who Strom Jr.'s Daddy was.

By the time we got the Senator home, the phone call came. They had voted. It was official. The Senator asked to speak to his son, so we got Strom Jr. on the phone. I happened to overhear the conversation. His son was thanking him profusely for helping him. You could tell the Senator really appreciated his son's remarks. He said, "You know son, I have always tried to do everything I could for you. Now, just live up to the example that I have set for you." It was a very poignant moment.

I've always been very fond of Strom Jr. He was always very deferential to his father. He showed him so much appreciation and respect. And his dad really did do a lot for him. When the Senator hung up the phone, I looked over at him. You could really tell he was a very proud father.

DEE SHORT

I remember being in the car with Senator Thurmond when he would phone his children. He was always supportive of them whether they were in school or starting a new job. He told them to work hard, study hard, and keep up the good work. He would often say how proud he was of them.

I remember one particular evening after the Senator hung up the phone with Strom Jr., I said to him, "Senator, I hope Strom Jr. will have you a little grandson one day, and I hope he will be just like you." He turned to me and in all seriousness said, "Dee, why don't you talk to him about having a grandchild for me?" I laughed and said, "Senator, you know I'd do anything in the world for you, but I don't think I should do that. They may tell me to mind my own business." He said, "I guess you're right." We all just laughed.

MARK GOODIN

I was in South Dakota when Nancy Moore was killed. Dennis Shedd called me from the hospital and said that Nancy Moore had been hit by a car and was in a very bad way. I said, "Where is the Senator?" He said, "He's on his way here now." I said, "How bad is she?" He said, "Mark, she's dead. She's on life support right now. But she's dead." I said, "Dennis, you've got to have a crash cart ready. I mean this! You've got to have a crash cart ready in case he has a heart attack over this. This kind of shock could put him over

Strom Thurmond, Nancy Moore Thurmond, Warren Abernathy, Duke Short on January 3, 1991 celebrating Thurmond's election to a seventh term.

the edge." I believe Dennis ordered up a crash cart or at least had a doctor on standby in case that happened.

I finally got to see the Senator several days later. He was sitting by himself. Holly had actually called me and suggested I come by. I stepped in the office, and he looked up and took one look at me and his eyes just watered up. I walked to the seat in front of the desk and sat for a moment. He said, "She was so good. She never hurt anyone. How could God let such a thing happen?" And he dropped his head and began to sob. I stood up and walked to the other side of the desk, and I put my hand on his shoulder. His head touched my chest, and he just sobbed.

I looked at him and said, "Senator, if I could answer that question I suspect I'd be the richest man in the world. I don't know. There are many, many things that God does that I don't understand and no one can because God is God." Before I could go any farther, something seemed to just click in at that moment, and the stoicism was back. He looked at me and said, "Let's talk about something else. How are things politically in the state?" He just turned the switch back on. That was his way. He took a deep breath. I sat back down, and we chatted some about politics.

ALAN SIMPSON

We all thought that the death of his dear daughter would just destroy him. Oh, that was such a tragedy. We just thought that would kill him. He grieved, but then he moved on. That was the way Strom was: no matter what he faced in his life, he persevered and moved on.

MARIO D'ANGELO

I went up to his office and sat with him for a little while when his daughter died. That poor man really went through a rough time. When I found out, I called Holly and asked if I could come express my condolences. He was sitting at his desk when I went in, obviously in deep mourning. We talked some. He cried. And we just sat there for awhile together. You could really see that the man was hurting deep inside.

BOB DOLE

One of the saddest things I ever experienced was the funeral of Strom's daughter. It changed their lives, and probably ruined Nancy's for awhile. He went after the liquor industry. I don't mean that in a mean-spirited way, but he understood there was a problem with drunk drivers and it should be addressed. So he became a champion in that area too.

JOHN WALSH

I spent time with Strom when their child was killed by a drunk driver. He said to me, "How ironic. I always admired you, and I always looked up to you for how you dealt with the loss of your child. Now I'm walking in your shoes, and I really feel the pain of it. I can understand now why you're so driven."

We talked a lot about losing a child. It breaks your heart. I talked to him a lot about that, about how to get through it. It really affected him and the whole family tremendously. It's a heartbreak. That girl had so much potential. I said, "You'll survive Strom. You have to; you're tough." He said, "John, this is the worst thing I've ever been through." I said, "Yeah, same for me. But you either let it break you and victimize you doubly or you pick up your bootstraps and you go on for the rest of your family. You're not a quitter Strom." And he said, "No, I'm not a quitter." And he didn't quit. And it didn't break him. But it sure took the wind out of his sails for awhile.

Senator Thurmond and Anna Tolles West,
August 6, 2000.

U.S. SENATE PHOTO

*Strom Thurmond genuinely loved babies. He loved to hold them and talk to them.
He just adored them.*

– David Black –

All God's Miracles

Many people remember Strom Thurmond's toughness. They recall his fighting behind enemy lines during World War II and his willingness to stand up to anyone — U.S. Presidents, foreign heads of state, or military leaders — for his beliefs. Senator Thurmond was always a force to be reckoned with.

The Senator also, though, had a remarkably tender and compassionate side. He cared deeply about people and always tried to treat everyone respectfully.

The affection Senator Thurmond felt for people and the delight he took in their company were greatly magnified with children. From tiny babies to high-school students, youngsters claimed a special place in his heart. Quite simply, the Senator adored them, and he was always looking for ways to give them something: advice, a hug, a hand-written note, a key chain, or especially help with any challenges they might face.

DAVID BLACK

The Senator loved babies. When little kids would come in, newborns to about two-years old, his eyes just lit up. People think that politicians show affection to babies because they're supposed to, part of the image or something. But Strom Thurmond genuinely loved babies. He loved to hold them and talk to them. He just adored them.

DARRELL G. SMITH

*was the Chief Investigator for the Senate Judiciary Criminal
Justice Oversight Subcommittee. He is also the former Assistant
Regional Commissioner for the Western Region of the Criminal
Investigation Division, U.S. Treasury Department.*

My wife Nell and I had the pleasure of going with Duke and Dee and the Senator a
few times to his favorite restaurant, Elsie's. He loved that place. He always ordered a
really big breakfast and cleaned his plate. I remember how he always took the time to
write a little note for each child who might be there that morning. He wrote them each
a little note of encouragement or best wishes, just something so that they could one day
remember the occasion. He really enjoyed the children.

FRANK NORTON

The Senator was so wonderful to me personally, and to my wife Carol, and our little
son Lee. I'll never forget we had Lee's picture taken with him when Lee was about
18 months old. I was nervous because Lee didn't like to go with other people. He was still
very clingy to his mother and me. Of course, we got to Senator Thurmond's office and
Holly, bless her dear heart, was there. Senator Thurmond said, "Colonel, I'm so glad to
see you and your lovely wife and this wonderful son. Come here; let me get a hug."

He reached out with those massive hands of his and took Lee. I thought, oh Lord, Lee's
going to pitch a fit. But Lee just snuggled right up to him like nothing you've ever seen in
your life. The Senator carried Lee around the office, finally sat down and put him on his knee.
Lee was sitting there, the happiest baby you've ever seen. Carol and I were amazed.

ROBERT "BO" SHORT

*is President of the American Leadership Foundation.
He is Duke Short's eldest son.*

I have a lot of wonderful memories of Senator Thurmond. In some ways he was like
an extra grandfather to me, my sister, and my brother. He was at my wedding, and he
wrote the foreword to my first book. My fondest memory with the Senator took place
when my little girl was born. After nine years of attempting to have a child, Sandy and I
were finally blessed with a little girl, Taylor Chilton Short. The first call we received in the

Bo and Sandy Short with their daughter Taylor,
Strom Thurmond and Duke Short.

hospital from a non-family member was from Senator Thurmond. He called to welcome Taylor to the world, to congratulate us, and to tell us he'd had a flag flown over the Capitol in honor of her birth. He also told us that the next time we came to Washington, he wanted us to be sure and stop by. "I can't wait to hold that baby!" he said. He was so excited for us.

A few months later, we got to Washington. Dad took Sandy, Taylor, and me down to see the Senator. He was in a conference with at least a dozen other Senators at the time, in a room just off the Senate Floor. We stood out in the hall and waited. The door was open, and you could tell it was a pretty intense discussion.

At one point Senator Thurmond looked up and caught our eye. He suddenly motioned to the other Senators that he had to leave for a moment. So he broke off the meeting, came out into the hall, and grabbed Taylor up in his arms. He oo'd and ah'd a little bit. Then the first thing he said was, "She is a miracle." He was right. He was so moved and so proud. He looked at my dad and said, "How about that Duke! That's your beautiful baby granddaughter!" Dad was smiling ear to ear. I will always remember that moment, when we all stood together and had our picture taken.

RON KAUFMAN

I have a daughter who is now twenty-two. She had the honor of twice interning in Strom Thurmond's office. I was just lucky enough that she could have interned in a bunch of different Senators' offices. But she chose Strom Thurmond. Let me tell you the reason why.

When my daughter was in the sixth grade, I brought her to work for a father-and-daughter day. She and her best friend came to work with me for a day in the life of a lobbyist. Naturally I had put together a kind of big day. I started off with a fund-raising breakfast for Senator Warner. Then we had some serious meetings on the Hill with a couple of clients. Before noon I did an interview with CNN, and the reporter put both girls on TV. Then we had lunch with a couple of members of Congress. That evening we had dinner with Mary Matalin and James Carville. I'd planned out quite a day for them.

I'll never forget two things from that day. The first is, around two o'clock in the afternoon, they were both sound asleep on the floor of my office, completely exhausted. The second is, on the way home I asked my daughter and her friend, "What was the best part of the day?" I thought they'd say being on TV or having lunch with the Congressmen. They both said, "Meeting Strom Thurmond!" You could have knocked me over with a feather. I'll never forget that as long as I live.

JACK DANFORTH

Strom was always polite and extravagant, even by Senate standards, in his expressions of esteem. I recall that he very frequently had a lot of school children and interns in tow. I distinctly remember one time being in an elevator with Strom and a whole bunch of kids. He said, "I want you to meet Senator Danforth; he's one of the South's very best Senators." I felt like saying, I'm not from the South. But that was Strom. That was just the way he was.

BECKY FLEMING

The Senator would often meet with groups of kids who came up from the state to see Washington. He always made a point to tell them to be proud, because they were from the finest state in the country. I recall one time when the Senator was nearly 100, he met with about 150 fifth graders who were up from Rock Hill, South Carolina. He shook every fifth grader's hand that day.

This one little kid came up to him and held his hand out. He was staring down at his feet. The Senator kind of grabbed that little kid's hand and said, "Son! When you shake a man's hand you need to look him in the eye!" If you could have seen that little fifth-grader's eyes. He looked right up at the Senator and said, "Yes sir!" The teacher was standing beside me. She said, "That child will never forget that as long as he lives." I thought, well neither will I!

JOHN DALTON

In the mid-term elections in 1994 the Republicans took control. Senator Thurmond became Chairman of the Armed Services Committee. In my role as Secretary of the Navy, I had a close involvement with the Chairman. I remember having him over for breakfast one time. It was when the Jon Benet Ramsey case was going on. I remember talking to him about what was going on in the world and that subject came up. He sort of looked off in the distance and almost got emotional about it. He finally cleared his throat and said, "Why in the world would anybody want to kill that little girl?" He was clearly shaken up over it. This had nothing to do with a constituent or Charleston or South Carolina. It upset him so because he was always so very concerned about people, especially children. It struck me as a moment that defined Strom Thurmond.

DEE SHORT

We took the Senator to brunch at Elsie's Restaurant every Sunday for many years. We often saw a little girl there who was eating with her family. We always stopped and said hello and visited with them a little each week. One Sunday the Senator signed a dollar bill and gave it to the little girl as a present. When we saw her the next Sunday, she was upset because no one at school believed her when she said she knew Senator Thurmond. I guess they thought she'd made it up.

So that week, Duke got together a goodie bag for the little girl: a signed photo of the Senator, some key chains, stationary, a letter opener, and some other things with the Senator's name on it. The little girl and her family were so appreciative of the gifts. The next time we saw her after that she said she'd taken the goodie bag to school for show and tell. She said everybody was so impressed. They believed her now! Of course that thrilled the Senator. He was so pleased that she was happy.

HELENA HUNTLEY MELL

worked for Senator Thurmond from 1980 to January of 2003.
She held a variety of posts, including Chief Clerk for the
Anti-Trust Judiciary Subcommittee, Legislative Correspondent,
and Staff Assistant.

There's a lot that's been said about Senator Thurmond. I have one story, about something that happened uniquely to me. And it happened the first time that I met him. The Thurmonds met in my home town of York at the Grape Festival Parade. I think they actually met at the York Country Club. He was Senator, of course, and she was Miss South Carolina. After they got married, they came back to York for the Grape Festival. I think that was August of 1969.

There was a small reception for them before they went to ride in the parade. I was there. We had all formed a line to meet them, and the Thurmonds were walking down the line speaking to everyone. I was 13-years old, and I was standing there with one of my brothers. I saw Mrs. Thurmond, and I just thought she was the most stunning thing I had ever seen. She was in a suit, and her hair was done up with a pillbox hat. I wanted to say something really nice and special to her. When she got to me, I got up my nerve and I said, "You are so pretty." Just at that moment, something distracted her. She turned away from me and left. And I was just standing there.

My brother started laughing at me. I was just mortified. I guess Senator Thurmond had seen the whole thing. He immediately stepped up, and he took my face in his hands and he said, "No, you're the pretty one. What's your name?" He made everything okay. He made me feel really special. I didn't know it then, but I certainly know it now, that he said that dozens of times a day.

"WHEEE!"

STROM'S SENSE OF HUMOR

Strom Thurmond wasn't funny in the sense that he told a lot of jokes and stories and could make a crowd laugh. He did not possess the quick dry wit of people like Senator Bob Dole or Senator Alan Simpson, who are two of the funniest men I know. But privately, one on one or with a small group, Senator Thurmond could at times be very amusing.

I remember being at a reception one night in Washington. There were a number of Senators, Congressmen, and celebrities present, including Charlton Heston. At one point during the evening I was talking in a small group with Senator Thurmond and Heston. There was a lull in the conversation. Suddenly in that distinctive southern drawl, and completely changing the subject, the Senator started talking to Charlton Heston about his role as Moses in *The Ten Commandments*. He asked, "How'd you manage to part the sea like that?" Heston chuckled and said, "Senator, I guess you just had to be there." Senator Thurmond laughed even harder and with a totally serious expression on his face he said, "Mr. Heston, how do you know I wasn't there when the real Moses did it? After all, some people say that I'm as old as Moses."

The Senator used to tell the story of the time when he was Governor of South Carolina and was on tour of a mental ward. A woman came running through screaming at the top of her lungs, "I need a man! I need a man!" Governor Thurmond turned to the head of the institution and said, "You let her out: she's sane!"

U.S. SENATE PHOTO

Senator Thurmond enjoying a good laugh.

BILL TUTEN

Whenever it was somebody's birthday in the office, we'd all meet back in the mail room for cake. On one of those occasions, I asked the Senator if he wanted to join us. So we started walking back towards the mail room. He stopped at one point, looked around, and said, "I don't usually enjoy sweets, you know." I said, "Yes sir, I know." Then he added, "Unless it's a sweet young lady." He thought that was so funny. He kind of caught me off guard. I said, "Yes sir Senator, there's no fat or cholesterol in that." He threw his arms up and just busted out with this big "WHEEE!" It's one of the hardest times I ever saw him laugh.

Senator Thurmond loved curly hair. There was a waitress we saw regularly when we went out to eat. Every time she came over to the table, he just stared at her. She had long, tightly curled hair. Finally one day he stopped her and asked, "How did you get your hair to do that?" Without batting an eye she said, "I bought it." He thought that was hilarious. He slapped the table and laughed up a storm.

I remember one day I was going with the Senator over to the Capitol so he could vote on a Defense bill. We both got on the elevator. He didn't look like he was enjoying himself. He was having a bad day. He was wearing a new suit, so I tried to cheer him up. I said, "Man, Senator, you are looking good today! Got a new tie on! You must be having a date tonight." He picked up his tie and sort of studied it. I thought well, he's just not interested in talking today. As we started to get out of the elevator I said, "You sure you don't have a date tonight, Senator?" He pointed a finger at me and got this great big old smile on his face and said, "You make 'em, and I'll keep 'em!"

JAMES D. GALYEAN

One day the Senator and I were headed over to the Senate Floor. I think Senator Thurmond liked Senator Mary Landrieu a lot, and she was always very kind to him in return. We came to the basement of the Capitol and got on the elevator to go up to the Senate. Just as the doors were about to close, Senator George Allen, the new freshman Senator from Virginia, came rushing up and jumped in with us. Right then Senator Mary Landrieu walked by. Senator Thurmond spotted her, quickly reached up and pushed Senator Allen back out of the elevator, and said, "George, get out of here! I want her to get on this elevator with me!" He was just joking, of course. Everybody got a big laugh out of that, including Senator Allen. Senator Thurmond was always quick with a joke.

ROBBIE CALLAWAY

Senator Thurmond had been selected to receive the Ellis Island Medal of Honor, which is a very prestigious award. So my wife, Sue, and I planned to meet him at his hotel in New York City early one morning, then go on over to Ellis Island together for the awards ceremony. It was being held in the morning, so we had to get over there early. We got to his hotel room at the Waldorf at around six o'clock in the morning. We knocked on the door. Senator Thurmond came to the door, opened it, and there he is standing there in his underwear. He looked at us and without missing a beat said, "Robbie, you stay out here. Sue, you come on in!" We all started laughing. He smiled and said, "I'll be ready in a minute," and closed the door. We still laugh about that to this day.

LEE BANDY

There were three reporters: myself, Joan McKinney, who was then the Washington correspondent for the Charleston, South Carolina paper, and a guy named John Larrabee who wrote for the *Greenville News*. All three of us were in Thurmond's office interviewing him about various subjects. Suddenly the bell rang for a vote in the Senate, and Thurmond said, "Come on; go with me." Well, you know how fast Thurmond walks. We hurried down the hall with Strom and interviewed him en route.

We came to the Senators Only elevator. He said, "Now come on; go over with me to the Capitol." So the three of us were standing there with Strom as the door of the elevator opened. Strom suddenly reached down and picked Joanie up, one arm behind her knees and one arm behind her shoulder blades. He picked her right up and hauled her onto the elevator. She was stunned. She turned beat red. Of course, John and I were laughing. Joan looked at me and said, "Bandy, don't you tell a soul about this." I said, "Joanie, it'll show up someday." She said, "I know it will, but not now."

I noticed a change in Strom after he married Nancy. I think she helped him develop a sense of humor. He loosened up a little bit, relaxed, and smiled more. He had something else to live for other than his life in the Senate. I remember Nancy when she was an intern in his office. She used to deliver press releases over to the Senate Press Gallery. She was the biggest flirt. Roger Mudd of CBS worked up there at the time. We both flirted right back. None of us had any idea at the time that she was dating Strom. That came as a total surprise.

But before he married Nancy he was always so serious. You couldn't kid him about anything. All that changed later. You could kid him, joke about things, and he'd return fire. He clearly enjoyed himself much more.

HENRY MCMASTER

We were sitting down there at the '96 convention. The Senator was sitting on the front row of our delegation. As usual, he had on a dark blue suit with an American flag in the lapel. I don't know if I'd recognize him in a sports shirt. Every couple of minutes, somebody would come over and speak to him, and he'd get up and shake their hand and chat for a minute. I remember at one point during the convention a man came over and shook the Senator's hand and said, "You won't remember this, but you were at a parade; it was about 50 years ago. My wife was a young girl then with a group of people. They had their picture taken with you. You gave her a big kiss right on the cheek. I know you don't remember that, do you Senator?" He said, "No sir, I don't. But if you bring her on down I'll kiss her again!" We all broke out laughing. That man was absolutely beaming.

JOHN A. GASTRIGHT, JR.

The Senator liked being involved with the staff. He enjoyed going out for breakfast or dinner with the staff. And of course it was an honor to go with him. One morning, right after I'd gotten married, we got a call. It was probably eight o'clock in the morning. I picked up the phone. It was Senator Thurmond. "Mr. Gastright, I'm going to breakfast this morning at Elsie's Skillet. I want to know if you want to go with me." I said, "Of course, Senator, we would be honored to go." He said, "You and your wife come on and meet me here in an hour." Well we lived 45 minutes away, so we hopped up out of bed and got dressed real fast and raced over to his house.

The Senator had his nephew and his wife there. My wife's father is Korean, and the Senator's nephew's wife is Korean. As we walked up, I noticed the Senator had a big grin on his face. He asked my wife, "You're Korean?" And my wife said yes. He turned to his nephew's wife, "You're Korean?" And the nephew's wife said yes. "Well, y'all might know each other!" I couldn't tell if he was kidding or if he actually thought they might know each other. But either way, he was clearly enjoying himself.

MARY CHAPMAN WEBSTER

Senator Thurmond could be quite funny, but he didn't know it. You know that expression, "He's dumb like a fox"? Sometimes I think he knew exactly what he was saying. There were other times he was funny, and I don't know whether he knew he was being funny or not.

JASON ROSSBACH

The Senator was walking down the hall in the Russell Building one day. An intern, who really wanted to meet him, walked up to say hello. She said, "Senator, you know my mother so and so." I could tell he didn't connect with the young woman, but he was being nice. He said, "Oh, that's wonderful. How is your mother? If I recall she was a lovely lady, and so are you. It's so nice to see you. Hope you enjoy yourself in Washington." She walked off as happy as can be. We got about five feet down the hall, he turned to me and laughingly said, "Her mother was homely and so is she."

Whenever he gave a speech, he had three or four jokes that he was really fond of. You could always tell when he was about to use one. But he used to get mad because he only knew those same three or four old jokes. They weren't even all that funny. Even he was tired of them. Every time he was working on a speech, he'd get upset that he didn't have better jokes to use. In fact, he came in one time all ticked off yelling, "I need humor! Someone's got to find me some humor! Go find it in a book; go find it wherever you want. Just someone find me some humor!" It really made me laugh. I said, "Senator, this is pretty funny right now." He shook his head, "No, that's not funny!"

SUSAN PELTER

I remember we were having a staff meeting one day. I guess car jacking had been in the news lately because the Senator told the staff, "There's been a lot of stories in the paper about these people that come and steal your car. I want you to know that your car is not worth your life. If somebody comes up to you and they want your car, then you give them your car!" Then he kind of rocked back on his heels, his eyebrows went up, and he got this little grin. He said, "Unless of course you got a gun in the car. In that case you open up right away!"

BUD ALBRIGHT

When Nancy Moore came home as a baby, I met them at the airport. There was a lot of confusion. They were carrying all sorts of stuff. There were suitcases, bags, hanging bags, you name it. And the Senator was, of course, saying, "Come on! Let's go! Let's go!" In the confusion, I threw one of the hanging bags on top of the car. I took them home out there in McLean, then I went home to bed.

About forty-five minutes later the phone rang. "Buddy! Where's my hanging bag? I had two fine suits in there, and one of Nancy's beautiful dresses! Where is it?" Well it hit me as soon as he mentioned it that I'd left that hanging bag on top of the car. I said, "Ah, Senator, I think I left it in my trunk." So off I go to the airport as fast as I could drive. Thank goodness Security had found the bag and kept it. The Senator teased me for a long time about how I almost lost their clothes. Then years later he brought it up and told me, "You know, I knew all along those clothes weren't in your trunk!"

BOB HURT
is the former Chief of Staff for Senator Sam Nunn. He is now with Hurt, Norton and Associates.

The first time I traveled with Senator Thurmond was in the late '70s for a hearing about the Savannah River Nuclear Site which is located in South Carolina just across the Savannah River from Augusta, Georgia. At the time I was working for the member of Congress who represented that part of Georgia. It was a large public hearing and had something to do with expanded activity at the site. So there was some controversy.

The hearing was held in a very large gymnasium that was packed with people. There was quite a long parade of public witnesses. Senator Thurmond was in his late 70s then. The hearing went on and on. He was doing a wonderful job presiding over the hearing, but he would not take a break. He just kept going, kind of oblivious to how long we'd all been sitting there. He was totally focused on making sure everyone got a chance to speak. Finally I watched somebody walk up and whisper in his ear. He frowned a little bit and said, "Well, we're going to take a break now. Some of the younger staff members have to go to the bathroom." It brought the house down.

CRAIG METZ
I never thought of Senator Thurmond as a particularly gregarious person that would regale people with stories. He had memorized a few jokes that he usually opened his speeches with. And when we were writing speeches, he'd always say, "Remember to put some humor in it!" But by and large he was a very serious business-like person, so the story I'm about to tell is very unique for him.

The Senator usually went in the same door of the Russell Senate Office Building every day. And usually the same Capitol policeman was on duty at that door. This one policeman had four or five daughters. His wife was pregnant again, and they were hoping for a boy. Senator Thurmond was very interested in people's personal lives. He'd ask that policeman every day, "Have you had that baby yet?" "No sir, not yet." Finally, one day, the policeman said, "Senator, we finally had our baby." The Senator said, "Was it a boy?" The policeman said, "No sir, Senator, it was another girl." That was their fifth or sixth girl.

So Senator Thurmond said, "Well, let me tell you what you need to do to have a boy." Now, the policeman knew the Senator had two boys of his own. So he got out his pad and started writing this down. Senator said, "First thing you do is draw your wife a warm bath with lots of bubbles. Then put on some romantic music. Then you help her take off her clothes and get down in the tub. Let her soak in there while she listens to the music. Then get you some wine and two glasses and put it on ice. And tell her, say, 'Honey when you're ready to get out let me know.' When she's done you go in there and wrap her in a towel and pat her dry and bring her out into the next room where you got the music and the wine. Then you pour the two glasses of wine and make a wonderful romantic toast. Then you drink that wine. Then when she's had a glass or two, then you get on the phone and call me I'll get you a boy!"

DENNIS W. SHEDD

People didn't usually see this, but the Senator had an extraordinary sense of humor. He was so quick with a quip. He always had a one liner or a come back. I never saw anybody one-up Senator Thurmond on one liners. One night I was working late with Senator Thurmond. We were just sitting around his desk. He sort of leaned forward and said, "You know Mr. Shedd, that Howard Metzenbaum, I don't really agree with him on anything." Metzenbaum was a very liberal Democratic Senator from Ohio. The Senator said, "I don't agree with him. But I'll tell you, you got to admire him because he stands up and fights for what he believes in." I said, "Senator Thurmond, in that regard, he and you are a lot alike." He said, "Well thank you, Mr. Shedd." And then I said, "Senator Thurmond, you and Senator Metzenbaum have something else in common." He asked, "What is that?" I said, "You both have excellent staffs." Before a second passed Senator Thurmond leaned forward and said, "Mr. Shedd, the roses you sent yourself have arrived."

LESLIE SEALY

Senator Thurmond was a very nice, kind man. And he treated me well. I remember when Nelson Mandela came to Washington to address a joint session of Congress. The Senator said, "Get all my black staff together. I want to take them to meet Nelson Mandela." So we assembled and went over to the Capitol to meet him. There were just two of us. The Senator walked up and said, "Is this it?! This is all my black staff? Are you sure?" We just died laughing. He obviously expected many more of us. It was very funny. I'll never forget that.

LAUCH FAIRCLOTH

was a United States Senator from North Carolina, 1993-99.

I was having a fund raiser in Winston-Salem one time, and Strom was scheduled to make a speech. He was delayed, and it was pretty late by the time he got there. He knew everybody had been waiting. So he said, "Well, I'm going to tell you all like Elizabeth Taylor told her husbands: I won't keep you long."

I remember one time Strom asked me, "What year were you born?" I said, "Strom, I was born in 1928." He said, "That was a good year. That was the year I was elected the Superintendent of Schools."

JAMES B. EDWARDS

We were at the Kansas City Republican Convention in 1976. We had all the Southern delegates there in one room for a meeting. I was Governor at the time and kind of MC'ing the meeting. Nancy Thurmond introduced me as "the greatest Governor that South Carolina has ever had." Well, I knew that Strom was in the audience, and I sort of gulped. I said to myself, I wish she hadn't said that. But Strom didn't bat an eye. He got up later and said, "You know, what Nancy said about Governor Edwards, the reason she can say that is because she wasn't born when I was Governor."

MATTHEW J. MARTIN

I always enjoyed watching Senator Thurmond and Senator Dole when they got together. They got along so well. I think they really enjoyed joking around and teasing each other. On Senator Thurmond's 98th birthday, Senator Dole came over to the office and brought him a shovel from the World War II Memorial ground-breaking ceremonies. Senator Dole told Senator Thurmond that over the Christmas break he could get out there with that shovel and get to work on the monument. Senator Thurmond laughed and said, "I'd put all you boys to shame!"

WILLIAM SCHACHTE

After I retired, I brought some clients to meet the Senator. We went into his office. I had the President and CEO of a company and some other people. I said, "This is so and so, Senator; he's from New Jersey. And this is such and such; he's also from New Jersey. And this is so and so; he's from Pennsylvania. And this is so and so; he's actually from Colorado." The Senator said, "Well, I'm glad to meet y'all. It's good you brought 'em in here Admiral because we're all in the Union now!"

MICHAEL BOZZELLI

I was one of the few non-South Carolinians who worked for the Senator. But he always made me feel right at home. Anytime I came in his office he'd always make me laugh because he'd yell, "Oh! There's that Italian boy! Italians are good cooks you know!" I remember one day I was helping him get dressed at Walter Reed. They always laid his clothes out. He was a very humble man, and he didn't have a very expensive wardrobe. But one day I noticed he was wearing a very fine French shirt. I said, "Wow Senator, where'd you get this beautiful French shirt?" He thought for a moment and said, "I don't know. Would it be better if it was from Italy?"

The Senator was a very witty guy. I remember there was a huge cemetery we always passed whenever James drove us back to Walter Reed, where the Senator lived towards the end. Every time we passed by there, the Senator would ask James, "Now James, where do you want to be buried? Do you want to be buried here?" James would say, "No Senator, I prefer to be buried in South Carolina." And the Senator would always nod his head and say, "Well, I'll see to it for you James. I'll take care of that for you."

ELIZABETH DOLE

Most people don't know that the Doles and the Thurmonds were "related by marriage" when the late Leader Dole was mated with Strom's schnauzer Chelsea-Marie. Later on, their offspring were introduced at a press conference on Capitol Hill. Bob, Strom, and I agreed that when the puppies were born they were Democrats, but once their eyes opened they became Republicans.

KEVIN SMITH

The Senator had this unique laugh; well, it wasn't so much of a laugh as it was a shout. Whenever he thought something was really funny he'd go "WHEEE!" If you said something he thought was funny, he'd give one of those shouts and slap his knee.

MICHAEL MISHOE

It's customary in Washington that the various lobbying groups send out invitations to members of Congress for events and receptions. Sometimes Senator Thurmond would attend an event and other times he would give the invitations to members of the staff so they could go.

In 1977 the prostitutes in Nevada formed a lobbying group. They sent out an invitation to the members of Congress to an event they were hosting. George Duckworth was on staff at the time, and he was responsible for going over all the invitations with the Senator to see which ones he wanted to attend. George knew the Senator wouldn't want anybody from the office to attend this event that was hosted by prostitutes. But he took it in anyway when he met with the Senator just to see how he'd react.

They went through the various invitations and finally got to the one from the prostitutes. George said, "Senator, I'm sure you're not interested in this one. But I wanted to make you aware that this group representing prostitutes sent us this invitation." The Senator said, "George, I just don't think anybody from my office should attend this function." George said, "I agree, yes sir, Senator. That's what I was thinking too." When they finished up, George headed towards the door. The Senator stopped him and said with a laugh, "George! If you go, tell them you're from Kennedy's staff."

James and Vanjewell Graham with Strom Thurmond.

*He was part of the family. You always had a soft spot in your heart for him. That's how a
lot of people felt about Senator Thurmond.*

– Dennis W. Shedd –

The Senate Family

M any people find it extraordinary that Senator Thurmond — Judge, Governor, Major General, President Pro Tempore, and the oldest and longest-serving Senator in the history of the United States of America — thought nothing of social position when he formed friendships. Although he associated regularly and comfortably with many of the most powerful people in the world, he was also very close to and cared genuinely about any number of individuals who lacked economic clout, political influence, or social connections.

No matter how high he rose in public office and esteem, Strom Thurmond never possessed a sense of superiority. In his view, it seems, people were simply people, and reaching out to them was a natural thing to do.

MARIO D'ANGELO

Senator Thurmond was very meticulous about his hair. He always wanted the color of his hair to be darker, but Nancy, Holly and the girls in the office always wanted it lighter, sort of a more natural look. So we tried to do what he wanted one month, and then the next month we would satisfy the ladies. That's why we kept changing the shade of his hair. It went back and forth from a light brown to a dark blonde. He always said, "I want it darker." Sometimes he would say "black"; I know he didn't mean black.

He just wanted it darker. He definitely didn't want any gray to show.

During the hearings on Justice Thomas, when the lights were very bright, I think a camera man caught him from a low position. With those bright lights behind him, it made his hair look reddish. That's where he got the reputation for having orange hair. The press used that a lot. Of course, it wasn't orange. But under those lights at certain camera angles, it sometimes looked like it.

The Senator didn't want people to know he was having his hair colored. But when you get to be 100-years old, it's almost impossible to deny it. Nancy came into the shop one time. We were back in a private room. I had just finished washing his hair. He looked at her and said, "Honey, it's just a shampoo, just a shampoo." I think he was trying to keep it a secret that he was getting his hair colored.

We always went through a routine after every haircut. I'd show him the mirror, and let him see how nice he looked, and I'd call him a handsome young man. He would always respond, "That's because you're the best barber in Washington." He was really a good friend, you know. A true friend. We all just loved that man.

Senator Thurmond's 90th birthday party was held downtown at a big hotel. I took care of him before the party, and he knew I was going to be there. He said, "Mario, I want you to get there early so I can introduce you to President Clinton." That night I found him in the crowd. The President was nearby shaking hands with a lot of people. Senator Thurmond said, "Mr. President." Bill Clinton was still shaking hands. He said, "Mr. President, Mr. President." But President Clinton still didn't respond. Finally Senator Thurmond grabbed the President by the shoulder and said, "Mr. President." Bill Clinton still went on shaking hands.

Well, all of a sudden, Senator Thurmond reached out and grabbed the President with both arms and shook him and yelled, "Mr. President! I want you to meet my barber!" Bill Clinton was so surprised. He looked at Strom. He looked at me. Then he burst out laughing. I shook his hand. We exchanged a few words. That's Senator Thurmond for you. He promised me that he was going to introduce me to the President, and he always stood by his word.

The Senator came in another time. He looked like he was mad at the world. I said, "Senator Thurmond, what's wrong?" He shook his head, "Nothing!" But you could tell something was wrong. I said, "Senator Thurmond, I'm your friend; what's wrong?" He said, "I told you nothing!" He was almost shaking. He was mad.

Then I said, "Senator Thurmond, there's clearly something that's bothering you really bad." He said, "My wife." I said, "What's the matter? It couldn't be that bad." He said, "She got caught drunk driving." It was really hurting him, because this was after his daughter got killed by a drunk driver. He was so shaken up by that. He was so mad he didn't know what to do. I didn't really know what to say.

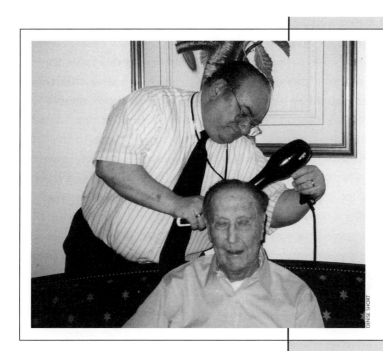

Mario D'Angelo and Senator Thurmond, 2003.

MANSEL LONG, JR.

I remember distinctly the day when Nelson Mandela came to the United States Senate. Senator Thurmond raised Mandela's hand as if he was raising a champion boxer's hand, like he was raising a hand in victory.

There was a woman who worked as a cashier in the cafeteria. When Senator Thurmond saw her, he motioned for her to come over so he could introduce her to Mandela. Well, after she met Mandela, that woman started walking away and she collapsed. She died right there. She had a heart attack or a stroke.

Senator Thurmond ran over, and he stayed right there. He made the paramedics keep working with her even though it was obvious she had died. He was so shaken by that. He had known her a long time. He didn't let up with those paramedics. He kept telling them to keep going, keep trying to bring her back.

DENNIS W. SHEDD

I don't think Senator Thurmond got credit for this, but he was one of a handful of the brightest Senators in Washington. He was also absolutely a man of his word. If he said it, he did it. You could count on him. He also cared more about the little courtesies than anybody else in the Senate. It didn't matter if you worked closely with him on his staff or policed the doors or worked in the cafeteria. He cared about you. He cared about saying "happy birthday" or about going to someone's funeral or a wedding. He did those things. He'd go and be with people at a time of need or celebration. He was a very smart man who had the common touch, and he had an unbelievable wealth of common sense.

He was sort of like one of your favorite uncles at the family reunion. He wore clothes that were a little bit different than most people. He always had time to talk to the kids, tell them a joke or give them a piece of candy. Now, he might embarrass you on occasion, but you just loved him anyway. He was part of the family. You always had a soft spot in your heart for him. That's how a lot of people felt about Senator Thurmond. He was sort of like the fun uncle. He wasn't like a father figure; it wasn't that kind of relationship. But he was sort of like a cousin or an uncle that you didn't see all the time, but when you saw him, you really enjoyed him. And you knew, despite his little odd ways, that he was a good man and really cared about you.

JACK BALLARD

It was about my sixth year with the U.S. Capitol Police when I found myself assigned to Delaware Avenue, Northeast, next to the Russell Senate Office Building. The officer on that post was not only responsible for maintaining a police presence in the area but also for making certain that no one poached on the parking spaces that had been assigned to high-level staff and about fifteen Senators. In between, you gave direction to visitors: "It's that building across the street, the one with the white dome." And in early October, as scores of young attorneys made their first pilgrimage to D.C, you'd always get the question, "How do we get to the Supreme Court?" With a little police humor, I would respond, "Appeal, appeal, appeal, then get a Writ of Certiorari; turn left at the corner, one block up and turn right."

On one particular day I heard the call, "Officer! Officer!" I looked across the street and saw Senator Strom Thurmond motioning me over. As I got closer he asked, "Are you going to be out here permanently?" My response was that it appeared that way. He pointed to the automobile next to Senator Magnuson's car and said, "Senator Magnuson is going to be leaving; is there any objection if I take that space?" I could not say "Yes sir!" fast enough. And as I recall, I even gave him a quick salute as he went back into the building.

Over the years that followed, we conversed at times, although not any more than with the other members as he was an early bird and always in a hurry. And likely as not, he was always carrying shopping bags full of work that he had taken home to review.

I recall one morning as a motorcycle passed by, he mentioned that many years ago when he was a school teacher he rode a motorcycle. He said he really liked going fast.

One August many years after I retired, I was on Capitol Hill with my wife. Duke Short spotted me and whisked us into Senator Thurmond's office to say hello. The Senator rose to greet us and pointed toward a couple of chairs saying, "Holly, hold my calls. I'm going to talk with my friends." We spent a good half hour in gentle conversation, and as we were leaving he hugged my wife (what would you expect) and shook my hand with a firm grip. I could feel the electricity. Senator Strom Thurmond, by his kind actions, gave me the experience that all could envy. That afternoon made me recall something my father, who was also a veteran of the Capitol Hill Police Department, used to say: "Working on Capitol Hill can be the best thing that will ever happen to you." He was right.

CLARENCE THOMAS

I met Senator Thurmond when I came to work for Senator Danforth in 1979. We all have our preconceived notions, and I had assumed just from his reputation that he'd be a terrible person to be around. Of course, I'm from Georgia and he's from South Carolina, and I grew up in the era when he had a decidedly different viewpoint. When I got there, the thing that was most interesting was just how polite and decent he was. If you were in the hall or walking through the tunnel to the Capitol or taking an elevator, he was not above stopping you and saying good morning or waving you on to the elevator. Back in those days if a Senator got on a public elevator, in many instances you had to get off. But if Senator Thurmond got on a public elevator, he invited you on. I was initially just impressed with how warm he was towards me and towards the other staffers, which wasn't true for a lot of the Senators.

HALEY BARBOUR

I am certain Senator Thurmond missed those old days when the Senate enjoyed a wonderful spirit of cordiality. When I was first around national politics in the late 1960s and early 70s, the civility and cordiality among Senators who voted very differently was routine. Senator Eastland, who was our senior Democrat Senator and one of Senator Thurmond's friends, almost on a daily basis had Senators by his office late in the afternoon for a drink — everybody from Teddy Kennedy to Roman Hruska, from far left Democrats to far right Republicans. Of course, you didn't have to drink, but the spirit of that cordiality is what was important. That spirit is missing today, and the truth is, we need to get it back. Our country would be better served. We need more of that.

MARK IVANY

I met a lot of people who didn't know Senator Thurmond personally and assumed he was some racist Southerner. I always tell them the story about James Graham, the Senator's driver, the most religious, sweetest man in the entire world. James went away every year in August for a family reunion back down in South Carolina. I would fill in for him and drive the Senator when he was away.

I was driving him home one time and the Senator said, "Where is James?" I said, "Senator, he's at his family reunion." He said, "Oh, oh yeah. That's right." Then he said, "Hey! Let's give James a call and see how he's doing!" That's the first time that I really realized how much James Graham meant to Senator Thurmond. He wasn't just his driver. He was a true friend, and the Senator missed him.

DAVID T. BEST

His treatment of people was very consistent. It wasn't a PR spin or a political calculation; that was the way he was. Whether it was the elevator operator, the subway driver, the door keeper, everybody held him in high regard because he recognized them and treated them as important individuals. There was one particular elevator operator that he rode with frequently and got to know. She was pregnant, and he noticed that. He always made a point to stop and talk with her. When she went on maternity leave, he frequently asked us how she was doing. When she got back he'd chat with her about her baby.

After Senator Thurmond died, I was going over to the Senate Floor, and I guess she'd been on vacation so she hadn't heard about his passing. She said, "How's the Senator doing?" I said, "Well, you haven't heard the news. He actually passed away last week." She was stunned and literally broke into tears right there. It struck me that this woman has been around probably close to 200 Senators during her time there, but this was like a personal loss to her. The Senate was his family as much as anything else, and it didn't matter if you were the doorkeeper or the Majority Leader; you got the same high regard.

MICHAEL BOZZELLI

There were lots of insensitive remarks there towards the end of the Senator's life that kind of sullied his retirement. I don't want this to go unmentioned. The Senator's driver, James Graham, is an African American. Any time we would go to the Senate Dining

Room, the Senator always made sure that James joined us. He would usually wait in the car until the Senate adjourned, but if they decided to go eat, Senator Thurmond always sent someone out to get James. He'd say, "Go get James. We're going up to the Senate Dining Room to get something to eat. I want him to come with us." He always thought about him and always remembered that he was there.

TERRY L. WOOTEN

We were at a big function down on the Mall. They had a barbecue and a lot of food. The Senator and I went to this event and had a big dinner. Then he got up and went back to the people putting on the event and asked them to put another plate together. He said, "I want you to fill it up real full. I want a plate for my driver." He had them load the plate up with barbecue, hush puppies, rice, and slaw. And the Senator carried that back to the car. He didn't hand it to me, and he didn't ask me to get it. He put it together himself, put it in his hands, and carried it all the way back to the car. He said, "Here James, I brought you something for dinner." Most people don't know that James Graham, the Senator's driver, was one of Senator Thurmond's best friends. He was like family.

JAMES FLOYD GRAHAM

One day Senator Thurmond and I were out alone in the car. He turned to me and said, "James, I really like you and consider you one of my closest friends." I said, "Thank you, Senator; I really appreciate that." He then said, "James, I have something I want to tell you." I said, "Sure Senator." He said, "James, when I was the Governor of South Carolina, you would not have understood some of the things I did. As Governor, I had to take an oath to uphold the law. At that time most of the Southern states had segregated laws, and the only thing I was doing was upholding the law. James, I could not take an oath and then not uphold the law. No one should be allowed to break the law and get away with it. If you break the law and get away with it, then the law does not mean anything." I thought about that a lot. I came to the conclusion that this was the kind of person I wanted to be around, listen to, and to take advice from. I don't know of any human being that I have more respect for than Senator Thurmond.

Tom Moss and Strom Thurmond.

*To truly understand how far Strom Thurmond came in his life, you have
to first understand where he started out.*

– Butler Derrick –

THE CENTENNIAL SENATOR

Doing the Right Thing

STROM THURMOND AND RACE

*S*trom Thurmond was born into a very differ-ent world than the one he lived through. As a boy, and indeed even as a circuit judge in the 1930s, he and others in his South Carolina com-munity still regularly traveled by horseback. He grew up in a town largely populated by Confederate veterans. When Strom Thurmond ran for U.S. President in 1948 as a States' Rights advocate, he doubtless considered himself to be defending the law as written as well as the South's rights and heritage. It is somewhat surprising that — of all the things Senator Thurmond did in the space of a century, nearly all of it in public service — his 1948 Presidential bid still looms so large in some people's image of him.

The fact is that Strom Thurmond changed with the times and became a legislative leader in support of Civil Rights. As Governor of South Carolina he advocated the elimination of poll taxes which had been used to prevent African Americans from voting. The voters of South Carolina agreed and repealed the poll tax. Also during his term as Governor, he used his political clout to direct more public investment in the predominantly black South Carolina State College in Orangeburg. He continued to lend his support to all the historically black colleges in the South throughout his political career.

Strom Thurmond was the first Southern Senator to hire an African-American person as a senior staffer. He accepted the Supreme Court's decision to desegregate schools as the law of the land, and encouraged all South Carolinians to do the same. He voted for the Martin Luther King Holiday and any number of other measures designed to convey respect for and improve the lives of African Americans. When considering Strom Thurmond's stance on race, his position in 1948 should not overshadow his activity during the next five decades.

BUTLER DERRICK

To understand Strom you have to understand Edgefield, because Strom is an absolute product of Edgefield County and the times that he grew to manhood. When he was born in 1902, Pitchfork Ben Tillman, from Edgefield County, was in the United States Senate. Strom's father, ol' Judge Thurmond, was kind of Tillman's man. You went to him if you needed something from the Senator.

They always tell the tale of ol' Judge Thurmond, that he had a big garden and was always out giving away vegetables. The people that he gave vegetables to always seemed to turn up on the jury list. Back then, women were not franchised. And of course the African Americans didn't vote. So there wasn't a large voting population. I think Strom learned a great deal from his father.

Also at that time, former Governor Shepherd was living right up the road, four or five houses from where he was born. And up at the top of the hill from where he was born was former Confederate General Matthew M.C. Butler. M.C. Butler was the only man in history who was a Confederate General yet died a Union General after the Spanish American War. And right down the street from where Strom was born was the home of Governor William Martin.

This was the kind of atmosphere that Strom Thurmond grew up in. He ran and was elected Superintendent of Education in the late 1920s. It is said that a large part of his constituency at that time was Confederate veterans. To truly understand how far Strom Thurmond came in his life, you have to first understand where he started out.

LEE BANDY

Thurmond proved one thing: he was very adaptable to change. The change became quite noticeable after Albert Watson, who was then a Congressman, ran for Governor and lost. Strom saw why the guy lost. That was a racist campaign. After that, Strom Thurmond saw the handwriting on the wall. The first thing he did was move to hire the first senior black staffer in the delegation. That was Tom Moss of Orangeburg. He was hired as a field representative to serve in South Carolina. He served with Strom until he died. He was Strom's main contact with the black community. No other Southern politician had hired a senior black staffer. Senator Thurmond was the first to break the color line.

After Albert Watson lost, Strom saw what was happening in South Carolina. He saw that the people were beginning to change in their attitudes towards race. One thing that changed a lot of Southern politicians was the passage of the Voting Rights Act, the result of which was thousands of black voters registering. One thing Strom could do: he could count. I definitely agree with the conclusion that Strom was more of a politician than he was a racist. He was the best politician I've ever seen. Early on in his Senate career, Strom was sort of the Jesse Helms of that era: Senator No, always voting against everything. But he began to change, to be a little bit more progressive.

GLADYS V. MOSS

On February 15, 1971 the official announcement about Thomas's appointment to the Senator's staff hit the newspapers and the airwaves. Senator Thurmond and Thomas set the record straight at the beginning. Senator Thurmond said that Thomas was a deep thinker and an asset to his staff. During that time Thomas was asked how he felt about the Senator. On a Saturday, March 13, 1971, Thomas spoke to the press. Thomas said he told the Senator he would take all the interviews at one time.

Thomas told the press he was not worried about the Senator's past activities. He told them that Senator Thurmond's history speaks for itself. He was very concerned about what the Senator was concerned about, and that was meeting the needs of the people of South Carolina. Tom was asked how he was going to go about helping the Senator. He told them that he was going to follow Jesus Christ's precepts and examples, and that he was sure he'd get it right as long as he did that. The record was set then, and it was time for them to get to work.

Thomas spent about a month in Washington, meeting with the different federal bureau-cracies and getting the information he would need to do the work back home. I'm holding in my hand a menu from the Senators' Dining Room where Tom ate with the Senator just before he came home. The Senator wrote on it: "Best Wishes to my newest staff member and my friend Tom Moss."

When Tom got home, we sat down as a family. He let us all know that he would be away a lot because he was the field representative for the entire state. He spent most of his time on the road working, but he always remembered to come home. That was wonderful.

Thomas said the Senator had asked him several questions about what they could do to help the people of South Carolina. Thomas mentioned to him about the plight of the black schools, and the Senator was very instrumental in helping to keep the doors open to the black schools here in South Carolina. Our motto at that time, and now: it's never too early or too late. Tom told people to contact him anytime, when and if they needed him. He was on call 24 hours a day. He was not asked to do that by the Senator. But he put himself on call like that to help as many people as he could. The Senator was very gracious, giving of him-self to meet the needs of the people of South Carolina. And he valued Thomas's judgment. He stated that many times.

I remember around two o'clock one morning, I got up and heard Tom talking. I went into the den. He was on the phone with the Senator. Tom was saying, "Senator, stay off the tube!

Stay off the tube!" There was a lot of controversy at the time about the Senator. He had been on the television a lot. Thomas told him to stay off the television and focus on the work at hand. What was important was not arguing things out in the press but helping the people of South Carolina. I knew that night that Thomas was not just a yes man. He was about trust. He was about guidance. He was about giving his opinion. And the Senator respected him for that.

WILLIAM W. WILKINS

As one of my duties working in his office, the Senator assigned me to assist the school boards who were coming to Washington. They'd been told by the Department of HEW (Health, Education, and Welfare) that all public schools had to be integrated, something that was long overdue. The process then, developed by the Nixon Administration, was that a school board would come to Washington and work with the Department of HEW to develop a desegregation plan that the Department would approve. If they could not come to an agreement as to how desegregation was going to be accomplished, then the matter was referred to the Department of Justice, and the Department of Justice was instructed to bring a lawsuit.

When the members of a South Carolina school board came to Washington, they invariably came to Senator Thurmond's office first. Quite frankly, a lot of them thought that Senator Thurmond would say, "I'm going to stand in the schoolhouse door," not literally, but at least give them encouragement not to cooperate with HEW. He did just the opposite. He told those school board members in no uncertain terms that the Supreme Court had ruled, the law was the law, and the people of South Carolina were law-abiding citizens. We were going to do the right thing. That gave the school boards a lot of support to go back to South Carolina and say, "We've been to see Senator Thurmond and he said he's going to help us. But he said that we have to do the right thing. He said, 'It's the law, and we're going to follow the law.'"

DENNIS DECONCINI

The thing I remember so well about Strom Thurmond was when he changed his position on Civil Rights. I recall a speech he made on the Floor when he talked candidly about how different it was when he was growing up. He was almost apologizing. He didn't say, "I'm sorry if I hurt anybody." But that's the feeling I got from it. It takes a big man to do that, particularly when you're a senior Senator from South Carolina. And then, he not only supported the Voting Rights Act renewal, but he became a leader in minority rights. When I saw him do that, I thought, this is a great man.

ED KENNEY

Very few people know what I'm about to tell you. In the early 1960s, when I was the Senator's Executive Assistant, a man came to see us about getting a job. He lived in Washington, but was originally from South Carolina. He was a black guy. We took him in to see the Senator, as we routinely did. I think he impressed the Senator with his manners, sincerity, and so forth. The guy really wanted to work on the Capitol Hill Police Force. But there were no blacks on the police force then. But the Senator said, "Ed, you take him down there and find him a job."

So I took him down to the police force. I think their jaws nearly fell off their mouths when I brought this guy in. To my knowledge, he was the first black man ever to apply to the Capitol Hill Police. It was crazy, you know. This was 1963. We didn't have any blacks on the police force. It was crazy, but that's the way it was. Anyway, we pressed on it, but they didn't budge. They did find him a really good job in the Superintendent's Office. The man made a career there.

I don't think people are aware that Senator Thurmond was the first Senator to recommend a black officer for the Capitol Hill Police Force.

BOB DOLE

When the South changed, Senator Thurmond wasn't in the back of the pack or the middle of the pack; he was leading the pack. Even though he was a segregationist at one time, when the time came and the country changed, Strom didn't wait to second guess everybody. He got out there and did the right thing for the people of his state.

DARYL JONES

I really do have high regard for Senator Strom Thurmond, at least for the way he conducted himself in the twilight of his career. I think he was a person who stood up for what he believed in throughout his career. I'm just happy that the things he believed in towards the end of his career were some of the things I supported as well.

DENNIS W. SHEDD

People ask me about Strom Thurmond running for President in the 1940s. I always say that you have to understand: the Strom Thurmond I worked for voted for the Voting

Rights Act; he voted for Voting Rights for D.C.; he voted for the Martin Luther King Holiday. That was the Strom Thurmond I worked for. I never knew the Strom Thurmond who ran for President in the '40s.

ROBERT MCNAIR

Senator Thurmond really got his early reputation from his presidential campaign. Most people don't remember him when he was Governor. He was a rather progressive Governor. He really helped get the state started in its economic development program during his administration. Then of course he got his reputation as a States' Rights candidate in 1948. Folks kept that image of him for years until he went to the Senate, but he changed with the times like a lot of people did during that period.

CLARENCE THOMAS

One of the lessons I've learned in Washington is that you really have to think hard sometimes before you pass judgment on people for something that happened long ago. You don't have to agree with it or think that it was the right thing to do. But when people go on with their lives and try to do what's right, try to do better, and they succeed, then I think you give credit where credit is due.

Every dealing I had with Senator Thurmond was positive, and I came to Washington thinking just the opposite. If you're going to judge someone, you make your assessment based on your own personal dealings and your own personal observations, not what other people say or what's been characterized in the media. There have been some people I've met in Washington who've been characterized in the media and elsewhere as good and decent people, and yet they've turned out to be really awful in their dealings with me personally. I can say this about Senator Thurmond: his dealings have always been honest and fair with me. From the day I met him as a staffer to the day I was sworn in at this Court, and even after, he was always fair, honest, decent and good.

SONIA HOLMES PRICE

Being an African American, many people ask me how I could have worked for Senator Thurmond. I grew to love him because I knew him on a personal level. To me he was a real beacon of hope. I saw first-hand what he did to help so many people. And anybody who knows me, knows I will go toe-to-toe with them on defending the man that I knew and cared for. I came to work with the Senator in 1991. He was a very different man, I'm sure, than the man who ran for president in 1948. I can't tell you about that man, or the man who did a filibuster on the Senate floor. I never knew that man. I'm not going to condone what he did, nor will I speak to it because I wasn't there. But I do know personally how he reached out to all people during the time that I knew him. He certainly earned my respect, my admiration and my loyalty. I'll always remember him, and I will forever just adore him.

LINDSEY GRAHAM

His political life is a testament to change. His early career was sort of a dark chapter in Southern politics. That was replaced by a man who grew and changed and became a driving force to improve the quality of life for everyone. He appointed the first African-American judge to the Federal bench. But his biggest legacy is not an appointment or a bill or a piece of legislation. It is that common touch. Most South Carolinians, regardless of political background, race, or region, felt that Senator Thurmond was on their side. They felt that he would try to help if he could. That's a great political legacy to leave.

HALEY BARBOUR

Strom clearly had the ability to adapt to change. He adjusted to integration. He started treating his black constituents just like he'd always treated his white constituents. It was genuine and they knew it. Don't confuse his adapting there with his not being tethered to great issues, because he was. I think one of the things that made Thurmond great is that he knew what he was for. He would stand up for what he believed in, and he'd stay stuck. His adapting to integration came with his recognition that this is the way things ought to be, not because it was politically significant. If he'd never gotten one African-American vote, he'd still have gotten elected. He thought it was right. He believed the change was right. He recognized that this was the right thing to do, that the time had come.

NADINE COHODAS

During my interviews with him for my book, I was kind of hoping that he would one day put his feet up on the desk and say, "Well Nadine, let me tell you how South Carolina politics works." But that's not Senator Thurmond. He said this to me more than once, "The past is past. You can't do anything about it. Look to the future." As Mark Goodin said, "That's the philosophy of someone who never got ulcers; he only gave them." I think too that was an ingredient of his success. He didn't dwell on the past. He only wanted to move forward.

JUDITH RICHARDS HOPE

The thing I remember most about Senator Thurmond is that he had the courage to change his opinion about things like segregation. And when he changed his opinion, he became a fighter, a fighter for equal rights and for minorities. I think it takes a very big man to say I was wrong for all those years and I'm going to make amends. I thought he was a man of principle, justice, integrity and courage. That's the way I remember him.

BO BLUDWORTH

For Senator Strom Thurmond, America truly was one nation under God. He was there to support all Americans, regardless of their race or religion or gender or whatever. He did a heroic job for all of us, and I am just proud I got to know him.

CHRIS KELLEY CIMKO

I was heartened by some of the remarks at the funeral, particularly Senator Biden's. I hope very much that the memories from the '40s and '50s do not shape his legacy one hundred percent. I hope people remember how much he did for the young people in the state in terms of schools and the scholarships. And I hope people remember everything he did for the state. He brought so many federal programs there. He really was someone who shaped that state into the wonderful and very vital and vibrant place that it is today. I think he showed that as the nation changed, he could change.

JIM DEMINT

He was the genuine article. My best thoughts of him are that he seemed to live many lifetimes and was able to change his mind as he developed a different understanding of things. He was constantly able to keep a perspective that was ahead of the time, even though he lived through so many generations. We didn't know each other that well, but I considered him a friend and I think he considered me a friend.

A leader of his stature who served for so long creates a certain stability in the state. His example of service, not just as an elected official but in the military and other ways, set an example for a new generation of elected leaders that are taking over now. I think he built the foundation in many ways for future service.

We will probably never see again a time when people in South Carolina serve so long. I think it was an anomaly to have two Senators serve so long, especially if you look at what's going on around the country. In many ways I think that was good for South Carolina. It provided stability. But it also opened the door for a future generation of leaders who are focused on change. Again, I think it goes back to his willingness to change in the middle of difficult times, whether it was changing parties or changing his views on segregation. He set a good example that we always need to keep reevaluating our positions and our points of view to make sure they're right.

JOSEPH R. BIDEN, JR.

I believe Strom Thurmond was a captive of his era, his age, and his geography.

I do not believe Strom Thurmond at his core was racist, but even if he had been, I believe that he changed. The news media says he changed, they think, out of pure opportunism. I believe he changed because the times changed; life changed. He worked with, saw, and had relationships with people who educated him, much as I have been educated.

I deem it a privilege to have become his friend. We were equals in the sense that our vote counted the same. Our influence on some issues was the same. But I am 60 and he was 100. There was always a 40-year chasm between us. I could say things to Strom and be irreverent with him. I could grab him by the arm and say, "Strom, don't" — which I would not have been able to do if there had been a 10-year difference. I was like the kid. It is strange — I find it strange even talking about it — how this relationship that started in stark adversarial confrontation ended up being as close as it was, causing Strom Thurmond to ask his wife whether I would deliver a eulogy for him. I don't fully understand it, but I do know it is something about this place, these walls, this Chamber, and something good about America, something good about our system, and it is something that is sorely needed: to look in the eyes of your adversary within our system and look for the good in him, and not just the part that you find disagreeable or, in some cases, abhorrent.

I did some research about Strom to find out about his background before I did this tribute on his 90th birthday — a combination tribute and roast. You know what I found? I found a lead editorial — I don't have it now — from the year 1947 or 1948 from *The New York Times*, and the title, if memory serves me correctly, is something like "The Hope of the South." It was about Strom Thurmond. The *New York Times*, the liberal *New York Times*, in the late forties — it must have been 1947 — wrote about this guy, Strom Thurmond, a public official in South Carolina, who got himself in trouble and lost a primary because he was too empathetic to African Americans. When he was a presiding judge, he started an effort statewide in South Carolina that tried to get better textbooks and materials into black schools, and he tutored young blacks and set up an organization to tutor and teach young blacks how to read. I think it was in 1946 or 1947. The essence of the editorial was that this is "the hope of the South." In the meantime, he got beat by a sitting Senator for being "weak on race."

I think Strom Thurmond learned the wrong political lesson from that and decided no one would ever get to the right of him on this issue again. But I also was sitting next to him when he voted for the extension of the Voting Rights Act.

The only point I want to make is that people change, people grow, and people react to crises in different ways. I choose to remember Strom Thurmond in his last 15 years as Senator rather than choose to remember him when he started his career.

I do not choose that just as a matter of convenience. I choose that because I believe men and women can grow. I believe John Stennis meant it when he said the Civil Rights Movement saved his soul. I believe Strom Thurmond meant it when he hired so many African Americans, signed on to the extension of the Voting Rights Act, and voted for the Martin Luther King Holiday.

I choose to believe that he meant it because I find it hard to believe that the many decent, generous, and personal acts that he did for me, did not come from a man who is basically a decent, good man, and the latter part of his career reflects that.

I choose it not just because I am an optimist. I choose it not just because I want to believe it. I choose it not just because I believe there is a chemistry that happens in this body. I choose it because I believe basically in the goodness of human nature and it will win out, and I think it did in Strom.

Lessons Big and Small

NUGGETS OF WISDOM FROM STROM THURMOND

O f all the things Senator Thurmond gave people — of all the help with legislation, contacts, and jobs, and of all the peaches, key chains, and letter openers — the gift they've usually kept the longest is the advice he offered them. Virtually everyone who knew the Senator recalls at least one invaluable lesson they learned from him.

Many people adopted a habit of striving for excellence in matters big and small from his personal example. Other people recall a saying the Senator used or a statement he made which struck them as so true and so important that they never forgot it. Strom Thurmond began his professional life in the 1920s as a teacher, and although his title changed many times thereafter, he educated people all his life.

KAREN HENDERSON

In the early '80s I ran into Senator Thurmond on a plane coming up to Washington from Columbia. He was sitting in the seat right in front of me. He was reading *The State* newspaper. As he finished each section, he tossed it over the back of the seat to me, wordlessly, but just having asked me ahead of time if I'd like to see the paper. Through the whole flight I managed to collect the whole newspaper and had put it back together in the proper sequence. When we landed, I handed him back the newspaper.

He told me I was one of the few people that he had ever met who knew how to

Senator Jesse Helms and Senator Strom Thurmond.
This photograph was taken October 16, 2002 at a
retirement reception hosted by Senator Biden for
Senator Helms in the Foreign Relations Committee
Room in the Capitol.

return a newspaper. He said when he was he was a student at Clemson, he and his friends would go into the library, and they would read the newspaper and leave it any way they wanted. The librarian would say, "Now you put that newspaper back the way you found it!" Sixty years later that lesson that he learned as a college student was still not only in his memory, but he saw fit to lecture other people about it. From then on, each time I would see him again, he would always say something like, "I remember how you folded that paper." Senator Thurmond had an incredible memory for the smallest things like that. That is one lesson that he learned and 60 years later was still teaching other people. As long as he lived, he must have picked up thousands of little lessons like that.

MANSEL LONG, JR.

Senator Thurmond always tried to help his constituents; that's what he was known for. He called it "Casework" or "Projects." It essentially meant that you help people who are having problems. One of Thurmond's greatest lessons is that by simply focusing on helping people, you can almost get enough votes to stay in office. There are a lot of politicians in Washington who learned that lesson from Strom Thurmond.

MARIE BOYLE BUCKLER

The Senator was always there for people. We staff members were like his extended family, and he was always there for us. He never let us down. And you could agree to disagree with him. He and I didn't always agree on political things, but that was okay; it didn't matter to him. We had interns who were staunch Democrats. That didn't matter to him. That's not what they were there for. They were there to get a first-hand view of what Washington was all about. Many times he would tell the interns, "It doesn't matter whether you're a Democrat or a Republican. It matters that you're willing to stand up for what you believe in, and that you're willing to put a voice to what you feel is right or wrong." The young people appreciated that. It was a true life lesson that I know many people learned from Strom Thurmond.

STEPHEN BREYER

I'll tell you something Senator Thurmond said to me once. We were discussing some ethical problems of a person who was going to be confirmed as a judge. The Senator remarked, "If you think you're going to be in public life and get rich, you better think of another career." In other words, stay ethically sound. You're helping the country and that's it. He stood for that.

ROCKY ROBINSON

*is a successful businessman from South Carolina and was a great
friend of Senator Thurmond for many years. He is Duke Short's
brother-in-law.*

This had to be back in 1991 or so. I went up to have lunch with Duke, and while I was there we went in to visit with the Senator for a little while. Well, we got to talking about houses. I had bought a house in McLean for $900,000 that I planned to tear down and replace with something better. Senator Thurmond found out about that and said, "What! What did you say?! You bought a house for $900,000 just so you could tear it down!"

I explained the deal to him, how I could come out better in the end if I built something bigger on that lot. He just couldn't understand it. He looked over at Duke and said, "You told me he was a smart businessman! He is not a good businessman! He's going to tear down a perfectly good $900,000 house!" He really lit into me about that and had a good time teasing me. By the time I left his office, the Senator was convinced I was nuts, and I was convinced he was so old he didn't understand how to make money.

You know what? In the end, Senator Thurmond was right. For other reasons, I ended up not tearing the house down. I put some money into it, fixed it up, and today that house is worth over $5 million.

SUSAN PELTER

I went to work for Senator Thurmond as a completely apolitical young graduate student. I didn't come to him as a political junkie like so many others did. What amazed me was his interest in everything, from the greatest to the smallest detail. He taught me to be meticulous in whatever I did. He wanted things to be a certain way. If you took him in a letter or a speech to look at, and you hadn't really done your homework and researched it well enough, he would frequently sense that and ask you some question you couldn't answer. He taught me as a young professional to get my ducks in a row and make sure I knew exactly what I was talking about. That has served me in good stead throughout my career. He really believed that if you're going to do something, it better be right.

DAVID T. BEST

I recall a time we were in a Veteran's Affairs Committee meeting. This would have been back in the 103rd Congress because Senator Rockefeller was Chairman. Democrats were in the Majority. I believe the bill before the Committee was a healthcare issue, something to do with tobacco-related illnesses. The Democrats had the votes. Frank Murkowski had five amendments. He offered the first one, but Rockefeller had the proxy votes and voted it down. Senator Murkowski offered the second amendment. Same result. By then he was pretty frustrated.

He stood up and said, "Mr. Chairman, I see you have all the votes on these. These are all very similar amendments. I don't see any point in wasting anybody's time debating these when you're just going to vote them down. I've got another obligation. You got your bill. It's clear to me it's going to pass. So, do your business and I'll stop." And he got up to walk out.

Just then Senator Thurmond said, "Frank! Sit down!" Everybody kind of held their breath. We didn't know what was going on. Senator Thurmond said, "Now Frank, you go

Rocky Robinson and Senator Thurmond,
July 2002.

on and offer those amendments!" Murkowski said, "Strom, it's pointless. The outcome is very clear to me. It's just a waste of time." And Senator Thurmond said, "Frank, a principle fought for is a principle never lost. It doesn't matter if we have the votes or not. You offer them!"

The room went silent. We were in awe of the power that was displayed there. Senator Murkowski sat down. He offered the remaining amendments. And they were all soundly defeated. But on the advice of Senator Thurmond, he had stood his ground.

DEE SHORT

Like so many others, I have been inspired by the Senator's advice and life lessons. Little things stick out in my mind. I recall one time he said, "I like dogs. But dogs don't belong in the house. Folks should keep their dogs outside." It really bothered him that they had become inside pets. He just didn't think that was proper. When it came to animals his absolute favorite was the horse. I remember a story he told me about a pony that he had when he was a young boy. The pony got into some "green pea vine hay" and gorged itself to the point that it later died. The Senator would always say, "Dee, if you ever have a pony, never let it eat green hay."

MELISSA KIRACOFE-LOW

worked for Senator Thurmond from May of 2000 until September of 2002. Her last position was as a Project Caseworker.

The biggest thing I learned from the Senator during my time as a page and when I worked in the front office as a staff member was the way that he treated people. From former Senator Dole to John Doe visiting from South Carolina, he treated everyone the same. That was my first job right out of college, and I was extremely nervous because of the people coming in and out of the office. He had very important, powerful people coming in and out at all times. But everyone who came into that office was shown the same amount of respect. That was an important lesson to me: that if you treat everyone with great respect, you'll get that in return.

MICHAEL BOZZELLI

After I started my internship, I was set up for a photo with the Senator. I went in to his office, which is a thrilling experience no matter how many times you've been in there. I asked the Senator, "What's the best advice you can give a young man like me?" He said, "Work hard; make a lot of friends, and do the right thing."

JOHN L. NAPIER

The first time I ever went anywhere with Senator Thurmond, he looked at me and said, "Where are we going?" I said, "We're going over to the Committee." We got down in the bowels of the Senate Office Building and he said, "Where are we going?" I said, "We're going to the Committee." He said, "Where is it?" We were going from the Dirksen Building to the Russell Building. I said, "It's over in the Russell Building." He said, "Where?" I didn't know the exact name or number of the room. I said, "Senator, I'm not exactly sure." He said, "You're not sure?! Any time you're going somewhere you need to be sure! You need to have it planned out. I don't have time for this. Come on, I know where we're going."

Then he led me right to the room. When we got there he turned to me and said, "Let me be clear; any time we're going anywhere from now on you need to know where we're going." He taught little lessons that way. He was not at all mean-spirited. But at the same time, he expected you to learn that lesson.

CRAIG METZ

A rather agitated group came up to Washington from South Carolina one time because the Republicans were opposing some type of welfare program. Senator Thurmond was on the other side of the issue from this group. He was in the Senate at the time, and met them in a reception room right off the Floor. Some of the members of this large group were ready to start shouting at him. He immediately stopped them, held up his hand, and said, "Now I'm happy to meet with you. I'm happy to discuss things with you. But I can't talk to people who are shouting and everybody talking all at once. So we have to have a spokesman. Who's your spokesman? Who is your spokesman?"

They started talking amongst themselves, trying to figure out who their spokesman was going to be. Of course, a lot of people thought they were most important so there was some disagreement. Senator Thurmond said to me, "You watch this. This will keep them busy for some time." He was exactly right. It took quite a while for them to decide who was going to be their leader. At last they produced somebody they could all agree was going to be the spokesman. By that time Senator Thurmond had a meeting to go to. He said, "Now I want to welcome you to Washington. And we want to help you in every way. This is Mr. Metz here; he's my attorney for the Committee and he's my detail man. He's going to discuss the details with you. I want to help you, and we're so glad to see you. I've got this other meeting to go to now. I'll talk to you later. Bye-bye." He certainly knew how to control and organize a crowd, no matter how unfriendly it might be. I thought, that's a wonderful lesson for life.

BILL TRAXLER

There are two things the Senator often said that I'm frequently reminded of. He said, "The higher a person goes in public service, the more humble he should become." And, "You should never expect to get rich working for the federal government."

BUD ALBRIGHT

The Senator told me a very interesting story about when he was in World War II and came up on someone who was about to shoot a prisoner. The Senator said he knocked the pistol out of the guy's hand. He said, "You just don't do that. I don't care where you are or what you are. Whether you're in war, politics, whatever, you always do the right thing." That's one of the biggest life lessons I learned from him.

My mom and dad instilled me with a good sense of right and wrong. But Senator Thurmond taught me what it was to have an opportunity and take advantage of it.

Another time he and I had flown into Charlotte. The Senator was still married to Nancy at the time, so this was before the separation. We were trying to get to Rock Hill. He was hungry and said, "I've got to stop and get something to eat." I said "Senator, let me call Nancy for you, and I'll let her know you're going to be late." He reached over and patted me on the shoulder and said, "Buddy, you never call a woman and tell her what you're going to do. You only call and tell her what you've done."

MICHAEL MISHOE

In all my thirty years working in Washington, I learned more about politics and about life from Strom Thurmond than I did from anyone else. He was extremely efficient and hardworking, and had a tremendous sense of what was happening at the moment. I believe the Senator would have been successful in anything he chose to do, because he would have applied that same level of effort and commitment to anything else. It was a wonderful opportunity to watch someone who was so successful and see how they accomplished what they did. I certainly learned a lot, and I appreciated the opportunity he gave me. You know, I was just a country boy. I grew up on a farm. My family had never really been involved in politics. The Senator gave me a chance to come to Washington and have those amazing experiences that I had. I will always be grateful to him.

WALKER CLARKSON

Senator Thurmond had the most wonderful handshake on the planet. He didn't do that little woman's handshake that I hate. He actually shook your hand like you were an equal. Whether you were a man or a woman, he gave you a good firm handshake. Age, race, gender, it didn't matter. He wanted to show you the respect of offering you a good firm handshake. I think that says a lot about a person.

TUCKER ESKEW

When Senator Thurmond campaigned for Carroll Campbell, he would stand and deliver what I call the Four Cs Endorsement. He'd say that Carroll Campbell was a man of *courage*, and he'd take on the tough issues. He'd say Carroll Campbell was a man of *capacity*, and he'd go on about his abilities. He'd say he's a man of great *compassion*, and he'd talk about his concern for the little man. And he'd say he's a man who respects the *Constitution*. Over the years, that speech became the Five Cs, as he added that Carroll Campbell was a man of *courtesy*. To people around the country who aren't from the South and who didn't know Strom Thurmond, that might sound pretty antiquated. But couldn't we all use a little more courtesy in politics?

For Strom Thurmond to say that courtesy was an important quality in a candidate for office, I believe, said a lot about Strom Thurmond. There's no question that was part of his formula. Treat people with respect, and they'll respect you in return. Treat people with respect, and they'll listen to you. Treat people with respect, and you can get things done. That was true for him working on both sides of the aisle. Sure, he wanted Republicans to win. I'm a loyal Republican and have been my whole life. But I learned the lesson from Strom Thurmond that you didn't have to be against somebody else to be for your own candidate or for your own principles. That's how he practiced his own brand of politics. And he demonstrated a great lesson about how politics ought to be practiced in this country.

ED KENNEY

The first thing that impressed me about the Senator was that he wasn't afraid to tell his family he loved them. When I was in the office, he called his family practically every day just to tell them he loved them. I think in a society like we live in, where everyone is so mobile and frequently gone from home, it's important to let your loved ones know that you love them. A lot of men have trouble saying I love you. Senator Thurmond was not that kind of man. He loved his family and he told them so.

He also did his very best to stay in touch with people. You knew that was an important value to him, and he wanted others to do likewise. He would frequently ask me about my sister-in-law, "How's Mary doing?" I'd say, "She's fine, Senator." "Well, are you keeping in touch with her?" I'd say, "Yes, I try to call her at least once a month." And he would say, "That's not enough. Call every week. There's no reason you can't call her every week."

He really pressed me to stay in close touch with those people who were dearest to me. I've tried to do that, and I've tried to pass it on to other people. That's good advice. At my age you realize that you may not be here tomorrow. So it's nice to have had a chat today.

General Quick, Duke Short, Senator
Thurmond and Chinese Opera performers
in Beijing, China, August 1997.

The Senator's reaction to the Great Wall provided a source of great humor on our trip: "Yep,
this is a big wall. Well, let's go!" And he was off to the next destination.

– R.J. Duke Short –

One Last Big Hurrah

THE 1997 TRIP TO CHINA

For as long as I'd known him, the Senator had always talked about how much he wanted to see the Great Wall of China. The man had seen most of the rest of the world, but China remained for him an exotic, enticing mystery that he sincerely wanted to visit before he died. Thanks to General Richard Quick, President of the U.S.-Asia Foundation, and Marsha Lefkovits, the Executive Director, a trip was planned for the summer of 1997.

Surprisingly, the Senator was reluctant to go at first. Over a series of big breakfasts on Sunday mornings down at Elsie's Magic Skillet, my wife Dee convinced the Senator he would enjoy the trip. So he finally agreed to go. Then the next week, he canceled. A few days later he agreed to go again. Then he canceled, telling me he just wasn't up for it. Then he came in one day and said, "When are we going to China?" It went back and forth like that for several weeks until finally the day arrived for our scheduled departure. It was to be Senator Thurmond's one last big hurrah — his final trip overseas.

A number of staff, as well as his daughter Julie, had planned to accompany the Senator on the journey to China. We all gathered at Andrews Air Force Base one Saturday morning. Everyone filed into the VIP Lounge, but Senator Thurmond was nowhere to be seen. Thanks to the Army's Senate Liaison Office and Colonel Randy Bookout, who handled travel for these type of diplomatic trips, we had a former Air Force One warming up out on the runway. But still no Senator. I started to think that perhaps he'd changed his mind again.

At last James drove up with the Senator. He bounded out, genuinely excited about going to China. As we started to walk towards the plane, Senator Thurmond yelled out "AH! I left my pocketbook!" That's what he called his wallet. "James! I left my pocketbook at home! I got to go get it." He turned around and started for the parking lot. I said, "Senator, let James go get it. We'll wait on the plane. He'll be right back." I wanted to keep him there. I was afraid if he got back home he might change his mind again, and the whole trip would be off. He said, "Nope! I got to go myself." And he was off. We all filed back into the airport and waited — fifteen minutes, thirty minutes, forty-five minutes. I honestly started to believe that he'd decided not to go. But about an hour later James raced up again and the Senator got out of the car. He came through the door and said with a broad smile, "Okay! Let's go to China!"

That was one of the best trips we ever had. The Senator met with a number of high-level Chinese officials, including President Jiang Zemin. He was treated with great respect by everyone we met. And yes, he finally climbed to the top of the Great Wall of China. His reaction to the Great Wall provided a source of great humor on our trip: "Yep, this is a big wall. Well, let's go!" And he was off to the next destination.

RICHARD QUICK

In my capacity as President of the United States-Asia Foundation, we had the unique honor of organizing Senator Thurmond's trip to China in the summer of 1997. He was 95-years old, president Pro Tempore of the Senate, and Chairman of the Armed Services Committee. It was really historic. I was told that this was the first time a sitting President Pro Tempore of the Senate had ever visited China. And Senator Thurmond was by far the oldest member of the United States Senate to ever visit China. This was a CoDel, or Congressional Delegation, so we actually flew over there on a U.S. Government aircraft. There were several other Senators in the group.

The Chinese accorded Senator Thurmond the courtesies that they would normally extend to a head of state in terms of security and hospitality. It was very impressive. He was hosted by the Chairman of the National People's Congress, who is one of the top three leaders in China. We also flew down to the President's summer residence where Senator Thurmond met with President Jiang Zemin. They had a long, successful meeting.

During the trip, Senator Thurmond wanted to be sure and see the Great Wall of China. We got out there, and the Chinese had provided one of the chairs that he could sit in and they would carry him up the steps. There were four young, strong Chinese guys in traditional dress who were prepared to carry him to the top of the Great Wall. They assumed that Senator Thurmond, who was 95-years old at the time, would not be able to make the climb. Well, you can just imagine Senator Thurmond's reaction when he saw that chair and four Chinese guys standing there waiting to carry him. There was absolutely no way he was going to ride in that chair. So we all started walking up the stairs to the Wall.

It just so happened there was a group of American tourists coming down as we

Senator Thurmond meeting with Chinese
President Jiang Zemin, August 1997.

were going up. We overheard one of them say, "I think that's Strom Thurmond!" And
another one said, "No, that couldn't be Strom Thurmond. He's too old to be walking up
these steps." So they got into a big argument about whether or not that was Strom
Thurmond climbing the Great Wall of China. I finally turned to them and said, "That is
Senator Thurmond; he's on an official visit to China." The next thing you know, all the
tourists are chanting, "Go Strom Go! Go Strom Go!" The Senator went right up the Wall.
Everybody was applauding and cheering. It's one of those events that I'll remember for
the rest of my life.

JOHN A. GASTRIGHT, JR.

In 1997 I accompanied Senator Thurmond to China which was his last big trip. There
was quite a delegation that went along. Senator Jeff Sessions and his wife went, Senator
Rod Graham and his Chief of Staff, and of course Mr. Short and his wife, Dee, went
along. Senator Thurmond's daughter Julie and one of her friends were there, as well as
a handful of staffers like myself.

When we touched down in China, they really rolled the red carpet out for us. A big motorcade drove us into Beijing. One of the most remarkable things I remember from that trip was that every ten yards, for the entire 20 miles into Beijing, policemen were posted on either side of the route. I'd never seen anything like that. It was breathtaking to drive that far with no other cars on the road and see policemen standing guard every ten yards. It was pretty much like that the whole week we were there, no matter where we went.

One of the highlights of that trip was Senator Thurmond's visit to the Great Wall of China. As I understand it, that's something he had always wanted to see. He was 95-years old at the time. The Chinese who accompanied us told us they thought he was the oldest man to climb the Great Wall. To get up there, you have to walk a series of steep steps. It's a pretty significant hike, but Senator Thurmond went to the very top.

We were surrounded by Chinese dignitaries. They had a camera crew there, and a security detail. It was a big deal. Plus, the place was swarming with tourists. When we got to the top of the Wall, everybody got kind of quiet because it looked like the Senator was going to say something. He looks around, sort of surveying the Wall, and he said, "Yep, this is a big wall. Well, let's go!" And we started back down. It was so funny. You could see him thinking, hey, this is just a big wall, so what! That was the Senator's Great Wall of China moment.

Another thing happened on that trip that kind of reminded us that we were in the PRC [People's Republic of China]. We were driving out to review a military base. Of course, there were policemen flanking the route the entire time. We were just flying down the road. At one point, our van clipped another vehicle. I think the other guy was making a lane change or something. Anyway, it was an old farmer in his truck. I guess he was taking his crops somewhere. It was just an accident, but in a matter of seconds, the policemen swooped in and grabbed the old farmer guy and off he goes. We never saw him again.

During the trip, I also remember that the limousine Senator Thurmond was riding in got a flat tire. A pit crew came out of nowhere and got to work. They just appeared, jacked up the car, and changed the tire. Senator Thurmond never even got out of the limousine; they were that fast.

JASON ROSSBACH

Senator Thurmond was so funny at the Great Wall of China. It was one of the few places left in the world he really wanted to see. But when he got up there, he was like, "Yeah, that sure is a big wall. Okay let's go!" You could just see him thinking, we can't stand out here on this wall all damn day!

A guy from the State Department rode with us. It was the three of us sitting in the

Senator Thurmond relaxes on the trip back
from China.

U.S. SENATE PHOTO

backseat of this car. About two minutes into the ride, Senator Thurmond looked at the guy and said, "You ever think about eunuchs?" The guy looked at me. I started shaking my head as if to say, "Don't even answer it; don't worry about it. He's just had a passing thought; let it go." Then the Senator said, "You think that's a choice? How do you think that works?"

Now, the guy was a very intelligent man. You could just see the smoke coming out of his ears, the wheels spinning, as he tried to figure out what Senator Thurmond was talking about. He tried his best to give the Senator a great State Department-like answer, but wasn't having much luck. I kept shaking my head. Senator Thurmond could be quite funny without even realizing it.

DEE SHORT

In August of 1997 I had the honor and privilege to be part of the Strom Thurmond Congressional Delegation to China. Prior to our trip, on several occasions, the Senator had mentioned that he would like to see the Great Wall of China. This was one of the last things he wanted to see and do. Walking up that magnificent Great Wall with him truly was an unforgettable experience and one I will always treasure.

Strom Thurmond meets the press.

It was once said that the most dangerous place to be was between Strom Thurmond and a TV camera. I mean, you could actually get hurt as the magnetic field pulled Thurmond inexorably towards the camera. He loved it.

– Mark Goodin –

Of the Nuclear Tripod, Black Socks, and More

SENATOR THURMOND AND THE PRESS

One of the problems I faced as Senator Thurmond's Chief of Staff was how to react when derogatory comments about the Senator came out in the press. The staff usually wanted to respond. But if you respond, you can keep a one-week story going for a month — you give the story legs, as they say. I remember the time another Senator made an unnecessarily unkind comment about Senator Thurmond, something about the Senate being his nursing home. The staff wanted to respond to that. But you just can't. If you respond, you make it worse. So we said nothing. And the truth of the matter was, Strom Thurmond was nearly 100-years old, and the Senate was his home. Dee and I thank God he had the Senate family to keep an eye out for him. He was much better cared for there than he would have been in any other place.

By and large we didn't have any major press problems. We always had very talented press secretaries who did a wonderful job for the Senator. And we didn't hold a lot of sit-down interviews. Senator Thurmond never saw that as a good investment of his time. He believed his time was much better spent on the phone trying to help someone in South Carolina than chatting with a reporter. I agreed with him. But if reporters stopped the Senator in the hall, he was happy to answer their questions.

A significant part of my job was to protect the Senator. I never wanted the Senator to be embarrassed or to regret following my advice. As he neared 100-years old, like anybody else, he had good days and bad days. He could get confused and tired at times, then just as quickly snap back to being quite lucid and energetic. It was unpredictable.

There was a press incident toward the end of the Senator's last term in Washington that has never been reported publicly and that very few people know about. I had agreed to allow a South Carolina TV news crew into the office so they could tape an interview with the Senator to use in a memorial story after he had passed away. But I insisted on one condition. If I said they had to turn the camera off, they had to turn it off. If I said they couldn't use the tape, they couldn't use it. No negotiating. I had the final say. The station owner agreed.

They sent a lovely young woman reporter to do the interview, which was a smart move. Senator Thurmond was much more likely to cooperate. I was in the office when they started rolling the tape. Within a few minutes they were moving around the room as the Senator pointed out various awards he'd received and discussed photos on the wall. I could tell he was really having a good time with the interview. Then they came to the photographs of all the Presidents that Senator Thurmond had served with in public office, going back to President Roosevelt. The young woman said something like, "Are these all the Presidents you've served under?" The Senator quickly corrected her, "Served *with*, served *with*! These are the Presidents I've served *with*. I didn't work for any of them."

Senator Thurmond shared an anecdote or two about the Presidents, starting with F.D.R. He was a delegate to his convention in 1932. Then he came to the photograph of John F. Kennedy. The Senator always liked the Kennedys. He didn't particularly like their politics, but he liked the family, individually, and as a group. He especially admired the fact that they were a big, close-knit family which encouraged public service to the country. He believed that was a wonderful model for any family.

The reporter asked him, "Senator Thurmond, where were you when President Kennedy was shot?" Without hesitating the Senator answered, "I was there in Dallas. I was in the motorcade. I heard the shot." The reporter stopped and looked at him. I think she knew better. "Are you sure Senator? Are you sure you were there?" He insisted. "Yeah, I was there. I was in the motorcade. My car was further back. I heard the shots."

I immediately stopped the taping. I pulled the Senator aside to discuss the matter. Senator Thurmond personally witnessed many of the historic moments of the 20th century. I can only believe that he assumed he was there. Plus, he'd seen the clip of the Zapruder film so many times, as we all have, that I guess he came to think he saw it actually happen in person — which he had not. I asked him, "Senator, are you sure you were in Dallas? I'm not sure that's right." But he insisted. "I was there Duke!" Well, I let the interview continue. But when they were wrapping up to leave I told the reporter they could not use that part of the tape. She understood. To my knowledge that tape has never been broadcast in its entirety. As the station owner is a man of integrity, he abided by our agreement.

Holly later checked the Senator's schedule book and discovered that he had in fact been in a parade the very day that Kennedy was shot — but it was in South Carolina, not Dallas, Texas.

LEE BANDY

When I went to work for *The State* newspaper in Washington, Strom Thurmond was not at all happy with my coverage of him. One weekend he came down to Columbia and went out to the home of my publisher, Ambrose Hampton. He lived out on Lake Berry for the summertime. Strom went out to his house and knocked on his door. Of course, Mr. Hampton was shocked to see Strom Thurmond on his doorstep. Strom said, "I need to talk to you about your Washington correspondent. We're not happy with his coverage." Mr. Hampton, being the nice guy that he is, told the Senator, "Well thank you very much, but I'm busy right now. I'll send my Executive Editor, Charlie Wickenberg, to Washington to sit down and talk to you about it."

So Charlie told me he was coming to Washington to see Senator Thurmond about my coverage. Wickenberg was in Thurmond's office for about 30 minutes. He told me later that he went in the office and the Senator said, "We're not very happy with your Washington correspondent, Lee Bandy. We don't think he's covering us like he should." Strom Thurmond opened up this file drawer in his desk and pulled out his Lee Bandy file, which was full of press releases he had given me. He had checked off the ones that I had written stories about. Needless to say, there weren't too many checked off. So Wickenberg said, "That's fine. That speaks well for Mr. Bandy, Senator, because we did not hire him to be your public relations agent." After that, I guess Strom Thurmond adjusted to the new way of covering politicians. He and I got along well after that. I had no problems, and I had total access.

DENNIS W. SHEDD

I was with Senator Thurmond one time when we did an interview with Dan Rather. Dan Rather said something to the Senator off camera. He said, "Senator Thurmond, I want to thank you. When I first started working as a cub reporter on Capitol Hill, nobody would give me an interview. I couldn't get anybody to stop and talk to me. I was getting kind of desperate. One day you came by, and I asked if I could talk to you. You stopped and gave me my very first interview on Capitol Hill. I've never forgotten that. It's something I'll always be grateful for."

ROBIN ROBERTS

We were shooting some TV commercials for the Senator's 1990 campaign. He was 88-years old at the time. We wanted to show that he was still active and physically fit, which he was. So in addition to showing him around the office, working in the Capitol, and down in the state, we arranged to shoot him at a health club working out. Well, he shows up in his workout clothes: a nice navy blue Adidas outfit. But he was also wearing black Army socks with moccasins. We didn't think that would be appropriate to have him jogging on the treadmill in black socks and moccasins. So we went down to the locker room and made a deal with a club member to borrow his tennis shoes and white socks.

We had arranged with the camera crew to film him from multiple angles so we'd be sure and have something we could work with. But we told them to be conscious of the Senator's age and not to wear him out. Hopefully everybody could get what they needed on the first take. So we set these shots up. We had him doing sit ups, lifting weights, calisthenics, and running on the treadmill. I said, "Senator, we're going to do this as quickly as we can so we don't wear you out." He said, "Wear me out? What do you mean? I worked out for an hour before I came here today."

MARK GOODIN

Senator Thurmond was fascinated by television, but he was not what you would call telegenic. He never really understood what television wanted from politicians, because he didn't grow up around it. Television was invented when Strom Thurmond was a young man. The way he got elected was walking from county to county and shaking hands, doing favors, and doing stump speeches. The age of television transformed all that and made it important that politicians look and sound good on television. But he never really understood that. The whole idea of a sound byte never made sense to him.

I remember one night, Tom Brokaw was on TV. There were a bunch of pages standing around his office. Thurmond yelled out, "Look at that! Look at that!" And he crouched down on his knees, got real close to the TV, and said, "You can see the wrinkles around that man's eyes! And he's 500 miles from here! It's a miracle!"

All the children started giggling. So I stepped outside the office with them and said, "Before you ladies and gentlemen start cackling at this, I want you to realize that this man was born before the airplane was invented. I want you to think about that for a minute. He was born before the airplane was invented; one whole year before Orville and Wilbur Wright got off the ground in Kitty Hawk, North Carolina. Television is a new thing to him. You grew up with it. You took it for granted. You saw it as a fact of life. It is indeed a miracle that a camera can transmit an image that clear for 500 miles. But the miracle is lost on you because you grew up with it. He did not."

He was consistently fascinated by the technology of television and thrilled by the fame-making quality of it. At the same time, he was dangerous in front of it because he didn't understand sound bytes. He never understood how to encapsulate a small mes-

Senator Thurmond answers a reporter.

THE STROM THURMOND INSTITUTE, CLEMSON UNIVERSITY

sage. He just wasn't built that way. He never mastered it. But he really loved to be on television. It was once said that the most dangerous place to be was between Strom Thurmond and a TV camera. I mean, you could actually get hurt as the magnetic field pulled Thurmond inexorably towards the camera. He loved it.

One day in the middle of the MX Missile debate, the little buzzer on my phone went off. I said, "Yes sir?" The Senator said, "I want to go up and talk to the TV about this missile." Before I could say anything the line went dead. That was an order. You saluted and did it. My objection was that he had had absolutely no involvement in the MX Missile debate. It was basically a Gary Hart stand-alone show. Nobody had asked him to make a statement about it. And one of the big rules of the Senate Radio and TV Gallery is that you don't go up there unless you're asked. You need to be invited. That territory belongs to the correspondents. So I called Brit Hume, who was working for ABC as a Capitol Correspondent at the time, and asked Brit, "I need a favor. Can you invite Senator Thurmond up to the Gallery to talk about the missile?" He very quickly and correctly told me, "Sure, be glad to. We're happy to have him up here. But we're not going to use it." I said, "Okay, I get it; he just wants to come up."

So we began the slow march from the Russell Building over to the Capitol where the Radio and TV Gallery is. It was a tiny, little room then, very different from what's there now. It was probably no bigger than about 600-square feet just packed with correspondents and cameras. We got about two feet from the door and Senator Thurmond stopped and turned to me and said, "Now tell me about this missile." My jaw dropped. "What do you mean, tell me about this missile? I thought you wanted to say something." He said, "What should I say?" I said, "Just say that the missile is a very important modernization of our strategic triad: of land-based, sea-based, and air-based missiles."

Well, the words *strategic triad* must have stuck in his head. We walked in, and the room was packed. Everybody was simply going through the motions. Nobody had any actual intentions of putting him on the air. He didn't know that of course. So Phil Jones of CBS News asked him, "Senator, what's so important about this missile?"

Thurmond looked into the camera and cleared his throat. He said, "Well I'm glad you asked that. You see, this missile, this cruise missile, is a very important part of our nuclear tripod."

The whole room began to laugh, including me. I was laughing so hard. It was one of those laughs where it hurts to laugh because you're laughing so hard you hyperventilate. I had to leave the room to compose myself, because I was creating more of a scene than he was. He had no idea why people were laughing. I went right back in and yelled out, "Thank you very much ladies and gentleman!" And I literally grabbed him and pushed him out the door. We got clear of the room, and he said in this gruff voice, "What were they laughing at in there?" I said, "Senator it's *strategic triad* not *nuclear tripod*." He said, "Triad, tripod, three legs, what different does it make? You want me to go back and do it again?" I said, "No!"

The buzz I got back from the Gallery was that the old man was senile, that he's gone over the edge. So I chose to make light of it. I got an old camera tripod from an ABC correspondent, taped a plastic missile to it, then covered it with a sheet. Over that I put one of those Top Secret government document enclosures which said: "Do Not Look!" I drug it up there to the Gallery after the deadlines were passed. I said, "You people doubt the existence of the nuclear tripod. Well I'm here to show you that it does indeed exist!" And I ripped the sheet off the thing. Everybody started laughing and the tension was broken. The only problem was, Lee Bandy was sitting there taking all of this down. He called me later and said he was going to write about the incident, including my little stunt.

So I had to go explain to Strom Thurmond why I did that. He said, "What do you mean?! You embarrass me by going up there and laughing at me?!" I finally told him, "Look, here's the deal; you either look senile or you just laugh about it." He said, "Well, laugh about this: you're fired!" I gulped real hard. He kind of looked up and smiled and said, "Oh, go on." He didn't care. That is the famous *nuclear tripod* story.

Growing Old Is Not For Sissies

*I*t was during Senator Thurmond's last term in office, which he won in 1996, that we started to notice he was really slowing down. We had expected these challenges; after all, he was approaching 100-years old. But that didn't make it easy to take, since he had always been the very specimen of fantastic health. His hip was giving him problems, making it increasingly painful to walk. Each year he seemed to have substantially less energy than the last. And he sometimes got severely dehydrated, which made for a couple of well-publicized fainting spells. There was one fainting incident, however, that was particularly troubling.

Holly burst into my office one afternoon and screamed, "The Senator! Duke! Come in here quick!" We ran back into his office, where I found him slumped over in his chair. I got him down to the floor. I elevated his feet. He looked horrible. I knew he was alive, but he had a deathly look about him. Holly called the Capitol Physician's office. They were at his side within minutes. We got him into an ambulance and took off for Walter Reed Army Medical Center. I held his hand on the way over, and I remember trying to talk to him. But he wasn't responding very well.

The folks at Walter Reed got him on IVs right away. They were wonderful with him. They deserve great accolades for all the compassion and care they showed the Senator during his last years in Washington. Within a few minutes the Senator was conscious, breathing normally, and talking. He asked what had happened. Then he told the doctor he had to get back to the office because there was so much work left to do. Dee, of course, had rushed to the hospital when I called her at home. She and I stood next to his bed. I reminded the Senator of the saying that my doctor, David Bernanke, has on display in his office: "Growing old is not for sissies." He

Duke Short and Strom Thurmond at Walter Reed
Army Hospital, 2002.

smiled and squeezed Dee's hand. You could see him thinking, that's the truth!

Strom Thurmond battled against growing old with terrific courage, just as he approached everything else in his life. But it was not easy, especially knowing he would never win. Since he was a young man he had prided himself on his superb health and physical fitness. He was a runner. He was a swimmer. He lifted weights. He liked to demonstrate his strength by doing one-arm push-ups. When his body started to fail him, he was frustrated and angry. He refused a wheelchair. He didn't like the idea of what it might look like in the papers. His greatest fear was that the people of South Carolina might start to think he was too weak to help them anymore.

So he insisted on walking, very slowly, typically holding onto the arm of a personal assistant. With his bad hip, each step was incredibly painful. You could see it in his face. He sometimes winced with each step. And yet if someone came over to say hello he quickly put a smile on his face, straightened up, and said with such cheer, "How are you? It's so good to see you!"

I vividly recall the moment when he and I were walking down the hall in the Russell Senate Office Building outside his office. He was having a difficult time getting one foot in front of the other. He stopped. He exhaled loudly. He leaned against me and said with such sad resignation, "Duke, I can't do it anymore. You've got to get me one of those rolling chairs." I sent a staffer to the Capitol Physician's office for a wheelchair. The Senator used one for the rest of his life.

He made the best of it. He learned to adapt to that "rolling chair;"and he got used to the "ear plugs," as he called them (hearing aids which he more often than not refused to turn on); and during his last two years in Washington he adjusted to spending his nights at Walter Reed, where he could get immediate care if needed. Dr. David McLeod, one of the Senator's personal physicians and one of Walter Reed's finest, deserves much of the credit for the superb care Senator Thurmond received.

"You want to know how to live to be 100?" Senator Thurmond used to ask visitors to his office. They would all nod with rapt attention and say, "Yes sir, please!" He'd throw his hands out and say with a hearty laugh, "Just keep breathing!"

NEWT GINGRICH

One of my most striking memories of Senator Thurmond was when he and I were meeting with President George H.W. Bush in the Cabinet Room at the White House with the leadership. I had become Republican Whip by that point. We were talking about education. All of a sudden Senator Thurmond said, "I was a school teacher." You could see everybody looking at each other trying to calculate, okay, if he was the Senator, the Governor, a Presidential Candidate, a Circuit Judge, a Major General in the Army Reserves, a State Senator, and an Attorney, when could he possibly have been a school teacher? Our best calculus was that he was a school teacher before George H.W. Bush was born. It was a marvelous moment.

MIKE TONGOUR

I was with the Senator one night, and I told him I needed to stop and get some money from the ATM. This was back when they first came out. I got some money. Senator Thurmond was absolutely fascinated with how the card worked, how the money came out, and how it automatically got deducted from your account. His eyes were glittering with this new technology. He wanted me to do it a second time, just to see how the whole process worked. He was amazed. Some of the newer technologies must have seemed like science fiction to him, having been born in 1902.

MANSEL LONG, JR.

I'll never forget a conversation I had one time with Senator Thurmond. It was about the time they were voting on the Martin Luther King birthday bill. He told me, "I always thought that birthday bill should have been for Booker T. Washington." Most people will remember that Booker T. Washington was the father of Tuskegee University. He was born in 1856. I said, "Senator, what do you know about Booker T. Washington?" He said, "My mother took me to hear him speak when I was a little boy." Imagine that! He continued, "Booker T. Washington taught that when you graduated from college you should walk across the stage with a diploma in one hand and a certificate in the other; a diploma to show that you know something and a certificate to show that you can do something." It was remarkable to me that not only did Senator Thurmond hear Booker T. Washington speak, but that he also knew about the man.

LESLIE SEALY

I used to take the Senator to lunch sometimes on the weekends. He was a funny guy. We would ride in the car, and he would always say, "Do you know how old I am?" I'd answer yes and tell him his age. He'd say, "How do you know how old I am?" I'd say, "Well, I know you were born in 1902, so I just added it up." He was always amazed that I knew how old he was.

DEE SHORT

It's funny, I never thought of the Senator as being old. I remember when he was approaching his ninetieth birthday I asked him, "Senator, do you feel ninety?" He chuckled and said no. Then he slyly looked at me and said, "You mean, I'm really going to be ninety? I don't look it do I?" And of course my answer was a truthful, "No sir, you sure don't."

I don't think I really accepted his growing older until his last year in office. During our visits with him at Walter Reed that last year, I began to accept the fact that this giant of a man was slowing down. In my mind, Senator Thurmond will never be old. His spirit was always young — young at heart, we often say. After all, age is just a state of mind.

ROBERT BENNETT

is a United States Senator from Utah, 1992-present. Senator
Bennett made the following remarks in June 2003 on the
Floor of the U.S. Senate.

One of our colleagues was in the Senate doctor's office, as we go in there from time to time, and he noticed Strom coming out of the doctor's office with a very worried look on his face. We were all very concerned about Strom and his health in his later years. So the colleague said to the doctor, "What's the matter with Strom?" The doctor said appropriately, "I cannot discuss the medical condition of one patient with another patient, so I can't say anything to you." He continued, "However, I don't think it would be violating medical ethics to tell you that Strom is a little worried about the fact that he can no longer do one-arm pushups."

SCOTT FRICK

The Senator was still walking to the Senate Floor when I first joined the staff. He was not yet in a wheelchair. We would walk alongside him and just assist him, give him an arm to lean on when he needed it. He was definitely getting more frail. The short-term memory loss was the thing you noticed most. He would ask the same question repeatedly, like five minutes apart. And yet he could remember things so clearly from many years ago. Constituents would walk in the office, and he could tell you the whole history of their family and all about the town they were from. And yet, he might not remember what day of the week it was.

Sometimes the Senate works late into the night. I don't remember one time that Senator Thurmond wasn't able to handle that. There he was, going on 100-years old, and he was still ready to stay as late as needed to do the job.

But no matter how old he got, he still had that strong grip! He never lost that. Sometimes he'd grab my arm as we were walking down that long hall in the Russell Building. He would squeeze my arm so hard, I'd have to stop and tell him to let up. I mean, it was painful!

R.C. PREACHER WHITNER

The Senator loved The 116 Club. Anytime he could get away, the Senator and Duke and I would go over there for lunch. Senator Thurmond knew I was from Rock Hill, South Carolina, so every time we got together he'd always ask me the same two questions: "Who is the President of Winthrop?" I never knew the answer to that one. Then he would ask, "How are those two Williams boys that owned the Gulf Station in Rock Hill?" I'd always say, "Well Senator, Harris died about twenty years ago and Wade is still clicking along."

He asked those same two questions every time we went to lunch. I told Duke, "If I had any brains at all, I'd find out who the devil is the President of that university." So I finally called down there to find out. It was Dr. Anthony J. DiGiorgio. Next time we had lunch I told the Senator, "I got a surprise for you. I know who the President of Winthrop is." And I told him. He just kind of thought for a moment and shook his head positively. That question never came up again. He just wanted to know.

DIRK KEMPTHORNE

I served on the Armed Services Committee when I was in the Senate, which was a tremendous honor. It was also an honor to serve under the leadership of Strom Thurmond. When you consider his military record and the different feats he accomplished, he was truly an incredible man and a great patriot. He not only believed in our country but in our military. It was not unusual for the Senate to go very late at night with a variety of debates or votes. One thing I will always remember about Senator Thurmond is the fact that even though he was in his nineties, he was always there no matter how late it got, sitting bolt straight at his desk, reading what material may have been provided, and was probably one of the more alert members of the Senate in those wee morning hours.

CHRIS KELLEY CIMKO

For all the things that people said about him during his last few years in the Senate, I can tell you that while I was there, Senator Thurmond had a strong mind and asked insightful questions. And he could still be very demanding about the quality of work that he expected from the staff.

TERRY L. WOOTEN

The Senator's press secretary was getting married in Columbia. Some of the staff and the Senator went down for the wedding. When I came out of the church after the ceremony, I noticed that the stairs were really old and narrow. I thought that if the Senator slipped or stumbled on those steps, it could be very embarrassing for him. So I thought I'd just wait at the top of the steps until he came out. That way I could walk close behind him and just be there in case. Of course, I wouldn't let him know that. I'd just kind of stand by and be there to catch him if he slipped so he wouldn't embarrass himself.

So people started coming out of the church. I heard the Senator talking. As he came out the front door I said, "Senator, how you doin'?" He said, "Fine Mr. Wooten; how you doin'?" I said, "Good, good," I tried to talk with him so as not to let him know that I was there to keep him from stumbling down those steps. I turned to start down the steps. Well, I was wearing brand new shoes that day and they had a slick bottom. I slipped in those new shoes. I literally started to fall forward down those steps. I reached over and grabbed the Senator. He grabbed me. He wrapped his arms around me in a big bear hug and walked me down the steps. We got to the bottom of the steps. He looked me straight in the eye and said, "Be careful! You're gonna hurt yourself!" Then he turned and walked away. That's a totally true story.

BOB HURT

In Senator Thurmond's later years you'd think his memory would be at its weakest. But that wasn't the case. You'd see discussions in the press about how he was losing his edge, as we all do when we get older. But it was quite the opposite. I remember we were having lunch one time at The 116 Club. I'm from Georgia, so we started talking about the former Senator and former Governor Herman E. Talmadge. Senator Thurmond, and this was probably during the last year of his life, told some stories about Talmadge when he was Governor. Right off the top of his head he said, "Herman and I were both Governors. He cut a bunch of taxes." And he quoted the exact figures.

I had actually reread Senator Talmadge's autobiography because I was helping Senator Nunn with some draft remarks for a eulogy for Senator Talmadge. So I came back and checked the book. Senator Thurmond had those numbers exactly right! I was kind of stunned. The man had a very vivid recollection of facts and details. When that light was on, it was quite amazing.

JASON ROSSBACH

As an older man the Senator had a stunning vanity for not wanting to wear glasses or hearing aids. But much to his disbelief, he was rather hard of hearing. So we finally convinced him that he needed hearing aids. He really didn't like wearing them, so he only wore them periodically. The challenge was, unless you'd been around him all day, you never knew if he was wearing them or not. Staff might walk into the room and talk in the normal way you usually talked to him, which was a little bit louder than you might talk to anyone else. He would sit there behind his desk and then look over at Holly and say, "Why is everybody yelling at me? Tell them to stop! Everybody's screaming at me today, and I don't like it!"

He would always tinker with the hearing aids too because he insisted he knew better than everyone else. They tell you not to mess with them, that once they're set they're fine; they'll adjust themselves. But he would always have his driver James tinkering with them. Then he'd put them back in. One day the Senator and I were walking down the hall in the Russell Building toward the elevators. He and James must have messed up the setting because all of a sudden he starts howling: "Too loud! Too loud! Make it stop!" I said, "Oh my God!" He yelled, "Take it out! Take it out! Too loud!" I took the hearing aids out. He shook his head and said, "Ah! I'd rather be deaf!"

ROBERT R. SMITH, II

The Senator made a trip down from D.C.; that was probably in 2001. Normally he didn't need or even ask for much help. But on that trip his hips were really bothering him. It looked pretty painful. Anyway, at one point during the trip, the car we were parked in was a little too close to the curb. So I said, "Senator, I'll help you get out of the car." Usually he didn't like that. He'd say something like, "I'm fine. I don't need help." But on that day he said, "Okay, sure. But I don't think you can lift me." I told him I'd like to try.

So I got outside the car and reached in and pulled a little bit. It was a little pull, nothing big. It was more like he just used me as leverage to pull himself up out of the car. Soon as he stood up on the sidewalk he wheeled around, slapped me right across the chest as he was known to do his male staff, and said, "I underestimated you!"

DONALD BALDWIN

In the year before he retired, the Senator and Duke joined me for lunch one afternoon at the Capitol Hill Club. The Senator was pretty feeble. Duke and I walked on either side of him down to the Grill Room. A few people came over and said hello, and he seemed to come alive for that. But otherwise he was only passively interested in his food and didn't have much conversation. He was showing his age, put it that way.

After we finished, we headed to the front door. Again, Duke and I were on either side of the Senator. He was kind of holding on to us, shuffling along. Well, there was a young lady who was coming in the door as we were going out. Suddenly, Senator Thurmond looked up and saw that girl. He perked up, stood straight up, dropped a hold of both our arms, walked up to the door and pushed it open for her and said, "Hi, can I open the door for ya?!" She really brought him to life.

JASON ROSSBACH

One night we were sitting at one of those big Republican dinners. I used to tease the Senator and call him "rock star" because every time we went to one of those events he was the biggest celebrity in the room. People flocked to meet him, young and old. And without fail, there would be groups of young women who would come over and have their picture taken with him. That made his heart leap a little bit because he enjoyed it so.

But that night, I guess he wasn't in a particularly grand mood. As usual there were different groups of girls who came over, fawned all over him, and had their picture taken. He was very nice to them. But when they all walked away he suddenly said, "Hah!" I said, "Yes sir?" He said, "Look at that cute little old man! Isn't he precious; isn't he sweet! Harmless!" He was really perturbed. He had that look on his face like, if only I was twenty years younger they wouldn't be calling me sweet and nice and treating me like some old man. I didn't say anything for awhile. He was very upset about it. You could see that bothered him.

DAVID T. BEST

The Senator's death brought a lot of memories back. I really thought of him as a grandfather. First and foremost, I respected him as a Senator. But I was privileged to be around him enough to get to know him personally. He was like family.

I remember one Saturday during December I took my daughter out to Walter Reed.

She was a senior in high school. I think she was doing an interview for a school project. She asked him a lot of questions about when he was younger. He told her how he used to crank up a car, and how one day the crank came back and broke his wrist. He said the worst pain in his entire life was the crank of a Model T snapping back on his hand. He talked about learning to ride horses and riding his motorcycle down unpaved country roads. And of course he told the story about why he became a cross-country runner: because the nearest women's school to Clemson was 22 miles away.

He was not the kind of man to reminisce a lot. But if you could find him in the right mood, there were times he opened up. I'll never forget that day, just he and I and my daughter talking. I remember she asked him what he wanted to be remembered for. He always answered that question the same way: "That I tried to help the people, all the people." It wasn't a political answer. He really felt that in his heart. He honestly wanted to be remembered as a man who helped others.

I've got a lot of very good memories of the Senator. I haven't been able to walk back by his old office in the Russell Building. I want to remember it the way it was. There are evenings when I'm over here late, and I really truly miss him. I miss going down and getting a bowl of soup together. We really were a family, particularly those last four or five years when we knew we were coming to a conclusion and everybody was working so hard to get the most done with what time we had left.

MARK IVANY

I was there on two different occasions when the Senator fainted. I'll be perfectly honest: the first time, down on the Senate Floor, I thought he had died. I had only been his special assistant for three or four months, so I was relatively new at the job. We were sitting next to each other. I was the only person from his staff down there. There really wasn't anybody else close to us. He started gripping his chair with both hands very tightly. His eyes started kind of rolling back in his head. I shook him, and I said, "Senator! Senator, are you okay?!" He turned his head to look at me but just had a total glassy expression over his eyes. I thought he was having a stroke. I'd never seen anyone have a stroke, but I assumed it had to look something like that.

The whole time this is going on, other Senators are debating on the Floor. I remember Senator Warner was speaking, so he was down there. I stood up in front of Senator Thurmond, because I didn't know if he was going to fall over. I kind of assessed the situation, and I quickly jogged to the Cloak Room. I told them to call the Capitol Physician. By the time I got back to him, Les Brownlee, who was working for Senator Warner at the time, had started walking over. So together we laid Senator Thurmond down and loosened his tie. Senator Frist came over.

Mr. Short made it down to the Senate Floor in zero seconds flat. At one point I just looked up and he was right there and took over. An ambulance came and Mr. Short rode with the Senator to the hospital. I spent the rest of the day out at Walter Reed with the Senator. He was fine. He just got badly dehydrated.

The second time was at Holly's funeral. The Senator, his daughter Julie, his son-in-law Martin, and Mrs. Thurmond were sitting in the front row. I was seated directly behind the Senator with James, his driver, and James' wife Vanjewell. It was an exceptionally hot day. We probably made it halfway through the service when the Senator sort of slumped over. I jumped up and walked around. He had obviously passed out. I told Martin to get the wheelchair. Martin and I picked him up, got him in the wheelchair, and pushed him out a door.

We got him back into a church hallway where there was air conditioning. Once he got a chance to cool off he came around, and we got some food in him. I always carried Nutrigrain bars and fruit drinks with a lot of sugar in them. We fed him some of that. The paramedics came, but he was okay by the time they got there. They didn't even do anything. He was fine. Unfortunately, as soon as they left, I think they called the newspapers. We all took him back to Walter Reed. We didn't even use the ambulance.

PHIL JONES

Let me tell you about the last interview I did with Senator Thurmond. I think he was 98 at the time. He'd been declining over the years. I had watched it happen and not done anything on it. Then one time he went on the Senate Floor as President Pro Tem and really screwed it up. I mean, they almost had to carry him down. So I said, okay, the time has come. I'm going to have to do a story on this.

I talked with Mark Goodin, because Mark and I are good friends, and I talked to Duke. I told them both that I was going to have to do a story about the Senator's old age. To get the interview, I'd probably have to stake him out somewhere. The next thing I know I got a call from Duke. He said, "Now listen; you don't have to stake the old man out and surprise him." Duke said he would let me know when the Senator was coming to work and I could get some pictures of him. I said okay.

Duke said, "Now, we'll probably pick him up about 11 o'clock in the morning and bring him to work. He'll be coming in the side door over there." I said, "Okay. And I'm going to ask him some questions." Duke said, "Aw, do you have to do that?" I said, "Come on, I've got to. Duke, relax. What good is it going to do me, Phil Jones, to be seen on national television beating up on a 98 year old man? That's not going to do me any good. But I need to ask him a couple of questions about how he's feeling." So Duke said okay.

The prescribed time came. We were in the Russell Building, a few feet from the elevator where he usually comes in. The door finally opened and Senator Thurmond came

As Strom Thurmond neared the end of his final term and celebrated his 100th birthday, he sometimes took naps in his office.

walking out. He was holding Duke's arm, or Duke was holding his. They walked along, shuffled along I would say. Finally I came up to him with the camera. "Good morning, how are you Senator? How are you feeling?" He said, "Oh, great." He kept on walking. We went right up to his office door. I asked him if he still enjoyed coming to work. He said, "Oh, I do. There's still so much work to do. Got to take care of the people."

At that point, I asked a few more questions. Then he and Duke went into the office and left the door wide open. I asked Duke if we could follow him in with the camera. Duke said okay. So the camera crew followed the Senator all the way across the office to his desk. He took off his coat, then went around behind his desk and sat down. He looked out at the camera and said, "Any questions?" So I walked into the office. I wasn't really prepared for a sit-down interview. But I said, "Sure, I've got some questions."

I said, "Are you reading all these stories about your health?" He said, "Oh yeah, they all got me one foot in the grave. But they're wrong. I'm going to outlive them all!" I said, "You've never seen a Senate this close." At that point it was 50-50. Senator Thurmond said, "Yeah, that's why it's more important that I keep coming in."

The story that I had started to do that day, which was going to be pretty rough, he well took care of. I couldn't really dump on him. I mean, it was obvious he looked feeble;

it was obvious he looked old. But the fact is, he answered all my questions. And he was funny. The story that went on the CBS Evening News was tender, not because I'd necessarily made it that way. That's the way that he handled it.

The next day I called Duke to thank him for helping me out on the thing. Duke said, "Well, it's a good thing you did it yesterday because he couldn't do it today." I said, "You know Duke, with all due respect, I think you're wrong. If I were there with a TV camera in front of him, I think he would rise to the occasion. That's exactly what happened yesterday. I think he saw the camera; he knew by God he had to perform, and he performed. That's the fight, the vigor in him." Whatever he had to do, he always rose to the occasion. Anyway, it was one of the most precious moments I ever had up there.

All the politicians of age complain that the press guts them and treats them unfairly. I've always been an advocate that a public official can kill a reporter with kindness. That's what Senator Thurmond did. There he was; he could hardly walk. But did he say "Get out of here; get out of my way," or did he leave the impression with his staff that they'd better prevent any reporter or camera from getting to him? No. It was just the opposite.

His most trusted aide felt comfortable in saying, "I'll help you get to him." Other public officials would have left the impression with their staff, the vibes would have been there, that by God you better not let Jones get close because the Senator's too feeble; he's going to make a mistake, and it's just going to be awful. But Strom never did that. I don't think he ever told a staffer to keep the press away. And he was smart enough to know, any time that I got to him, just to talk, to tell it the way he was thinking. He didn't need a briefing on anything. Strom Thurmond always felt, no matter how old he got, that he could handle it. And my God, just look at the issues and the firefights that he'd been through during his career, and you can see why. He was not battle weary: he was battle prepared.

LINDSEY GRAHAM

It was a really big day when he came out and endorsed me for the Senate race. I can't express what an incredible honor that was for me. Duke set up the announcement with Bob Dole and Senator Thurmond. That was in 2002. But Senator Thurmond was doing very poorly that day. We were all worried whether or not he would be able to make the event and participate. He was laying on his couch in the office. Holly was still in good health then. You know, she doted on him like no one else. We were talking about maybe going ahead without him and letting him rest.

All of a sudden he opened his eyes and said, "Is it time to go?" Duke said, "Yes sir." He got up slowly off the couch and made it out to the car. We drove over to the RNC headquarters. The Senator shuffled slowly into the building, and slowly went up to the podium. James Brown was there singing "God Bless America." Bob Dole was there. At that point I was more of an afterthought, just standing in the background. I was stunned by this array of people that had come out to support me.

Senator Dole introduced Senator Thurmond like only Senator Dole could. When that camera light went on, Senator Thurmond lit up. He became a different person. He looked at the camera and said, "Vote for Lindsey Graham! I am! He's a good man!" And that sealed the day. He rose to the occasion.

JASON ROSSBACH

A lot of people thought Senator Thurmond was just a curious, old man. But even well into his late nineties he had tremendous instincts. No matter how old he got, you could never really slide something by him. If you ever gave him an argument on something that had a weak point, for example, he would instinctively go right for the weak point. If you wrote something that you weren't sure about, he would jump all over those very two sentences you weren't sure about. He would say, "Why did you write this? What does this mean?" That's why he lived through as many political ups and downs and changes in society as he did. He had remarkable intuition and instincts that served him well his entire life. He gave people that, "I'm just a good old guy from Edgefield, South Carolina, aw shucks" act a lot of the time. But truth is, Strom Thurmond had incredibly sharp instincts right up until the end.

PATRICIA KEMPTHORNE,
was the First Lady of Idaho and is the wife of Governor Dirk Kempthorne, who presently serves as the Secretary of the Interior.

I was so fortunate to attend Senator Thurmond's 90th birthday party, and even luckier to share a dance with him. While we were dancing, I told him what a great honor it was for me to be there. I said, "I hope you'll reserve a dance for me at your 105th birthday." I expected him to say, you bet, I'll be there! But he said, "Sweetheart, I don't want to live that long. I'm getting tired." It was really surprising to hear him say that. It gave me some insight that perhaps reaching 100 was his goal.

DARYL JONES

Senator Thurmond was using a wheelchair when I was in Washington. He would stand up and try to make his way as best he could, but it was difficult for him. Some days were better than others. There were days we had discussions, and I was absolutely impressed with how coherent he was. And there were days when he did not seem to be feeling his best. But through it all, the gentleman always worked at the very best his body and mind could give. I was impressed with that.

It makes you wonder, what it is that drives a person like that? What keeps them going? You'd think most people might want to relax at some point in their lives and have a little fun. But Strom Thurmond always wanted to be the Senator. He never wanted to stop trying to help the people of South Carolina. And he certainly was not going to let old age stand in his way of performing that duty.

That takes a special kind of person to keep going like that. Critics might say it was out of fear, fear of not knowing what to do if you retire. But I don't believe that was true in his case. I think Strom Thurmond was just driven, right up to the end.

Governor Mark Sanford of South Carolina, Duke Short, Senator Lindsey Graham, and Senator Strom Thurmond, January 2003. (This is also the last photo that was ever taken of Duke and Strom Thurmond together).

DENISE SHORT

It was thrilling. His voice was strong; it was loud. He made it through the entire speech. That was the last time he spoke at length on the Senate Floor.

– Scott Frick –

Senator Thurmond's Last Speeches on the Senate Floor

WEDNESDAY, OCTOBER 9, 2002
TUESDAY, NOVEMBER 19, 2002

Human Events Weekly News reported on October 14, 2002: "In what was probably his last speech on the Senate Floor, Republican Senator Strom Thurmond of South Carolina last Wednesday brought an end to his storied 48-year Senate career by calling Senate Judiciary Committee Chairman Patrick Leahy a liar. Thurmond's ire was sparked by Leahy's broken promise to send the appeals court nomination of Federal District Judge Dennis Shedd to the full Senate for confirmation. 'I was hurt and disappointed by this egregious act of destructive politics,' said Thurmond. 'Chairman Leahy assured me on numerous occasions that Judge Shedd would be given a vote. I took him at his word.'"

*U*nlike countless other erroneous and slanted stories that had been published about Senator Thurmond during his lifetime, this is one time the press got the story exactly right. They were dead on accurate. I wish I could say that the Senator's last speech on the Floor of the U.S. Senate was under happier circumstances, but it was not. When he pulled the consideration of Judge Shedd from the agenda of the Judiciary Committee that week, virtually killing the nomination with a procedural trick, Senator Leahy broke a promise he'd made to Senator Thurmond and to other members on that Committee. Senator Thurmond had no choice then but to go to the Floor and call Leahy to task for his actions.

If there's one thing I learned from three decades on Capitol Hill it is this: in the United States

Senate, a member is only as good as his or her word. Strom Thurmond himself enjoyed a formidable and well-deserved reputation among his colleagues as a man of great reliability. If he said he was going to do something, you could absolutely count on it. If he said he supported you, he was in your corner to stay. As the Senate's longest-serving, most senior member and its standard-bearer for integrity, Strom Thurmond bore the responsibility to remind his younger colleagues that their good word was a critical and necessary component in the health of our democracy. It was to underscore this message that he came to the Senate Floor to make his last major address, just a few weeks shy of his 100th birthday.

President Bush first nominated Judge Shedd to the appeals court bench in May of 2001. But thanks to the political maneuvers of some Democratic leaders, they managed to put off a Committee vote for well over a year, thus refusing to allow his name to go to the full Senate for consideration. What was particularly disappointing to Senator Thurmond and me was that these very leaders knew Dennis Shedd personally and had for many years.

Dennis went to work for Senator Thurmond right out of law school in 1978. He came highly recommended and possessed a sterling academic record. Over the course of the next decade he held various positions, including Chief Counsel and Staff Director for the Judiciary Committee. He also worked as Senator Thurmond's Administrative Assistant. After he left Washington, he served for eleven years as a U.S. District Court Judge in South Carolina. Dennis Shedd is a fine judge and a good man. The American Bar Association gave him its top rating. I know for a fact that Senator Thurmond thought very highly of Dennis and believed he was more than qualified for the position on the appeals court. That he was unfairly attacked by some who had known him, worked with him, and depended on him for many years was terribly disheartening.

Senator Thurmond was not the only one who felt slighted by the political machinations that kept Dennis from getting an up or down vote in the Senate. I recall that Senator Orrin Hatch was extremely upset by it as well. "This is all politics," Hatch told a reporter, "and it's rotten politics at that." Senator Fritz Hollings, a Democrat from South Carolina, had known Dennis Shedd for many years. He knew what Senator Thurmond knew: Dennis Shedd was a fine man and an excellent candidate for the Fourth Circuit Court of Appeals. Senator Hollings was a powerful force in moving Shedd's nomination forward. Without his unwavering support, Judge Shedd may never have been confirmed. Hollings, admired by so many in South Carolina, in true statesman-like fashion, cast politics aside and supported Shedd.

After a year and a half of politically motivated delays, Judge Shedd's nomination was finally scheduled to get a vote by the Committee on October 8. We were all assured by Chairman Leahy that the vote would indeed take place. In fact, Senator Leahy had told me to my face on the Floor of the Senate, "Duke, we're going to have that vote. Dennis is going to be passed out of committee. If the nays are louder than the yeas, don't worry. He's going to be voted out." But the night before the meeting, I learned from Senator Leahy's Chief Counsel that Shedd's name had been pulled from the agenda. Leahy later said that the only reason he delayed the October vote was that he knew it would spark debate and delay seventeen other nominations. Not many really believe that Leahy was very concerned about Republican nominees becoming federal judges.

Senator Thurmond spoke out at the meeting the next morning. And a few hours later he rose to his feet on the Senate Floor. I must admit being pretty nervous about that speech. I didn't know if he could do it or not. What concerned me most was the Senator's energy level. He had been very tired that day and his hip had really been bothering him. I was worried fatigue might prevent him from making a sustained, powerful statement that the event demanded. But as usual, Strom Thurmond rose to the occasion.

He did a fantastic job. It was a great moment. We were all very proud of him. Despite his age, despite the challenges to his health, Strom Thurmond had stood his ground with great stamina and an inspiring presence. In his next-to-last address to the United States Senate, he dutifully reminded everyone present and all those who would come after him that a successful democracy depends on the integrity of its leaders. It was just one of many historic moments where I was so fortunate to have been present.

I was sitting beside the Senator during his statement. When he sat down, he turned to me and asked, "Was that okay?" I told him, "Senator, that was great." He gave me a quick smile and a nod. I will never forget the look on his face. He was energized. He was happy. I could see in his eyes the fiery spirit of that once great orator. He was ready for more. I know that if he had to, he could have kept going.

Senator Thurmond's speech galvanized the issue of judicial nominations for Republicans. Following the speech, President Bush called Senator Thurmond and other senators to the White House to discuss judicial nominations, and for the next month leading to the 2002 elections, judicial nominations became a central issue in campaigns around the country. Senator Thurmond's last major speech thus found a nationwide audience and helped frame an important campaign issue.

Judge Dennis Shedd was later confirmed by the full Senate on November 19, 2002. Prior to that final vote, the Senator made a brief and his last statement on the floor of the U.S. Senate:

> Mr. President, I rise today to express my strong support for the nomination of Judge Dennis W. Shedd to the Fourth Circuit Court of Appeals. Judge Shedd is a man of great character who will make an outstanding addition to the federal appellate bench. He possesses the highest sense of integrity, a thorough knowledge of the law, and a good judicial temperament. I want to assure my colleagues that Judge Shedd is committed to upholding the rights of all people under the Constitution. This fine man is truly deserving of such a high honor, and he will serve the people of the Fourth Circuit with distinction.

After the Senator finished this statement, the entire Senate, members and staff, stood and gave him a lengthy ovation. The next day, the *Charlotte Observer* reported:

> When he finished, all the senators, clerks and staffers stood in long applause for Thurmond's final Senate action. From the other side, Sen. Patrick Leahy, the Vermont Democrat who fought against Shedd and will give up the chairmanship of the Judiciary Committee when Republicans take control of the

Senate, looked at the press gallery with a sneer and clapped with just his finger-tips. … Sen. John Edwards, D-N.C., was the only Carolina legislator to vote against him.

Judge Shedd has proven that Senator Thurmond knew what he was doing; he was right to insist on confirmation for Shedd. He is now one of the finest judges on the United States Court of Appeals, and our nation is lucky to have him there.

DEE SHORT

I vividly remember the evening of November 19, 2002. I was in the office with Duke when Senator Thurmond called to invite us over to the Senators' Private Dining Room. Duke was too busy to go, so he asked me to take some of the staff and join the Senator for dinner. Walker Clarkson and Emily Dorrah accompanied me. When we arrived, Senator and Mrs. Helms were sitting with Senator Thurmond and some other Thurmond staffers. Senator Helms regaled us with wonderful stories of his long-time friendship with Senator Thurmond. He also made it clear that he had returned to the Senate to support his old friend and make sure Judge Shedd would be confirmed to the Fourth Circuit Court of Appeals. What an historic moment it was, having dinner for the last time in the private dining room with these two icons.

After dinner, we hurried to the Senate Gallery to witness yet another historic event: Senator Thurmond and Senator Helms casting the final votes of their Senate careers. After the Senate voted to form the Department of Homeland Security, Senator Thurmond stood and offered Judge Shedd's nomination for a vote. The Senator gave a sincere statement as to why Judge Shedd should be confirmed, after which the entire Senate vigorously applauded. I was moved to tears.

Senator Thurmond really rose to the occasion. He had the fire in him that was reminiscent of so many of his great battles as he stood up for his beliefs. Some of the things he was most passionate about were judges and the laws of the land.

When the roll call was taken and Senator Thurmond's name was called, he all but shouted, "AYE." Duke was sitting by his side, and I watched as he broke into a big smile. Judge Shedd was confirmed by a 55-44 vote.

Shortly thereafter, Senator Jeff Sessions, in a gesture of kindness I will always remember, came up to the gallery; he gave me a big hug and said that he wanted to personally thank Duke and me for our devotion and service to Senator Thurmond. I knew that Duke had always admired and respected him. When I told Duke what had happened, he was pleased and said that Jeff Sessions is not only a fine Senator, but also a gentleman in the likes of Strom Thurmond. He is someone to be admired.

SCOTT FRICK

Senator Leahy promised Senator Thurmond that he would place Judge Shedd's nomination on the agenda for the Judiciary Committee to report the nomination out to the floor so that the full Senate could consider the nomination. Senator Leahy had promised Senator Thurmond that he was going to do this on a particular date. At the last second he went back on his word and pulled Judge Shedd's nomination off the agenda. So Senator Thurmond made a speech at the Judiciary Committee meeting, and he also made a speech on the Senate Floor.

We had to be careful about those speeches. They had to be short. You couldn't get them very long because simply standing and talking on the floor would take a lot out of him. We drafted a speech for him to give on the Senate Floor about Judge Shedd's nomination. It was rather long. We used a very large font, and it came out to two pages. I was scared to death that he wasn't going to make it through that speech, that he would simply get tired.

Duke kind of gave the Senator a little pep talk before the speech. Just before we walked through the doors onto the Senate Floor, Duke said, "Senator, your voice has got to be loud. It's got to be loud and it's got to be strong." It was tough to sit through the speech, because we were just hoping he had enough strength to get through it. But he did. It was thrilling. His voice was strong; it was loud. He made it through the entire speech. That was the last time he spoke at length on the Senate Floor.

The Senator celebrates his 100th birthday with friends:
Duke Short, Myrna Whitner, Dee Short, Preacher Whitner
at the South Carolina State Society.

DENISE SHORT

How many people celebrate their birthdays at the White House, let alone have two
Presidents in attendance to wish them a happy birthday?

- R.J. Duke Short –

The Happy Birthday Heard 'Round the World

THURSDAY, DECEMBER 5, 2002

Strom Thurmond turned 100 on Thursday, December 5, 2002. His estranged wife Nancy and some others organized a birthday celebration for him. It was held in a large room in the Dirksen Senate Office Building. The event did not have the black tie pomp like his 90th birthday party which was a magnificent Washington affair, but it certainly proved to be memorable nonetheless.

The Senator's staff was in no way included in the organization of this event. However, I was very concerned when I learned that C-SPAN had been invited to cover it. I didn't think it was appropriate to have the birthday broadcast on television. It was not a show. It should have been a private gathering for family and friends. I strongly encouraged one of those involved with the planning of the event to cancel the television coverage. They insisted. In any regards, it was a regrettable decision.

I want to be perfectly clear on this point. When Senator Lott made the comments he did regarding Senator Thurmond, he was doing nothing more than trying to make an old man feel good. That was all. Nothing else. To assume that he was making some grand political statement — like some reporters made it out to be — is not only woefully ignorant; it is mean-spirited. Trent Lott adored Strom Thurmond. He was trying to say something nice on the man's birthday. He was congratulating him on a life well lived. And that is precisely how it was received at the time by all of us in attendance. There were no gasps from the audience, as some in the press have written. That is simply not true. We all enjoyed the comments by Senator Lott and Senator Dole. It was a wonderful, warm occasion, and members of the press should be ashamed for having so aggressively and unnecessarily sullied it.

Senator Thurmond was especially disappointed in the reaction of the political operatives at the White House to the attacks on Trent Lott. Unfortunately the Administration not only opted not to defend him; they essentially threw Senator Lott to the wolves. Senator Thurmond and I were both saddened by that demonstration of timidity. In my opinion, Senator Lott should regain his position of leadership. He is a very decent and honorable man who loves this country and wants the best for all Americans. He was an excellent leader, and the United States Senate would be fortunate to have him back at the helm.

The lack of support by the Administration for Lott, however, in no way detracted from the respect and admiration that the Senator felt personally for President George W. Bush, Former President George H.W. Bush, and the entire Bush family.

President Bush most graciously hosted a private birthday celebration at the White House for the Senator on December 6, 2002, the day after he turned 100. The President, a few days earlier while in the Oval Office and during a meeting with a number of Senators and members of the Administration, turned to Senator Thurmond and said, "I understand you have a special day coming up." The Senator replied, "I will be 100-years old on December fifth." The President then turned to Andy Card, his Chief of Staff, and asked what he had on the calendar that day. Andy replied that he was fully booked and could not break the engagements. The President told Andy to find the best day. President Bush then turned to me and said, "Duke, I am serious; I want to have something special at the White House for the Senator, so you and Andy work out the details." I thanked the President and did just that.

Once the day was set, the entire Thurmond staff was invited, along with a number of dignitaries, including members of the Senate and House as well as members of the Cabinet. The Senator was very pleased when Former President George H.W. Bush walked into the Red Room and expressed his warmest greetings.

Senator Thurmond was most honored by this special event and later told me that he considered it one of the highlights of his career. I told the Senator that I understood and said, "After all, how many people celebrate their birthdays at the White House, let alone have two Presidents in attendance to wish them a happy birthday?" He just smiled.

BOB DOLE

I spoke at his 100th birthday party. And Senator Lott spoke. Senator Lott got crucified for nothing. We were all just having fun, carrying on. Senator Thurmond was laughing and smiling.

RUTH BADER GINSBURG

We all went over to the Dirksen Senate Office Building on that disastrous day of his birthday celebration. By we, I mean Justices O'Connor, Kennedy, Souter, Breyer, and me. The official part of the program was long delayed. We all had Court work to do, so we left just as Trent Lott arrived to deliver his ill-fated remarks. We'd been waiting and waiting. At the Court, when things are supposed to start at a certain time, they start. It's a little different in the First Branch. David Souter and I were sitting behind the place from which Trent Lott would be speaking. We were very glad to have exited before his remarks.

DENNIS W. SHEDD

I thought that his birthday celebration was overdone. I thought the better way to do it was to have a little meet and greet with the press, if he was up for it, then go into a private celebration. I don't know him well enough to defend him, but I think Trent Lott just got carried away. Everybody was celebrating, and everybody was saying good things about Senator Thurmond. But then people, politicians especially, try to one-up one another. That's just not the way his birthday should have been handled. It should have been done privately.

I think what it did was revisit on Senator Thurmond some of those issues that would be better left unvisited on him. When he stood up and made his final speech on the floor for me, I thought it was good for Senator Thurmond because he was going out the way he came in, fighting for what he thought was fair. He was weak, but he made the speech. I thought that was a great way for him to end his career. But it was completely overshadowed by all this that happened later.

CLARENCE THOMAS

It's sad the way his last hurrah was affected by the Trent Lott controversy. I told my wife, sometimes you let people rest in peace, you know what I mean? It was a shame. It's unfortunate that things turned out like that in the end. What should have been a eulogy turned into a controversy.

CHRIS KELLEY CIMKO

I have been very distressed over the Trent Lott incident. Our hearts were broken when that became such a tempest in a teapot. Quite frankly, when we heard Senator Lott say it we really didn't think anything of it. We just saw it as what it was, honoring a man who had given a great deal of himself for this nation, in a lot of different ways, most of them good. We were very disheartened by all the news coverage. It made us ill to think that Senator Thurmond's legacy would be marred by that last incident. It opened up a very old wound.

PHIL JONES

The whole Trent Lott thing was more tragic for Strom than it was for Trent Lott. I say that because those remarks, at the end of his career, left the impression that he was still the old redneck racist that he'd been. And that was unfair because he in fact had changed. He should have been commended and remembered for the turn around. But instead he was tarnished by Lott. His memory was really a casualty. His reputation was a casualty of Trent Lott's gaffe.

Trent Lott's young enough and should have known better, and I suppose can still recover from it. But it was too late for Strom to recover. A whole new generation has that impression of him now. And because he was never out seeking headlines, there weren't that many stories along the years praising him for his contributions to Civil Rights. So there he goes. And that incident is following him. And that's too bad.

TRENT LOTT

It was a very unfortunate set of circumstances. I had nothing but good intentions. The media made the worst of it. When I talked about what a great President he would have made, I talked about his sense of fiscal responsibility, his commitment to Country, his war against crime, his support for a strong national defense, his integrity. That's the way I view Strom Thurmond. That's what I meant. If you are a conservative Republican from the South, the media is out to get you. For thirty years they have not been able to nail me. They used this occasion, very much out of proportion, to undermine my efforts. But because I'm from the South and proud of it, I know that you have to be prepared to get knocked off your horse and get back up and ride again. That's what Senator Thurmond would do, and that's what I'm doing.

"That's All!"

FAREWELL TO THE SENATE
NOVEMBER 22, 2002

S enator Thurmond was given the honor of gaveling to a close the 107th Congress. Floor privileges were given to the entire Thurmond staff for that historic event. I think we were all thrilled and honored to be a part of the end of this magnificent era.

BILL TUTEN

I will always remember the moment Senator Thurmond adjourned the Senate for the end of the 107th Congress. He hit the gavel, there was some applause, and then he said, "That's all!" The entire staff was down on the Senate Floor to witness the event. Everybody was getting upset. It was a very emotional moment for a lot of people. He came down into the well of the Senate, and everybody was coming up to shake his hand or give him a hug.

JAMES D. GALYEAN

The last day of the session the Senator took the Chair and gaveled the 107th Congress to a close. We all stood there and applauded, not really believing that it was all over. He waved his hands in the air and said, "That's all!" It was a very historic moment.

There were Senators who had come down to the Floor just to stand there and watch it happen — his last moment in the Senate.

DEE SHORT

It meant so much to be on the Senate floor with Senator Thurmond's staff and witness such an historic event. It was so moving, watching the Senator gavel out the Senate for the very last time. I don't think there was a dry eye in the crowd. After gaveling out, in true Strom Thurmond fashion and without missing a beat, the Senator walked down into the well where we were all standing and asked the ladies in attendance, "Would any of you ladies care to dance?" We all erupted into laughter.

Senator Thurmond bids Senate colleagues farewell.

Home to Edgefield

Throughout December of 2002 all of us on the staff worked overtime to get the office packed up and ready to close. My beautiful wife Dee, bless her heart, was there with us, working late into the night and on the weekends packing and taping the boxes. None of us had any idea that the Senator hung onto as much stuff as he did. Just when we thought we had it all under control, someone would casually open a closet door only to find it filled to the ceiling with files, books, and papers of all kinds — all of which had to be gone through item by item and recorded before it left the office.

Alan Burns, Thurmond Archivist at Clemson University, made numerous trips between South Carolina and Washington as he transported decades of Thurmond memorabilia and papers to the archives at Clemson. Alan was a dependable and inexhaustible member of our team during those last few weeks, and we couldn't have done it without him.

The Senator rested in his office during most of this time. I encouraged him to stay at home, put his feet up, and take it easy. But he insisted on being at work in case he was needed. In my heart, I knew he preferred to be at the office because he got lonely at home in his apartment at Walter Reed. He occasionally looked at all the boxes stacked high in his office with raised eyebrows and a puzzled smile — as amazed as any of us that there was so much stuff that needed to be packed up.

On December 15, James Graham, his wife Vanjewell, Dee and I took the Senator down to Elsie's Skillet in Alexandria for what turned out to be our final Sunday brunch together. Henry Sacks and Preacher and Myrna Whitner met us there. That was a sad day. We reminisced with

Dee Short and Strom Thurmond in his apartment at Walter Reed.

Elsie about the ten-plus years of Sundays we had all enjoyed together.

We knew of Mrs. Thurmond's plans to remove the Senator from Washington and take him back to Edgefield. Neither Dee nor I agreed with those plans. We would have loved to have seen the Senator remain in Washington. The attention he would have received at Walter Reed was far superior to anything he had access to in Edgefield. But the family naturally wanted him to return to South Carolina, and I can understand their feelings.

The following Sunday, December 22, Dee and I visited the Senator in his room at Walter Reed. We had thought we might try going down to Elsie's again that day, but he was too tired to get out of his bed. I remember Dee rubbed his head, and we talked about his upcoming trip home to Edgefield.

At one point Dee asked him, "Would you be happier staying here with us, Senator?" He said weakly, "Dee, I'd be happier here with you, but you understand the circumstances." Dee started to cry. She said, "Well, if you get down there and you're not happy, who you gonna call?" The Senator looked at Dee and smiled. "You." His eyes glistened.

On December 23 we were still busy packing the office, rushing to get everything ready for our official closing on January 3. My two sons, Bo and Coy, paid a final visit to my office that day. We all went in and sat with the Senator for awhile. Both of my boys had known the Senator since they were small children, especially Coy, who remembers sitting on Senator Thurmond's lap when he played Santa Claus at an office Christmas Party in the mid '70s. In some ways, they were saying goodbye to a man who had been like a grandfather in their lives. And it was very much like I was saying goodbye to my dad.

Watching the Senator over the course of that last year was like watching a once mighty engine run out of steam. Every month he grew more tired, weaker, and quieter. By December of 2002 he often spoke only in a whisper. He frequently pulled me aside while we packed the office to ask, "Duke, what can I do for you? Tell me, how can I help you?"

I told him he had already helped me. I told him I was going to write a book about him one day. He cleared his throat and said, "You just be sure and say that I worked hard, and that I tried to help the people, all the people." I promised him that I would.

We closed the office on January 3, 2003. The Senator left for Edgefield a couple of weeks later. I spoke to him a few times on the telephone. But Dee and I never saw him again.

DEE SHORT

I must have cried a million tears in those final months before closing the office. For the last fifteen years the Senator's office had been a huge part of my life. Being the wife of Strom Thurmond's right-hand man, "the 101st Senator" as Duke was affectionately referred to by some of the Senators, meant that I also was part of the Senator's office family. Not being good with good-byes, this one was really taking its toll on me, as it did with Duke. Duke is the most loyal, dedicated, and devoted man I have ever known. The Senator relied on him most heavily and told me on many occasions that he trusted Duke more than he had anyone else. Senator Thurmond knew Duke looked out for his best interests and would never do anything to jeopardize him in any way.

We spent the better part of that last year in the office packing boxes of the Senator's memorabilia to be taken to Clemson. The Senator's staff worked diligently to help get the office packed up. Those kids are awesome. In many ways they were like my kids. Duke and I think so highly of them.

Packing up the office was like saying goodbye to Holly again. It was so hard to pack up her desk and personal belongings. Nobody knew that office better than Holly Richardson. She knew what was in every box, in every closet, and in all the files in every file cabinet. She was so much a part of Senator Thurmond's life — of all our lives. The Senator loved and missed her dearly.

I'll never forget the last time we saw Senator Thurmond. It was January 7, 2003 at the Capitol for the swearing in of the Senators. Senator Thurmond wanted to be there with Lindsey Graham, who was taking his Senate seat. I was having difficulty fighting back the tears, and to be quite honest, Duke was too.

After the swearing-in ceremony Duke took the Senator back to the Senate Floor for one last look. I will never forget that moment, looking across the Senate floor and watching Duke wheel the Senator in his wheelchair for the final goodbye. That would be their last time together on the Senate Floor.

On their way out I bent down to give the Senator a big hug and kiss. I told him how much I loved and appreciated him. It was so hard to say goodbye, and deep down in my heart I knew that this would be the last time we would see him. I cried all the way home.

MARK IVANY

During his last few months in office, the Senator's sister Mary Tompkins sent up a Baptist prayer book, a daily reflection book. I didn't know if he ever really had time to read it. So one day I said, "Senator would you like to read today's passage?" Then usually every day of the week we would sit down, either at his desk or on the couch, and I would read the passage from the Bible and then the commentary that followed. He would sit back and visualize it, think about it, and sometimes we'd talk about it. Sometimes he'd say, "That was a good one." He even might tell a quick story about how that applied to life. I'll always remember that time we had together. I'm actually a pretty religious person myself. I'm going to be a Catholic priest. I kind of think that I was put in Senator Thurmond's office for a reason.

ELIZABETH DOLE

I will always remember that Strom came by my office before he left Washington the last time, to say good-bye and wish me the best. That meant a lot to me, and I'll never forget that special time together. He was always so considerate, caring, and supportive of Bob and me. That was just the kind of man he was.

JAMES A. BAKER III

Once we won in Florida in 2000, we had a reception in D.C. before the Inaugural, and Strom was there. At that time, he was probably 98 or so. I never will forget that he showed up. We'd been out of power for eight years, but he hadn't lost his touch one bit. He remembered everybody's first names. He was quite sharp right up till the very end.

MATTHEW J. MARTIN

I remember towards the end, when we started going through all of the Senator's things and packing them up, we found his Army cap from World War II. The Senator was wearing it around the office; he was quite proud of it. At one point, Duke tried it on. The Senator laughed and said, "I think it looks better on me."

The saddest day was of course January 3. That was the last day we were there. It was Duke, Dee, Eliza Edgar, myself, and the Senator. We literally held the door open for him on the way out. His daughter Julie was there when we left, and he reached up from his wheelchair and took her hand as they went down the hall.

DAVID G. MCLEOD

Senator Thurmond received such good care at Walter Reed. It really is a fantastic place. They were honored to have him. From the doctors to the support staff, everyone there did a fantastic job with him. When it did come time for him to leave Walter Reed and go home to Edgefield, I recall that one of the cooks commented to me, "Doctor McLeod, if they take him out of here, he's not going to last a year." She was right. He passed away less than six months later.

ELIZABETH MCFARLAND

When the Senator retired to Edgefield, I assisted him with a lot of his correspondence. He continued to get letters and cards from around the world, and from all 50 states. I recall one Christmas card in particular. It was from an Army officer who said he had been at Walter Reed with his wife recently for a medical appointment. They had gotten some very bad news that day, and his wife was sitting in the hallway crying. The Senator had come walking down the hallway, noticed the man's wife crying, and had stopped and sat with her and consoled her. The officer just wrote to thank the Senator and let him know how much that had meant to them both. That was right before Senator Thurmond turned 100.

One time I went up to visit the Senator at the Edgefield hospital where he lived. When I walked in the room, he looked up at me and smiled and winked. It was the greatest wink. There he was, over 100-years old, and he's still got that charming little wink.

HENRY SACKS

The last time I saw him was at his office. Duke and I were sitting there talking with him. Then Duke got called away to the phone. So he and I talked for a bit. Then he said, "Henry, I think I'm gonna take a little nap." And he laid down on that couch. He went right to sleep. I couldn't resist. I took a picture of him sleeping there, just like a baby.

I hated that they moved him back to South Carolina. Duke and Denise were so upset about it. I know Denise cried for two weeks. It tore her heart right out of her. I told him before he went to sleep on the couch that day, that was the last time I saw him, I said, "Senator, I want to write to you. Don't you dare think about returning my letters. I just want to write to you." And I wrote him three times while he was down there in Edgefield before he died. The first two letters he answered, but when the last one arrived he had already passed. I was extremely honored to be his friend, a little ol' nothing like me. He was a great American.

DENNIS W. SHEDD

I was really more moved by his death than I thought I was going to be. We didn't just lose a Senator; we lost a close personal friend. He told me one time he never had a better friend than me, but that was a shock to me. He was my employer. Until then I had never really thought of him in terms of a friend. He was 50 years older, and he was my boss.

I went over to visit him a couple of times in Edgefield. When I saw him, I just thanked him for everything he had done for me and my family and for all the good he had done for South Carolina and the nation. I let him know how much we all appreciated everything he had done. I'm so glad I had that last chance to thank him before he died.

C. BRUCE LITTLEJOHN

I went to visit him in Edgefield about a month before he died. He was in a little apartment they had arranged for him in the hospital there. He was very frail physically but mentally alert. We reminisced about things that happened when he was Governor, about things that happened when we were in the Legislature together a long time ago. His mind was perfectly good. I will always treasure those last moments we had together.

JESSE HELMS

I hope he passed in his sleep. I'd hate to think that he suffered. Bless his heart. I have so many fond memories of him. I'm so thankful he was my friend.

James Strom Thurmond died in his sleep at 9:45 p.m. on Thursday, June 26, 2003. He was 100 years old.

Strom Thurmond
U. S. Senate – S.C.

When he saw the entourage coming, he had parked on the side of the road, gotten out of his
truck, and stood there in the rain with his cap over his heart. In his other hand he held a
sign which said: "Goodbye Senator Thurmond. Thank You."

– James B. Edwards –

Final Respects

THE FUNERAL OF JAMES STROM THURMOND
JULY 1, 2003 IN COLUMBIA, SOUTH CAROLINA

After a century of energetic work for constituents and the nation, Senator Strom Thurmond was laid to rest in his native Edgefield, South Carolina, on July 1, 2003. His funeral was held in Columbia, and the people of South Carolina came out along virtually every road between Columbia and Edgefield to watch the funeral procession pass. They stood in a drenching rain to pay their respects to the Senator who had done so much on their behalf, many of them with signs reading — simply but aptly — "Thank You."

STAN SPEARS

As I understand it, the Senator had left word in his burial instructions that I was to present the American flag to his wife and family. I can't express what a great honor that was for me. I will never forget that. It was a magnificent honor, and I was so proud to have that role on that important day.

MARK GOODIN

I think Strom Thurmond would have been appalled that at his funeral the Vice President of the United States and the Secretary of Defense were forced to stand while the State Legislature left. It was just a measure of disrespect. So many people saw Thurmond as this aging Confederate that was still fighting the Civil War, which was absolutely untrue. I think Thurmond was a Union man in his heart. He understood the causes of the South and cherished many of the sacrifices that were made for States' Rights. But he also supremely understood the need for the United States of America. He wasn't a Confederate; he was a Unionist.

Strom Thurmond understood the mission of the United States of America, and the mission of a federated government. You don't go on active duty after you're over the age limit and you're exempt from military service because you're a Circuit Judge, and then volunteer for D-Day service because you somehow believe that the South will rise again. You do that out of a supreme sense of patriotism and love of country that superseded everything. So people who want to paint a Confederate flag on Strom Thurmond's back or make these kind of stupid gestures like that at his funeral, I think he would have been appalled by that. He was an unapologetic Unionist.

BILL TUTEN

Senator Thurmond loved to drive fast; everybody knows that. At the funeral, Jason Rossbach rode down with me from Columbia to Edgefield. A buddy of mine, who was up ahead of us down the road, called on the phone and said, "Listen, I just got up to the funeral procession. I'm going 80 miles an hour and they're pulling away from me!" I said, "Well, good!" At least he did get that last fast ride in the car.

JAMES B. EDWARDS

I fully believe that there has never been a politician in the state of South Carolina that has built up the reservoir of support and love of his constituents like Senator Strom Thurmond. I doubt there will ever be another one like him in South Carolina. My wife Ann and I drove over to Columbia for the funeral. It was pouring down rain when we left town, but the streets were lined with people — all races, all walks of life — showing their support for Senator Thurmond. They were standing on every overpass between Columbia and Edgefield. Some people were holding signs that read: Goodbye Strom, Thank you Strom, Hail to Strom, Thank God for Strom.

I remember so vividly one person we saw. He was standing right there on the out-skirts of Columbia. He was a young black man standing next to an old beat-up pickup truck. When he saw the entourage coming, he had parked on the side of the road, gotten out of his truck, and stood there in the rain with his cap over his heart. In his other hand he held a sign which said: "Goodbye Senator Thurmond. Thank You."

The Life and Legacy of J. Strom Thurmond

1902-2003

Assessing the legacy of Strom Thurmond will doubtless busy historians for many years to come. On one level his principles were clearly defined, but on another level he was a complex figure.

People who knew him well often remember different key features about him and imagine his legacy somewhat differently. Some remember him primarily as an American patriot, others as a politician who served South Carolina first and foremost. Some recall his courage, intelligence, and conviction; others his courtesy, gentleness, and affection.

All of these people are right in their memories of Senator Thurmond and in their estimation of his legacy. He was all of this, and more.

ELIZABETH DOLE

My mother passed away on January 14, 2004, just four months short of her 103rd birthday. She was alert right to the end, just as Strom was. For many years young people had flocked to her den for long visits, and she always gave them understanding and wise counsel. She and Strom both reached out to people, expressing a keen interest in others. They always took time to really listen to people. Strom, like Mother, was so thoughtful and kind, never missing births, weddings, and birthdays. His constituent service was the best, and one I'm striving to emulate.

Kathryn Hook, President George Bush, Senator Thurmond, Duke Short, and Holly Richardson on the occasion of the Senator's receiving the Presidential Medal of Freedom, 1992.

GEORGE H.W. BUSH

was President of the United States, 1989-1993.

My memories of that great man Strom Thurmond are less specific, more general. Anecdotes I am short on. Memories I am long on. I remember Strom's fantastic support when I was President. I remember his extraordinary courtesy to me, to Barbara, indeed to all in our family. I remember attending events in South Carolina — events benefiting a race he might be in, or benefiting the Republican National Committee, or helping some other candidate. I also remember Duke, Strom's most loyal friend, a man for whom I have not only warm good feelings in my heart, but respect as well.

I loved watching Strom as we stood in receiving lines together. He had a flattering or encouraging word for all who went through the line: "This little lady is the best volunteer in South Carolina," or, "This pretty young girl just won great honors in her school." Even when he was along in years, Strom stood patiently so as to make every person in attendance feel glad he or she came to the event.

LINDSEY GRAHAM

Senator Thurmond lived a rich life. He lived at times a controversial life. But the biggest testament I can give to Senator Thurmond is that he changed. He changed with the times. He won his last election by getting more African-American votes than any Republican in the South. His legacy in my state, across party lines, across racial lines, and across regional lines was that he was the go-to guy. Whether you owned the company or you were the janitor; whether you were black, white, rich or poor, his office and he as a person had a reputation of going to bat for individuals. To me, that is his greatest legacy. This man, your friend, my friend, South Carolina's favorite son, is gone. But he will never be forgotten. We thank God that He provided us with a great public servant.

TRENT LOTT

Senator Thurmond will be remembered for many years to come for his work ethic, his courtesies, and his conduct as a Senator serving the people of the United States. Historians will write of him often, and future leaders will strive to emulate his example.

ORRIN HATCH

This is a poem I wrote about Senator Thurmond:

A man of inestimable charm
And physical strength with cleverness instilled
Through long years of battling for the truth as he sees it,
And also, much native intellect,
Refined through the tumultuous years,
During which he has served the people as he saw fit,
Which fact is doubted by none who know this great man.

JOHN WARNER

I remember so well when I was Secretary of the Navy and I would come up before the Armed Services Committee at various times, of course, in connection with budget requests; but at other times I was called on the carpet pretty thoroughly by Senator Thurmond during the war in Vietnam. I served five years and four months as the Navy Secretary. He used to question me. As the hearing ended, he would pull me over and say:

"Why don't you think about coming to the Senate someday?" I owe Senator Thurmond a debt of gratitude for instilling in me the thoughts that eventually led to my election to the Senate.

Senator Thurmond has touched every life with whom he has served in this Chamber these many years. He has touched mine very deeply. He was sort of like the older brother I never had. There is not a Senator here who, from time to time, does not quietly go and talk to the elder statesmen in the Senate about problems they have. I have certainly shared many conversations with Senator Thurmond. How well I always remember Strom Thurmond and what he has done for America and what he did for this humble Senator.

GEORGE ALLEN

My best memory of Senator Thurmond will always be his smiling, sparkling eyes which were a window to his happy heart and his love of life.

JAMES B. EDWARDS

Strom Thurmond was one of the greatest Americans I've ever known. He's already terribly missed. Unfortunately for us, we'll probably never have another one like him.

ROBERT MCNAIR

Strom was always campaigning. He was very warm and friendly. He would stop a parade, actually get out of the car, and go speak to people. Everybody recognized that was the way he was. He was a true friend. And that friendship extended beyond party lines. I believe the strength of his legacy will center around his constituent service, representing his people well, and serving his country. He always had the people of South Carolina first in his mind. We will not forget that.

DAVID WILKINS

I'm like every South Carolinian; I have great admiration for Senator Thurmond, and always had. But the more I got to work with him and know him personally, the greater the admiration became. He'll always be in my mind, and probably everybody else's too, the greatest statesman this state has or will ever produce. I don't think that will ever change.

JUDITH RICHARDS HOPE

Senator Thurmond was very respectful of the Judiciary and the legal system in our country, as he was for those who served in the military. My father-in-law was Bob Hope, and Senator Thurmond always expressed tremendous gratitude for all the things that Bob Hope had done for our servicemen and women over the years. I saw Senator Thurmond as a true American who was dedicated to the principles of justice, law and service.

DONALD BALDWIN

I never met anybody in Washington who was more honest, direct, and effective. I don't think anybody would ever tell you different. He was determined in what he did, and he had terrific integrity. He was a great American.

KAREN J. WILLIAMS

I don't know that we'll ever have anyone in Congress again that can forge so many strong friendships like Senator Thurmond. He made it possible to do so much for the state of South Carolina. The friendship between him and Senator Biden is indicative of what a great man Senator Thurmond was. I don't think anyone else will be able to mirror that degree of constituent service he offered, though I am sure people will try. He set the bar very high. He was such a fine, nice, genuine man.

R.C. PREACHER WHITNER

I believe Strom Thurmond will be remembered for the honorable approach he took to his office. He held every office he occupied with the highest esteem and integrity. That's just the way he was. I don't think he would have ever considered compromising that. He was true from the heart. It's been a real enjoyment for me to know Duke Short and Senator J. Strom Thurmond. It's been a real positive point of my life. I can't thank the Senator enough for all the little things that he did for us. I like to reflect about the Senator now that he's gone and looking down on all of us. He was a great American. He surely set an example that others can follow.

JOHN A. GASTRIGHT, JR.

When it comes to remembering Strom Thurmond, a lot of people are always going to think about Civil Rights. You don't have to look any farther than the *Washington Post* to figure that out. No matter what article was written about him, they always go back to 1948. But the people of South Carolina have a better feel for what Strom Thurmond was all about. It will be hard for South Carolinians to get over the hangover of losing Strom Thurmond as their Senator. When he was there, it was like you had somebody in Washington, D.C. who considered you family, and was going to do whatever he could on your behalf. His number-one focus at all times was to take care of the people of South Carolina. When Strom Thurmond was there, you knew you had somebody in Washington who sincerely cared about you.

PHIL JONES

I'm happy that he got to do what he really wanted to do, be in the Senate when he was 100-years old. I'm sure that is an achievement that will never happen again in this country; it can't, with politics as brutal and expensive as they have become. I just don't see anybody ever lasting that long again.

I should add though, it's sad that he did not get out earlier because he had achieved so much. For him to hang around and look so feeble at the end, I think he ended up diluting his impact by not having a sense of timing. That's unfortunate. He understood everything about politics. He really had that mastered, but he had no comprehension that there was life after the Senate. And that's tragic, because I've seen too many of these people go out and make great contributions after their time in the Senate; people like Howard Baker, Warren Rudman, or Sam Nunn.

Now, that's me looking at him and thinking how tragic, how unfortunate. But I honestly don't think Strom Thurmond would have cared too much for serving on commissions or doing anything other than taking care of the people back home. All Strom Thurmond ever wanted to do was to bring the bacon home to the people of South Carolina. And he did that like no one ever had before and no one probably ever will again.

ROGER MILLIKEN

Strom Thurmond was a man of real principles. You always knew that you could count on the fact that if he told you he would do something, he would do it. He was just not momentarily trying to acquiesce to please the audience. I think that's a very

President Bush, Senator Thurmond, and Duke Short in the White House, October 2002.

GEORGE W. BUSH
is President of the United States, 2001-present.

Senator Strom Thurmond led an extraordinary life. He served in the Army during World War II, earning a Bronze Star for valor and landing at Normandy on D-Day. He served his country as Senator, Governor, and state legislator, and was a beloved teacher, coach, husband, father, and grandfather. While campaigning across South Carolina with him in 1998, I saw first hand the tremendous love he had for his constituents and the admiration the people of South Carolina had for him. He was also a friend, and I was honored to have hosted his 100th birthday at the White House. He will be missed.

admirable character position to take. It means a very great deal to the governance of our country. Simply put, he was a man of his word. You could count on him. He became known for that. He was also tireless when it came to serving his constituency. And he not only wanted to help them; he wanted to be with them. He never did become overwhelmed by the inside-the-beltway politics or socializing. His heart and his thoughts were always with South Carolina.

I can never forget the day when he came up and rang the doorbell on my house in Spartanburg on Otis Boulevard. He was there to tell me he was going to run as a write-in candidate for the U.S. Senate. That goes far, far back. I knew him from that day forward. And I always respected him as a man of strong conviction who was never afraid to stand up for his beliefs.

BUTLER DERRICK

Senator Thurmond took care of South Carolina and South Carolina took care of him. He brought incredible opportunities to many young people in the state. I think he will be remembered as a kind of godfather to the state, and I mean that in a positive way. It's actually hard for me to realize that he's not still with us. If anybody in the state had business with the Federal government, the first thing that came to mind was, well, we'll just call Strom. Multitudes of people in the state felt that he was a very close friend. And he was a friend. That is what his legacy will be. I don't think his legacy will be that he took a big part on the national scene. I think his legacy will be that he took care of his people for almost a century.

ANTHONY PRINCIPI

Senator Thurmond achieved excellence and set a high standard for all of us. He threw the beacon to us and now it's our turn to carry on, to serve others and work to make America and the world a better place, as he did nearly his entire life.

JOE WILSON

represents South Carolina's Second District in the United States Congress, 2002-present.

With the death of Strom Thurmond, South Carolina lost its greatest statesman of the 20th century. Strom Thurmond will never be replaced in the countless hearts of those who loved and respected him. He will endure as the leading example of a public servant due to his love and devotion to all the people of South Carolina regardless of status, race, politics, or region. He was our living legend. The legacy of Strom Thurmond will always be felt in South Carolina because of his steadfast integrity and the meaningful results of his thoughtful constituent service. He was my personal hero, and I will miss him dearly.

DENNIS DECONCINI

Strom Thurmond obviously had aspirations at one time to be President and to be a national figure. After that campaign, I gathered that he completely dedicated himself to being a good provider to the state of South Carolina. Now there were many other issues, because he'd been around so long, that became important to him — women's health, the defense of the nation, the temperament of judges — but as long I knew him, Strom never put anything in front of South Carolina.

TUCKER ESKEW

For a short time, late in Governor Campbell's second term, my office became the repository of a then new portrait of Senator Thurmond. I think they were awaiting a more public place to install it. The portrait had been painted recently, but had been done from photographs of him perhaps when he was in his forties or fifties. I commented to friends at the time that it looked a lot like Paul Newman in his heyday.

One day I walked in to find a man standing there. He had his back to me, and he was looking up at that portrait. That man was Strom Thurmond. We stood and chatted awhile about the portrait and about his career. I believe the Senator was fond of that portrait. He thought that it did him justice.

Knowing Strom Thurmond and his energy and drive, I think he saw a face like that in the mirror every morning. He saw a smiling, upbeat face with many years to look forward to. No matter how old he got, I think that he held that outlook all the way. He always had a horizon ahead of him and goals to achieve. I believe that outlook is what really propelled his great career of service. That portrait gave me a small window into that.

BAKTYBEK ABDRISAEV

Senator Thurmond was a person to admire, not only for the people of the United States but for people around the world. He was a great statesman, a great father, and one of the greatest sons of the United States.

GERALD R. FORD

was President of the United States, 1974-1977.

I have nothing but the highest regard for Strom Thurmond's career in the Senate and overall. He was an outstanding Senator from South Carolina at a very critical time. He was staunch in his beliefs, and as a result felt obligated to switch from the Democrat to the Republican Party. I applaud that change because it opened the door for others in the Democratic Party in the South to do the same. When I was in the White House, I could count on him one hundred percent. We both shared a conservative ideology that served and continues to serve our country well.

JACK KEMP

One of the things I remember most about Strom is how courteous he always was to people. I did a couple of favors for him in politics, made a couple of speeches for candidates in South Carolina that he wanted me to support. He would call you himself to say thank you; he never went through his staff. He was so gracious in thanking you beforehand, afterwards, and even sending notes and flowers to my wife. Strom Thurmond was the epitome of Southern charm, Southern grace, and Southern hospitality. I don't think Ronald Reagan could have been as successful as he was without Strom Thurmond in the United States Senate. He was one of the most courageous men I ever met in my life.

C. BRUCE LITTLEJOHN

Strom excelled at all his undertakings. He was a teacher and promoted to Superintendent of Education. He was a lawyer and got promoted to judge. He was a candidate, and the people elected him Governor. He was a candidate, and they elected him a United States Senator. He was a soldier, and he ended up a General. How was he able to rise to the top of all his endeavors? First among the reasons, I think Strom was a man of unimpeachable integrity. He had a knack for making people like him. He had a knack for making people feel confident in him.

I will never forget a trip I took to Washington; it must have been around 1985. On the way to my meeting I stopped by to watch the U.S. Senate. I sat in the balcony. The Senate was opened by a country lawyer from Edgefield County. He came in, picked up the gavel, and brought the United States Senate to order. I said to myself, could this possibly be my old, country lawyer friend from Edgefield County, South Carolina presiding over the great deliberative body known as the Senate of the United States? The answer was yes. It was my friend, Strom.

DAN QUAYLE

Clearly his longevity will give him a place in history. People will recall his love of the public arena, which can be a rough and tumble place to live all those years. He passed a lot of legislation, and engaged in a lot of discussions that shaped the course of our country. But I believe he will be remembered most as being a steadfast stalwart when it came to serving the public. He really believed in giving to the community, and he did just that for decades. We'll miss him. He was a great public servant.

WILLIAM W. WILKINS

Senator Thurmond's legacy will be one of a patriot, a patriot who passionately loved his country. He didn't just mouth words about patriotism; he lived it in military service and in the Senate of the United States. His life was fundamentally about service. He believed that service to others is the highest calling one can have. In my judgment, he excelled in that calling without equal.

DENNIS W. SHEDD

In all the stories that people told about the Senator at his memorial services, I think they kind of missed something that was essential, and that is the personal connection that Senator Thurmond had with people who lived in South Carolina. He had a personal connection with them that in many regards was much more important than the position he took on issues. A lot of people down here agreed with Senator Thurmond on almost everything. A lot of people disagreed with him on one or more issues, but they still liked him because their personal association, their personal dealings, and their personal memories about him just made those disagreements mean almost nothing. They just sort of faded away.

To be honest, I suspect his legacy in the country won't be much other than an oddity; you know, that he was so old and served that long. But in South Carolina, he is a legend. People will still be telling Strom Thurmond stories for many, many years to come. But his real legacy will be his impact on public service in the state and across the South. There are so many people who, in some way or another, were associated with him and who are now in public service themselves: judges, representatives, governors, and on and on. These people are now encouraging the next generation of public servants. That's Strom Thurmond's greatest legacy.

NADINE COHODAS

Over time, Senator Thurmond had to redefine in his own mind who "the people" were, and for him, "the people" came to embrace black and white South Carolinians. That is what I think his strongest legacy is in the area of racial politics, that accommodations are possible. I don't think that's a bad legacy, to show that the vote makes a difference. It's a very powerful legacy.

PAUL LAXALT

We often hear descriptions of people as patriots. As far as I'm concerned, I never saw one that came close to Strom Thurmond. Strom Thurmond is properly described as one of the last, perhaps the last, genuine patriots in America.

WILLIAM C. PLOWDEN, JR.

He loved his people. He loved his state. He loved his country. He was a real patriot. And we miss him terribly. We won't have another Strom Thurmond.

MARY CHAPMAN WEBSTER

There will never be another Strom Thurmond. He was absolutely one of a kind. You just never knew what he was going to do or what he was going to say. And I do believe that he was more than a Senator. I think he was a true statesman. He had beliefs, and he stood by them. He didn't play all those political games. His word was his bond. We won't see the likes of a Strom Thurmond ever again.

JOSEPH R. BIDEN, JR.

Strom Thurmond was a brave man who in the end made his choice and moved to the good side. I disagreed deeply with Strom on the issue of Civil Rights and on many other issues, but I watched him change. We became good friends. I went to the Senate emboldened, angered, and outraged at age 29 about the treatment of African Americans in this country, what everything that for a period in his life Strom had represented. But then I met the man. Our differences were profound, but I came to understand that as Archibald MacLeish wrote, "It is not in the world of ideas that life is lived: Life is lived for better or worse in life."

Strom and I shared a life in the Senate for over thirty years. We shared a good life there, and it made a difference. I looked into his heart and I saw a man, the whole man, and tried to understand him. I learned from him, and I watched him change. I believe the change came to him easily. I believe he welcomed it. This is a man who was opposed to the poll tax. This is a man whom I watched vote for the extension of the Voting Rights Act. This is a man whom I watched vote for the Martin Luther King Holiday. It's fairly easy to say today that that was pure political expediency, but I choose to believe otherwise. I choose to believe that Strom Thurmond was doing what few do once they pass the age of 50: he was continuing to grow, continuing to change.

I was honored to work with him, privileged to serve with him, and proud to call him my friend. His long life may well have been a gift of his beloved God, but the powerful and lasting impact he had on his beloved South Carolina and on his nation is Strom's legacy, his gift to all of us. He will be missed.

BOB DOLE

Here's one important thing I've learned in my life: it's not how many titles you have or how much power you have; the question is, did you take care of the guy at the bottom of the ladder, the guy who couldn't hire a lawyer and had to turn to his Senator for help? Did you take care of him? Strom took care of that guy. He did it all his life. He never cared what party they were registered with, what color they were, or anything else. If you had a problem, it was his problem. And it was his problem until he got it fixed. When people are writing about the Senate 100 years from now, they won't be writing about many Senators, but they'll be writing about Strom Thurmond. He'll be right there on the A list. Strom was my buddy. I really miss him.

MARK GOODIN

Most people made a habit of underestimating Strom Thurmond. Throughout his whole life, he was constantly underestimated. People wanted to see him as this hokey, Southern politician. And in some respects, he was. Some people wanted to see him as the wily political strategist who was wise beyond his years. In some respects, he was that too.

But at the very core of his being, he was guided by a strong sense of humanity, by the fact that he was in a position to do something about personal problems. Big national issues, absent the '48 campaign, were not the mainstay of his life. And yet he did some tremendous things that are overlooked by most historians who want to see him merely as a guy who reached the pinnacle of power through sheer constituent service.

All of those things that I just said are true. He was a master of constituent service. He was a wily legislative strategist. He could be a hokey, back-slapping kind of guy. But at his core, he never surrendered one thing; and I believe it was an innate, almost primordial sense that he had a mission to help people. It was a mission that would not be denied.

HENRY SACKS

The guy was a genuine American icon. He was a hero. And he just loved the fact that he was a native son of South Carolina and a citizen of the United States of America. He was proud of that until the day he died.

DEE SHORT

As we all know, Strom Thurmond will forever be remembered for his willingness to help people and for always looking out for the welfare of his beloved South Carolina. I am one of many South Carolinians who will never forget him. I personally witnessed during the last fifteen to twenty years he was in office that he never wanted to slow down. During his last term, even during the last few days before he left office, he repeatedly asked Duke, "Who can I help?" "Is there anybody I can help?" "Have I done everything I could do?" That was always on his mind, to the very end. The last three days in office, several times during these three days, I remember the Senator calling Duke into his personal office and telling him how much he appreciated him, thanking him profusely for his loyalty, dedication, and all he had done for him throughout the thirty years they were together. He was so gracious.

To quote our and Senator Thurmond's good friend Henry Sacks, "If there's such a thing as reincarnation, Senator Thurmond would like to come back as the same: in the Senate with Duke, Holly and staff by his side, and play it all over again. Good night Senator Thurmond, wherever you are."

JESSE HELMS

I believe Strom would have found it acceptable for me to refer to him as "my great friend" because that was how he referred to me when speaking to many, many others. He was a friend as well as colleague because, when all is said and done, there wasn't a bit of pretense about this remarkable man; and while the rest of us knew that he was a legendary political leader, he didn't let it bother him.

It's always difficult to write about fallen friends. But as I look back on the years, it was particularly meaningful for this Senator to have enjoyed a personal relationship with the Honorable Strom Thurmond of South Carolina. My feeling about Strom is that every breath he drew was a pro-American breath, and that — in my book, and I believe in his — is what counted!

Four years ago, a young, unsophisticated lad alighted at Cherry's Crossing. He, too, was contemplating a plunge into the "sea of knowledge." Little did any one dream that this same person was to write his name in indelible print on the records of this institution. Nor did any one think that this handsome young man was to become a ladies' man of the "first water," and was to provoke so many extra heart beats among the "fairer sex."

Strom's athletic ability found expression on the cinder path. Although having to work hard, he proved to be a good point winner and a fair representative of the purple and gold.

May success ever be yours, Strom, old boy.

– *from the 1923 edition of Taps, the Clemson University annual*

BUD ALBRIGHT

I don't know how history will treat the Senator. If history treats him as a man who was guided by principles, it will be a true telling of the past. If, on the other hand, history focuses solely on the times of segregation, and not the later times when he realized he was going in a wrong direction, that will be most unfortunate; history should speak to the whole man.

For those of us who were fortunate to have known Strom Thurmond personally, we know he was a genuine war hero, a true statesman, a great leader, and a man guided by deeply held principles. I only hope that history will treat him fairly. He was not a man without faults. None of us are.

It is my sincere hope that history will remember all the good that he did; the development and progress that he brought to South Carolina; the love he had for the people; and the understanding that he had for those who were less fortunate. He understood what it was to labor in a cotton mill, to go barefoot, to work hard and not get enough sleep, to have too many children and not enough money. He cared very deeply for people like that, and he never gave up trying to help them. To grow our economy and keep the country safe at the same time, that's a difficult challenge. But the Senator took it on with all his energies. I hope that will be his legacy.

When you work in the nation's capital, you see a lot of great people who do great things. Sometimes you are lucky enough to work with them, perhaps even get to know them. I have been very fortunate to have known some great people in my life. But I really do have to say that Senator Strom Thurmond is up there at the very top.

ALAN SIMPSON

Strom was unique. He was a comet across the political sky. There will never be another one like him, ever.

THE CENTENNIAL SENATOR

Farewell, Old Friend

Against Dee's wishes and better judgment, in early 1996 I gave serious consideration to leaving Senator Thurmond's office and taking a job in the private sector. I knew the Senator was gearing up to run for office one last time, and I was not prepared to spend another six years on the Hill. I knew I could make more money in a new job, and frankly, I was tired. Keeping up with the Senator all those years had flat worn me out.

I shared this line of thinking with him late one afternoon in his office. "But I want you to stay," he said flatly. "Just think Duke, I'll be 100-years old when I leave office!" He was thrilled at the very idea.

"I know," I said, "And I'll be seventy! I'm getting too old for this."

He chuckled. "Seventy?! Ah, that's not old! You're just a young man. Do you know what I would do if I was your age?"

I said, "Yes sir, I know. And I'd have to be there to get you out of a lot of trouble too!" We both laughed. But the issue was on the table.

I discussed the matter with Senator Dole, a man whom I have always admired and whose judgment I've always trusted. He admitted that there were real pros and cons, but encouraged me to stay. In a sense he told me what I already knew: if Senator Thurmond won that last election, which he certainly would, he was going to need the support of his entire staff, including me.

A few months later, at President Clinton's second inaugural ball in January '97, the Senator pulled Dee aside and said, "Dee, you can't let him leave. Please, we've got to keep him here. Help me convince him."

In the end, of course, I did stay with the Senator until his very last day in office. Looking back, I know it was the right decision. When it got right down to it, the single most important issue was this: he was my friend. In fact, he was in many ways like a father to me. But he was first and foremost my friend, and you don't leave your friends when they need your help. It was an honor and a privilege to work with him for so long. When his family moved him from Washington to Edgefield, it really hurt me to see him go, because I knew that I would never see him again.

For the first ten or so years in my career with him, I really didn't have much of a personal relationship with the Senator. He was my boss. I worked for him. That was that. But in those last fifteen to twenty years, we became very good friends. I give most of the credit for that change to my wife Dee. She often sent him meals at night which James happily delivered. She did his laundry. And she made sure he had something to do on the weekends. I got used to seeing the Senator at our dinner table. We grew to really know and like each other. But Dee loved him like a father. And he absolutely thought the world of her. I'm sure Strom Thurmond had countless close friends over the course of 100 years, but I'm proud to say that his very last, very best friend was my wife Dee.

When the totality of Strom Thurmond's life is fully assessed, I believe people in the future will envy his accomplishments. They will wonder how one man could do so much in one lifetime: teacher, attorney, soldier, governor, senator, father, and statesman. He led a remarkable life. He will be remembered as the most outstanding South Carolinian in the state's history.

Near the end of the Senator's last term in office, we went over to the Senate Floor for a final vote. When we got back to the office, I was standing with some others quietly talking about how many times we had taken that trip over to the Capitol and back. The Senator looked up from his desk across the room and shouted with a laugh, "What are y'all planning over there, some kind of coup? What kind of revolt y'all got planned?"

We told him we were just reminiscing about all the trips we'd made over to the Capitol. He said in all seriousness, "You shouldn't spend your time thinking about what you've done. You should be planning what you're going to do tomorrow." If there was ever a theme for Strom Thurmond's life, that was it.

The greatest tribute that we can give to the memory of James Strom Thurmond is to plan for tomorrow how each of us, in our own way, can work hard to help the people, all the people, and to continue to make this the greatest country in the world.

Gone but Not Forgotten

On April 28, 2006, Dee and I were returning to Virginia from a visit to Chesnee, South Carolina. We stopped in Gaffney for gas. Just as I pulled up to the pump, an older African-American man about my age pulled in directly behind me. We exchanged pleasantries, and both of us voiced our opinion about the high cost of gas.

The gentleman went inside the station and when he returned, he stopped at my car and said, "Well, I'll tell you one thing, if *Strong* Thurmond was still in Washington, we wouldn't have this problem today. There is no way he would put up with people in South Carolina having to pay so much for gas."

He went on to tell me how the Senator had helped him with a Social Security problem. He also said that at one time many years before, he'd almost lost a job until Senator Thurmond came to the rescue. He said, "*Strong* Thurmond didn't care who you were. He just wanted to help all the people."

I shared with the man that I had worked for Senator Thurmond for almost 30 years. He couldn't believe it. At this point, Dee, who had overheard the conversation, got out of the car. She told the man that she too had been a good friend of Senator Thurmond. Dee said, "Since you spoke so nicely about my favorite Senator, I want to give you something." Dee then gave the man her own personal Strom Thurmond keychain and a Strom Thurmond pencil we had in the car. The man was genuinely appreciative. He said, "I'll put my keys on this right now!"

With a parting thanks the man added, "Do you know why they nicknamed him *Strong* Thurmond?" I said no. He replied, "Because he was a strong man — a strong man who would do anything to help folks."

Duke Short and Strom Thurmond on a final walk through the Capitol.

WASHINGTON POST

"You shouldn't spend your time thinking about what you've done. You should be planning what you're going to do tomorrow."

– Senator J. Strom Thurmond –

Senator James Strom Thurmond

1902	Born December 5 in Edgefield, S.C.
1923	B.S. Degree from Clemson University (held 34 honorary degrees)
1923–29	Teacher and Athletic Coach; McCormick, Ridge Spring and Edgefield, S.C.
1924	2nd Lt., U.S. Army Reserve; commissioned on January 9, 1924 upon becoming 21-years old.
1929–33	Superintendent of Education, Edgefield County, S.C.
1930	Admitted to S.C. Bar (studied law under his father, Judge J. William Thurmond)
1930–38	Attorney at Law, Edgefield, S.C. (City Attorney and County Attorney)
1933–38	State Senator, representing Edgefield County, S.C.
1938–46	Circuit Judge of South Carolina (four year leave of absence for World War II service)
1942–46	World War II: First U.S. Army — American, European and Pacific Theaters. Landed in Normandy on D-Day with 82nd Airborne Division, awarded 5 Battle Stars. For his military service, earned 18 decorations, medals and awards, including the Legion of Merit with Oak Leaf Cluster, Purple Heart, Bronze Star for Valor, Belgian Order of the Crown, and French Croix de Guerre.
1947–51	Governor of South Carolina
1947	Married Jean Crouch of Elko, S.C., November 7: deceased January 6, 1960.
1948	Candidate for President of the U.S.; carried 4 states and received 39 electoral votes as States Rights Democratic candidate (third largest independent electoral vote in U.S. history)
1951–55	Attorney at Law, Aiken, S.C. (City Attorney of North Augusta, S.C.)
1954–2003	U.S. Senator; elected as write-in candidate; first person ever elected to major office in U.S. by this method; Served Dec. 24, 1954 to April 4, 1956 when he resigned to run in the Democratic Party primary election, pursuant to a promise made to the people during the 1954 campaign. Re-elected U.S. Senator and resumed duties November 7, 1956; re-elected 1960, 1966, 1972, 1978, 1984, 1990 and 1996; President Pro Tempore, U.S. Senate 1981-1987, January 3, 1995-January 3, 2001, and January 20-June 6, 2001.

1959	Major General, U.S. Army Reserve; served 36 years in Reserve and on Active duty. (Past National President, Reserve Officers Association, 1954-55).
1964	Switched from Democratic to Republican Party, September 16. Delegate to 6 Democratic and 6 Republican National Conventions.
1968	Married Nancy Moore of Aiken, S.C., December 22. Four children: Nancy Moore (deceased 1993), J. Strom Jr., Juliana Gertrude, and Paul Reynolds
1983	President's Commission on Organized Crime (appointed by President Reagan, Nov. 28)
1985	Commission on the Bicentennial of the U.S. Constitution (by U.S. Senate, Sept. 29)
1996	Became the oldest-serving member of the U.S. Senate, December 5
1997	Became the longest-serving member of the U.S. Senate, May 25
1998	Cast 15,000th vote, September
2001	Named President Pro Tempore Emeritus, June 6
2003	Retired from the U.S. Senate, January 3; returned home to Edgefield, S.C.
2003	Died June 26 in Edgefield, S.C. at age 100

U.S. Senate Committees

- **Armed Services Committee** (member since 1959)
  - Named Chairman Emeritus, 1999
  - Chairman, January 1995-January 1999; Ranking member, January 1993-January 1995
- **Judiciary Committee** (member since 1967)
  - Chairman, 1981-1987; Ranking member, 1987-1993
  - Ranking member of the Judiciary Subcommittee on Constitution, Federalism, and Property Rights
  - (Chairman, January 2001-June 2001)
- **Veterans' Affairs Committee** (member since 1971)
  - Named Chairman Emeritus, 2001

Member: Baptist Church, South Carolina and American Bar Association, Masons (over 50 years), Lions Club (over 50 years), Rotary Club, and numerous defense, veterans, civic, fraternal, and farm organizations

Index of Contributors

JOHNNY MACK BROWN is the U.S. Marshal for the District of South Carolina. He first met Senator Thurmond in 1972 when he was asked to represent law enforcement in the Senator's reelection campaign.
PAGES: 225, 270

LES BROWNLEE, Colonel, U.S. Army (ret.) was the Acting Secretary of the Army under President George W. Bush and the former Staff Director of the Senate Armed Services Committee. A highly decorated veteran, Colonel Brownlee was a good friend of Senator Thurmond's.
PAGES: 254, 317

MARIE BOYLE BUCKLER served as a Personal Assistant to Senator Thurmond and was a Director of his Page and Intern Program. She worked for the Senator from 1988 to 1999.
PAGES: 108, 314, 319, 324, 371

GEORGE H.W. BUSH was President of the United States, 1989-1993.
PAGES: 430

GEORGE W. BUSH is President of the United States, 2001-present.
PAGES: 435

ROBBIE CALLAWAY is the CEO of Technology Investing, Inc. and Chairman of the National Center for Missing and Exploited Children. Robbie was for many years a close and devoted friend of Senator Thurmond's.
PAGES: 49, 81, 84, 275, 342

ASHLEY HURT CALLEN worked in Senator Thurmond's Washington office from 1999 until January of 2003. Her final title was Legislative Assistant. She is now General Counsel to Congressman Gohmert.
PAGES: 296

DR. NED CATHCART was a life-long friend and supporter of Strom Thurmond's. He practices obstetrics and gynecology in Spartanburg, South Carolina.
PAGES: 32, 266

CHRIS KELLEY CIMKO served as Senator Thurmond's Press Secretary from 1993 to 1997, and also worked as Communications Director for the Senate Armed Services Committee.
PAGES: 17, 34, 168, 366, 397, 416

WALKER CLARKSON worked for Senator Thurmond from January of 2001 until his retirement.
PAGES: 134, 274, 376

ERNIE COGGINS was a Legislative Assistant for Senator Thurmond, 1999-2003. He is now on active duty as a Lieutenant Colonel with the U.S. Army Reserves.
PAGES: 26, 102, 109, 226, 251

NADINE COHODAS is a former reporter for *Congressional Quarterly* and the author of *Strom Thurmond and the Politics of Southern Change*.
PAGES: 140, 365, 440

GARRETT CUNEO is the Executive Vice President of the American Chiropractic Association.
PAGES: 289

JOHN DALTON was Secretary of the U.S. Navy, 1993-98.
PAGES: 150, 293, 337

ALFONSE D'AMATO was a United States Senator from New York, 1981-1999.
PAGES: 150, 176, 223, 308

JACK DANFORTH was a United States Senator from Missouri, 1976 to 1995, and is a former Ambassador to the United Nations. He is now a partner with the law firm of Bryan Cave.
PAGES: 109, 117, 251, 308, 323, 336

MARIO D'ANGELO, the Senior Barber at the U.S. Senate Barber Shop, was Senator Thurmond's personal barber for 25 years.
PAGES: 250, 331, 351

DENNIS DECONCINI was a United States Senator from Arizona, 1977-1995.
PAGES: 69, 90, 119, 138, 196, 284, 362, 437

JOHN DECROSTA is a former Senior Policy Advisor and Press Secretary for Senator Thurmond. He worked for the Senator from 1991 to 2001.
PAGES: 7, 15, 39, 226

JIM DEMINT is a United States Senator from South Carolina, 2004-present. He previously represented South Carolina's 4th District in the U.S. House of Representatives.
PAGES: 33, 316, 366

BUTLER DERRICK was a United States Congressman representing South Carolina's Third District from 1975 to 1995.
PAGES: 119, 180, 194, 221, 281, 360, 436

MIKE DEWINE is a United States Senator from Ohio, 1995-present.
PAGES: 175, 237, 298

BOB DOLE was a United States Senator from Kansas, 1969-1996. He served as either Majority or Minority Leader from 1985 to 1996. He was the Republican Nominee for President in 1996.
PAGES: 32, 68, 237, 252, 274, 283, 331, 363, 414, 442

ELIZABETH DOLE is a United States Senator from North Carolina, 2003-present. Her career includes her service as the Secretary of Transportation under President Reagan, Secretary of Labor under President George H.W. Bush, and President of the American Red Cross.
PAGES: 151, 348, 422, 429

JOHN DRUMMOND is President Pro Tempore of the South Carolina State Senate, a highly decorated veteran of World War II, and was a life-long friend of Strom Thurmond's.
PAGES: 165, 181, 281

ELIZA EDGAR was the Assistant to the Chief of Staff as well as the Page and Intern Coordinator for Senator Thurmond's office from 1996 until January of 2003.
PAGES: 15, 29, 106, 147, 168, 296

JAMES B. EDWARDS was Governor of South Carolina from 1975 to 1979. He later served as the President of the Medical University of South Carolina from 1982 until 2000.
PAGES: 51, 162, 196, 214, 246, 291, 318, 347, 428, 432

TUCKER ESKEW served as the Deputy Assistant to the President and Director of the White House Office of Global Communications under President George W. Bush and, prior to that, as Press Secretary and Communications Director to South Carolina Governor Carroll Campbell. Mr. Eskew served as a Page for Senator Thurmond in the summer of 1978.
PAGES: 188, 376, 437

LAUCH FAIRCLOTH was a United States Senator from North Carolina, 1993-99.
PAGES: 347

BECKY FLEMING served as Senator Thurmond's Press Secretary. She worked in his office from 1997 until January of 2003.
PAGES: 18, 24, 46, 107, 223, 336

GERALD R. FORD was President of the United States, 1974-1977.
PAGES: 283, 438

DON FOWLER is a former Chairman of the Democratic National Committee. He is now President of Fowler Communications.
PAGES: 34, 48, 131, 146, 178

SCOTT FRICK worked for Senator Thurmond from 2000 until he left the Senate in 2003. Mr. Frick served as the Minority Chief Counsel on the Senate Judiciary Subcommittee on the Constitution.
PAGES: 10, 99, 395, 411

JAMES D. GALYEAN is a former Legislative Assistant to Senator Thurmond. He worked for the Senator from 2001 until the day he left office in January of 2003.
PAGES: 100, 341, 417

JOHN A. GASTRIGHT, JR. served as Projects Director for Senator Thurmond, 1995-2002. He is now Deputy Assistant Secretary of State for South Asian Affairs.
PAGES: 27, 42, 47, 52, 343, 381, 434

MARK GOODIN worked as Senator Thurmond's Press Secretary and Spokesman for the U.S. Senate Judiciary Committee, 1981-87. He later served as Deputy Assistant Secretary of Transportation under Ronald Reagan and as George H.W. Bush's Campaign Spokesman.
PAGES: 23, 38, 58, 127, 176, 312, 329, 388, 427, 442

NEWT GINGRICH served as a U.S. Congressman from Georgia, 1979-99 and as Speaker of the United States House of Representatives, 1995-99.
PAGES: 148, 158, 393

RUTH BADER GINSBURG is an Associate Justice on the United States Supreme Court, 1993-present.
PAGES: 299, 415

JAMES FLOYD GRAHAM was a close friend as well as Senator Thurmond's personal driver from 1986 until the Senator's last day in office in early January of 2003.
PAGES: 204, 326, 357

LINDSEY GRAHAM is a United States Senator from South Carolina, 2003- present. He succeeded Senator Thurmond in office.
PAGES: 45, 189, 252, 365, 403, 431

VANJEWELL GRAHAM is the wife of James Floyd Graham, Senator Thurmond's personal driver from 1986 until 2003.
PAGES: 260

ORRIN HATCH is a United States Senator from Utah, 1977-present.
PAGES: 75, 114, 431

JOHN F. HAY, Lieutenant Colonel, U.S. Army (ret.) is the former Vice President of Government and International Affairs for Westinghouse Electric Corporation. He is currently a partner with P3 Consulting, LLC.
PAGES: 132, 147, 239

JESSE HELMS was a United States Senator from North Carolina, 1972-2003.
PAGES: 33, 187, 284, 425, 443

CRAIG HELSING is the Vice President of the BMW (U.S.) Holding Corporation. He previously served as an assistant to Lee Atwater in the Political Affairs Office at the Reagan White House.
PAGES: 242, 296

KAREN HENDERSON is a Judge on the United States Court of Appeals for the District of Columbia Circuit.
PAGES: 89, 235, 369

KATHRYN HOOK worked as Chief Receptionist in Senator Thurmond's Washington office from 1967 to 1997. Senator Thurmond gave her the title "Dean of Women."
PAGES: 118, 163

JUDITH RICHARDS HOPE is a Senior Advisor to Paul, Hastings, Janofsky & Walker, an Adjunct Professor of Law at Georgetown University Law School, and President and CEO of Oncovir, a biotechnology company.
PAGES: 91, 252, 268, 313, 366, 433

GEDNEY HOWE, III and his family were long-time friends and supporters of Senator Thurmond's. He practices law in Charleston, South Carolina.
PAGES: 34, 191, 283, 325

CHRISTIE DENISE HUMPHRIES was a page for Senator Thurmond in 1995 and 1997, an Intern at his Columbia, South Carolina office during her college years, and later worked full-time in the Columbia office. She is the niece of Duke and Dee Short.
PAGES: 108, 260

BOB HURT is a former Administrative Assistant for Senator Sam Nunn. He is now with Hurt, Norton & Associates.
PAGES: 345, 397

MARK IVANY is a former Special Assistant to Senator Thurmond. He worked for the Senator from 2000 until January of 2003.
PAGES: 159, 356, 400, 422

DOUG JENNINGS represents District 54 in the South Carolina House of Representatives. He has continuously served in that capacity since he was first elected in 1991.
PAGES: 33, 63

COY JOHNSTON, II was a long-time friend of Senator Thurmond's and the father of Holly Johnston Richardson, Senator Thurmond's Personal Secretary. Holly worked for the Senator from 1979 until her death in September of 2002.
PAGES: 126, 178, 228, 240

DARYL JONES, Colonel, U.S. Air Force Reserve, served in the Florida State Senate from 1992 to 2002. Colonel Jones was nominated by President Clinton to be Secretary of the U.S. Air Force but was not confirmed by the Senate. He is now an Attorney with Adorno & Yoss.
PAGES: 315, 363, 405

PHIL JONES was a Correspondent for CBS News for 32 years, which included his tenure as the Chief Congressional Correspondent on Capitol Hill.
PAGES: 41, 124, 135, 277, 301, 401, 416, 434

STEPHEN L. JONES was the Executive Assistant to Senator Thurmond, 1974-81. He is now the Principal Deputy Assistant Secretary of Defense (Health Affairs).
PAGES: 68, 124, 198, 203, 205, 300

RON KAUFMAN is a former Deputy Assistant and Political Advisor to President George H.W. Bush.
PAGES: 121, 158, 336

P.X. KELLEY, General, US Marine Corps (ret.), was Commandant of the Marine Corps, 1983-87, and a member of the Joint Chiefs of Staff. He is currently the Chairman of the American Battle Monuments Commission.
PAGES: 152

JACK KEMP is the Co-Director of Empower America. He was the Republican Nominee for Vice President in 1996. He was Secretary of Housing and Urban Development under President George H.W. Bush and served nine consecutive terms in the U.S. Congress.
PAGES: 198, 439

DIRK KEMPTHORNE was a United States Senator from Idaho, 1993-1999. He served as Governor of Idaho from 1999-2006. Since May of 2006 he has served as U.S. Secretary of the Interior.
PAGES: 71, 255, 396

PATRICIA KEMPTHORNE, the former First Lady of Idaho, is the wife of Secretary Dirk Kempthorne.
PAGES: 404

ANTHONY KENNEDY is an Associate Justice on the United States Supreme Court, 1988-present.
PAGES: 94

ED KENNEY was an Administrative Assistant to Senator Thurmond. He worked for the Senator from 1960 to 1970, and later served more than a decade as a Professional Staff Member on the Senate Armed Services Committee.
PAGES: 17, 249, 363, 377

CLAUDE M. "MICK" KICKLIGHTER, Lieutenant General, U.S. Army (ret.), is Director of the Department of State and Defense, Iraq/Afghanistan Joint Transition Planning Group.
PAGES: 154

MELISSA KIRACOFE-LOW worked for Senator Thurmond from May of 2000 until September of 2002. Her last position was Project Caseworker.
PAGES: 374

MELINDA KOUTSOUMPAS worked for Senator Thurmond for almost 20 years, from 1984 until his retirement in 2003. She served as the Chief Clerk of the Senate Judiciary Committee and then later as Chief Clerk for the Senate Armed Services Committee.
PAGES: 6, 18, 120, 133, 174, 234, 268, 326

GEORGE LAUFFER, Lieutenant Colonel, U.S. Army (ret.), worked for Senator Thurmond from 1989 to 2002 as his Designee on the Senate Armed Services Committee.
PAGES: 16, 47, 100, 134, 149, 209, 297

PAUL LAXALT was a United States Senator from Nevada, 1974-1987.
PAGES: 115, 240, 441

C. BRUCE LITTLEJOHN was the former Chief Justice of the Supreme Court of South Carolina and a former Speaker of the South Carolina House of Representatives. Judge Littlejohn was a close friend of Strom Thurmond's for well over sixty years.
PAGES: 89, 167, 245, 280, 424, 439

MANSEL LONG, JR. served as a Legislative Director for Senator Howell Heflin in the 1980s.
PAGES: 24, 353, 370, 394

TRENT LOTT is a United States Senator from Mississippi, 1989-present, and served as Majority Leader from '96-02.
PAGES: 108, 176, 272, 416, 431

DAVID LYLES is the former Democratic Staff Director on the Senate Armed Services Committee. He is now the Chief of Staff to Senator Carl Levin.
PAGES: 139, 303

GARRY D. MALPHRUS was appointed as an Immigration Judge for the Arlington, Virginia Immigration Court in 2005. From 2001 to 2004 he served President George W. Bush as Associate Director of the White House Domestic Policy Council. Judge Malphrus served as Senator Thurmond's Chief Counsel on the Senate Judiciary Committee from 1997 to 2001.
PAGES: 73

MATTHEW J. MARTIN was the Military Assistant to Senator Thurmond from 2000 until January of 2003.
PAGES: 16, 118, 149, 270, 347, 423

ELIZABETH MCFARLAND was the Office Manager for Senator Thurmond's Aiken, South Carolina office from 1986 until his retirement.
PAGES: 130, 204, 221, 238, 423

DAVID G. MCLEOD, Colonel, Medical Corps, U.S. Army, Walter Reed Army Medical Center. Colonel McLeod is Chief of Urology and Director of the Center for Prostate Disease Research at the Uniformed Services University.
PAGES: 150, 423

HENRY MCMASTER is the South Carolina Attorney General and a former U.S. Attorney, having been appointed by President Reagan. He also worked as a Legislative Assistant for Senator Thurmond in the 1970s. He and his family were good friends of the Senator's for many years.
PAGES: 62, 124, 179, 196, 227, 343

ROBERT MCNAIR was Governor of South Carolina, 1965-71.
PAGES: 180, 309, 364, 432

HELENA HUNTLEY MELL worked for Senator Thurmond from 1980 to January of 2003. She held a variety of posts, including Chief Clerk for the Anti-Trust Judiciary Subcommittee, Legislative Correspondent, and Staff Assistant.
PAGES: 338

CRAIG METZ served as Senator Thurmond's Counsel on the Labor and Human Resources Committee from 1988 to 1990. He was also Deputy Assistant Secretary for Congressional Liaison at the Department of Education, and later served as Chief of Staff to Congressman Floyd Spence of South Carolina.
PAGES: 9, 19, 38, 159, 208, 247, 269, 318, 326, 345, 375

HOWARD METZENBAUM was a United States Senator from Ohio, 1976-1995.
PAGES: 98

ROGER MILLIKEN is the Chief Executive Officer of Milliken & Company in Spartanburg, South Carolina and was a life-long friend and supporter of Senator Thurmond's.
PAGES: 282, 434

MICHAEL MISHOE was a Legislative Assistant for Senator Thurmond, 1976-77.
PAGES: 7, 20, 24, 100, 202, 208, 302, 349, 376

GLADYS V. MOSS is the wife of the late Thomas Moss, Senator Thurmond's Field Representative for South Carolina from 1971 to 2001. Mr. Moss was Director of the South Carolina Voter Education Project and a veteran of the Korean War. He was the first African-American staff member to be hired by any U.S. Southern Senator.
PAGES: 132, 361

JOHN L. NAPIER is a former U.S. Congressman from South Carolina (1981-83), and was appointed to the U.S. Court of Federal Claims by President Reagan. Mr. Napier served as Counsel and Legislative Assistant to Senator Thurmond, 1972-79. He now practices law in Washington, D.C. and South Carolina.
PAGES: 19, 61, 120, 315, 374

FRANK NORTON, Colonel, U.S. Army (ret.), is former Army Legislative Liaison to the United States Senate and served on the staff of the Senate Armed Services Committee. Colonel Norton was a great friend and supporter of Senator Thurmond's.
PAGES: 151, 158, 246, 251, 334

SAM NUNN was a United States Senator from Georgia, 1972-1996. He now serves as Co-Chairman and Chief Executive Officer of the Nuclear Threat Initiative which works to increase global security by reducing the threat of nuclear, chemical, and biological weapons.
PAGES: 115, 273

SANDRA DAY O'CONNOR was an Associate Justice on the United States Supreme Court, 1981-2006.
PAGES: 93

JOHNNY PALEOLOGOS is the General Manager of The 116 Club on Capitol Hill in Washington, D.C., one of Senator Thurmond's favorite restaurants.
PAGES: 234

SUSAN PELTER is a former Press Secretary for Senator Thurmond. She worked for him in the mid 1980s and again from 1990 to '93.
PAGES: 22, 35, 162, 180, 222, 254, 276, 312, 344, 372

WILLIAM C. PLOWDEN, JR. was the Assistant Secretary of Labor for Veteran's Employment under President Reagan. He was a close friend of Senator Thurmond's for over fifty years, and served as Chairman for three of his Senatorial campaigns. Mr. Plowden now holds the position of State Director of Veterans Employment Training for South Carolina, under the U.S. Department of Labor.
PAGES: 185, 195, 207, 224, 246, 280, 441

ELSIE PLUES is the former owner of Elsie's Magic Skillet in Alexandria, Virginia, where Senator Thurmond and Duke and Dee Short went for brunch nearly every Sunday for over ten years.
PAGES: 236

JOHN R. STEER is a former Legislative Director and Administrative Assistant to Senator Thurmond. He is now Member and Vice Chair of the U.S. Sentencing Commission, having been appointed by President Clinton in 1999.
PAGES: 22, 175, 208, 230, 257, 308

JOHN PAUL STEVENS is an Associate Justice on the United States Supreme Court, 1975-present.
PAGES: 92

SHELL SUBER is a former Staff Assistant for Senator Thurmond, 1990 to 1993.
PAGES: 11, 14, 36, 40, 44

PATRICIA RONES SYKES managed Senator Thurmond's Charleston office from 1995 until he retired in 2003.
PAGES: 10, 135

CLARENCE THOMAS is an Associate Justice on the United States Supreme Court, 1991-present.
PAGES: 95, 111, 302, 309, 355, 364, 415

MIKE TONGOUR is a former Legislative Director for Senator Thurmond, 1985-97. He is now with Tongour, Simpson, Holsclaw.
PAGES: 72, 262, 394

BILL TRAXLER is a Judge on the United States Court of Appeals for the Fourth Circuit.
PAGES: 133, 230, 309, 375

BILL TUTEN is a former Projects Director for Senator Thurmond. He worked from 1997 until January of 2003.
PAGES: 9, 14, 102, 190, 195, 206, 235, 273, 274, 297, 341, 417, 428

JOHN WALSH, founder of the National Center for Missing and Exploited Children, is a globally recognized advocate for victim's and children's rights. He is the host of the television program America's Most Wanted, which has helped law enforcement capture over 900 fugitives.
PAGES: 79, 123, 331

JOHN WARNER is a United States Senator from Virginia, 1978-present.
PAGES: 164, 431

MARY CHAPMAN WEBSTER worked as an intern in the Senator's office in the summer of 1968. She and her parents were dear friends of the Senator's for many years.
PAGES: 106, 139, 168, 182, 210, 224, 235, 241, 247, 260, 285, 311, 343, 441

TOGO D. WEST, JR. was Secretary of Veterans Affairs, 1998-2000, and Secretary of the Army, 1993-97. He also served as General Counsel of the Department of Defense under President Jimmy Carter.
PAGES: 145

R.C. PREACHER WHITNER is the Founder and President of R.C. Whitner & Associates. He and his family were long-time friends and supporters of Senator Thurmond's.
PAGES: 184, 249, 396, 433

DAVID WILKINS is Ambassador to Canada and former Speaker of the House of Representatives, State of South Carolina. He served on every one of Senator Thurmond's campaigns for the U.S. Senate, beginning in 1972, and was Chairman of his last campaign in 1996.
PAGES: 40, 163, 183, 191, 228, 432

WILLIAM W. WILKINS is the Chief Judge of the United States Court of Appeals for the Fourth Circuit. He has the distinction of being the first Federal Judge appointed by President Reagan (1981). Judge Wilkins served as a Legal Assistant to Senator Thurmond from 1970-71.
PAGES: 5, 20, 45, 48, 123, 184, 202, 207, 316, 362, 440

J. HARVIE WILKINSON III is a Judge on the United States Court of Appeals for the Fourth Circuit.
PAGES: 91

KEVIN WILKINSON is a Senior Congressional Affairs Specialist with the Federal Bureau of Investigations. He has been with the FBI's Congressional Affairs Office since 1980.
PAGES: 302, 323

KAREN J. WILLIAMS is a Judge on the United States Court of Appeals for the Fourth Circuit.
PAGES: 96, 228, 310, 433

JOE WILSON represents South Carolina's Second District in the United States Congress, 2002-present.
PAGES: 436

TERRY L. WOOTEN worked with Senator Thurmond for over a decade, beginning in 1986. Before he left the Senate, he held the title of Minority Chief Counsel and Staff Director for the Senate Judiciary Committee. He is now a Federal District Judge in Florence, South Carolina.
PAGES: 18, 37, 64, 204, 206, 238, 250, 253, 314, 357, 397